The Making of an African Working Class

Anthropology, Culture and Society

Series Editors:
Professor Vered Amit, Concordia University
and
Professor Christina Garsten, Stockholm University

Recent titles:

Claiming Individuality: The Cultural Politics of Distinction
Edited by Vered Amit and Noel Dyck

Community, Cosmopolitanism and the Problem of Human Commonality
Vered Amit and Nigel Rapport

Home Spaces, Street Styles: Contesting Power and Identity in a South African City
Leslie J. Bank

In Foreign Fields: The Politics and Experiences of Transnational Sport Migration
Thomas F. Carter

Dream Zones: Anticipating Capitalism and Development in India
Jamie Cross

A World of Insecurity: Anthropological Perspectives on Human Security
Edited by Thomas Eriksen, Ellen Bal and Oscar Salemink

A History of Anthropology Second Edition
Thomas Hylland Eriksen and Finn Sivert Nielsen

Ethnicity and Nationalism: Anthropological Perspectives Third Edition
Thomas Hylland Eriksen

Small Places, Large Issues: An Introduction to Social and Cultural Anthropology Third Edition
Thomas Hylland Eriksen

What Is Anthropology?
Thomas Hylland Eriksen

Discordant Development: Global Capitalism and the Struggle for Connection in Bangladesh
Katy Gardner

Organisational Anthropology: Doing Ethnography in and Among Complex Organisations
Edited by Christina Garsten and Anette Nyqvist

Border Watch: Cultures of Immigration, Detention and Control
Alexandra Hall

Corruption: Anthropological Perspectives
Edited by Dieter Haller and Cris Shore

Anthropology's World: Life in a Twenty-First Century Discipline
Ulf Hannerz

Humans and Other Animals Cross-cultural Perspectives on Human–Animal Interactions
Samantha Hurn

Flip-Flop: A Journey Through Globalisation's Backroads
Caroline Knowles

Cultures of Fear: A Critical Reader
Edited by Uli Linke and Danielle Taana Smith

The Will of the Many: How the Alterglobalisation Movement is Changing the Face of Democracy
Marianne Maeckelbergh

The Anthropology of Security: Perspectives from the Frontline of Policing, Counter-Terrorism and Border Control
Edited by Mark Maguire, Catarina Frois and Nils Zurawski

Cultivating Development: An Ethnography of Aid Policy and Practice
David Mosse

The Gloss of Harmony: The Politics of Policy Making in Multilateral Organisations
Edited by Birgit Müller

Contesting Publics: Feminism, Activism, Ethnography
Lynne Phillips and Sally Cole

Food For Change: The Politics and Values of Social Movements
Jeff Pratt and Peter Luetchford

Race and Ethnicity in Latin America Second Edition
Peter Wade

Race and Sex in Latin America
Peter Wade

The Capability of Places: Methods for Modelling Community Response to Intrusion and Change
Sandra Wallman

Anthropology at the Dawn of the Cold War: The Influence of Foundations, McCarthyism and the CIA
Edited by Dustin M. Wax

The Capability of Places: Methods for Modelling Community Response to Intrusion and Change
Sandra Wallman

Anthropology at the Dawn of the Cold War: The Influence of Foundations, McCarthyism and the CIA
Edited by Dustin M. Wax

The Making of an African Working Class

Politics, Law, and Cultural Protest in the Manual Workers' Union of Botswana

Pnina Werbner

First published 2014 by Pluto Press
345 Archway Road, London N6 5AA

www.plutobooks.com

British Library Cataloguing in Publication Data
A catalogue record for this book is available from the British Library

ISBN 978 0 7453 3496 7 Hardback
ISBN 978 0 7453 3495 0 Paperback
ISBN 978 1 7837 1178 9 PDF eBook
ISBN 978 1 7837 1180 2 Kindle eBook
ISBN 978 1 7837 1179 6 EPUB eBook

Library of Congress Cataloging in Publication Data applied for

This book is printed on paper suitable for recycling and made from fully managed and sustained forest sources. Logging, pulping and manufacturing processes are expected to conform to the environmental standards of the country of origin.

10 9 8 7 6 5 4 3 2 1

Typeset by Stanford DTP Services, Northampton, England
Text design by Melanie Patrick
Simultaneously printed digitally by CPI Antony Rowe, Chippenham, UK
and Edwards Bros in the United States of America

For Ben and Donna

Contents

List of Figures

List of Abbreviations

ANC	African National Congress (South Africa)
BALA	Botswana Association of Local Authorities
BCC	Botswana Council of Churches
BCSA	Botswana Civil Servants' Association
BCP	Botswana Congress Party
BCWIS	Botswana Core Welfare Indicators Survey
BDP	Botswana Democratic Party
BMD	Botswana Movement for Democracy
BNF	Botswana National Front
BFTU	Botswana Federation of Trade Unions
BIAC	Botswana Institute of Administration and Commerce
BLLAWU	Botswana Land Board and Local Authorities Workers' Union
BMWU	Botswana Mine Workers' Union
BOCCIM	Botswana Confederation of Commerce, Industry and Manpower
BOGOWU	Botswana Government Workers' Union
BOFEPUSU	Botswana Federation of Public Sector Unions
BONEPWA	Botswana Network of People Living with Aids
BOPEU	Botswana Public Employees' Union
BOSETU	Botswana Secondary School Teachers' Union
BTU	Botswana Teachers' Union
BTV	Botswana Television
BULGASA	Botswana Unified Local Government Service Association
BURS	Botswana Unified Revenue Service
CEDA	Citizens' Entrepreneurial Development Agency
CKGR	Central Kalahari Game Reserve
COSATU	Congress of South African Trade Unions
DCEC	Directorate on Corruption and Economic Crime
DIS	Directorate of Intelligence and Security
DMSAC	District Multi-sectoral Aids Committee
DPSM	Directorate of Public Service Management
GSS	Gaborone Secondary School
HIES	Household Income and Expenditure Survey
HLCC	High Level Consultative Council
ILO	International Labour Organisation
IMF	International Monetary Fund
ISPAAD	Integrated Support Programme for Arable Agriculture
ITUC	International Trade Union Confederation
LIMID	Livestock Management and Infrastructure Development
LRC	Legal Reform Centre (South Africa)

MWU	Manual Workers' Union (National Amalgamated Local and Central Government, and Parastatal Manual Workers' Union of Botswana)
NACTU	South African National Council of Trade Unions
NASM	new alternative social movements
NEC	National Executive Committee
NEMIC	National Employment, Manpower and Incomes Council
NGO	non-governmental organisation
NJICC	National Joint Industrial Coordinating Council
NPSBC	National Public Service Bargaining Council
NSM	new social movement
NSMU	new social movement unionism
PBRS	performance-based remuneration schemes
PSI	Public Service International
OECD	Organisation of Economic Cooperation and Development
RIPCO	Rural Industries Promotions Company
SADC	Southern African Development Community
SATUC	South African Trade Union Coordinating Council
SHHA	Self Help Housing Agency
SMU	social movement unionism
SWAPO	South-West Africa People's Organisaton
TAC	Treatment Action Campaign
TAWU	Trainers' and Allied Workers' Union
UCCSA	United Congregationalist Church of Southern Africa
ZCC	Zionist Christian Church

Series Preface

Anthropology is a discipline based upon in-depth ethnographic works that deal with wider theoretical issues in the context of particular, local conditions – to paraphrase an important volume from the series: *large issues* explored in *small places*. This series has a particular mission: to publish work that moves away from an old-style descriptive ethnography that is strongly area-studies oriented, and offer genuine theoretical arguments that are of interest to a much wider readership, but which are nevertheless located and grounded in solid ethnographic research. If anthropology is to argue itself a place in the contemporary intellectual world, then it must surely be through such research.

We start from the question: 'What can this ethnographic material tell us about the bigger theoretical issues that concern the social sciences?' rather than 'What can these theoretical ideas tell us about the ethnographic context?' Put this way round, such work becomes *about* large issues, *set in* a (relatively) small place, rather than detailed description of a small place for its own sake. As Clifford Geertz once said, 'Anthropologists don't study villages; they study *in* villages.'

By place, we mean not only geographical locale, but also other types of 'place' – within political, economic, religious or other social systems. We therefore publish work based on ethnography within political and religious movements, occupational or class groups, among youth, development agencies, and nationalist movements; but also work that is more thematically based – on kinship, landscape, the state, violence, corruption, the self. The series publishes four kinds of volume: ethnographic monographs; comparative texts; edited collections; and shorter, polemical essays.

We publish work from all traditions of anthropology, and all parts of the world, which combines theoretical debate with empirical evidence to demonstrate anthropology's unique position in contemporary scholarship and the contemporary world.

Professor Vered Amit
Professor Christina Garsten

Preface

This book began with an interview in 2001 with Elsinah Botsalano, a salaried officer of the Manual Workers' Union (MWU) of Botswana. The interview inspired me to return for a study of the MWU in 2005 for six months, and subsequently for shorter periods in 2006, 2007, 2011 and 2012/13. In between these trips, I read local newspapers online and tried to follow the never-ending saga of union affairs. I first went to Botswana in 1972, so by the time I met Elsinah I had spent a considerable amount of time in the country alongside my husband, living in a small rural village, Moremi, in a valley at the foothills of the Tswapong Hills. But studying the MWU opened my eyes to a new world I could not have imagined existed. I have tried in this book to conjure up that world as seen from the perspective of an anthropologist who has not only lived in Botswana's rural hinterland, but has researched for many years elsewhere in the world, in Pakistan and among Pakistani migrants in Britain. In writing this book, I owe an immense debt to the MWU's leaders and to the ordinary members who figure in it. It would be impossible to thank them all but I want in particular to thank Johnson Motshwarakgole, Elsinah Botsalano, Lydia Tlhong and Samuel Molaudi for their huge contribution to the research. Andrew Motsamai was unique in answering e-mails and was very generous with his time and thoughts. Mosala Phokontse, Bina Tsalaile, Neo Joel and Motseothata Gopane were always welcoming and enlightening. The study would not have been possible without their generosity and help. My research assistants, Queen, Mama and Tshepo were just amazing in every respect, and often helped me see the humour of it all when the going was tough. My husband, Richard Werbner, the true Botswana expert, not only introduced me to the country he loves but supported me intellectually and emotionally. The 2005/6, research was conducted with support from the ESRC's Programme on Non-Governmental Public Action. I owe an immense debt to Jude Howell and other participants in this programme, especially Simon Clarke, for enlightening me about the world of labour unions. Individual chapters received insightful comments from a range of readers and reviewers. Earlier versions of chapters 2, 3, 5, 6 and 10 have been published elsewhere (P. Werbner 2008, 2009, 2014a, 2014b). I delivered some chapters, particularly Chapter 10, at various seminars and conferences. I acknowledge my debt to reviewers separately alongside the chapters. I am grateful to the ESRC for supporting the initial fieldwork, and to the Wenner Gren Foundation for supporting the research in 2012/13. Keele University's Research Institute administrative staff gave me immense support, and I would like in particular to thank Judith Garside, who over the years gave me huge backing in my research endeavours.

As this book goes to press, the Manual Workers' Union, 45,000 workers strong, is threatened with losing many of its members through government privatisation of cleaning, laundry, catering, gardening and other services. At the same time, despite costly court cases, the union has prospered, with large-scale investments and continued activism within the Botswana Federation of Public Service Unions.

Pnina Werbner, Gaborone, April 2014

CHAPTER ONE

Introduction

E.P. Thompson famously remarked in his opening to *The Making of the English Working Class*, 'The working class did not rise like the sun at an appointed time. It was present at its own making' (Thompson 1963: 8). The emergence of class and class consciousness, he stressed, is an active process, 'which owes as much to agency as to conditioning' (ibid.). Class was not merely a 'structure' but a historical phenomenon, unifying 'disparate and unconnected events, both in the raw material of experience and in consciousness' (ibid.). Following Thompson, Iliffe argued that dock workers in colonial Tanzania developed class consciousness through the very act of working together and acting together to advance their interests (Iliffe 1975: 50).

In deliberately echoing Thompson's title, my aim in this book is to describe the historical emergence of class identity and class consciousness in an African postcolonial nation as an *active* process, forged in the struggle of low-paid workers for public dignity and a living wage. I trace this struggle through a series of historical events that have shaped Botswana's low-paid public service workers' individual and collective identity in what Thompson called a 'historical relationship' – above all between workers and the Botswana government, their employer, but also with churches, the opposition parties, fellow unionists and other key actors in civil society. As in industrialising England, in Botswana, too, the working class, newly formed after national independence in 1966, cannot be regarded as a fixed, reified social entity, measured by 'concrete indices' (Talib 2010: 230). It is, instead, 'multiple and contradictory' (Kasmir 2005: 81). Above all, it is a constantly evolving imaginary, created through concrete interactions among workers, in practice and performance, vis-à-vis a dominant, hegemonic employer. The *experience* of class is mediated by cultural images, songs, vernacular oratory, public meetings, rallies, strikes and popular culture that contribute to a sense of continuity, linking past and present, even as these images and discourses are refigured and reincorporated into new discourses whenever workers encounter new cosmopolitan ideas about labour rights or face new local crucibles. This changing yet continuous repertoire of signs orders experience and infuses it with meaning (Harries 1994: xvi).

As a public anthropologist, my aim in the book is to recover the cultural dimensions of trade union and worker activism often neglected in other labour studies.[1] In particular, I show – against a simplistic unidirectional 'proletarianisation' thesis – that the fusing of cosmopolitan and local popular culture has created a distinctive, vernacular way of being a worker in Botswana that does not deny workers' roots at 'home', in the countryside. Although E.P. Thompson's humanist interpretation of class consciousness and of the 'acting subject' has been questioned, this critique has itself been questioned. Sharryn Kasmir, for example, rejects the widespread 'end of ideology' view that charts a decline in class consciousness, allegedly replaced by non-class, identity-based social movements. Citing Thompson, she proposes that anthropologists are particularly well placed to understand the 'ideas of working people in specific social and historical contexts' (Kasmir 2005: 79). Chapters 2, 3 and 9, which portray the personal life histories of union activists, women and men, underscore manual workers' evolving agency as they shape their futures by strategising and struggling against the handicaps of low pay, working poverty and a lack of formal education.[2]

Unionists gain the capacity to act not simply through their daily struggle as workers. Their horizons expand as they come to be aware of worker struggles elsewhere, join and draw support from international labour organisations and gain consciousness of their rights, enshrined in international law. The need is, then, to move beyond Judith Butler's notion of agency as merely resistive performativity (Butler 1993) to illuminate the way that a mastery of knowledge through trade union activism authorises public leadership positions.[3] I draw here on Foucault's later work, in which he developed what might be called an ethical theory of leadership, first hinted at in the second volume of *The History of Sexuality* and developed more fully in the third volume (Foucault 1987, 1990). In this final volume, Foucault outlines his view on ethics, not simply as aesthetic self-fashioning through personal asceticism, as in the first volume (Foucault 1980), but as a theory of alterity, leadership and power beyond the limits of the polis, as the Greek world expanded. Ethics thus moved from being almost entirely monological, focused on the autonomous self, to being dialogical, egalitarian and cosmopolitan.[4]

A somewhat parallel move is evident when workers of village origin transform rural values of *seriti*, dignity, into values of honour and responsibility in the workplace, in their relations with government, their employer, and above all as they become leaders within the trade union movement. Hence, the book shows that trade union politics are a passionate politics, deeply concerned with dignity, justice and fairness. Workers feel strongly that their labour should be respected and adequately recompensed. Although in Botswana, unlike neighbouring South Africa, strikes have been conducted peacefully, this should not lead us to underestimate the bitterness of the union's conflict with their employer, the government of Botswana.

The Extended Case Study Method

The present book examines these issues through the prism of a detailed case study of a blue-collar industrial-class, public service union, the National Amalgamated Local and Central Government, and Parastatal Manual Workers' Union, widely known in Botswana as the Manual Workers' Union (hereafter the MWU, or simply 'the union'), over a period spanning some 20 years, from 1991 to 2013. By focusing on a single union's development over time, I adopt the Manchester School's extended case study method. This mode of micro-analysis in time allows us to see a society in all its complexity as it is becoming and changing. Situational analysis highlights points of resistance to change, cultural encounters, conflicts between rules, instability, anomie, and how these are played out in public and even in the intimate relations of everyday life. It also allows us to study the effects of external forces, including global change, on a micro-society. Hence the relation between micro and macro is played out differently in this methodological approach.[5] The key point stressed by all commentators is that the extended case study is not simply an 'apt illustration' or an interesting 'ethnographic vignette' – writing strategies favoured by many anthropologists. The extended case study is an analytic construct that, by abstracting directly from an ethnography of practice, generates a theory of social process, change and conflict, often by following a series of encounters or social situations involving the same or related actors. Each social situation is an indexical event that records relations between social categories, ideologies and modes of practice. Seen in its totality, the extended case study method allows us, in other words, to think outside the box, to recognise the rules and values constituting a complex, changing social field, one characterised by shifting borders and political alliances, and hence also by a kaleidoscopic play of identities and competing normative and ethical assumptions. Practice in this method incorporates both discourse and symbolic action, including performance, ritual and ceremonial, as well as political actions such as elections, mass protests and strikes, or violent clashes.

In the first section of this book I examine the cultural and moral economy of the MWU as it is refracted in women unionists' portrayals and narratives in the context of the political economy of the nation. This fresh vantage point on African labour opens a window on the often unseen army of manual workers who underpin the state's daily functioning. Moving beyond that, in the second and third sections of the book I aim to elucidate the relationship between law and politics – the legal, ethical, religious and popular cultural values animating union activism and its mythologised history. From a legal anthropological perspective, the book adopts a post-realist, critical-legal theoretical approach to explore the dialectics of judicial morality and political influence as these are reflected in Botswana High Court argumentation and judgements, themselves influenced by changing international legal notions of cosmopolitan justice, ethics and fairness, interpreted in a local setting. In particular, I challenge the sceptical view adopted by many leading anthropologists and socio-legal scholars who argue that court decisions, even on the rare occasions when they favour workers or other marginal groups, have little impact; that is, that the law is a mere 'fetish', a source of mystification. Against this view I propose that the relatively recent international development of more robust legal instruments in judicial review has made it possible to challenge arbitrary state decisions – and sometimes win significant victories against the odds.

The book's narrative underscores a perennial question in labour studies: to what extent are trade unions the radical vanguard of the working class or, on the contrary, conservative actors concerned primarily with the immediate bread-and-butter interests of their members? Seen overall, the narrative structure of the book tells a story of an apparent abandonment by the MWU of its radical, dissenting politics and co-optation by the ruling party in the face of internal factional divisions, only to recover its oppositional mission in the events leading up to the great strike of 2011, explored in the last section of the book.

The complexity inherent in African workers' identities and subjectivities is highlighted in studies that challenge simplistic assumptions about popular worker mobilisation and strikes, or the emergence of a long-term proletarian consciousness.[6] Repeatedly, unions are revealed to be divided by internal racial, class and educational divisions, with clerical and skilled workers often suspected of being stooges or sell-outs. In the early colonial period, sustained consciousness was said to be weakened by workers' double-rootedness as circulatory labour migrants.[7] Another source of division was the divergence of local union and national union interests (Cheater 1986; Kapferer 1972), leading to worker suspicion of union official political rhetoric. Such divisions have been apparent most recently in the platinum mine strikes in South Africa in 2012, with tragic consequences.[8] In Botswana, anthropologists have increasingly challenged the supposed homogeneity of Botswana as a 'Tswana' nation, and have highlighted the need to study marginalised social groups and intersections of ethnicity, class and gender.[9] But despite their multiple ethnic and linguistic affiliations, worker members of the MWU who are the subject of this study appear, on the whole, to minimise divisions among themselves. In transcending ethnic and regional divisions, their project could be constituted paradoxically as one of nation-building, even as they struggle against the government, their employer.[10]

African Trade Unions and the Public Sector

The rise of African trade unions, perhaps the first truly modern organisations in colonial Africa, has been extensively documented by social historians, anthropologists and sociologists. Most early studies focused on the largest organised unions, those involving miners, dockers and railway workers functioning in industries established by the colonial government. These included studies of, for example, the Zambian Copperbelt mine workers (Epstein 1958), East African railway workers (Grillo 1973, 1974) and Dar es Salaam dock workers (Iliffe 1975), but there were also studies of factory workers in Zambia, Nigeria and South Africa (Kapferer 1972; Peace 1979; Simons & Simons 1969). Cooper's monumental comparative study of the history of African trade unions in Anglophone and Francophone colonies from the 1930s to 1950s highlights both the internationalisation of the trade union movement in Africa within the context of colonial labour relations in the period leading up to decolonisation, and the awkward relations between unions and nationalist leaders once independence became imminent (Cooper 1996).

With all this, the present book addresses a remarkable hiatus in the study of trade unions in contemporary Africa – that is, the role played in civil society by public sector unions. Seen worldwide, unions in the public sector are some of the largest and most influential, especially when it comes to enabling new, more progressive labour laws.[11] More than other trade unions, public service unions are likely to engage in public policy issues relating to the welfare state and universal social justice (Carpenter 2000). They are also adept at using judicial review in the High Court and Court of Appeal to hold the government accountable. In Botswana, unions in the public sector form a dominant numerical presence, with low-paid public sector workers being at the forefront of the struggle for a 'living wage'. Despite this, with the possible exception of Jeffries's study of Ghanaian railwaymen (Jeffries 1978), few African studies have looked specifically at public service unions, and particularly those of low-paid industrial class, blue-collar manual workers, the subject of the present book.

Their neglect is significant: public sector unions form a special class of unions. They have certain inherent advantages (for example, job security), are subject to specific legal regimes and mirror in the span of their spatial organisation the outer reaches of the state. Unlike mine, factory or dock workers, usually concentrated at specific sites, public sector workers are dispersed nationwide, in large cities and small towns, in the capital's government enclave and in remote border outposts, in urban and rural areas. In this respect too, the work of the MWU, even when it mobilises for a national strike against the government, as it did in 1991 and 2011, can be construed as the work of nation-building. Public service unions' influence in Botswana grew as they came together in a federation, the Botswana Federation of Public Sector Unions (BOFEPUSU), in 2010.[12]

Historically, African trade unions were at the forefront of liberation struggles, including the fight against apartheid in South Africa,[13] the liberation struggle in Namibia (Moorsom 1977) and, since the 1980s, of political struggles for democracy in Zambia (Bratton 1994: 66–7, 71–2; Larmer 2006, 2007) and Zimbabwe (Raftopoulos and Phimister 1997), reflected in the Movement for Democratic Change's challenge to Mugabe's tyrannical rule. In Ghana, railway and other public workers developed an independent, radical consciousness, across ethnic and tribal divisions, during the colonial era, which persisted after independence (Jeffries 1978). Following independence, however, workers in African postcolonial nations were often subjected to patriotic appeals in the name of broader, national interests, most recently in South Africa (see Barchiesi 2011). Botswana, a multi-party democracy since independence, started off as one of the poorest countries in the world, and for this reason, anti-state protests were defined as a betrayal of the solidarity needed to build a new nation.

Most studies of unions in Africa have stressed tensions and conflicts based on the complex intersections of class, race and colonialism (see Cooper 1996; Schler et al. 2009), classically in South Africa (Berger 1992; Simons & Simons 1969) but elsewhere as well, in Zambia, Tanzania and Nigeria (Epstein 1958; Grillo 1973, 1974; Peace 1975). African union militancy in these studies was understood in the context of the struggle not simply with 'management' but with colonial authorities or white workers. Few studies, however, have analysed conflicts among unions and employers where race is *not* an issue. Equally absent have been analyses in contemporary Africa of the way the factional politics of national political parties intersect and 'infiltrate' union factional politics, an issue discussed in Chapters 6 and 7.

Botswana is perhaps unique in Africa in not having a legacy of race-inflected industrial labour relations during the colonial era, or a brutal history of racism, as in neighbouring South Africa – though Batswana men did, of course, work in large numbers in the South African mines until quite recently, and were employed by white storekeepers and farmers (Mazonde 1994). Unlike other African countries, Botswana's national struggle for independence was far less bitter and at no time involved union mobilisation. Although many early labour disputes concerned unequal pay for expatriates (see Cooper 1978; Mogalakwe 1997: 116–18), the current absence of a racially based labour politics has meant that labour relations are wholly African and thus mainly class based, so that radical politics too are framed ideologically in the language of class warfare versus (neo)liberal democracy.

Studies of trade unions by sociologists, historians and political scientists in Botswana have stressed issues of class and civil society (Makgala et al. 2007; Maundeni 2004; Mogalakwe 1997). Across Africa, however, there has been little analysis of how black African public service unions are able to transcend divisions among themselves in order to bargain with the state or challenge it in court. In part this is because so few state workers have been allowed to unionise across sub-Saharan Africa (see Saidy Khan n.d.). In this respect, Botswana is both an exception and an exemplary case, which charts a future trend for other African countries.

The book highlights the apparent paradox that in their struggles for a living wage, small items of expenditure are converted by unions into overarching principled discourses of human rights and state responsibility. This was evident in the negotiations leading to the first union strike, in 1991, analysed in Chapter 6. It applies equally to the need for insurance against job loss. Hence, alongside their struggle for a living wage, a perceived threat faced by low-paid workers in Botswana relates to the consequences of losing their jobs in the absence of state unemployment benefit. Privatisation and job retrenchment in the public services have made this threat all too real for public sector industrial class workers, the majority uneducated and unqualified. They, in particular, are positioned on the edge of a precipice: their capacity to find alternative employment with commensurate pay is restricted by their lack of qualifications in a job market characterised by unemployment rates of 25 per cent or more. As Chapter 2 documents, even minor rises in salary only underline the enormity of the fall that the loss of their job in government service would entail – from worker to destitute.

The extent to which unions are moved by the bread-and-butter interests of their members or mobilise for more radical socialist or reformist agendas is a central question preoccupying theorists of labour relations. Unions are Janus-faced, positioned precariously between the two poles of political protest and economic expediency.[14] Van Holt (2002) has argued, in relation to post-apartheid South Africa, that social-movement unionism in alignment with other community activists is no longer in any simple way an appropriate model to describe the erosion of worker solidarities there in the face of post-apartheid black elite formation, a point I return to below. In the case of Botswana, both

Mogalakwe (1997) and Maundeni (2004), writing more broadly on civil society actors, reflect on the overall absence of confrontational politics. The Manual Workers' Union, the subject of the present study, is, however, singled out for its willingness to engage in openly defiant public conflict with the government (Mogalakwe 1997: 104–5, 119). Indeed, in my very first interview with a woman trade unionist officer, in 2001, she told me the inspiring tale of the union's courageous struggle for a decent wage against the government of Botswana, which lasted for over ten years. Her narrative highlights the role of the union as a leading actor in the fight against poverty and for workers' rights in Botswana.

The Manual Workers' Union

The Manual Workers' Union is the largest public service union in the country, comprising industrial-class workers employed by government, local government and parastatals.[15] The vast majority of its members are relatively uneducated, with many of the older workers barely having completed primary school and none having tertiary educational qualifications. Many speak only Setswana, the national language, which is also the language in which most union business is conducted.[16] They constitute the lowest-paid workers in the formal government sector, earning even today, after pay demands were finally settled in 2001, just over £100 a month (1250 pula), rising to just over £350 (4400 pula), though workers in the commercial sector, like shop assistants and casual workers, earn even less.[17] They are the counterpart of UNISON members in the United Kingdom, without skilled workers such as nurses.

The MWU was formed in 1968, two years after Botswana's independence in 1966. Its members occupy the lowest ranks in government service. Among union members, women comprise 50 per cent or more of the workforce, and many are among the lowest-paid workers. They work as cooks, cleaners, porters, messengers, telephone operators, hospital orderlies, storekeepers, library assistants and drivers. The men work, in addition, as night watchmen, handymen, auto mechanics, agricultural extension workers, pump attendants, technicians, ambulance drivers, grave diggers and gardeners. They work in local authorities and in all the different government departments, from health, education, industry and agriculture to water and sewage, local government and home and labour affairs.

Despite the low wages of its members, the MWU was remarkable during the initial period of my study, in 2005, for being the largest in Botswana – at its peak, in 2003, it had some 70,000 paid-up members, and even in 2005, in the face of an extremely painful factional split, it still had some 45,000. For a small country of 1.5 to 2 million people, these figures are impressive, especially in a period when union membership in the West has been in decline. In Britain, for example, only a quarter of all workers belong to a trade union. This comparison underlines the immense achievement of the MWU in recruiting virtually all government industrial-class worker employees into the union. Its success has partly been due to the fact that, in 2005, union dues were low, 5 pula (about

50 pence), though they have since risen slightly, yet the income from this paltry sum had made the union rich – its officers invested union income wisely, in property and shares. Hence, paradoxically, the union of some of the lowest-paid workers in Botswana was also historically the wealthiest in the country, and the best organised. Knowing their rights has made union officers unflinching, tenacious negotiators who have gained the respect of university-educated, top Batswana civil servants. The achievement is all the more notable in a developing country in which formal education is regarded as an essential requirement for effective public action.

Ironically, as is often noted, while African nationalism often arose from alliances between unions and African political parties – as between the Congress of South African Trade Unions (COSATU) and the African National Congress (ANC) in South Africa – most African unions were subsumed and suppressed after independence. In Botswana during the early years after independence, unions, never strong, were actively discouraged and the demand for workers' rights construed as unpatriotic, striking at the country's development effort.[18] It thus took an act of moral courage to challenge the status quo from the lowly position of a manual unskilled worker, as the MWU did in 1991, when they went on strike to demand a 'living wage'.

Such workers were not the subject of common esteem. Seretse Khama, the first president of Botswana, extolled rural work while suppressing the demands of miners and government public manual workers. Thus, in a speech made in 1976 to celebrate ten years of independence, Khama said:

> the future of Botswana lies in the rural areas, in the land, where our forefathers eked out a living, where the majority of our people still eke out a living, and where we must make life more attractive not only for ourselves but for many future generations. To do this – to develop our rural sector – we must, first and foremost, appreciate the dignity of labour, and be instilled with a clear social conscience. We must come to grips with our true identity as a traditionally rural people who are being lured to the towns by the largely false promise of a better style of life and a more secure standard of living ... Botswana is a democratic country founded on the ideal of *kagisana* (harmony) ... rooted in our past – in our culture and traditions. (quoted in Vaughan 2003: 134)

Dignity, in Setswana *seriti* or *tlotlo*, is here represented as a feature of rural 'traditional' labour. Against that, the struggle of the MWU has been for dignity and a fair wage in modern, manual, non-agricultural work, mainly outside the rural sector. As I argue in Chapter 4, against Khama's idealisation of farming, there was a redemptive quality to the self-conception of struggle in the union, expressed in their labour songs and the pervasive sense that their ultimate aim was to liberate the poor and oppressed – this, despite the fact that union daily activities were marked by nitty-gritty, pragmatic negotiations over wages and rights. Members of the union never tired of telling me that despite their poverty and lack of education, they could 'teach' the other unions and occupational associations in Botswana how to be unionists, how to protest, how to mobilise effectively.[19] This was a source of pride and distinction for them.

The redemptive quality of their vision may be linked in part to members of the Manual Workers' Union's almost universal affiliation to churches, whether established churches like the Anglican, Congregationalists (UCCSA) and Roman Catholic, or local 'Spiritual' churches, 'Zionists' or Pentecostals. Many union leaders stressed that they had cut their teeth in church preaching and organisation. 'Political prayers' were a common feature of union rallies, as I discuss in Chapter 8. Indeed, the 'dignity of labour' bears Christian connotations, rooted in Puritan ideas of vocation and calling (Constantin 1979). The International Labour Organisation (ILO) headquarters in Geneva has a large mural painting by Maurice Denis entitled *The Dignity of Labour*, commissioned in 1931 by the International Federation of Christian Trade Unions, showing Christ in his Nazareth workshop talking to a group of workers, dressed in twentieth-century work clothes, who are easily identifiable as key leaders in the Christian trade union movement (WTO 2007: 12).

The Manual Workers' Union and National Politics

The majority of the salaried and elected officers of the Manual Workers' Union were at the time of my study supporters of the opposition, particularly the Botswana National Front (BNF), a party that began its life with strong Marxist tendencies but has since moderated its stance considerably, advocating social democracy and the rights of the poor. The BNF has had a tendency to splinter, unlike the ruling party, the Botswana Democratic Party (BDP), which has historically been able to absorb opponents and has regularly been returned to power in democratic elections every five years since independence.[20] The BDP has in the past ruled the country on a pragmatist liberal, developmental, social welfarist platform, though in recent years it has begun to adopt more neoliberal policies, including a government programme to push low-paid government workers into the private sector through privatisation.

For most of Botswana's short history, the various opposition parties have been unable to form a united front against the ruling BDP (Basedau 2005: 410). In the 2004 elections, the opposition won collectively 48 per cent of the vote, with the BNF winning 26 per cent, or 12 out of 57 seats in the National Assembly. The BDP won all but one of the remaining 45 seats. Despite its dominance, the considerable and growing opposition vote appears to have shaken the BDP leadership, by now entrenched in its hold on power, with all the perks and privileges this entails. When I first met some of the union officials in April 2005, they assured me hopefully that the BNF was 'bound to win' next time, 'as long as it stays united'. Both the MWU's legal firm and their auditors had strong BNF connections. Virtually all of the national elected and salaried officers of the union had been BNF councillors at one stage or another, and the elected general secretary of the union had also run as a BNF candidate for parliament in Serowe, a stronghold of the BDP. At the start of my research in 2005, however, only one of the salaried officers was a BNF councillor, in Kgatleng District. The general organising secretary of the MWU and its most prominent leader, Johnson Motshwarakgole, a salaried union officer, whose story is told in Chapter 9, told me privately that he had been sought by the BNF to run for the National Assembly, but he hesitated to do so.

In Botswana, much like late-nineteenth-century Britain before the formation of the Labour Party, strong opposition has repeatedly been expressed by the ruling BDP, the party in power, to the involvement of unions in party politics.[21] The Friedrich Ebert Stiftung Foundation notes that, 'To the extent that the trade union movement does not have alliances with any political party, it does not have any political power. Neither does it yield any influence of a political nature. But political parties are struggling to win support of union leaders for membership drives of their parties' (FES 2004: 25–6).

Although in Britain and the USA it would not be very surprising to find a trade union associated with one or another political party, in Botswana a widely prevalent public rhetoric castigates any involvement of so-called civil society actors in party politics, a discourse that evidently favours the party in power. Most NGO activists I knew agreed that overt links with political parties were unacceptable for NGO leaders. Even in the MWU, the official line is that the union is politically neutral since it represents members of all political persuasions. The national organising secretary and effective union boss, Johnson Motshwarakgole, told to me at our first meeting, in 2005:

> J.M.: They [the government] associate the union with the opposition, as though we were the mouthpiece of the opposition. There is no respect for us. I am 50 years [old] now. If someone says my ideas are someone else's, I resent it. They think we are being put up by the opposition.
> P.W.: By which party?
> J.M.: The BNF. Yes, as individuals we do belong to the BNF, at least some of us do.[22]

Johnson is a large man who speaks forcefully, with passion and commitment. A charismatic leader and man about town, he is well-known in the capital and throughout Botswana, his picture often appearing in the media. He is reputed to be a sharp negotiator, tough opponent, effective manipulator and uplifting speaker. A battle-scarred warrior, I was soon to discover that he is adulated by ordinary members of the union who have absolute faith in his ability to win their grievance cases and settle their disputes.

The long tradition of Batswana 'living their lives in courts' (Gulbrandsen 1996, 2012) has been widely documented by contemporary anthropologists (e.g. Comaroff & Roberts 1981; Kuper 1970b; Richards & Kuper 1971), following Schapera's early path-breaking work (Schapera 1938, 1956). With Griffith's work on divorce (Griffiths 1998), this observation has been extended to a consideration of legal pluralism, but so far there have been few detailed legal anthropological studies of the often high-profile use of judicial review in Botswana – that is, of the suing of the state by its citizens (though see Hitchcock et al. 2011; Saugestad 2011; Solway 2009; R. Werbner 2004). Anthropologists in Botswana have looked at state commissions on minority cultural rights (Solway 2002, 2010; R. Werbner 2002b, 2002c, 2004) and at the intersections of gender and generation (Durham and Klaits 2002). Urban class is implicit in the study of churches (Klaits 2010; R. Werbner 2011). Elsewhere, particularly in India (e.g. Parry 1999, 2010; Subramanian 2009; Talib 2010) and the United States (see Durrenberger & Reichart 2010), the anthropological study of labour unions is a topic of growing interest. Chapters 5, 7 and 12 in particular look at the way the MWU challenged the government and other unions in Botswana's High Court and Court of Appeal.

Neoliberalism and the Citizen-as-worker Moral Discourse

It has become almost a truism to argue that globalisation and structural adjustment have generated neoliberal policies in both OECD (Organisation of Economic Cooperation and Development) countries and the developing world. As a market-driven approach, neoliberalism advocates that government divest itself of responsibility for costly, universally allocated, public services and, alongside that, the responsibility to care for all its citizens. The neoliberal ideological vision thus substitutes for the welfare state's caring role a monetary policy and a market-driven private sector, justifying this shift by contending that 'liberalised' economies deliver more efficient services. Rather than the state being responsible for its vulnerable, less-fortunate citizens, then, neoliberals call on citizens to make themselves responsible for their own futures.

Neoliberalism is thus not simply an economic theory but a moral discourse which repositions citizens vis-à-vis their governments. Rather than citizenship being a 'status' in the 'community', as conceived of by T.H. Marshall, key architect of the post-war welfare state in Britain, with the nation-state community delegated to care for all its vulnerable members, citizens are redefined as consumers and producers of goods and services. Part of the moral discourse of neoliberalism, then, relates to the central place of productive work in the national polity. This comes alongside the castigation of non-workers: non-producers who nevertheless remain 'consumers' of welfare. A second, related moral discourse advocates the privatisation of the public sector, blaming public servants for being wasteful and inefficient, hence a burden on the nation. By contrast, critics of neoliberalism argue that it is a vision that leads to ever-growing inequality, economic and social polarisation and grinding deprivation, even in countries like the USA. At the same time, the global growth of the financial sector and multinationals within this liberalised regime has divested many states of much of their effective power to make meaningful decisions.

This is evident in developing countries. In tandem with the introduction of neoliberalism in the North, indebted countries in the South were advised by the World Bank and International Monetary Fund to cut their rudimentary welfare services in order to balance their budgets. Taking South Africa, Botswana's closest neighbour, as an example, neoliberal policies have led to the privatisation of large parts of the public sector and the casualisation of labour in private industry, resulting in very high rates of unemployment and precarious semi-employment, low-paid contract work and growing income polarisation (see Barchiesi 2011). The ranks of trade unions representing the working class have been decimated as jobs have been shed in their tens of thousands. Equally strikingly, welfare services and utilities' provision (water, electricity, roads and municipal rubbish collection) have declined or been privatised, with many workers in the post-apartheid era having no access to health, housing, basic amenities and free education, despite the country's relative wealth (ibid.). The South African ANC government justifies this betrayal of the promise of liberation by deploying a moral discourse that defines the citizen as a productive worker contributing to the 'new' South Africa, while stigmatising the unemployed as scroungers or at best, hopefully but unrealistically, potential petty entrepreneurs, while the government refuses, ostrich-like, to recognise that most workers earn near-starvation wages (ibid.).

Despite close links and ongoing relations with its neighbour however, Botswana cannot be compared to South Africa and, not surprisingly, the moral discourses in the two countries differ. This was true even after the post-2008 financial crisis outlined in Chapter 11. In Botswana, the state is all, the private sector still in its infancy. Botswana defines itself as a liberal democracy and modernising developmental state, not a socialist state, but it has also nevertheless conceived of itself throughout as a welfare state, responsible for the well-being of all its citizens. Without a legacy of racism and discrimination, Botswana at independence in 1966 was, perhaps because of its extreme poverty, one of the most inclusive countries in Africa. It relied initially and almost exclusively on development loans which were efficiently used and later converted by donors into grants. After the momentous discovery of diamonds and copper, however, the government gradually began to build a welfare state. Over time this came to include the free provision of health, education, including school meals, and, more gradually, social welfare services, roads, water, electricity and telephone grids, along with municipal services. However, as I document in Chapter 2, a universal national insurance scheme for unemployed workers remains lacking. Instead, in 2012 there was a patchwork of welfare benefits directed at those deemed most vulnerable.

Diamonds allowed the government to build up substantial foreign reserves until, as a result of the 2008 global financial crisis, Botswana ceased to trade in diamonds for almost a year and needed to appeal to the African Development Bank for a substantial loan, at which point the country's reserves began to be depleted at alarming speed.[23] This drove home the high dependency of Botswana, now a middle-income 'developed' country, on diamonds, a diminishing resource. Despite longstanding government attempts to diversify the economy, granting special dispensation to foreign investors and large loans to 'citizens' for entrepreneurial ventures, the private sector has remained very small, restricted to banking, retail and wholesaling or importing, with most goods imported from South Africa. This led to moves towards privatisation, artificially boosting the private sector, with a potentially dire impact on labour rights.

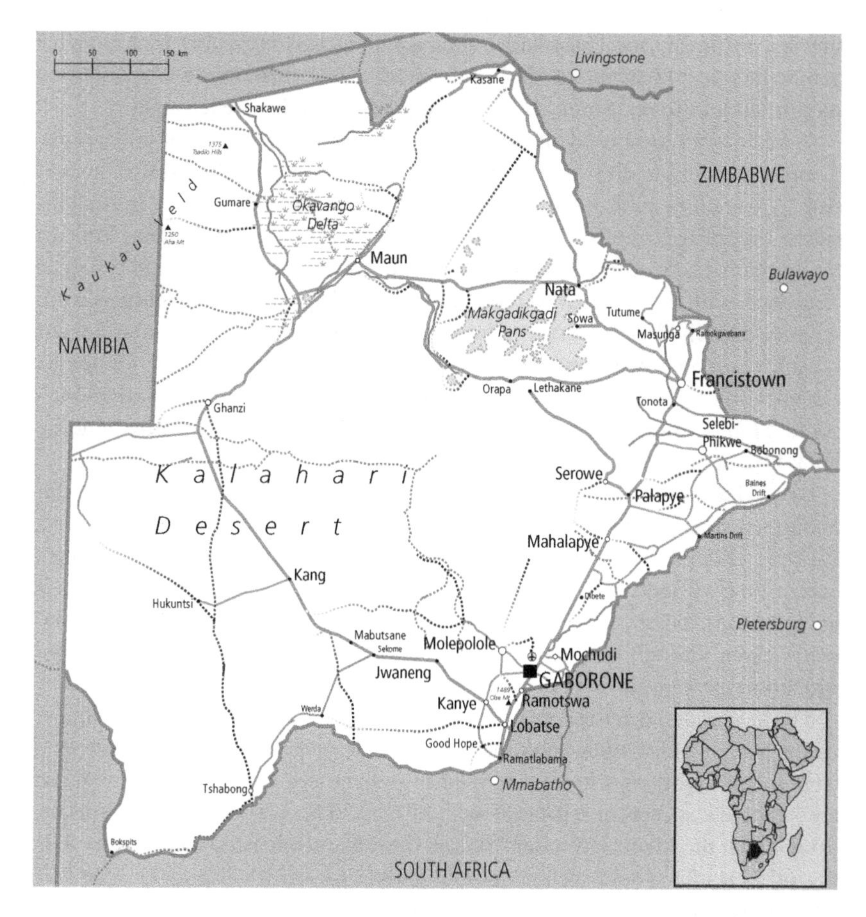

Figure 1.1 Map of Botswana (map by Peter Blore).

The Reliance on Government Wages: Moremi Village

Botswana is a country of villages. To give an idea of citizens' heavy reliance on government wages beyond the capital, an example can be taken from Moremi, a small village 50 kilometres east of the line-of-rail town, Palapye, in the Tswapong Hills, a village which my husband and I have known for almost 40 years.

In 2005, Moremi, officially a village of some 500 to 750 persons, including many absentee residents working in town, had ten industrial-class workers all living in the village, working as cooks, cleaners, pump attendants, night watchmen and drivers who each earned around 1000 pula a month (less than £100). Members of the Village Development Committee and the Home Based Care Committee received 120 pula a month, while 70 local persons were receiving a range of welfare benefits, of whom around 30 were defined as destitutes.[24] Local villagers could also earn 200 pula once a year, working for 20 days at 10 pula a day, on drought-relief projects. Many of the elderly living in the village over the age of 65 received state pensions. These amounted to 220 pula a month in 2012, a substantial sum by local standards, with grandmothers invariably looking after grandchildren who went to the local school while their mothers worked or sought work in town. Some children also received orphan-relief support.

In addition to local residents, there were primary-school teachers and a nurse living in the village who were born elsewhere in Botswana. By 2011, there was also a *kgotla* office with a clerk administering the planned game park in the hills facing the village, another government initiative. A lodge was being built in the hope that tourists might visit the reserve and the beautiful village spring at Manonye, with its cascading waterfalls. But a very large number of villagers were supported by children who were labour migrants working in town, among them a bank manager, several miners, two high-level civil servants and numerous casual workers, living precariously, who sent remittances when and if they could. Highly paid urban workers and miners signalled their success by building brick houses in the village, providing much needed work for local builders.

Beyond government employment, the village also had several successful traditional diviners, two tiny stores, a van owner who carried passengers to Palapye, a brick-maker, a potter and a few local builders or cattle owners. More enterprising villagers had planted fruit trees and vegetables in their yards, and grew melons, beans, corn and sorghum in their 'fields' (*masimo*) during the rainy season, though frequent droughts and lack of manpower made extensive agriculture precarious, with low returns for back-breaking labour.

The key point is that the core of the village – the active, energetic, civic-minded younger men and women who manned its wide range of village committees – were manual workers who earned regular government incomes, along with the few relatively successful self-employed villagers. This was the pool of workers from which the Manual Workers' Union drew its membership nationwide. The loss of their jobs would spell economic disaster for small villages like Moremi. This book is about the trade union that fought to protect their interests.

The class gap between the elite salariat and manual workers in Botswana's public service is evidently huge. Top civil servants are paid at least ten-fold the salary of industrial-class workers employed by the government, and often a good deal more, a gap that has continued to widen. Indeed, the gap in salaries created in the past a chasm between manual workers and civil servants, who were regarded as mere government stooges. Despite this, Chapter 2 argues that given the precariousness of unskilled work in the private sector, public service manual workers in Botswana could be considered a labour 'elite' in comparison to most other Batswana workers and potential workers. This was true even of women, on average more poorly paid than their male counterparts in the public service. In his study of Indian public sector workers in the steel industry, Parry found that workers' privileges militated against union protest (Parry 2008). As this book highlights, however, unions are neither the radical leaders of the proletarian struggle against government nor, alternatively, a co-opted body neutralised by government – historically, the MWU has been both at different times. The point is rather that the minimal security afforded by regular wages privileges state manual workers by comparison to unskilled workers in the private and informal economy. In the past, however, the educational and income gap between manual workers and other civil servants seemed unbridgeable, both ideologically and practically. The Botswana Federation of Public Sector Unions' 'mother of all strikes' in 2011 changed all this. In creating cross-class solidarities through popular culture, workers across the educational and income spectrum forged a new, vernacular working-class consciousness, clearly cognisant of and receptive to wider cosmopolitan influences, as I show in Chapter 10.

Outline of the Book

Chapter 2 interrogates and critiques the 'African labour aristocracy' thesis, and proposes that public service industrial-class manual workers in Botswana form, if not a labour 'aristocracy' in the sense first defined by Arrighi and Saul (1963),[25] then a marginal worker 'elite'. They are privileged in having a regular salary above the minimum wage, augmented by periodic lump-sum gratuity payments. This sets them apart from other low-paid workers in the private sector, casual workers in the informal economy and a vast army of unemployed job-seekers. In the absence of a national unemployment benefit scheme, the inventive strategies deployed by unionists attempt to contend with the potential spectre of future unemployment and impoverishment. Both Chapters 2 and 3 foreground women and feminine accomplishment. A gendered perspective highlights the independence, autonomy and decision-making capacity of women trade unionists, who straddle the worlds of workers' rights and citizens' rights, and manoeuvre their way through the maze of rules and regulations they encounter in both.

Chapter 3, tracing the careers of two Batswana women trade union leaders, explores ideas of ethical leadership in Botswana. Such leadership is understood as essentially dialogical, embedded in notions of dignity and responsibility, while activism has created an impetus for the women to expand their cosmopolitan political imaginaries. Against Michel Foucault's 'negative paradigm', proclaiming the illusion of agency, it argues for a more dialogical understanding of subjectivity, suggesting that an alternative reading of Foucault's later work provides insight into an ethics of the other, beyond the self.

Chapter 4 introduces the *kgotla la babereki*, 'the court of the workers', as trade unions are called in Botswana. As the name implies, the MWU is the workers' public forum or assembly, marked by elaborate procedures and structures determining union governance and charting some of the issues preoccupying low-paid public sector workers. Public culture was forged by the union through debate, popular songs, shared activities, grievance cases, meetings and rallies, beginning in 2005.

Chapter 5 charts the events leading up to the first Manual Workers' Union strike, in 1991, and the significance of the High Court and Court of Appeal judgements of the union's challenge to the government to reinstate dismissed workers with all their past benefits. The role of public ethics and morality in Botswana is reflected in key notions used by High Court judges, such as 'the duty to act fairly' and 'legitimate expectations'. Such ideas have not been adequately scrutinised by legal anthropologists, despite becoming a bedrock of contemporary judicial reasoning (Riggs 1988). While there has been a renewed interest in ethics in anthropology (Laidlaw 2002), issues of public ethics and morality in legal anthropology remain relatively untouched in contemporary debates. One has to go back to the work of Max Gluckman (1967) on reasonableness in judicial decision-making among the Barotse to find foundational anthropological insights into the morality and ethics of law in non-Western societies. In developing a contemporary legal anthropology of judicial reasoning inspired by these early insights, I draw on critical-legal theory, taking cognisance of the way politics, economics and notions of justice interact to affect judicial reasoning in postcolonial states. Against the argument that postcolonial litigation by human rights NGOs is a mere 'fetish' (e.g. Comaroff & Comaroff 2006) disguising disorder, I demonstrate that, on the contrary, the widening remit of judicial review in both the West and developing countries has critically challenged the arbitrary power of the state, even if it sometimes fails.

Workers' struggles for fair working conditions and wages are often conducted against huge odds, and failures are intensely felt as deep injustices, since they affect the very livelihood and dignity of workers. This is true in Botswana where the government, with its immense authority, legal power and financial clout, has repeatedly refused to recognise the validity of public sector manual workers' claims to a living wage. Notions of fairness and unfairness permeate relations with employers, and hence also litigation and negotiation in labour disputes. Judges in Botswana – especially in the High Court and Court of Appeal – must recognise these ethical considerations even if conservative judges find ways to reject them.

Chapter 6 examines the historical factors that led to a factional dispute within the MWU in 2004, which grew in subsequent years to involve a series of court cases and drew into it factional cleavages within the ruling party. The growing wealth of the union, despite the low pay of its members, the embourgeoisement of its employed officers, the domestication of ILO treaties, the limited success of Botswana's opposition parties, and internal divisions within the ruling party all combined, the chapter argues, to create an enduring split within the MWU in a dispute that ramified well beyond its local beginnings. In attempting to win its battle, the union was faced with the possibility of abandoning its sacred working-class ethos, built in the course of a constant defence of workers' rights. Seen as a social drama, the factional conflict extended as the 'breach widened', until it became co-extensive with a 'dominant cleavage' in the nation (Turner 1957: 91). ILO legal reforms newly introduced into Botswana meant that schisms within unions no longer required eventual reconciliation as they did in the past, when each union was a closed shop. This allowed the rebel faction to hive off and create a rival union.

Chapter 7 examines the political battle with the rebel faction following the legal victory in the courts. To make the court victory a political reality, MWU officers undertook a month-long arduous tour of the whole of Botswana, seeking to mobilise support in the 'regions', especially those backing the rebels. Their tour highlights the national reach of the union: the vast size of Botswana, its heat, dust, bumpy roads and out-of-the-way places came to be inscribed on the very bodies of unionists during the 2005 regional tour. The tour underscored the practical limitations of court judgements and commissions of inquiry to right a wrong without determined political mobilisation.

Chapter 8 describes the mobilisation of the entirety of Botswana's trade union movement in 2005 against the dismissal in 2004 of 461 miners by Debswana, the Botswana diamond company, following a strike deemed illegal. The struggle for workers' rights in Botswana drew 'spiritual' legitimacy from biblical truths learnt in the myriad churches workers regularly attend. As in American and British trade unions, in Botswana too the Christian God justifies and sanctions workers' claims and 'ennobles' their labour. Christian faith and current politics are interwoven in Botswana's union activism into a seamless whole, as God is beseeched in 'political prayers' to protect workers from greedy employers who rob the workers of their fair wages. Cooperation among the different unions and the Botswana Federation of Trade Unions (BFTU) during the 2005 protest rallies ended with the later formation of BOFEPUSU, a federation of five public service unions.

Chapter 9 examines the sources of charisma of the leader of the Manual Workers' Union, Johnson Motshwarakgole, who repeatedly figures as a mover and spokesman throughout the book. A man of humble origins, by his own admission, he is much admired and loved by rank-and-file workers, who believe he has almost magical powers to win against the odds in disputes with the employer, namely the government. An orator and man of the people, Johnson has dealt with other, more highly educated trade unionists, and with the employer, in trickster-like fashion, while balancing his conflicting positions as leader of Botswana's working-classes' struggle with the government-as-employer, and the increasingly powerful pressures on individuals living in Botswana's capital towards consumption and bourgeois living. The chapter considers the grounds for the evidently powerful charisma of this African organic intellectual in the light of these contradictory forces.

Chapters 10 to 12 are devoted to the 2011 public service strike, dubbed by the press the 'mother of all strikes'. Called by BOFEPUSU, the strike lasted for more than eight weeks. Chapter 10 explores the popular cultural dimensions of the strike. Like other protest movements in 2011, the strike in Botswana was aestheticised through a process of 'citation',[26] a fusing of past images and images from the spatially distant protests in North Africa and elsewhere with currently invented images in new bricolages and assemblages. The 'political' thus came to be powerfully inserted aesthetically by encompassing such displaced tropes, often subliminally, through performative acts of (re)iteration, 'doubling up' and mimesis, into the new context of the strike.[27] In particular, strikers and the media aestheticised the false pretensions to equitable pay of the government and its leaders while prefiguring, through performance, the 'just' society. The Botswana strike resembled new social movements in forging a shared identity across a wide occupational spectrum and in mobilising the whole of civil society in a call for dialogue and justice.

Chapter 11 looks at the political economy of the strike and its competing moralities from the perspectives of both unions and the government, a divergence which became more pronounced as the strike progressed.

Chapter 12 revisits the debate about the effectiveness of the law and of court judgements in the face of brute politics. Sceptical legal anthropologists have failed, I argue, to recognise that court trials are part of a wider campaign of social mobilisation and the struggle for social justice (McCann 1994; Snarr 2011). Legal mobilisation during the strike, and long after it had been 'suspended', was only one strategic part of a more comprehensive campaign to call on the government to pay its workers a living wage. The post-strike legal battles with the government through the High Court and Court of Appeal continued into 2013. The book concludes with a call for anthropology to re-examine some of its assumptions about the role of the law in postcolonial nations. Despite the possibility that judges may be biased or vulnerable to political influence, and despite the courts' restricted ability to implement their judgements, it is nevertheless the case that ethics, morality and the law, when mobilised alongside concerted political and civic activism, play a critical role in advancing the cause of citizens' rights and legal reform against an apparently all-powerful state.

CHAPTER TWO

A Labour Elite? Strategising Women and the Spectre of Unemployment[1]

A Labour Aristocracy?

The 'labour aristocracy' thesis, first proposed by Arrighi and Saul (1963), has been repeatedly and thoroughly discredited.[2] However, the need still remains to theorise the crucial differences between permanently employed, unionised African wage earners, even manual workers, and low-paid workers in the private sector, and beyond them the ever-increasing number of casualised workers in the informal economy of Botswana.[3] If industrial-class public sector workers are clearly not a labour 'aristocracy', they do nevertheless constitute a labour 'elite', signalling a critical rupture among low paid workers between those having agency, dignity and hope, and those lacking these basic aspects of well-being.

Against the view that unionised workers are necessarily co-opted into the ruling elite, critics point out that the labour aristocracy thesis ignored the huge pay gap between highly placed civil servants and other workers, whether miners or factory workers (Sandbrook & Cohen 1975). Reiterating this, Cooper says that 'the argument was misplaced from the start, confusing urban workers with a truly affluent city-based elite of politicians, senior bureaucrats, and others with access to power' (Cooper 1996: 461–2). The top echelons of the African 'salariat' were, Cohen concedes, both in lifestyle and ideology, a 'true labour aristocracy' (Cohen 1991: 85–6). This echoes studies elsewhere of the rise of an influential 'salariat' in newly independent South Asian nation-states (Alavi 1987), and of a 'state-made middle class' in newly independent Israel (Rosenfeld & Carmi 1990).

Arrighi and Saul's thesis, echoing Frantz Fanon, also posited a historically developing dichotomy between an urbanised proletariat and a potentially revolutionary rural peasantry. Against this polarisation, Adrian Peace proposed in his study of factory workers in Lagos that workers were never fully 'urbanised' (or permanently 'proletarianised') but remained embedded in multiple township and rural relationships, and dreamed of becoming self-employed entrepreneurs (Peace 1975).[4] This 'double rootedness' of urban migrant workers has been repeatedly noted, but less recognised is the fact that elites in Africa too continue to invest both symbolically and materially in the countryside.[5] Moreover, despite a wealth of evidence to the contrary, the linear historical view of urbanisation posited by Arrighi and Saul – from peasants to proletarians, urbanites and, indeed, 'cosmopolitans', still persists, as demonstrated in James Ferguson's analysis of the predicament of urbanised miners in the face of Zambian economic decline, who allegedly had cut off their links to the countryside during times of plenty (Ferguson 1999). Finally, rejecting the view that trade unionists are bourgeois organisations primarily focused on consumption (Sandbrook & Cohen 1975: 3), scholars widely agree that there is evidence in Southern and Central Africa and elsewhere of unionised workers mobilising in political struggles against social injustice and autocratic regimes.[6]

Saul subsequently reconsidered the labour aristocracy thesis and conceded that proletarianised workers may be distinguished from the 'bureaucratic bourgeoisie', and that under some circumstances the former may develop a more 'revolutionary' 'downward orientation' (Saul 1975: 305–6). This view is echoed by research on public service unions in Botswana by Monageng Mogalakwe, who cites an interview with a leader of the Botswana Federation of Trade Unions (BFTU) in 1991:

> The white collar workers are the least dedicated ... but look at the manual workers. They are the most militant and disciplined, and they support their union all the way. These are the most exploited workers ... They have nothing to lose. They do not start thinking about housing and car loans when they have to take industrial action. They do not start worrying about where they will get the money to pay their instalments if they are fired. They have no loans with the company or the banks. (Mogalakwe 1997: 104)

Mogalakwe concludes from this observation that in Botswana the civil service may indeed be labelled a 'labour aristocracy', positioned 'on the side of capital'. Unlike public sector manual workers, they have 'internalised a white collar mentality' based on the ownership of housing and consumer goods (ibid.: 104–5). But a stance of radical labour militancy may be misleading, as we shall see, misrecognising aspirations for long-term stability, house ownership and consumption among manual workers in Botswana.

A further message implicit in the interview cited above is that – since manual workers have nothing to lose – they need not fear unemployment. In a scathing critique of Ferguson's interpretation of the Zambian miners' predicament, Miles Larmer argues:

> although Ferguson clearly understood the underlying reasons for Zambia's economic decline and its devastating effect, he had virtually nothing to say about mineworkers' understanding of the decline, nor their resistance to its effects. In depicting mineworkers' lack of alternatives to rural retirement, Ferguson ... failed to explain that the [Mukuba pension scheme] strike was one expression of *an enduring demand by mineworkers for a sustainable urban retirement*. Such an approach reflects Ferguson's unduly sweeping generalisations, for example his claim that 'Copperbelt residents in the late 1980s did not inhabit a well-known and stable social order. They did not know what

was happening to them and did not understand why it was happening. *Neither did I*. (Larmer 2006: 25, emphasis added)

Here, Larmer is making the important point that workers, even blue-collar workers as in the case below, are fully conscious of the need to secure a decent retirement; indeed, part of their trade union activity is devoted precisely to this project. It is in this sense, we shall see, that permanent waged government employees, even those at the bottom of the scale, are a privileged cohort.

There is little doubt that African independence led to the rise of a state-made, affluent black salariat in many parts of sub-Saharan Africa. The elite included top politicians, senior civil servants and corporate managers, district and high court judges, army generals, professionals in the health service (senior doctors, hospital administrators), academics in state-funded universities, and managers, lawyers, accountants and engineers in state-owned mining companies or parastatals. Alongside these, in Botswana, senior civil servants, members of this educated elite, have tended to venture into business when they retire.[7] Many sit on the directorates of banks and other large companies. A few have moved into politics and have been elected as members of parliament. Nevertheless, they do not automatically support the political elite, as Cohen or Cooper assumed. Some of their interests are in good governance and, forming a distinguished cohort of the great and the good, they have frequently been entrusted to head government commissions of inquiry vis-à-vis the political elite.[8]

A further point needs to be made in advance of my argument. It is easy for anthropologists and other social scientists to disdain the fine details of policy issues in favour of the big picture. But when one lives on a minimum income, on the margins, details of wages and welfare payments are critical life-changing facts that cannot be ignored. The class gap between the elite salariat and manual workers in Botswana's government public service is huge, and growing. Top civil servants are paid at least 30-fold the salary of industrial-class workers employed by the government, and the salary gap has continuously increased with every cost-of-living settlement 'across the board'.[9] Despite this, I intend to show in this chapter that public service manual workers in Botswana are to be regarded as a labour elite in comparison to most other unskilled or semi-skilled Batswana workers and job seekers. This is true even of women, on average more poorly paid than their male counterparts in the public service.[10]

This is not to say that the Manual Workers' Union is either the radical leader of the proletarian struggle against the government or, alternatively, a co-opted body neutralised by government – historically, it has been both at different times, as will be seen in Chapter 7. Rather, I am suggesting that the minimal security afforded by regular wages and periodic lump-sum gratuities has given at least some members of the MWU the capacity to build their futures, which lower paid workers in the private sector and workers in the informal economy almost always lack. To fully appreciate my argument, it needs to be put into the context of wider debates on social welfare rights and the rise of trade unionism in Africa. Related to this is the question of the evolving, complex relations between town and country that industrialisation and urbanisation have created.

African Trade Unionism, ILO Conventions and Social Citizenship

As trade unions in colonial Africa increasingly began to mobilise and organise workers, their demands for improved pay and working conditions soon came to be framed in terms of international conventions applicable to workers anywhere. In the period following the Second World War, at a time when British and French colonial powers began to rethink their relationship with their colonies, the International Labour Organisation (ILO) based in Geneva became a key actor formulating the social rights of workers internationally (Cooper 1996: 216). In their attempt to portray themselves as progressive, British and French colonial powers accepted the new labour discourses, outlined by the ILO, as being applicable to the colonies, with dissent coming mainly from white settlers in these colonies. Among the range of issues brought to the fore in the ILO recommendations of 1944 were social security, job security, pensions, a minimum standard of living for workers and their dependants, and the 'stabilisation' of migrant labour (ibid.: 217–21, 364). Later, these recommendations were converted into a Convention (ibid.: 218–19), and they influenced the inclusion of social rights in the United Nations' 1948 Universal Declaration of Human Rights. The ILO thus became, as Cooper points out, the forum for the formulation of what T.H. Marshall called social citizenship as the right of the 'universal worker' (ibid.: 467).

The ILO 102 Convention of 1952 identified unemployment benefit among nine branches of social security.[11] Rather than recognising its essential necessity for the future of Botswana as a decent, caring society, Ntseane and Solo comment dismissively that the definition of these benefits is 'narrowly focused on individual risks arising in the work place', and does not include environmental factors affecting Southern Africa such as drought, floods or war (Ntseane & Solo 2007: 24). Nor does it take into consideration, they say, 'informal' social security arrangements such as mutual insurance funeral societies, which are widely prevalent in the region (ibid.: 24, 29–33, 48–84). Indeed, it appears that some 65 years after the ILO recommendations were first formulated, there is still a reluctance by the Botswana government, despite its caring record in other respects, to introduce a central pillar of the social security vision of the ILO: a national insurance scheme for workers which would guarantee them adequate unemployment benefit in case they lose their jobs. In this Botswana is not alone. Most of the 16 African governments in the Southern African Development Community (SADC), the exception being Mauritius, have failed so far to introduce the social benefits stipulated in SADC's Code on Social Security.[12] Although Botswana is a leader in Africa in providing free health and education,[13] accident and injury insurance, drought relief, maternity leave and a range of benefits for so-called destitutes, orphans, pensioners (over 65), war veterans, HIV/Aids sufferers, needy students, remote-area residents and other vulnerable groups, such benefits, usually in the form of food rations, cannot compensate for losing one's job, and are set well below the official poverty line or minimum pay set by the government itself. If a living wage in 1991 was deemed to be 600 to 700 pula a month, in 2002 so-called destitutes were entitled to a food equivalent from the state of 181.90 pula per month in the case of 'temporary destitutes' or 256.40 pula for 'permanent destitutes' (ibid.: 90–91). In 2009/10, food coupons were introduced instead of food rations, to the value of 524.25 pula, along with a cash allowance of 81 pula per month (rising to 90 pula in 2013), a substantial increase on the allowances I had earlier witnessed, but still inadequate, given inflation and the rising cost of living.[14]

This huge gap between salaried work as a low-paid government industrial-class manual worker and – in the absence of unemployment provision – risible destitute allowances, forms the context for the present chapter. It explains the entrepreneurial spirit displayed by the more fortunate among the government manual workers discussed here, and their bourgeois aspirations, which come not at the expense of but in tandem with their simultaneous long-term commitment to their status as workers and trade unionists. It also highlights the complex ways in which they manage their rural and urban assets and networks, alongside their claims to loans and other entitlements available to them as citizens of Botswana.

By contrast to civil servants, monthly wages for industrial-class workers varied in 2011 from a low of 1200 pula a month (about £110) to a high of 3400 pula for a storekeeper who has passed a vocational training course (about £300). Until their federation with the newly formed civil service union in 2008, union workers were not defined as civil servants and were not eligible for retirement pensions.[15] Instead, they were awarded a gratuity payment every five years according to a formula agreed between the government and the MWU, which amounted to five weeks' pay multiplied by five years of service. Hence a worker earning 2000 pula a month would get a gratuity of approximately 12,000 pula (around £1100) in a lump sum. Union officials explained to me that this was a far better arrangement than a final pension, which would be a risible amount, impossible to live on.[16]

The point I want to make here is that, despite their low earnings, the very fact that their wages are predictable, that they have bank accounts and that they receive occasional, large lump sums of money, makes public service manual workers in Botswana a labour elite among the country's working classes. In a society where, in the absence of national insurance and unemployment benefit as an entitlement, the loss of a job threatens instant destitution, the spectre of unemployment and with it the inevitability of losing one's home, usually mortgaged, and of the need to rely on very meagre state handouts or family philanthropy for bare subsistence, pushes those industrial-class workers who are able to save into entrepreneurial investments for the future. There are other public sector manual workers within this cohort, however, particularly women, who are the mainstay of a large number of dependants. These workers barely manage to make ends meet every month on a salary largely regarded by union members as starvation pay. According to Greener et al. (2000), even before the onset of the HIV/Aids pandemic, the income dependency ratio in Botswana for the poorest groups was 1:15.8 and this has risen to 1:23.7 following the pandemic.[17] Many families rely on the meagre state pensions of their elderly members. This means that a large number of people, many of them living in rural areas and including children, are often dependent on a single wage earner.

By drawing on case studies of women public service workers, most of whom were active in union affairs, I hope to show how some of the women have used their incomes and gratuity payments in order to raise themselves and their families into the entrepreneurial African middle class. Whether they have been able to do so depends in some measure on how many earners and how many dependants there are in their joint household.

One further point needs to be made in advance of the detailed case studies. It concerns the sharply declining importance of agricultural subsistence production in Botswana. This is partly due to the capacity of workers to earn much higher incomes in salaried employment, and it also relates to new consumer demands, even among rural households, with a rising expectation of minimum standards of living, mostly based on imported goods. During the 1970s, when my husband and I first arrived in Moremi, a small village in the Tswapong Hills, young men from the village, up to the age of about 40, worked on short-term contracts as miners in the South African gold mines. Many would come home to the village every October or November to plough, and stay for Christmas, before leaving again on a new contract. At that time, agriculture, including sorghum and maize cultivation combined with raising small livestock, mainly goats and more prestigious and expensive cattle, was the main form of long-term investment, and most people lived in compounds, in self-built mud huts made of locally gathered materials, with locally manufactured chairs, tables, stools, water pots, sand sleds and sleeping mats. Usually, they bought ploughs, basic utensils such as cooking pots and pans, plastic four-gallon buckets, radios, candles and blankets. The rise in earnings from regular rather than short-term jobs within Botswana after the discovery of diamonds, and following a succession of drought years, led to a decrease in agricultural production, which was never reversed. According to a recent report, between 1979 and 2001 Botswana's per capita production of cereal fell by 64 per cent (Earthtrends 2003). During Ian Khama's presidency, a range of incentives for agricultural production was introduced, but droughts continue to make even this unviable. Despite the country's vast tracts of land, and despite the considerable economic achievements of the country, one third of the population lives below the poverty line, and the government is the largest employer, employing 40 per cent of the workforce (Hansen 2008).

It is true that over the years Botswana has instituted a range of social benefits for what are termed 'destitutes' and, since the Aids pandemic, for orphans. Until recently it ran an annual drought-relief public works with pitiful pay (10 pula or £1 a day),[18] but as stressed already, there is no national insurance contribution system, and no unemployment benefit for workers who lose their jobs. Allocations for destitutes and orphans tend to be mainly of inadequate food rations, alongside 81 pula a month (in 2011) (see Figure 2.1). The status of destitute is highly stigmatised and, from my observation in Moremi village, even being categorised as destitute is often dependent on the whims of a locally elected village welfare committee, which judges its neighbours' entitlements to welfare, sometimes quite harshly. Most people thus try to avoid becoming stigmatised as destitute if possible.[19]

Figure 2.1 Monthly destitute rations at village shopkeeper's store.

Figure 2.2 The Manual Workers' Union Women's Wing (2005).

For some time the government of Botswana has been trying to formulate new comprehensive legislation on social security, in accord with the regional SADC code, coupled with its own national 2016 vision of a 'caring and equal society based on social justice', but there appear to be no plans at present to introduce unemployment benefit based on a comprehensive national insurance scheme for those losing their jobs. Such benefits are absent from the package being discussed. Nor is the Botswana Federation of Trade Unions demanding this, although now and then a member of the opposition or some other public speaker invokes the need for a national unemployment benefit scheme. What is carried over from the earlier phase of short-term contract labour migration to the South African mines is the implicit assumption that migrants who lose their jobs will simply return to the countryside, presumably to resume work in agriculture. Despite widespread recognition and repeated official laments that 'the extended family' no longer provides a reliable safety net (Ntseane & Solo 2007: 51), state policy seems to take for granted that workers, including women, who lose their jobs in town, despite owing mortgages on their houses, with children in local schools, will simply abandon everything, up sticks, have their homes repossessed, and return 'home' to the village and the welcoming arms of the mythologised extended family to subsist on agricultural production. Nor is it fully acknowledged that town is where the jobs are, and that the unemployed must stay there if they are to find another job. This is as true for middle-class women employed by NGOs as it is for other workers. It is equally true for manual workers, currently threatened by redundancies and transfers as government 'retrenches' or privatises many of its departments and parastatals.[20] The case studies below document the potentialities and limits available to low-paid government manual workers who must mobilise all the resources available to them as workers, often spanning town and country, and drawing also on their entitlements as citizens.

The Financial Strategies of Industrial-class Women Workers

The following cases illuminate the personal finances of four women, all active trade unionists in their local or regional branches, who live in widely separated parts of Botswana.[21] All four women combine voluntary union activism with full-time work. Their activism expresses their commitment as leaders. Their financial strategies express their complex sense of positioning: on the one hand, their consciousness of the precariousness of their jobs, and on the other, their bourgeois aspirations and shrewd understanding of how to access land and finance through multiple old and new government schemes for citizens. Three of the women were members of the Women's Wing of the MWU at the time of the interviews (see Figure 2.2).

Pillars of their Families

I begin by discussing two cases which demonstrate the limits posed by the lowly wages commanded by public service manual workers.[22] In both cases outlined here, the women interviewed are the mainstays of large families, and both are therefore unable in their present circumstances to use their earnings to lift themselves out of poverty.

Supporting Multiple Dependents: MaSeriti

In 2005 MaSeriti[23] was the voluntary, unpaid chair of the Women's Wing who sat on the National Executive Committee as a co-opted member (also unpaid). She also sat on the Public Service International's women's committee, again as an unpaid member.

A tall, somewhat angular woman, MaSeriti conveys a sense of calm, of being an able and responsible person, clearly a stickler for procedure. Although usually serious, she has a broad smile which lights up her face. Educated to Form 3 in her home town in northern Botswana, she was a primary school teacher for three years. Since then she has worked in a college of education as a library attendant. She has six children, all by the same father. She and her partner never married, she said, because his parents refused to pay the *bogadi* (bridewealth). Her partner was an alcoholic, who died of liver poisoning.

She remained with the children. The oldest was born in 1976 and was 30 at the time of the interview. He was a welder who did casual jobs and lived at home. But, she told me, 'children of nowadays look after themselves only'. Her daughter, born in 1980, was not working. However, she was completing Form 4.[24] A third child, a son, born in 1983, finished Form 5 and was completing a secretarial course in 2005. By 2011 he was in his fourth year of IT training. The fourth child was in the vocational brigades, studying carpentry. He too had finished Form 5. MaSeriti's fifth child was in Form 2, at a junior community college, while her sixth, born in 1993, was in Standard 6. Gilbert, her husband, a Kalanga (a different ethnic group) was from Musojane in the north-east. Broadly speaking, then, her children not only brought in little or no income; in fact, they were a drain on her resources. They were not the only dependants she had, however.

Her sister died leaving six children. She hadn't been married, so MaSeriti was looking after them as well. At the time of the first interview, one sister's son was a soldier, but he was still a private, she told me. He was the only one with an income. The older son did piece work. 'I am everything', she told me. 'The other children of my sister are attending school, one is doing NCC carpentry, the second farms, one is in Standard 6, and there are a boy and girl who are not working, aged 29 and 33. They have children'. All these nieces and nephews and their children lived with her. Her daughter too had children – four of them – but no husband. She too stayed with her. By 2011, the nephew who was a soldier had trained as an architect and subsequently left the army to start his own firm.

MaSeriti's mother never married, though she lived with the same man all her life. MaSeriti's parents died in 1983 and 2001, and her sister passed away in 1999. Now she was alone, she said. Her deceased partner's sisters and brother did not care about the children. The last time she visited Musojane was in December 2003. It was not a good visit, she recalled. She said it pained her because her children thought of her own father, their grandfather, as if he was their father. He was a good man, an electrician.

MaSeriti's circumstances were not unusual in Botswana. Her job as a public service worker saved her from destitution. Her job as a library attendant was defined as industrial work, even though the work that she did would seem to be better defined, she said, as 'P and P' ('permanent and pensionable', that is, being a civil servant). She told me she did the whole range of tasks in the college library, including cataloguing, shelving and serving customers. The librarian and assistant librarian were not industrial-class workers (that is, they were defined as civil servants). But in order to be promoted, she said, she needed to complete a one-year diploma. Even now, she told me, she was always attending workshops. MaSeriti never tried to go to university.

As a library attendant she was paid, in 2005, 1000 pula (less than £100) a month. Her husband left her nothing. She had a small house, where her mother used to live. There was a tap in the yard (a minimal luxury). I figured that MaSeriti is responsible for 18 dependants, in total. Some received orphans' rations but these were never enough. The previous year she had paid 4000 pula for her son's computing course in Gaborone, the capital. For the new course that year her son needed 300 pula but she hadn't paid that yet. He lived with her sister's son at the Botswana Defence Force camp just outside the capital.

MaSeriti joined the Manual Workers' Union in 1990, and in 1991 she became the assistant secretary of her branch. Tonota, in Central District, was made a region in 1995, and it was then that she was elected regional secretary. Since then she had been elected repeatedly, and had now been secretary for ten years. In 2004, at the union's annual national delegates' conference at Kang, she was elected as Women's Wing representative to the union executive along with MaSiame, whose story is told elsewhere (P. Werbner 2010a). All these positions are voluntary and unremunerated.

As secretary of Tonota Region, she said, she had been disputing the low pay for college library assistants for some time but had yet to enter into full negotiations with the Ministry of Education, which was dragging its feet. Library assistants at the Botswana National Library Service were paid 2000 pula a month, she explained – double her pay as an employee of the Ministry of Education.

MaSeriti was, above all, a committed trade unionist, conscious of her rights as a worker. Her leadership skills and qualities emerged in the course of fighting for workers' rights. Hence, she told me:

> People look at the work you are doing in your region. You have to work hard. You have to deal with the cases of the people there, without talking to Motshwarakgole [the national executive secretary]. Perhaps with advice, you can get to the bosses. When you talk to management they will agree if you give them the correct rules and regulations.[25]

This statement enunciates the bedrock of union negotiating principles: management will relent if you convince them that you are in command of the rules and regulations relevant to the case in hand. The task of union representatives is to persuade management of the fairness of your case. MaSeriti continued:

> You have a local works committee. I was shop steward for a long time; they elected me time and again. There are seven people on the management side, seven industrial-class [representatives]. But you must not show them that you are standing with them [i.e. backing the management's point of view]; they must follow the rules. You must be fair and tell them that 'you [i.e. the management] must do what you are supposed to do', and similarly [to] the worker. They [management] respect that. It's a difficult job. I'm still training the new shop steward. I am still training her. Some [union members] think they must [always] fight [the employer].

As chair of the Women's Wing and secretary of her region, MaSeriti had to speak in public and in committees, despite her relatively modest educational background. I asked her how she had acquired her rhetorical skills. Her explanation underlined once again the qualities of diplomacy, tact, patience and determination needed to become a union leader:

> How did I come to be able to speak in public? I got that from the union. When I started I was so afraid to talk in front of people. When you are a leader you are working with separate minds [internal divisions among members] and some are disruptive, but you must just understand them, be patient, and you will see that they will work with you patiently. It's bad to lose your temper, it leads to shouting. You mustn't follow people who are shouting. Nobody will know who the leader is then.

She commented on the behaviour of union dissenters at a recent general council meeting, which had erupted into a shouting match, that 'those who lose their temper lose "respect"':

> They were losing their temper. The Francistown [representative] – [she was] acting in a childish way, not taking us anywhere, even though she is an old woman.[26] People do respect you when you respect yourself ... She was shouting in bad ways. Women lose their temper. Even men do. But other women don't. They hold themselves. MaBotsalana [Elsinah, the salaried accounts officer in the central office of the MWU who facilitates the Women's Wing] doesn't lose her temper, she talks softly. [Did you see] how they were treating her, during the conflict? How they were talking to her? But she talks softly. That's why she's still here [has survived the union's factional divisions]. She doesn't show her feelings.

In the next chapter I outline the centrality of 'respect' (*seriti*) and honour in modern-day Botswana's union affairs. In MaSeriti's comments we see that respect is an intrinsic feature of achieving union leadership. It implies a capacity for self-control and rationality in dealings with others. This is also what endows persons with the needed qualities and capacity to lead and control others.

It was clear that MaSeriti's overwhelming financial commitment left nothing for entrepreneurial investment. Nevertheless, she had invested in her children's education and they appeared to be successfully acquiring skills and training that would equip them for better paid careers. In 2011, when I met her again, she told me she was on a two-year bi-weekly part-time librarianship course in Francistown. Once she completes the course she will double her pay from around 1200 pula per month to 2400 pula, she told me. She will then be on the B scale, B1 or B2. I asked her what she would do with all the money? She said she would build a house for her children.

Hence, despite the family responsibilities with which she was burdened, ultimately MaSeriti's job as an industrial-class worker did open up a path towards greater social mobility. In this case she utilised the route of adult education that many manual workers choose to pursue. Diplomas and certificates open up employment possibilities at higher grades within the Botswana government.

Investing in Property: Grace MaMolemo

My second case study is of a similarly burdened industrial-class worker. At the time of the interview in 2005, Grace MaMolemo was elected voluntary vice-chairperson of Gaborone Region, the biggest in the country, with almost 10,000 members. With the apparent defection of the chair to a rival union faction, she had become the *de facto* chair of the region, and in this capacity had attempted to unite the region behind the official leadership.

I met Grace during her lunch hour. She worked as a cleaner in the Ministry of Labour and Home Affairs. Grace is a mature and outspoken woman, a mother of eight, all with the same father, she told me. Unlike the case of MaSeriti, Grace's children appeared to have found work in Botswana's expanding economy. Only three of her children were living at home in 2005, two studying technical subjects in college, while the other five had jobs. Her husband had left her eight years ago and died four years later from Aids, she said. Since she had only completed Standard 7 (primary school), she was not eligible for promotion to other jobs, such as a messenger or switchboard operator, she explained. On the relatively meagre salary of a cleaner, Grace told me how she had managed: 'I paid for all my children at school. I had no allowance [from the state]. Transport is expensive. I don't buy them mobile phones, just toiletries'.

Nevertheless, taking advantage of her strategic location in the capital, with its rising land prices, Grace had claimed land through the Land Board and obtained investment loans:

> I have two plots, undeveloped. One is in Block 8 [in Gaborone] and one [at] Metse Mothaba [a village near Gaborone] – I got them from the Land Board [in fact, two different land boards]. Later, when all the children are working, I will develop them. The one in Gaborone, I applied for a loan from the Council of 20,000 pula for it, [I pay] 215 pula per month over six years. I spent the money [i.e. the original loan]. I pay [medical] insurance [104 pula],

> funeral cover [150 pula]. My salary is only 500 to 600 pula net [after all these outlays], just enough for food for the family and school things. In my life God is the only one who knows about me [i.e. no one else cares]. If I can work, I have money for food. I have no parents; my parents died. My two brothers and one sister are in South Africa … They are doing well, better than me. My brother is a government inspector of health. My sister is a nurse. The last one is working [there] in the First National Bank. Botswana is better but life in South Africa is better. The electricity connection is free [there].[27]

Grace worked her way up the union hierarchy to become the regional vice-chairperson. She told me:

> If anyone rings me having a problem with management, I try to follow that until I solve it. I am not afraid of talking to the management because I know our rights – regulations guide me in everything. I have to know how to read it [the book of regulations], to know all the sections.

Grace was critical of the rules that blocked her promotion. Even when she helped out as a messenger or switchboard operator, her pay remained that of a cleaner. In 1955, when she completed Standard 7, this was a reasonable educational achievement. However, the government, she said, 'blocks promotion for the uneducated'.

She herself was a strong supporter of the Botswana National Front, the opposition party supported by many of her fellow unionists, and she also had clear opinions about union affairs. Above all, she loyally supported the leadership during the factional dispute (see Chapter 6), endorsed the salaried officers' right to much higher pay than ordinary members, and denied allegations of their corruption made by the breakaway faction. 'They are tribalists', she said about them. At the same time, she was critical of the deal reached by the MWU on funeral insurance with a local commercial insurance company, arguing that it was 'too expensive' and that the union should manage its own insurance scheme (the scheme was later replaced by a better one). A forceful, energetic woman, I watched her chair a large general meeting several hundred strong in Gaborone Town Hall, with confidence and aplomb.

MaMolemo's case underlines the capacity of even the lowest-paid manual workers not only to support their children's education, but also to invest in land and housing for the future.

Citizens, Workers and Entrepreneurs

If MaSeriti and Grace MaMolemo are burdened with large families and no spouses, and hence do as best they can with very limited resources, other women are more fortunately placed to capitalise on their earnings as government manual workers and invest in the future, drawing on all the resources currently available to enterprising citizens in Botswana. One of these, MaSiame, had acquired prime tourist land from the Land Board at Chobe, and traded goods across the border with Zambia.[28] After attending a Public Service International (PSI) workshop, she explained the value of union work:

> You learn. Then you can do it in your country ... [L]ast time in South Africa – it was my first time to hear about fe-mi-ni-sm, women's struggle. It was there that I learnt something. It's good. Being a unionist is in the blood (*Union e mo madi a mi*). One day I want to see a regional chairperson who is a woman. In our region [Chobe] the chair and secretary are always men.[29]

Entrepreneurial Acumen: MaPelotona

My third case is of a manual worker who chose to take extreme entrepreneurial risks in her desire to advance herself economically. MaPelotona, a storekeeper employed in the central Gaborone store depot, earned 2000 pula (about £200) a month in 2005 when I first interviewed her. Two years later, having passed a storekeeping course with merit at the Botswana Institute of Administration and Commerce, she was in line for successive promotions over the following three years, which she said would raise her pay to 3400 pula.[30] MaPelotona was divorced, with three children. She came from a relatively prosperous rural family. Her mother and brother owned a minibus (a 'kombi') that ferried people from her village back and forth to the nearest line-of-rail town. Remarkable in her story is the extent to which Batswana in the know, with little collateral, can tap into loans for citizen enterprise, and access the higher echelons of the state for support.

She first embarked on her entrepreneurial career after she got married, and naively transferred the ownership of her plot in Block 8, granted to her by the Gaborone Land Board, to her husband ('it was a romantic gesture', she commented wryly). When they divorced, her husband claimed the property while the local council refused to grant her another plot on the grounds that she had already been given one. Eventually, her husband agreed to sell her their (second) plot in Tlokweng, formerly a village and now a suburb of the capital, for 65,000 pula, to be repaid in monthly instalments of 900 pula a month. She accepted the deal, she told me, even though at that time her salary as a storekeeper was only 800 pula a month. She used her rural income initially to pay the monthly instalments. She also managed to claim back money she had lent people (35,000 pula), with which she bought a kombi, driven by her brother, on Route 4 to Tlokweng.

In 2002, two years after the divorce, she received a 10,000 pula gratuity lump sum. She used the gratuity to build huts in the yard of her Tlokweng three-bedroom brick house, where she lives with her three younger children. In 2005, she had seven rooms in the yard which she let at 250 pula a month each, bringing her a total monthly income of 1,750 pula. In the meanwhile, she was promoted and her salary increased to 2000 pula a month. She thus succeeded, against the odds, in buying a substantial house and building up a minor property empire despite being a single woman.

The next venture she embarked upon was far more ambitious – to build a state-of-the-art storage warehouse in one of Gaborone's industrial zones. As a citizen, she borrowed 1.3 million pula from the National Development Bank, due to be paid back over 25 years in instalments of 25,000 pula a month (the debt subsequently rose to 1.5 million and then 1.8 million pula). When she took the loan, she told me, 'I prayed to God all night'. She had signed the contract just a few days before a 12 per cent devaluation of the pula, a terrible blow. Her plan was to rent out the planned warehouse's five units for 5000 pula each. To achieve this she first entered into partnership with an Indian and later with a Chinese builder. When I saw her again, in 2007, the warehouse had been built on a smaller scale than originally planned and the builder was refusing to hand over the keys, claiming she owed him 148,000 pula. She was also finding it hard to discover firms wanting to rent the units while the bank was threatening to repossess, due to mounting arrears. Perhaps hoping for divine intervention, she was attending a week's crusade of TB Joshua's Holy Ghost Prosperity Church. Her problems did not deter her, however, from investing in her daughter's wedding, which took place in South Africa. When I spoke to her, just before Christmas 2009, she told me she was suing the government in the High Court for repossessing the building.

Then, in 2011, she told me mournfully over the phone that she had 'lost my building'. Next, she came to see me in Gaborone, arriving in her own car straight from work in the stores, as elegant and beautifully presented as ever, with her smart clothes and a ready smile. She was now a supplies officer on the B1 pay scale, she told me, earning about 4000 pula a month.

She then recounted the amazing story of her warehouse. After I left Botswana in 2007, she said, she let the warehouse to the same Holy Ghost congregation whose meetings she had been attending. They paid her rent, 30,000 pula a month, for several years. Then, while she was working outside the capital, in Mahalapye, they failed to pay the rent for three months in a row, and the bank, the National Development Bank, said they would auction off the building. When they rang her, she first went to see the Directorate on Corruption and Economic Crime (DCEC) in the president's office, and from there, because they put her off, she went to see the finance minister, Gaolathwe, who referred her to someone in the bank, phoning the person in question and telling him the missing money could be drawn from the Citizens' Entrepreneurial Development Agency (CEDA). Her story was a little unclear on this point. Anyway, it seems that the official waited until the very day of the auction, which was a Friday. At the time, MaPelotona owed the bank 1.8 million pula. Officially, the property was auctioned off for 2.5 million pula.

MaPelotona was thus owed 700,000 pula, minus deductions for legal costs. But when she checked with the buyer, he told her he had actually paid 2.75 million pula – more than the declared sum. The bank had hidden 250,000 pula, she said, but all this came out in the High Court case, which MaPelotona won. When she met me, she still hadn't been paid the money because the lawyer who needed to be paid was delaying. She said that in actual fact the building was worth 3 million pula – and she still seemed to regret losing it. She told me that Ian Khama had been elected with a mission to root out corruption, which was rife and of which the sale of her building was an example. According to the new rules, a building cannot be auctioned off at less than its estimated value. Meanwhile, the church was still there, not paying rent because they said it was not clear whom they should pay. The net result of this complex chain of events was that she was set to get almost 1 million pula minus costs (for lawyers and auctioneers) as profit from the warehouse!

Despite all her capitalist ventures, MaPelotona remained a committed trade unionist. In 2005 she explained that she was chairperson of her branch, the headquarters of the depot with more than 100 to 300 members. It included not only storekeepers, but groundsmen, cleaners, night watchmen, drivers, switchboard operators, machine operators – as many as 200 workers. The vast majority of workers, she said, were industrial class, but there were also many 'P and P' (permanent and pensionable). There were seven big warehouses in the depot, and they were dusty and cold during the winter. As the chair of the union, she told me:

> We are complaining about a risk allowance. For three years they haven't responded because they don't do any maintenance. Dust, you can die from it after ten years! How did I become a leader? I think it's the way I used to call them [management] and talk with them and sit down with them.[31]

Social Mobility and Double-rootedness: MaJune

My final case is that of MaJune, the elected national treasurer of the Manual Workers' Union, who told me her story first in 2005 and then in 2011, during the great public service strike. A nurse orderly at the Marina Hospital in Gaborone, as union treasurer she had continued striking in 2011 in the face of a court order instructing all essential services to go back to work. Now, she had received a letter of dismissal. I was concerned about her: what would she do if the dismissal was not revoked? A woman of around 50 with few qualifications, what prospects would MaJune have of future employment?

MaJune had worked her way up. When I first met her, in 2005, she was living in the squatter settlement of Old Naledi in a rented ground-floor flat consisting of a well-furnished living room cum kitchen, with a TV, a picture of her Zionist Christian Church (ZCC) prophet, and at least one bedroom. At the time, MaJune was very apologetic about her accommodation. She clearly felt that living in Old Naledi, as she had for at least 15 years, stigmatised her. People from work, she said, never came to visit her at home. When people heard she lived in Old Naledi, they were afraid.

MaJune has five children, the youngest and oldest being girls. She was born in a village in the south, near Metsemotlaba in Balete District, not far from the capital, and is married to a Kalanga from Zwenshambe in the north-east. She told me that all the Kalanga she knew there had married Tswana women from the south. Until recently, her children had gone to school in Old Naledi, but in 2004 she moved them to live with her parents and attend the village school. The oldest was doing Standard 7. One lived with the grandparents in the north-east and spoke Kalanga better than Setswana. She moved them to the village school because in town there were no extracurricular activities like football, and the teachers, rather than working hard, tried to blame the pupils for their own failings. In the village, her older son had risen from being twenty-ninth in the class to being placed fourth. He was also very good at sport. In the village, the teachers really attended to the children, checked their corrected homework and so forth.

She met her husband walking down the road, she said. She wanted to marry first, before having a child, but he said, 'No, your younger sister has a child. I want to be sure you can have children'. The upshot was that she had three children (or more) before they finally got married, in around 2000. He paid 4000 pula in *lobola* (bridewealth in Kalanga), the equivalent of four head of cattle, on top of one head of cattle in damages (for impregnating her). Her parents said that that was enough since he had been supporting the children all this time. She was staying at her aunt's place when she met him, and used to sneak out during the day to visit his home. She hadn't realised that he too was in the process of joining her church, the ZCC. On one trip to South Africa, her friends told her, 'Your boyfriend is here'. He had come with friends. Then she met him at the border in his ZCC uniform. That weekend, the church was due to travel to Pilekwe, a south Tswapong village. Like many of the other unionists, MaJune was in the church choir.

By 2005, she and her husband had built a house in Zwenshambe, his home village. Since she was in government employment, they managed to borrow 20,000 pula and paid the brigades to build the house.[32] MaJune and her husband were only charged 12,000 pula, as she bought the materials herself. The house had three bedrooms and running water, but initially no electricity; they could not afford it though it was present in the village. They owned a car, and by 2011, a 'bakkie' (a pick-up truck), bought with her five-year gratuity lump sum payment, for 20,000 pula.

All these expenses, plus five children, meant that they lived very simply in Gaborone. Her husband was a salesmen. The children, she told me, do not like living with her mother, who is very strict, even with her, despite the fact that she is a grown woman and married. The children come home for the holidays and on weekends, and she and her husband visit the village quite often during the week, since it's not far. She explained that her children were considered Kalanga because of their father. But Kalanga were 'rude', she said, and you had to know how to handle them. Her mother-in-law demanded things from her rather than asking for them politely. But she had learnt to be rude herself, she told me.

MaJune was originally educated to Standard 7. She then took a course by correspondence and gained a Junior Certificate with a C grade.[33] She would have liked to continue to 'Cambridge' – the equivalent of GCSE, awarded in Botswana when graduating from senior high school – but her husband persuaded her to leave education for the moment. She explained that to get promoted at the hospital you had to keep doing courses. Thus she has done a course in being a receptionist and one in computing. She was now a nurse orderly, promoted from cleaner. In 2005 she was earning 1700 pula a month plus overtime for night shifts. By 2011, this had risen to 2600 pula a month, but with nights and overtime her take-home pay amounted to 6000 pula a month, more than double her regular wage. Working overtime was common among industrial-class workers at the hospital. They regularly worked night shifts, twelve-hour shifts, and weekends. MaJune told me she realised that she would not be able to earn as much as a receptionist, but she would like to be promoted to an ECG technical assistant. Her husband had been educated only to Standard 7.

Nowadays the hospital expects cleaners and orderlies to have a Junior Certificate – clearly an absurd policy when there are so many foreign nurses and doctors who can barely even communicate in English, or, if they speak English, their accents are incomprehensible. They come from China, Cuba and Kenya. Batswana nurses look down on them, so these newcomers turn for help to orderlies and cleaners like herself (in other words, low-paid manual workers play a critical mediating role).

We discussed the legendary rudeness of Botswana's nurses, highlighting the social gap with manual workers. She said that if someone comes for her, the nurses won't bother to look for her, they'll just say, 'She's not here', knowing perfectly well that she is. This got so bad that the cleaners asked to be told about all inquiries about themselves. Once her husband came to take her to a private doctor because she was ill. The nurse was very rude to him and said, 'She is not sick'. She told the nurse, 'I didn't tell you I was feeling sick, because you wouldn't have cared anyway'.

She stressed several times that the Manual Workers' Union was very powerful. Having been the Gaborone regional branch secretary, she was now the national treasurer, repeatedly elected since the Kang conference in 2005, and utterly loyal to the union leadership.

Sitting on a sofa in 2005, she showed me papers of her different committees, in order to explain how the events of the union factional conflict between 2003 and 2005 had unfolded. In 2005, the Botswana Women's Committee, set up by Public Service International via Elsinah, a union officer, included two other unions or associations besides the MWU: BULGASA (the Botswana Unified Local Government Service Association, which includes amongst its members nurses as well) and the Civil Servants' Association (BCSA). Although the MWU had initiated the Botswana branch, and was most experienced in union affairs, the others thought they could take over because they were more educated. They did not recognise that, as she put it, 'to be a unionist gets into your blood and reaches the whole body' (she made a gesture, moving her hands over her body). In any case, several things made the women's committee less than successful from her point of view. First, the previous treasurer of the union was one of the leaders of the rebel faction. She had dismissed Elsinah: 'Why are you here? You are going to be fired!' Elsinah was excluded from the committee, not at the SADC level but just in Botswana. After that, MaJune felt unable to attend and the committee fizzled out. Money, given initially to the rebel treasurer, seemed to just vanish. In 2005, MaJune planned to ask the committee what activities they had undertaken with the money.

The other thing she was unhappy about in 2005 was the Aids committee at the hospital. Management refused to give the committee the go-ahead, though money was available from the District Multi-sectoral Aids Committee (DMSAC), and despite the efforts of the coordinator. The deadlock blocked plans to sensitise workers, encourage them to test, advise them on their rights and hold a series of workshops. She herself had been to an Aids workshop in Johannesburg, initiated by UNISON.

Despite her achievements, in 2011 both her job and her position as MWU treasurer were threatened by her dismissal following the strike. What would she do? To my surprise, she answered a little enigmatically that she would 'sell vegetables'. By this time the family had left Old Naledi and built a new family-sized brick house in a developing neighbourhood in the capital, on land allocated to her by the Land Board. She had used her gratuity payment to build the house, moving in with all her children. As yet, it had no electricity, and only a tap in the yard. By 2011, her house in Zwenshambe had all mod-cons, including electricity and water, she had 20 'cows' and 50 goats, and her husband was under pressure to accept the village headmanship. Her fallback plan was to use her redundancy pay to expand and let the house in the capital. The large neighbouring houses were fetching rents of 5000 to 6000 pula (around £500) a month. She would go back with her children to Zwenshambe, grow vegetables and sell them in the local market.

Like the other women unionists discussed here, MaJune had used her gratuities wisely. Rather than flaunting her wealth, she had invested in houses and a 'bakkie', as well as in her own education and that of her children. She was paying life, medical and funeral insurance for herself and her family. During our conversations in 2011, I was impressed not only by her command of the union's financial affairs, no longer a novice, but by her command of English, as when she spoke easily of the union's salaried officers being 'mandated to work on behalf of the executive', or when she analysed Elsinah's qualities as a 'visionary' unionist (see Chapter 3). A confident orator who was among the few women to address the crowds at the Gaborone Secondary School grounds during the strike, she remained outspoken.

Conclusion

There is a growing literature on the predicaments female casual workers face in the informal economy.[34] Responding to the exponential rise in the number of casualised workers in post-apartheid South Africa, many of them women, Pauline Dibben has argued that 'South African trade unions should renew their focus on employment security, and in doing so should embrace "social justice unionism"' (Dibben 2007: 111). On closer reading, however, it appears that social justice unionism fails to address the challenge unions face to protect the rights of former members once workers lose their jobs. In the absence of a collective union struggle for national insurance and unemployment benefit, the four cases presented here highlight a range of *individual* potential strategies open to low-paid women manual workers in public service, with meagre but secure and predictable incomes. In the light of these findings, I argue in this chapter that, paradoxical as it may seem, industrial-class workers in public and local service in Botswana, though marginal, nevertheless form a labour elite among low-income, blue-collar industrial and casual workers.

There are no statistics to indicate how the tens of thousands of industrial-class public service women workers in Botswana manage their financial affairs. But it seems evident from the cases outlined here, and others I know like them, that such women seek or access certain privileges: virtually all have private health and burial insurance; all invest as best they can in their children's continuing education; all tap into citizens' rights to plots of lands; most have mortgages, and many are additionally now applying for development loans. At the same time, it is equally clear that whether or not they have a stable partner with a reasonable income, their lives remain precarious, and much of their investment is intended to protect them against the eventuality of retirement or job loss.

The women portrayed here were privileged in having a regular salary, well above the minimum wage though often below the poverty line, augmented by periodic lump-sum gratuity payments every five years. This set them apart from the vast jobless lumpen proletariat seeking work in Botswana's towns, or unemployed rural women dependent on remittances and occasional beer brewing. It also distinguished them, with the exception of miners, from other low-paid workers employed in blue-collar work in the private sector, or casual workers in the informal economy where salaries are much lower and often intermittent.

In the absence of a national unemployment benefit scheme in Botswana, the chapter has explored some of the strategies deployed by women members of the Manual Workers' Union in their attempts to evade the spectre of future unemployment, impoverishment and destitution. Seen in gender terms, the chapter highlights the independence, autonomy and decision-making capacity of women trade union leaders, who straddle the worlds of workers' rights and citizens' rights, and manoeuvre their way confidently through the maze of rules and regulations they encounter in both these worlds.

CHAPTER THREE

Women, Leadership and the Dignity of Labour[1]

From Subjection to Dialogical Agency

A key question not pursued in the early literature on labour relations concerns the extent to which a politics of honour and distinction is at stake in worker and trade union activism. The present chapter traces the historical evolution in Botswana of the notion of *seriti*, personal and collective honour and dignity, in the wider context of the emergence of what Iliffe has called a 'modern code of honour' (Iliffe 2005: 280). My approach echoes Lonsdale's analysis of the historical evolution of the Gikuyu notion of *wiathi*, self-mastery in labour (Lonsdale 1992), and that of Foucault's analysis of the changing meaning of *askesis*, self-fashioning and self-mastery, from the Greek to the Hellenistic period (Foucault 1987, 1990).[2] Unlike these two latter notions however, *seriti* even in its rural setting in Botswana, is not only a matter of self-mastery, but of recognition by others. *Seriti* is, in other words, an intrinsically dialogical notion, often related to the notion of *botho*, compassion or humanity. Tswana say that, *Motho ke motho ka batho*, 'a man [or woman] is a person through people'. This chapter moves from a broader discussion of current debates on subjectivity and ethics to a focus on the ethical subjectivities of two trade unionist leaders.

The poststructuralist turn in the social sciences, including social history, anthropology and feminist studies, has questioned E.P. Thompson's humanist conception of the acting subject, whose consciousness is embodied culturally 'in traditions, value systems, ideas and institutional forms' (Marks & Rathbone 1982: 8), and defined in struggle. In a far-reaching critique of Thompson's notions of experience, consciousness and agency, Joan Wallach Scott has argued that 'Thompson's brilliant history of the English working class, which set out to historicize the category of class, ends up essentialising it' (Scott 1991: 786). In particular, she castigates Thompson for ignoring women in his stress on an allegedly masculinist universal definition of class (Scott 1988: 68–92). In this respect, the project of the present chapter, to explore the subjective and public ethics of manual worker subaltern women leaders in post-independent Botswana, must necessarily contend with feminist responses to the early Foucault's deconstructive unmasking of the modern individual as inserted into inescapable discursive formations. These construct embodied subjects and subjectivities (see esp. Foucault 1972, 1977, 1980), allowing at most for a 'plurality of resistances' (Foucault 1980: 95–6).

Recent feminist scholarship has, however, questioned the constraints of this 'negative paradigm' of the subject, limited to describing subversive strategies or partial resistances to hegemonic normative regimes. Acts which 'transcend their immediate sphere in order to transform collective behaviour and norms', Lois McNay suggests, require a '*more dialogical understanding of the temporal* aspects of subject formation' (McNay 2000: 4, original emphasis). She thus proposes theorising a creative, active subject transformed not merely discursively (that is, in language) but through embodied action, self-narrativising and a capacity to imagine the social creatively (ibid.: 4 *et passim*).[3] A limitation in McNay's own work, however, is that she bases her critique on Foucault's first volume of *The History of Sexuality*, and thus does not attend to his later theorising of an ethics of the self in the second and third volumes (Foucault 1987, 1990). In this later work, Foucault developed what might be called an ethical theory of leadership, first hinted at in *The Uses of Pleasure* (Foucault 1987) and developed more fully in *The Care of the Self* (Foucault 1990), in which he theorises ethics not simply as aesthetic self-fashioning through personal asceticism, as in the first volume of *The History of Sexuality*, but as a theory of alterity, leadership and power beyond the limits of the polis, following the dissolution of its boundaries, with political space becoming much vaster, more discontinuous and less closed.

Citizenship, Honour and Dignity in Modern Botswana

Post-Foucault, we may conceive of subjectivity as the product of subjection and creativity co-existing historically in dialectical tension. In the present chapter I consider the careers of two women as trade unionists in the Manual Workers' Union. I locate their rise to positions of leadership in an epistemic shift in the history of citizenship in Botswana, relating to the grounding of citizenship in the right to a living wage. Chronologically, the shift was associated with the nascence of a collective working-class ethos and identity in Botswana, rooted in what Thompson, as we have seen, called a 'historical relationship' – in this case, with the black, African-governed, postcolonial state. Inserted as workers in Botswana's changing historical and political landscape, the women portrayed here sought, in different ways, to act and think in terms of wider social universes of discourse, expanding their current understandings of citizenship in the face of the state's failure to deliver what they came to regard as basic rights.

This process highlights the fact that subjectivities need to be grasped in temporal and creative terms – they are made and remade dialogically through tests and ordeals overcome. I mean 'dialogical' here in two senses: first, to refer to women's political engagement and struggle within the wider social field; and second, as reflecting vernacular notions of honourable ethics as they have come to be incorporated historically into Botswana's political discourse and 'modern code of honour' (Iliffe 2005: 280). My notion of dialogical also refers to Charles Taylor's argument (Taylor 1994: 27 *et passim*) that in the shift from feudal notions of 'honour' to notions of citizen 'dignity', secure hierarchies of ranking and respect have been replaced by the need for recognition, and that winning such recognition might fail (ibid.: 34–5). So too in modern Botswana. As Botswana has become more egalitarian and democratic, dignity (*seriti* in Setswana) – from being embedded in rural notions of ancestral protection and contingent on local prestige, gender, and seniority – has come to be a fragile achievement among strangers for both men and women. If, as McCaskie proposes, the 'Asante historical subject existed in dialogical consciousness', embedded in implicit collective 'background understanding[s]' (McCaskie 2000: 43–44), it is likely that modern Ghanaians, like modern Batswana, must win recognition in the public arena, and that this attempt may, and often does, fail.[4]

Seen in dialogical terms, then, I aim to show that the activism of the women described here emerged in response to the hard times they encountered, in contention with authoritarian or conservative voices and the perceived predicaments of vulnerable others. In ethical terms, their dignity (*seriti*) is linked by them to a sense of their rights and responsibilities as compassionate citizens (an ethos captured by the Tswana term *botho*). Notions of dignity, distinction and compassion define the qualities of the rightful leader in Botswana's modern-day political discourse, as they did for chiefship in the past (Schapera 1956: 137–8). Indeed, Botswana's most recent president, Ian Khama, has declared *seriti* one of his five principle aims in his platform for the nation (the other four, in addition to dignity, are democracy, development, discipline and delivery). Modern citizenship itself is a discourse that emerges dialogically; it is not frozen in a timeless set of principles, but encapsulates 'specific, historically inflected, cultural and social assumptions' as these emerge over time (Werbner & Yuval Davis 1999: 2 *et passim*; P. Werbner 1998).

I use embedded personal narratives to illustrate my argument. In doing so, I draw on a long tradition of African scholarship which stresses the centrality of narrative for recording the history of ordinary subjects alongside the 'morally determined, intellectually convinced, pioneers of a new Africa' (Lonsdale 2000: 6–7).[5] African narratives of selfhood embody different genres of telling the past, Richard Werbner argues. These emerge inter-subjectively, embedded in wider social relations (R. Werbner 1991).

A common historiographic strategy in Southern African scholarship is that of telling women's life stories or micro-histories, whether in order to recover their voices (Kompe 1985), to exemplify social change, highlight (racial) difference, or connect the global with the local (Marks 2000). Thus, for example, Deborah Gaitskell portrays the individual lives of mission women, white and black, and relations across the racial divide (Gaitskell 2000a, 2000b).[6] The shift in such narrativising by African historians has been, Hay argues, 'from queens to prostitutes' – from heroic narratives of prominent individuals to narratives of silent victims (Hays 1988). One problem in such micro-histories, as Shula Marks points out, is to underline both the commonalities and contrastive positioning of the women portrayed (Marks 1988).[7] As C. Wright Mills has argued, the value of biography lies in the way it brings forth recognition that one's personal troubles are shared by others and determined by wider structural forces; that the personal is also the political. Hence the biographies of particular individuals, he says,

> cannot be understood without reference to the historical structures in which the milieux of their everyday life are organized ... [T]hat is why culture and politics are now so intimately related; and that is why there is such need and such demand for the historical imagination. (Wright Mills 1959: 87)

The cases portrayed here are exemplary in the sense that they link the emergent recognition of shared predicaments to a widening sense of social responsibility, a move from the private domain to public activism, and the expansion of political imaginaries encompassing increasingly widening discursive horizons. My argument is thus that, for the women portrayed here, a sense of social responsibility for a vulnerable other is not simply pre-given. It is discovered through ordeals, which test the human capacity to act. This is an argument I have made elsewhere, in my development of the notion of 'political motherhood' (see P. Werbner 1999a). Political motherhood, as I have interpreted it, refers to the active move of women from their traditionally defined domains of *seriti* in familial care and social responsibility – from being a mother and wife – to being actors in the public sphere, often in the face of authoritative male resistance. Such processes lead them to 'discover' their role as public actors when they face hard times (Schirmer 1989; 1993: 58–9).

Writing about the rise of large-scale women's protest movements in South Africa, Gisela Geisler writes that in their heyday during the 1950s they were predominantly 'motherist'. Hence Lilian Ngoyi, the first president of the Federation of South African Women, a multi-racial organisation, 'called on women to be at the forefront of the struggle in order to secure a better future for their children' (Geisler 2004: 67). As Tom Lodge too argues, 'The most powerful sentiment was matriarchal, captured most vividly in the magnificent phrase of Lilian Ngoyi's: "My womb is shaken when they speak of Bantu Education"' (Lodge 1983: 151). It was only later that more explicit feminist agendas were developed by women.[8]

In theoretical terms this means that the subject, from being the object of subjection, becomes an acting agent over a lifetime. This transformation, it is argued here, occurs in active participation, in the challenge posed by hard times, by the encounter with oppression and discrimination, or the misfortunes of vulnerable others. Particularly in the case of women, activists often begin as wives and mothers in the domestic sphere, only 'discovering' their role as public actors when they face hard times. Ultimately, this activism leads them to engage with more universalist knowledge regimes and gendered or human rights discourses.

In this chapter I extend the comparative argument about political motherhood further by examining the unfolding ethics of contemporary African women activists. My acquaintance with the women portrayed here has been long term, based on many conversations and shared participation. Each of the women was interviewed formally at least once (in 2001, 2005, 2006 and 2011) at some length. Both trade unionists are (or were) union officers, firsts among equals in their union's collective action. Elsewhere I have compared them with a woman politician and international civil servant whose more elevated status enabled her to initiate major national and international policies in her own right (see P. Werbner 2009b).

Generational Consciousness: Two Women

While it may be true that postcolonial African women have moved into the public sphere in confronting hard times, these hard times have differed considerably for elite and subaltern women. The two cases discussed here trace the evolving subjectivities of subaltern women workers in Botswana in their involvement in the collective struggle for a decent wage. Elsewhere I show that for an elite woman in Botswana her subjectivity evolved as she felt compelled to respond to the HIV/Aids pandemic ravaging her country, and the world.[9] In each of these cases, the women's life histories reveal a dialogical movement in which they reached consciousness and self-consciousness of wider global or cosmopolitan discourses, whether of labour or human rights.

One could equally well, of course, talk about Batswana men who faced the same sorts of ordeals. I do so in Chapter 6, but I believe that a dialogical understanding of women's subjectivities as leaders is important precisely because the distances they have had to travel from being daughters, wives or mothers to public actors are often much greater, and because their interpretations of global discourses are inflected by their femininity. We see this in the remarkable autobiography of Emma Mashinini, a pioneering black woman trade unionist and activist in apartheid South Africa (Mashinini 1989). If, as Nancy Fraser argues, 'many of us who had been "women" in some taken-for-granted way have now become "women" in the very different sense of a discursively self-constituted political collectivity' (Fraser 1992: 179), this discursively constructed counter-hegemonic identity has nevertheless come alongside an identification with, and command of, broader discourses of social justice which encompass men as well as women. In this sense, the 'her-stories' presented here are not intended to relegate women to a 'separate sphere', isolated and apart from men, as Scott (1988: 20–21) suggests.

Both unionists were born just before 1966, the moment of Botswana's independence. They thus grew up in a time of scarcity and relative poverty, before Botswana's diamond wealth created a boom in personal consumption and its associated politics of desire. Although both have relatives in South Africa, they are committed Batswana citizens, dedicated to the country's project of nation-building, and share its ideology of development, as promoted by successive Botswana governments. If they opposed government policies, it was for the sake of just citizenship as they envision it. To the extent that they were also cosmopolitan subjects, they see the wider world as embodying values of justice and human rights which they believe should apply at home. Their careers, in many ways typical, portray the encounter of positioned individuals vis-à-vis their own African elected government in changing historical circumstances.

Seen sociologically, the women are thus part of a single 'generation' in the sense defined by Mannheim (1997). Mannheim argued that generational consciousness is always positioned temporally and socially. This means that those exposed to the same historical and cultural circumstances have, he proposes, a generational 'location'. In this sense members of a generation are 'sited'; they are 'held together by the fact that they experience historical events from the same, or a similar, vantage point' (Edmunds & Turner 2002: 2). At the same time, however, people may respond quite differently to the same historical events in terms of their class, status and political attitudes. In other words, their interpretation of these events may differ quite markedly. They may be liberal or conservative, religious or secular. This creates, according to Mannheim, generational 'units' or identity cohorts within the broader generational cohort (Mannheim 1997: 306–7).

In addition to generation, then, actors may also be positioned by class and status, as the cases below illustrate. I begin my account with the personal life story of a union activist, who rose to be vice chairperson of the Manual Workers' Union, based on research conducted between 2005 and 2011.

The Case of the Feisty Unionist

Many members of the Manual Workers' Union of Botswana are uneducated, relatively speaking, and they work in unskilled or menial jobs for very low pay. Not surprisingly, many, at least 50 per cent and probably more, are women. If anything, women trade unionists occupy even lower employment positions than their male comrades. They are certainly positioned below other public service women employees such as teachers and nurses. Unlike nurses in South Africa during the apartheid era who constituted the nascent black middle class (Marks 1994), both men and women in the MWU identify explicitly with the working class and with the international workers movement.

Their moral courage in claiming their rights as workers was displayed by the MWU in what has come to be mythologised as a glorious history of struggle. The struggle proved that although the union's workers may be uneducated, they cannot be intimidated, above all because they are rights experts. Against the grain, the union demanded a fair wage from government. At the time its members were earning as little as 236.72 pula a month, which amounted in those days to less than £50 in 1991.[10]

The 1991 strike, which lasted for four or five days, discussed in detail in Chapter 5, is a remembered heroic fable of worker solidarity. It took a further ten years, until 2000, to achieve the minimum-wage settlement demanded during the strike, in many ways by then a pyrrhic victory, and it involved the union taking the government to the High Court of Botswana and then to the Court of Appeal.

It was during those heady days that Lilian Mamoshe (a pseudonym) chaired and led the MWU in her region before becoming, in 2004, a nationally elected vice-chair. Lilian was a messenger in a government office. She was excluded from school at 16 when she became pregnant, and was a union leader by the age of 22. By the age of 30 she had been widowed and left to bring up four children.

Despite her lack of formal education, over time she succeeded in mastering basic word-processing skills, Excel, the internet and e-mail, and acquired competence in spoken English.

I first noticed Lilian as an outstanding singer of union songs. Never a great reader, the songs were for her a bridge to those other worlds of struggle, to a wider consciousness. She told me: 'When you sing these songs, you feel very happy, that you are very strong and it gives you the bones [i.e. the strength], like medicine. You feel at one with other workers'. As a woman, she had suffered. She was the victim of arbitrary rules which first removed her from education, then left her without compensation when her partner, who never married her, was killed in a road accident. Even when he was alive, although he professed to loving her deeply, he was, nevertheless, something of a philanderer. She managed her household and brought up her children alone. But she did not see her agency in her womanhood. She told me:

> I'm a man. I've never gone to those things of the Women's Wing. I just act like a man. I chaired the region for many years. Men like performing, standing in front of people. Women, I've noticed, like being the secretary, supporters behind the scenes ... To me, I've never been in these women's councils pushing men away from us. I don't like working on one side – from experience, when we women get together, we fight. There is a lot of jealousy, yes, even witchcraft – too much. Men like a big base, they want to be respected, honoured (*ba batla seriti, ba batla go tlotlwa*). Women are not so worried about that. They show off, they just show off ... That's not *seriti*, just to shine! Myself, I want to act like a man.

Lilian prided herself on her oratorical skills. When she stood up in front of an audience, she said, she was listened to intently, she held her audience. At my request, she described the time of the great strike, the moment of remembered heroism.[11]

> I started on 122 pula a month. When we went on strike, in 1990 [the strike began in November 1991], I was on 322 [or 276, unclear] pula. Myself as a politician I had once been in a seminar with Mr Marambo [a union official] who taught me about inflation and the poverty datum line, which was 276 [pula] a month, which means I was being paid at the poverty datum line. That is why I had the strength to teach my colleagues why the salary was so low. I was the vice-chair of the region, but in fact acting as chair because the chair was never there ... Sometimes I attended the union's general council. When we came close to striking I started to attend. The decision came after the government went back on their agreement [with the union]. Some members didn't really understand, many had never been to school ... we just made a simple example, so they could understand. We took three plates, and we put *bogobe* [traditional porridge], on the first plate just one teaspoon, on the second four teaspoons and on the third a huge quantity. The huge one represented

> the ministers and perm secs [i.e. permanent secretaries], the medium [plate], the supervisors. We the workers had just one teaspoon.

Her account highlighted the claim often stressed by union leaders that, although they were uneducated, they understood their rights. Lilian went on to highlight her own personal struggle against injustice in the workplace.

> We had a lot of general meetings. Here [at her workplace], they knew me, first when there was a lady who was our administrator, at the district office, who was very corrupt and I exposed her. When you are a chair you have to arrange for the meetings, cases and so on.

She described the sense of solidarity and shared commensality as memorable aspects of the strike:

> We went on strike for four days. It was long [for us] because it was our first time to strike … We were at the DC's [district commissioner's] office every morning, just to stay down, with our breakfast and scoff tins [lunch boxes] … and we sat on the ground, on the grass, sleeping, but with exact times: we ate breakfast at 8, lunch at lunch time, all [of us] together. The DC was instructed to fire us from the place, to expel us, (so) then we went outside to the trees, there were some big trees outside the magistrate's court … [That is] also where political rallies were held, we went under the trees. We agreed that all of us, every morning, should come and report there. We took the register. First we prayed, then we sang union songs, me and my secretary, we are both Roman [i.e. Catholics].

Communication and coordination across the whole country was a key challenge; and strikers required ingenuity and cunning to overcome the obstacles put in their way. They were helped by the Catholic church:

> The DC had left an instruction that we could not use the phone, so there was no communication. In those days there were no mobile phones in Botswana. So we went to see the Father at the mission to tell him our problem – can we use your fax and your phone? He even came and prayed for us the second day. That was after we'd been expelled. There were so many journalists, and Radio Botswana!
>
> Then we phoned Motshwarakgole to know the news. What the government was deciding. So we could stop the strike. That time Mabutsane [a remote village in southern Botswana] was under me, and then all the way to the Barolong farms and Moshupa. The regions were very big. 'Where are you? Roger Roger, under the tree! Go on, Roger'. It was very tough, we tried our level best, we stole the roger roger [i.e. the walkie-talkies] from the government – radio communication [i.e. the people working in that department], they stole it. And when we talked to Mabutsane all the other places could hear us.

> All of us were fired, on the third day, the government announced they were firing us. On the fifth day when we went to work we found the letters dated two days previously.

Her vivid memories underline the enormity of the achievement the strike represented for union members. Although the strike itself was brief, it was followed by nine years of litigation and political struggle in Parliament, represented by the opposition parties and through the press and media: 'The cases [against government, in the High Court] went on and on …'

Achieving Equity: Labour Grievance and Dispute Settlements

Shop stewards and branch and regional officers like Lilian are experts on the laws and regulations governing employer–employee relations. Disputes may be frequent and time-consuming. Reporting on the pressure union activism entails in the USA, Suzan Erem says:

> In Metropolis, I put out fires daily … Many of my co-workers put in ten- and twelve-hour days regularly. We don't get overtime. Hell, we don't even get comp time though we might spend six months in negotiations getting it for our members. We never have time to catch up on our paperwork … We barely have times to get to the meetings we're expected to attend, including interminable staff meetings that provide us with no useful information. (Durrenberger & Erem 2005: 39–40)

Erem shows how complex defending a worker's interests can be (ibid.: 66–9), a 'ritual dance of power as intricate as any' studied by anthropologists (ibid.: 74).

Like all judicial processes, workplace dispute settlements resemble 'rituals', but only in the sense that they follow elaborate procedures which union reps must master to be effective. The intricacy of the grievance disputes handled by Lilian as a union representative demonstrate the ingenuity required to reach a satisfactory resolution, her willingness to appeal cases to higher levels, to different ministries, and with a range of different officials. The cases also underscore the human, humane, ethical dimensions of case settlement, beyond sheer legal technicalities. In several cases, Lilian acted out of compassion and concern for workers and their families, even when the law appeared to be against them.

Lilian worked for the Land Board, but the cases she recorded for me extended to other departments as well. Her outstanding ability to negotiate tough cases is a remarkable but not unusual testimony to the acumen and knowledge acquired by industrial-class workers. Despite being self-taught, she was fully in command of labour laws, pay formulas and due process. Her report of the cases was striking for the briefness of its description, its focus on the key issues at stake, and how to resolve them. She stripped away extraneous details irrelevant to the case, much as a lawyer would, even though each case involved several meetings, singly with the worker or employer and then in joint hearings. I present the cases in the first person, as they were reported to me (for more cases, see the Appendix, pp.256–9).

The Case of the Inebriated Fieldworker

This case concerned an officer employed by the Department of Roads as a fieldworker. He was dismissed 15 years ago. He approached me through referral by his peers, since we were not in the same union. Because he came with such a pathetic case, I had to represent him for the sake of the worker's rights. In his case statement he said he was dismissed by his then immediate supervisor, who stated, according to the allegation, that he was under the influence of alcohol while on duty. He was given a dismissal letter on the spot.

I appealed to the officer in charge, Kanye, who claimed that, to his dismay, it was a new case to him, which he had never dealt with, under the pretence that he did not know the whereabouts of the fieldworker. He simply clarified his statement that he thought the officer had absconded. The fieldworker's personnel file had no copy of any dismissal letter. We had to build the case out of his dismissal letter.

The matter was taken further by the officer in charge to the director of roads headquarters. We had a meeting – myself, the immediate supervisor, the officer in charge, the fieldworker and the director. Initially, they insisted that there was no case to deal with because the matter was taken over by events. I raised my concerns that the case from the beginning was not properly dealt with. The arguments of the case were: first, it was based on allegations; second, there was no medical report as evidence or proof that the field officer had reported for duty under the influence of alcohol; third, the then immediate supervisor took advantage of the field worker's ignorance of the law.

Resolution: The fieldworker was reimbursed and reinstated. He was paid his salary for the past 15 years in full, amounting to the sum of 280,000 pula, and he was additionally awarded his accumulated leave days.

The Case of The Decent Accommodation Allowance

The Department of Roads had a case of 50 employees, all fieldworkers. For the past eight to ten years they were employed and stationed outside their duty stations, with their salaries not attracting decent accommodation allowances, equivalent to 850 pula per month per employee. I was approached to handle the case by the officer in charge, Department of Roads, Kanye. This was prompted by a directive from the Directorate of Public Service Management (DPSM) that a decent accommodation allowance be paid to every government employee designated as filling a fieldworker post and stationed outside their duty stations.

The arguments during our discussion were: First, the officer in charge, Department of Roads, Kanye, pleaded with me to negotiate to pay fieldworkers at least five years in arrears instead of their actual years served. I stood by my word to advocate for the workers' right to be appropriately paid for the full eight years. Second, the officer in charge took the matter further to the Department of Roads head office, arguing for the absence of source funds to pay the 50 fieldworkers, involving a huge sum of money outside the Department's budget.

Resolution: The 50 fieldworkers were appropriately paid all their outstanding money, and today they receive a decent accommodation allowance.

The Case of the Alcoholic Driver

A driver employed at the Department of Food Resources was caught under the influence of alcohol and in possession of a whisky bottle while on duty. The management took him to hospital to be tested for alcohol levels in his blood. He had no control at the time because he was so intoxicated. I came on board as his union representative. During the disciplinary hearing he admitted that he was guilty, and I had no grounds for defence because of the medical report, which was brought as evidence. I could see no way to defend his case. I had to seek a loophole so that at least he would gain his benefits. Under the regulations of employment, his 21 years of service benefits would be forfeited in case of dismissal. Looking at his social grounds, the fact that he was an alcoholic and had a family to look after as a bread winner, I took the initiative of going to his family to have a serious talk, especially with his wife. I was in a rush to at least let him resign from work before the final response from the permanent secretary came, since I realised that this was the only way he could save his benefits.

Resolution: I advised him together with his wife to resign within 24 hours in an effort to protect his benefits before the permanent secretary's final response. The management refused to accept his resignation letter, and I took over the matter and persuaded them to accept the letter. I personally called the permanent secretary, asking him to instruct them to accept the letter. The employee managed to get all his benefits. The payments were issued under the wife's name, because he himself was confused, out of frustration and not being in a stable condition of mind, having lost his job. But at last he coped with the situation to authorise the cheque in his wife's name.

The Case of the Pregnant Hospital Employee

At Kanye Seventh-Day Adventist Hospital, the management had a rule regarding female members of staff who were not married: when they went for maternity leave they would be compulsorily sacked. This rule of sacking unmarried pregnant female employees had been in effect for a long time. I came on board to defend one of the employees expecting a baby. The hospital management had a verbal discussion with me about this gender discrimination, and in confidence they disclosed the rule.

Resolution: The employee was paid maternity leave on condition that she was given three months' salary in advance and would be able to come back to work and resume her duties after the baby was delivered. I had to agree with this condition because I felt it was better than having her sacked. Even today the hospital is still using the rule of sacking unmarried expectant women employees, and some concerned MWU officers in the hospital do not come to the union for assistance to try to resolve this. They just accept the ruling.

The Case of the Rude Secretary

The senior typist at the Land Board was dismissed by management on the alleged grounds that she had used vulgar language towards her immediate supervisor during an argument in the office. She was dismissed right away, without being given the opportunity to defend herself or seek assistance from her union representative.

She called me on board to represent her as shop steward. I appealed the case to the permanent secretary of the Ministry of Lands and Housing.

Resolution: The permanent secretary resolved the case in favour of the senior typist, who was to be reimbursed and reinstated following three months absence without pay. The arguments were as follows: first, the case was not procedural, and did not deal with any charge quoted under the employment regulations; second, the dismissal letter contained no charge as per the employment regulations; third, the case had no minutes of its proceedings; fourth, the employee was denied her rights by the employer in terms of standard disciplinary procedures. Because I defended the typist in this case, my boss – who had tried to fire me – decided once again on my transfer, and this led to events described below.

Lilian's Ordeals

The final case I discuss here involves Lilian herself. Although she did not see herself as acting like a woman, and indeed had easy relations with male union comrades, Lilian's victimisation on this occasion was very much that suffered by assertive women in lowly positions. She told me:

> The union destroyed my future because of the strike. I am unlucky with bosses, every time I meet a tough boss who refuses to promote me. I'm at the top notch of A2 [a pay scale], on the bottom scale. My bosses refuse to promote me. I would prefer to be a field assistant. They think I'm a bully, that I'm tough.

Lilian did not allow men to dominate her. She demanded respect. She expected that her dignity and self-dignity, her *seriti*, be recognised. She was no longer the young girl expelled from school. But in her position as a manual worker, even as an elected national officer of the Manual Worker's Union, she seemed repeatedly to be forced into a clash of wills with dominating men. While she was the elected regional chair she led the union, she had the power of office. She represented members and settled their disputes with management with great skill. She told me, 'to be the chair of a region is tough'. But it was also rewarding. In her new, somewhat ambiguous status as elected vice-chairperson in 2005, she often felt marginalised and continuously struggled to find a role and voice. Eventually, in November 2006, she was compelled to leave the union after a confrontation with two union leaders, one a former colleague and friend from her own region, who had 'insulted' her. She began supporting a breakaway rival union. But through it all, through all her struggles, she saw herself as first and foremost a unionist, part of a heroic self-narrativising that gave meaning to the daily slog, and vision to her life.

Lilian's greatest ordeal as a worker came about as a result of a familiar conflict the world over: the clash between boss and underling. As a messenger for many years at the Land Board, she had seen bosses come and go. As a union leader, she had dealt with many of them in her feisty way. One of her bosses was particularly difficult, and she had a series of clashes with him culminating in a public stand-off which led to an extended series of disciplinary hearings, listed below. These exemplified the tenacity unionists must have in their dealings with government. It also exemplified the vulnerability of manual workers who lose their jobs in a time of high unemployment and government lay-offs, as we saw in the previous chapter.

The Case of the Offending Beret

The incident that sparked the case against Lilian happened during a public meeting with the permanent secretary of the local branch of the Ministry of Lands and Housing. Lilian attended the meeting wearing a beret and refused to remove it when asked to do so by the head of the local branch of the Ministry (she explained later that she had not groomed her hair). In retaliation, her boss had her physically moved to the back row. Henceforth followed a series of confrontations and internal disciplinary hearings which ended with the decision to fire her. When I first discussed the case with her, she was cavalier about it, invoking the length of time she had worked at the Land Board, which she felt gave her a measure of job security. Gradually, however, it became evident that her boss was determined to get rid of her. She had heard that he was accusing her of bewitching him, and had even treated the walls of his office against sorcery. He would not allow her to enter his office.

Despite her reluctance to mobilise the MWU officers, she asked fellow unionists to represent her. In a series of meetings involving the permanent secretary and his deputy over a prolonged period, her case was repeatedly heard, and the decision that her dismissal had been illegal repeatedly reiterated by the permanent secretary and his deputy. But her boss dug his heels in and, having been suspended initially with pay, her salary was stopped and she was compelled to manage for several months without any income at all. In effect, she was destitute. She had no savings, no unemployment benefit (non-existent in Botswana), no income from the union, which does not support unemployed members, and no job. The house she was living in was rented and belonged to her employers, and three of her four children were still attending school at the time and could not be easily shifted.

Just before the last scheduled hearing, her boss had a road accident while driving with two colleagues in a government vehicle. He was laid up in hospital, seriously injured. Lilian told me over the telephone that the final hearing had been postponed. She also told me that colleagues in the local branch of her workplace had been coming to her with information about the boss – in particular, that he had bought a vehicle without tendering, breaking regulations and hence subject to charges of corruption. She felt sure his days in the civil service were numbered. His accident, she speculated, had convinced him that her witchcraft powers were huge, but, although she heard rumours about this, he had not come out with a public accusation, since witchcraft accusations are against the law in Botswana.

After so many dashed hopes that the case would be settled, Lilian finally rang me one day when I was England to tell me that she was going back to work. Her boss had been ordered by the permanent secretary to pay her the wages she had lost over the previous months from his own salary, and she had been reinstated. When he asked why she had refused the 'reasonable request' (as set out in her job contract) to attend prayer meetings, she showed him the Constitution of Botswana, she said, which guarantees freedom of creed and assembly. During this time she continued to be an elected officer of the MWU, though increasingly critical of some decisions made by the executive.[12]

I asked Lilian how she was welcomed by the other workers when she finally returned to work? 'So well', she said. 'They say I am a hero' (*mogaka*, i.e. the bravest, a champion). Her boss was still in hospital, being treated for severe injuries. One of the other passengers had injured his back and remained hospitalised several months after the accident.

It is, perhaps, ironic that a year later, Lilian had made friends with her boss, supported by the local chief, also a friend or even distant relative. On a trip to Botswana in 2007, I found her position amazingly transformed: her boss had even selected her to represent the local manual workers in her department at a national meeting to discuss changes in the structure of public salaries. But a year later she again clashed with him, this time over his treatment of a fellow woman worker, and once again she was suspended without pay. When I talked to her in July 2008, she reported that she had joined another union (BLLAWU, the Botswana Land Boards and Local Authorities Workers' Union) which was handling her case, as her boss had finally been transferred. He and several other supervisors had, as predicted, been taken to court on charges of corruption over land and vehicles. By 2011, she had been shifted from the central to a local branch of the Ministry while still retaining her house. In her new job she had an easy relation with her woman boss (whom she described as a 'little girl'); her boss admired her skills, and she was advising her on the handling of local work disputes. The incidents in this case are here told in her own words.

The Case of the Thrice-dismissed Messenger

I, Lilian Mamoshe, employed as a messenger, was dismissed three times over three consecutive years. I was dismissed on the basis that I refused to be transferred from the head office to a Sub-Land Board. This dispute went on during the years 2007, 2008 and 2009, and in each case the dispute was settled in my favour. I was reimbursed and reinstated. The arguments of my case were based on the following reasons:

I was employed as an unskilled labourer. According to the directive from the DPSM, the conditions of work of the industrial classes are that all unskilled labourers are not transferable, therefore I was non-transferable.[13] The management ignored the directive and pressurised and intimidated me to move. This was because, in my view, I was disturbing them by revealing their corrupt dealings over land allocations and over leases awarded for rental expenses. They wanted to transfer me to the local Kanye Land Board because they needed my expertise there, but they didn't promote me. When I refused they threatened to take away my house, which was the property of the Land Board. They said they would demolish it. I then went to the late Kgosi Kgolo Seepapitso IV (the house was ultimately under the authority of the chief), and he went to the council chair. The council chair brought the matter for debate to the council. The council instructed the Land Board not to demolish the house because it belonged to the Bangwaketse tribe.

I appealed to the permanent secretary in the Ministry of Lands and Housing to reconsider my case, and her advice was that the Land Board must re-employ me and leave me as I was. I stayed in the house, but then they fired me again. I appealed this time directly to the Minister. The Minister resolved that I should be re-employed, then I should move to the Kanye Sub-Land Board, and I should appeal from there. I did that, but up until now the Minister has not responded to my appeal. In the meanwhile, the allegations of corruption that in my opinion started this problem have gone to court, with one person sued on nine counts!

Resolution: The matter is still pending.

During the disciplinary hearing prior to my refusal to move to a Sub-Land Board, I felt that the union representative I had was biased and his arguments were on the management's side. I decided therefore to take up my case on my own. In the first case I was represented by the union, but in the following two cases I represented myself. I currently have a good relationship in the Sub-Land Board, where I am also involved in worker dispute resolution as a trade unionist advisor. I'm a shop steward for BLLAWU (Botswana Land Board and Local Authorities Workers' Union), having left the MWU.

Lilian's case is exemplary rather than unique. Winning such cases for relatively uneducated manual workers due to confrontations with their educated, Westernised bosses is the reason for union support among its rank-and-file members, the basis for its formidable reputation. As I show in Chapter 6, attempts by the current government (or the ruling party, the BDP) to infiltrate and undermine the MWU's strength by engineering factional splits and accusations of corruption have had to contend with the belief of ordinary rank-and-file members, based on past experience, that only the union could protect their interests and their vulnerable, low-paid jobs.

Subjection and Agency

Lilian's case illuminates the complexity of self-knowledge and personal agency that manual workers in post-independence Botswana may develop. On the one hand, Lilian saw herself as an actor and leader, hence a man; on the other hand, she was a vulnerable victim, suspected and discriminated against, hence a woman. In Botswana, subjectivities are perceived to be affected interactively, with people's hostilities and animosities impacting physically on a subject's sense of self (see Klaits 2010). They are also formed through interaction with a close circle of kin and ancestors (R. Werbner 1989: 19–148). Empathy and antipathy are bodily emotions that affect others. In this sense, Richard Werbner argues, persons in Botswana are 'dividuals' rather than discrete individuals (R. Werbner 2011).

Clearly for Lilian, the 1991 strike was an empowering moment of heightened consciousness, solidarity and camaraderie, an ordeal successfully overcome. The Manual Workers' Union was for many years a primary source of her identity and dignity as an acting subject. Nevertheless, she was also active in a variety of other public forums. Indeed, as a civic-minded villager, she fostered good relations with the local chief. In 2007 she was engaged in setting up a local community-based organisation to help HIV/Aids orphans. By 2011, in this capacity she had been elected honorary chair of the Botswana Network of People Living with Aids (BONEPWA), a national umbrella organisation. She chaired national meetings in Gaborone, and attended regional conferences and workshops in Johannesburg on a regular basis, staying at five-star hotels and flying overseas. She had mastered the arts of word-processing and e-mailing, and now carried a laptop on her frequent trips to the capital. She had successfully raised funds for a building to house her project for Aids orphans. She was also a long-term supporter and member of the main opposition party, the BNF. Despite all this, she was constantly broke, and often dreamt of leaving her job and going to work in England so that she could afford to build herself a house in her natal village. Although a manual worker, some of her closest relatives were middle-class nurses, teachers and civil servants.

The active participation of women in the MWU alongside men supports Iris Berger's observation, against the argument that women workers tend to be 'incompletely' proletarianised, that in Botswana as in South Africa the predicament of very low wages for men, and women's responsibility for basic household livelihood, create 'a basis for solidarity between men and women' and women's trade union militancy (Berger 1986: 220–1). In their confrontations with government, the MWU, like Lilian, drew on a rights ethic that presumes that justice should and must prevail, that their rights were fundamentally and intrinsically sacrosanct. These rights were defined internationally by the ILO, by long traditions of labour struggle, and by notions of *seriti* rooted in rural Tswana notions of justice.

A Cosmopolitan Working-class Leader

Although recent research in Africa has begun to look at the role of contemporary African elites, intellectuals, civil society pioneers and activists (e.g. Hodgson 2008; P. Werbner 2009b; R. Werbner 2004, 2008; Yarrow 2008, 2011),[14] in a cosmopolitanising world of increased mobility and so-called space–time compression, there may also be working-class cosmopolitans (see P. Werbner 1999b). They too share a global subjectivity. As her career developed, Lilian increasingly became a cosmopolitan. So too, during the period of my study in 2000 and 2005, Elsinah Botsalano, a salaried officer of the Manual Workers' Union, rose from her role as coordinator of the Women's Wing of the union to become the elected representative of the Southern Africa region, and elected 'titular' for the whole English-speaking African region of Public Service International (PSI), an international trade union of public workers with its headquarters in Geneva.

Elsinah, like Lilian, was of Barolong origin, a tribal group spanning Botswana's international boundary with South Africa, and half her immediate family lived across the border. She herself came from a settlement in the Kalahari, and she began her career in the trade union as a typist in 1982. Later, she organised workshops on women's issues, and trained as an accounts officer. She was one of a team of four MWU salaried officers, who ran the union on a day-to-day basis.

As the union's strength grew, it was reaffiliated with the Botswana Federation of Trade Unions (BFTU) and PSI, despite the heavy costs of membership.[15] PSI represents millions of workers worldwide. It has five major regions, Africa and the Middle East being one such. As 'titular', Elsinah travelled regularly to Geneva, Johannesburg and throughout the Southern African Development Community region for PSI executive meetings, workshops and seminars. She also travelled to Italy for an ILO course, to Beijing as part of the Botswana delegation for the UN International Conference on Women, and to Canada for a PSI international meeting. Later, in 2009 and 2010, she also travelled to Britain, Spain and Denmark. At the same time, she participated in union struggles at home against redundancies and the looming privatisation of the public sector.

Elsinah is, I suggest, a working-class cosmopolitan. Given her modest education (to high-school level), she is deeply conscious of the inequalities in Botswana, and is part, perhaps, of a tiny labour elite, well-travelled and knowledgeable about the kinds of rights to which low-paid workers, and women in particular, are entitled. She and her fellow trade unionists have made a genuine difference to the alleviation of poverty in the lives of ordinary Batswana women, indeed arguably far more so in economic terms than other initiatives of the more sophisticated, university-educated cohort of women who have led Botswana's feminist movement.[16] In Gaborone, her position in the established church, the United Congregationalist Church of Southern Africa (UCCSA, formerly the London Missionary Society), its committees and women-run burial society, which included many wives of the great and the good in Botswana, seemed to prove her membership in the bourgeois middle class of the capital. Yet she was not really a sophisticated cultural cosmopolitan, and although she was part of the Botswana delegation to Beijing, she was often marginalised by the group of highly educated elite women activists, feminists and global travellers who shared that experience with her. Although she was and is quite explicitly a feminist who promotes gender equality within the MWU, and despite her international status and role as coordinator of the union's Women's Wing, as a union officer and labour activist Elsinah accepted that her role was to lend unquestioning and loyal support to Johnson Motshwarakgole, the charismatic national organising secretary of the union, who throughout my research was regarded by ordinary rank-and-file members – and even by many government negotiators – as having almost mystical powers to settle disputes, as he travelled up and down the country.[17] He, in turn, admired and relied on her, in an enduring partnership.

Elsinah is an example of a new type of cosmopolitan – the procedural cosmopolitan or 'cosmocrat': a person of admirable competence who knows all the procedures (*tsamaiso* in Setswana) and is familiar with constitutional structures; a skilled negotiator who is meticulous in her observance of rules and procedures. She enunciates the PSI ideology which promotes women and youth participation, and is imbued with political correctness; for example, when I asked her if she was a Kgalagadi, a low-status group living in the Kalahari (where some members of her family live), she explained that no, she comes from the relatively high-status Barolong tribe, but added immediately that she would not mind being a Kgalagadi.

In what senses was Elsinah a cosmopolitan? When she travelled, she rarely ventured out beyond the Geneva airport hotel or the PSI offices located near the hotel, mainly for lack of time. Despite the arduous flight from Botswana to Geneva of some 20 hours, she stayed only as long as meetings lasted, usually a couple of days, moving between her hotel and PSI headquarters by public transport. Like most other workers in Botswana, virtually the whole of her *per diem* allowance was saved up to support her immediate and extended family back home, and she was almost always called back urgently to attend to the mundane day-to-day business of the union, or to care for her own children, her ailing mother (who subsequently died in 2007) or one of her numerous siblings.

The briefness of her forays abroad, however frequent, meant that she never felt at home there; she was not a connoisseur of art, music or foreign cuisines. For example, when I asked her how Barcelona and Copenhagen had been, she commented that they had been 'very cold'. Her role was not that of a pioneer, a mover and shaker in global affairs, although her election as 'titular' was a first for Botswana. Instead, she was an actor in an emergent bureaucracy of global governance and, given her class background, a person who had advanced quite remarkably into global affairs through the esteem of colleagues for her dedication, religious piety and procedural knowledge. She was a person of evident moral integrity and meticulous commitment to fair procedures. She achieved her position as elected 'titular' for the English-speaking African region of PSI in the face of competition from far more educated trade unionists, men and women, civil servants in local and central government, and despite Botswana's insignificance by comparison to larger African countries like neighbouring South Africa, which houses PSI's regional headquarters in Johannesburg. Her achievement was all the more remarkable because in public meetings she was often soft spoken and diffident, frequently the tireless behind-the-scenes worker lending support to an event rather than being its charismatic leader. As chair, she was practical, down to earth and matter of fact. If she expressed emotions, this was only when she joined in the singing of trade union songs or led public prayers.

Like other women unionists, Elsinah was weighed down by family commitments. In addition to her children, husband and parents, she had at least a dozen still-living siblings and half-siblings, resident on both sides of the border, who regarded her as an elder sister, and expected her to take command at family funerals or during illnesses. She juggled her obligations to them, the Church and the union as best she could, always on the run. Her consciousness as a worker (and feminist) had emerged, over time, though her work, particularly in the endless rounds of meetings negotiating workers' rights, and in repeated legal adversarial action with the government, in the High Court and Court of Appeal, and with internal union dissenters and trouble-stirrers who on occasion had even questioned her own integrity. As with her family commitments, she was dedicated and loyal – above all to the union, its leader and ordinary members. Her consciousness had evolved through constant learning, but her instinct was always to play safe, not to rock the boat – to follow the rules and procedures.

Sitting with Elsinah and the union treasurer MaJune (see Chapter 2), in July 2011, I wondered what had made Elsinah such a sought-after leader, repeatedly selected to represent Botswana or the PSI in international forums? MaJune reflected on the paradoxical qualities of leadership Elsinah had:

> You know how Elsinah works? A unionist is a visionary person. So according to the Manual Workers' Union, one aspect to being a member is how she handles things, one; two, the vision she has or he has; three, one who cares for the workers. You can ask me why am I saying 'the one who cares'. You'll find that some of us people, when you are sent to a workshop, you'll just go for luxury. You can say that – just to enjoy [things]. You can't even tell your friends what was happening there. You might be even in the classroom or the workshop, you'll be there doing nothing. When you come back, [there is] no implementation of what you have learnt there. That is the weakness. So, for the past many years [during which] Elsinah has been working in the Manual Workers' Union, the first priority for her are the members. The achievements of the members. The second thing is to ensure that what is supposed to be done should be done. That is why she went to the workshop when HIV started in 2004, but she managed to implement those HIV objectives.

I commented that her election was a great achievement, since she was competing against bigger countries and more educated unionists. Elsinah merely nodded. MaJune went on to say of Elsinah that 'she encourages me to work with people, to agree with people, to commit yourself to people, however and wherever possible'.

During one conversation, I asked why workers were still joining the Manual Workers' Union from other unions.

> MaJune: We are the best negotiator.
> P.W.: Elsinah is the best negotiator.
> MaJune: She's the best of them all. A short, single woman [i.e. on her own].
> P: So quiet [MaJune laughs]. You don't hear her, you don't see her, she hides behind her scarf.

> MaJune: She is quiet, she hides. But by the time of the negotiation, you won't believe that this is a cat-mouse that sits next to you. You wouldn't know who is the cat and who is the mouse. You wouldn't know. She is not quiet when it comes to negotiation. She knows the law. She thinks quickly, slowly, but reasonably. She's always reasonable.

As we roamed from one topic to another, it was evident that Elsinah was always in command of the facts as well as the language of governance. About the 2010 Climate Change Summit she attended for the International Trade Union Confederation (ITUC), first in Barcelona and then Copenhagen, alongside three other Southern African country representatives, she commented that there were:

> critical issues [of climate change at stake] because trade unions, the ITUC had to make [present] a paper on the transition. When things are becoming worse, all the workers shouldn't be affected because workers are mostly affected, so we need to bring this to attention, that workers will be the first to be affected. So that when workers are affected, workers could be trained to do other jobs rather than be retrenched. Let's say you are a cleaner, you could be trained to do another job. If you are a machine operator, or whatever. There should be money for workers to be retrained. Also, some money from the developed countries. The developed countries were asked to provide money for underdeveloped countries that were affected [by climate change]. So all of us should know what we're supposed to be doing. Like forestry and agriculture, those are the first to be affected. That money should be there in the country, and the union should have access to that money and train the workers.

Her commitment and international exposure to debates about social justice in the fields of gender, HIV, the environment and labour relations have evidently expanded Elsinah's horizons, just as she continues to be a member of the select team that negotiates with the government as employer. Through all this she has remained a down-to-earth, warm and generous person.

Conclusion

Writing about South African labour leaders such as E.S. Sachs of the Transvaal Garment Workers' Union and Ray Alexander of the Cape Food and Canning Workers' Union, Iris Berger suggests that 'any sense of identification with others is not simply a given fact, inherent in people's material lives, but rather needs to be constructed conceptually, emotionally and historically' (Berger 1992: 11). In South Africa's long history of repeated mass strikes, protests and marches, the theme of trade union activism as historically leading to a sense of expansive agency and personal empowerment is one repeatedly stressed in the scholarly literature. As Jennifer Fish comments in relation to post-independence South Africa, 'Domestic workers' unionisation – while replete with struggles for both recognition and financial viability – continually reflected women's agency' (Fish 2006: 120). Yet as Emma Mashinini notes, almost as an aside in the story of her struggle to build a trade union and gain recognition for it in the face of apartheid, despite her national achievements and international recognition, and despite the fact that the majority of black workers were women, when it came to electing the national executive of the newly formed Congress of South African Trade Unions or choosing its logo women were absent, so that, as Mashinini concludes, 'it means that our presence – our efforts, our work, our support – was not even recognised' (Mashinini 1989: 118).

Botswana's short history is far less conflictual, and thus lacks, on the whole, the mass populist elements so prominent in the historical activism of its big neighbour. Nor have worker politics been imbricated in race politics as they almost invariably were in apartheid South Africa and other colonial societies. Nevertheless, I have argued in this chapter that in Botswana as elsewhere there are many public actors, among them women, whose subjectivities have been formed in interaction and confrontation with the government and state in response to local conflicts, injustices and crises.

Schirmer warns against a Eurocentric tendency to elevate Western feminism as 'a superior understanding of the 'truth' (Schirmer 1993: 63) vis-à-vis other forms of women's activism. Instead, the need is to reveal the alternative scripts and conjunctions that emerge in action, in particular contexts, as subaltern women in the global South create political imaginaries that make sense of their citizenship and gendered worlds in specific political or social circumstances. In the face of poststructuralist, post-Butler feminist suspicions of essentialised unities of self, class or gender, the present chapter thus follows Schirmer and McNay in arguing for the need to reclaim concepts such as agency, consciousness and experience, but as sited, embodied, participatory, dialogical and conjunctural.

In his book on postcolonial subjectivities in Africa, Richard Werbner reminds us of the slipperiness of the cluster of terms around the idea of the subject. Nor, he says, 'can we claim to have resolved the ambiguities by imposing a standard vocabulary, given the richness of the literature around these terms' (R. Werbner 2002a: 3). Nevertheless, he argues, we can say, broadly, that subjectivities are political, moral and realised existentially in consciousness (ibid.).

The emergent postcolonial subjectivities I have portrayed here draw on modern discourses: of class oppression, normative cosmopolitanism, labour rights, human rights and contemporary Christian humanist religiosity. But as I proposed at the outset of this chapter, the easy opposition between overdetermined subjects and free autonomous individuals cannot be sustained. Instead, the chapter has highlighted a dialectic between autonomy and heteronomy, emancipation and subjection, by tracing the evolving ethics and postcolonial subjectivities of subaltern women in Botswana. I have argued that these subjectivities need to be understood dialogically, as historically inflected in struggle in the face of hard times, and that therefore it can be said that there is no subject in and for itself, 'no subjectivity prior to intersubjectivity' (ibid.: 1). Above all, the women I have described here sought dignity and self-worth through a sense of responsibility for more vulnerable others.

CHAPTER FOUR

Lekgotla la Babereki, The Court of the Workers: The Trade Union as Public Forum

Singing Their Way into the Public Sphere

The first gathering of the Manual Workers' Union's general council that I attended, in May 2005, representing all 32 regions of the union, was fraught with tension. Despite a court victory by the official union leadership against a breakaway rebel faction, many prominent rebels were present at the meeting. Even so, the meeting opened with a prayer followed by union songs. The songs spoke of oppression and of the fight for workers' rights and liberty. There was an element of *déjà vu* in the songs for me,[1] of bygone eras and dead ideologies; but sung with passion in Setswana, the songs re-emerged like a phoenix from the ashes, to bear real meanings in the real world. 'We work in suffering/Creating Botswana's wealth/We work, not eating/We die in poverty'. Or, in another stanza: 'We die of hunger/Without healthcare/Without a home/Or education for our children'. And finally: 'We live in grief/We live wretchedly/We live like strangers/We live like beggars'. There was a tension conveyed by the songs: we, the workers, create the wealth of the new nation, yet we live like beggars and strangers in the land of our forefathers. As one song goes: 'We (only) want our rights,/In a land that is ours'.

The only solution to this injustice is to join the MWU and fight for liberty. So the singers sing in Setswana, in a translated version of the English song: 'The Union is our shield – we shall not be moved,/We are protected by it – we shall not be moved,/Just like a tree that's planted on the waters – we shall not be moved'. There was sometimes a local colouring to the songs: 'If you see workers (or women) sleeping in the bush,/[Know that] all they want is their rights'. Every MWU meeting begins with a song and a Christian prayer, followed by more songs. And it ends with a song and a prayer. Prayers are sometimes passionate and highly politicised. The workers stand up, often dressed in red MWU T-shirts, and sing in easy harmony, as in a church choir. It is indeed an uplifting, moving moment of hope, unity and solidarity. Members are used to harmonising their voices – almost all are active members of Christian churches. Unions and churches are deeply symbiotic in Botswana.[2]

The singing conjures up a consciousness of faraway worlds – of workers' struggles in Europe at the birth of the Industrial Revolution, but also elsewhere in Africa, particularly South Africa. Here in Botswana, however, workers know that the struggle is very concretely against their own government, and not against white privileged capitalists. It is the workers' own African government which is felt to be oppressive. Workers work for the government, and they experience on a daily basis this oppression and the hardship caused by their meagre salaries.

Union leaders are proud of their capacity to win against the full might of the government despite their lack of education. A question worth asking, nevertheless, concerns whether this echoes postcolonial narratives of subalternity, or merely mirrors more universal narratives of class conflict? Throughout the MWU meetings I attended, the stress was on the fact that the Botswana government did not respect international human rights and labour laws; it had not yet, as it were, come of age. Thus it thought it could dictate working conditions to workers with impunity. This narrative no longer bothers about a colonial past, in the sense that it demands full accountability and responsibility from the people's own African government. In all these conversations and meetings, the pre-independence era seemed totally irrelevant and long forgotten. Colonialism was neither mentioned nor invoked to excuse the government for its current failings. What was mentioned repeatedly was a new cosmopolitan world of rights, including workers' rights, which the state should acknowledge and respect.[3]

In demanding procedural accountability from government and the right to strike, organise, unionise and negotiate for fair wages, workers were also inserting themselves into a complex bureaucratic and legal regime that defined the parameters of their rights as citizen-workers. In this discourse, the idea of the dignity of labour, as we have seen, echoes rural ideas about *seriti* or *tlotlo* – self-respect and embodied selfhood, dignity and well-being. These have been transposed from their rural context and incorporated into the demand for worker respect and well-being in modernised urban contexts.

'When We Say Democracy, We Mean It!': Union Organisation

The Manual Workers' Union must be understood as both a public forum (a *kgotla*) and a hierarchical organisation whose long arm reaches to the far limits of Botswana. As a *kgotla*, the union opens a range of forums for discussion, debate and decision-making among workers. As an organisation, the union has a constitution, which specifies its office bearers' roles, election procedures and the hierarchical division of labour within it, from the centre to the regions and from the regions to local branches. Union representatives at different levels handle worker disputes with the employer and sit on local and regional joint negotiating committees. At the union's headquarters, union officers, both paid and elected, meet and negotiate conditions of work with representatives of government departments, parastatals and the central government, including the office of the president, the minister of labour and home affairs and the head of the Directorate of Public Service Management (DPSM), the official employer of public sector workers.

The union's elaborate constitution is relatively standard and follows an ILO-cum-British model. The bare outlines of the union's structure were explained to me during one of my first meetings at the union's offices. The supreme body of the union is the annual delegates' conference, which now meets every three years and elects the union leaders. Below it is the General Council, which consists of chairpersons and secretaries of the regions. There are 32 regions, and each is represented by two delegates; along with the overall general secretary and chairperson, these comprise the General Council, which has 66 members.[4] The annual delegates' conference is composed of two delegates from each of the local branches, elected by a secret ballot, making altogether about 1500 delegates. They represent branch committees.

Each region has several branches. For example, the Botswana Institute of Administration and Commerce (BIAC) has a branch of its own. Parastatals and local authorities also have their own branches. The minimum required to form a branch is 20 or 30 members. Where there are fewer in a particular work place, they can join together with other work places to form a branch. Branch officers are elected for three years and branch committees are expected to meet at least once every two months. In addition, workers at each workplace elect a shop steward annually. Shop stewards may further elect from among their numbers a senior shop steward. Shop stewards collect dues, represent members in grievance and disciplinary cases, and participate in negotiations with management.

According to the Manual Workers' Union's Constitution, the 'business' of the delegates' conferences is 'to receive reports from the General Secretary, the Treasurer and the Executive Committee'. The National Executive Committee (NEC) is elected by the delegates' conference and meets at least once every four months. It is quite distinct from the general council. It consists of 18 members, 16 elected, men and women, plus two *ex officio* members from the union's Women's Wing, and includes the elected office holders. One of the NEC's responsibilities is to 'protect the funds of the union against any misuse'. The General Council meets at least twice a year and 'transacts the business of the union' between delegates' conferences, or if the NEC fails to reach an agreement.

The union's secretary general, the chairperson and their deputies are also elected at the congress, for a period of three years. The secretary general is head of the union's administration, responsible for the day-to-day running of its affairs, for keeping the minutes and conducting the union's correspondence. The chairperson is the political head, who also chairs meetings of the union's executive. Decisions are made in consultation. As one union officer explained to me:

> The trade union is the most democratic [of all] movement[s]. At the end of the day, what is most important is consultation, and this must be respected. The labour movement is truly democratic. Always, though this is time consuming. When we say democracy, we mean it!

Figure 4.1 The old Manual Workers' Union headquarters in Gaborone until 2013.

Figure 4.2 The general council meeting.

In addition to the five elected officers – chairperson, vice-chairperson, general secretary, assistant general secretary and treasurer – the MWU also employs several paid officers. At the start of my research in 2005, there were four such officers: Johnson Motshwarakgole (national organising secretary), Samuel Molaodi (administration officer), Elsinah Botsalano (women and accounts officer), and Mosala Phokontsi (organiser). These four ran the day-to-day business of the union, and were often chief negotiators with the government over pay or grievance cases.

The price for democracy at all levels of the MWU was the time spent in meetings and deliberation. The attempt was always to reach a consensus, and this meant that internal union meetings were invariably numerous and long.

Meetings, Meetings and More Meetings

Even this cursory, superficial summary of the Manual Workers' Union's organisation gives a sense of the hundreds of union activists throughout Botswana all engaged, on a day-to-day basis, in union affairs. A corollary of this is the dozens of meetings convened on any one day all over the country for purposes of consultation, negotiation, arbitration, dispute settlement and administering or governing the union. This had implications for my fieldwork. An all too familiar refrain throughout my research was the voice of my union friend Elsinah, whispering into her mobile phone: 'Shhh ... I'm in a meeting'. Alternatively, she would tell me on her ever-busy mobile, that, unexpectedly, having arranged to meet with me in the capital that day: 'I'm on my way to Francistown [or Maun, or Kanye] with Johnson [or Molaodi, or Tsalaile]. We set out at 3 AM [or even earlier] for a meeting at 8'. Catching union officers was like catching the wind – even their families often barely knew where they were or when they would arrive home.

During 2005, and for much of the period that followed, in addition to bitter internal factional battles, MWU officers were preoccupied with challenges to blue-collar, industrial-class workers' positions arising from the introduction of two major policies: performance-based remuneration schemes (PBRS), and retrenchment or privatisation, as government departments were converted into parastatals or industrial-class work such as cleaning or rubbish collection was contracted out to private companies. There were also issues related to the renegotiation of overtime rates and the reclassification of educational colleges. All these involved union officers in day-to-day negotiations with the employer, and entailed calling meetings with workers in particular localities, industries or departments in which issues relating to these changes were discussed and aired publicly. I attended several such meetings over five months in 2005.

What was particularly striking about the meetings was the open, democratic mode of participatory debate they encouraged. Possibly the very first such meeting I attended, on 22 April 2005, was with cooks employed at a local community college. The following account of that meeting is taken from my fieldnotes.

Overtime Pay: The College Cooks' Meeting

I arrived at the MWU office in the early afternoon to find that the union had been called in to discuss a possible strike at TTS (the Teachers' Training College) at Tlokweng, near the capital city. We drove there in heavy rain, Johnson still with his foot in a cast from a fracture (he had jumped, reviving an old injury). The meeting was attended by about 40 unionists alongside the deputy head of the college. Many of the women were cleaners or cooks, working in the kitchen. The men were mostly groundsmen or guards. The women were mostly in their fifties, large matrons, with a scattering of younger women, a couple smartly dressed. Johnson chaired the meeting, and unionists were invited to speak in turn, either to put their case or ask questions.

The meeting opened with a prayer, led by one of the men, and closed with a prayer by one of the women, who had been very vocal at the beginning and had demanded a prayer. The branch leader was not self-evidently in attendance, and it was said that the branch meets rather rarely.

The complaint appeared to be that the college was refusing to pay the cooks overtime. At present the college was teaching University of Botswana students who were non-residential (in 'distance learning'), which evidently cut down on the need for overtime. The kitchen staff were saying that since they were feeding students they should be paid University of Botswana rates.

Johnson led a lengthy discussion about shifts, pointing out that the workers should be paid according to their shift.[5] A deal had been negotiated in December for the whole educational sector, uniformly applicable to all industrial-class workers, a concept he kept repeating. He mentioned the precedent of a college in Tonota in the north. I got the feeling he was not in favour of strike action.

Despite being relatively uneducated, women as well as men spoke forcefully, one by one, with authority and at length, without notes. There were no fumblings, and they displayed no hesitation as they explained their position and the hardship they were suffering. Public speaking is clearly part of an oral tradition in Botswana, which the MWU's culture of debate and discussion incorporates. In this first encounter with a union forum, I reflected that this could have been a village *kgotla* (assembly, court) meeting, or *merero* (caucus).

The decision was made to postpone any strike decision and to meet again, having first selected a new shop steward for the branch committee.

Retrenchment: The BURS Meeting

The next meeting I attended took place a week after the college cooks' meeting, in the Gaborone government enclave. About 80 people, more than half of them women, some quite young, trickled in rather slowly. The meeting concerned the privatisation of the Department of Taxes, Customs and Excise, and the transfer of all their employees to a new parastatal, the Botswana Unified Revenue Service (BURS). Three days earlier, MWU leaders reportedly had a 'stormy meeting' with the Ministry of Finance and Development Planning's management and its permanent secretary, Serwalo Tumelo, regarding the Ministry's exit 'package'.[6]

Workers had been asked to sign a letter of agreement to transfer to the new body before a 'package' had been negotiated and finalised. The deadline was the following day, 30 April. This left unclear, according to the MWU, the possible shedding of jobs in the new parastatal, and what compensation and benefits would accrue to retrenched workers. It was also unclear how workers' accumulated benefits would be transferred and calculated by the new parastatals, and what would happen if they chose to remain in government service, which they were entitled to do.

Botswana's *Daily News* reported on 26 April that, in a meeting with MWU representatives, 'After an acrimonious exchange at the City Hall in Gaborone, the two union leaders [Motshwarakgole and Molaodi] then left, saying they did not want to be seen to be selling out on their members'.[7] In the report, the Ministry's permanent secretary, Tumelo, denied that workers would be disadvantaged by the move to BURS – they would have enhanced salaries and benefits in the private sector, their accrued benefits would be preserved and their years of service used to compute their gratuities and other benefits. The MWU responded by demanding that a retrenchment package should be signed before workers agreed to be transferred. In the end, as Johnson Motshwarakgole announced to the assembled workers, the MWU achieved a postponement of two weeks. He advised them to tell the employer: 'We are not going to be BURS before we talk to the MWU. We can only sign after we have talked'. He went on to warn the government not to threaten workers, not to play games with them: 'We are not playing *morabaraba* [a local board game]. As for me, I don't feel pain if you have signed for the BURS as long as you just go home with this package'.

The meeting discussed the case of workers who had already signed the letters of transfer. Johnson advised that, 'Those people who signed the papers, you should go and take them [back] and tell them that you have changed your mind (*ferekanye*). We are not forcing you (*pateletse*) but it is the right way to help you. We have to agree first!' The meeting was clearly united in regarding Tumelo as a villain.

People expressed concern: When would the two week postponement start? What if their letters were destroyed? Johnson assured everyone that they could rely on the union's great experience negotiating such packages. The MWU were their 'parents', he said:

> We have more than 35 years doing this work. If you want to know more about it, we helped people at the Postal Services, Botswana Housing Corporation and Botswana Telecommunication Corporation ... This Tumelo knows nothing about the package and we at the MWU are going to make him learn about the package. We are 'consultants' when it comes to the affairs (*merero*) of the workers. We will lead BCSA! [the 'educated' Botswana Civil Servants' Association] ... There is no one who can chase you from work, just because you ask where you are going after retrenchment and what your kids are going to survive with. A draft is not the equivalent of a contract of employment!

The MWU officers then left to continue their meeting with the new BURS management, started the previous day. They would report later. Having reviewed what had been said, the meeting dispersed. No decisions were taken and no date set for a further meeting.

After the meeting, I talked to a woman who was a driver with Customs and Excise at the airport. She was very concerned about what would happen to her since she was nearing 45, the age of retirement. She said she felt a little reassured by the meeting. She would report to her colleagues at the airport, since most had not attended.

Experience versus Qualifications: The Storekeepers' Meeting

The following day, Saturday 30 April, a national meeting gathered storekeepers working in government service at a community hall in the capital. They came from all over Botswana, with delegates arriving from some distance, trickling in gradually – from Francistown, Phikwe, Mahalapye, Gantsi, Tsabong, Molepolole, Kang, Good Hope. Many also came from Gaborone, from different ministries. The meeting was scheduled to start early, at 8 AM. By 11 AM there were some 50 storekeepers present. Most were women. Johnson apologised for not preparing food for those who had travelled some distance.

The meeting had been called after three women came to the MWU to complain that the BIAC had advertised a course for storekeepers open only to applicants with 'Cambridge' (the exam equivalent of GCSE, completed in the last year of senior high school). There was a need to act fast, Johnson explained, if they wanted to change the qualification demanded; the employer could not just change an earlier agreement without consultation. The MWU had to renegotiate with the employer to clarify the rights of people without 'Cambridge', but who had been working for a long time. This was the first meeting the MWU had ever held specifically for storekeepers, and they were very pleased with it (normally, storekeepers would have been part of the MWU branch in their place of work). The meeting appointed a steering committee and a secretary to take the minutes. It opened with addresses by the committee members:

> Mr J.S. (committee member): We are not making progress (*tswelele*) [not being promoted] and we don't know what the problem (*mathata*) is. Why don't we make progress? The reconstruction of BIAC – most of us don't have 'Cambridge'. We asked a question but did not get an answer. Then we asked ourselves what should we do? We went to the MWU office to tell them that our employers say we don't have Form 5 qualification. At the union they said that we should gather ourselves because we know each other. We should have one soul (*mowa o le mongwe*). We are fighting the same fight.
>
> Ms M.B. (committee member): We have started fighting for our rights (*ditshwanelo tsa rona*). There is no way you can climb the tree without starting from the bottom before you reach the top. We have come for one thing. [The people here] have long (*boleele*) years of work. What do the employees say about this? They have to consider (*akanetsa*, reflect upon) all the years we've served!

Mr Molaodi (MWU officer, previously a storekeeper himself): You have been troubled in your progress [promotion]. The requirements have been changed. To enter storekeeping (nowadays) you need 'Cambridge'. DPSM has approved this new 'scheme of service'. You know that children [in Botswana] who finish Form 5 and other graduates have no work. There should be some changes here and there in the public service [i.e. he admits the need for raising qualifications]. For example, Form 2 was required for those trained at that time, when I was still a storekeeper, but today there is confusion (*tlhakatlhakano*) about who comes first [who is in line for training and promotion]. MaSebitla [the director of supplies] at that time decided who is supposed to go for a course, who should be promoted. [Nevertheless] all those old people at work are very important. It can be painful [for established workers with long years of experience] to teach a [new] person how to work and then [that new person] is promoted and you are left behind!

Johnson: In life there should be changes. Storekeepers in those times were Standard 7 (primary school) leavers, but today they want those who have attained Junior Certificate. If you increase those requirements to 'Cambridge' you also have to think about those at the bottom. You can't make changes that hurt people. You shouldn't be harsh on them (*felelwe ke pelo*). [In the Bible it is said:] Something that is neither warm nor cold should be thrown away [i.e. ambiguity is not acceptable]. We have a 'collective agreement' that the government should inform us if there are any changes to the conditions of work. When they say that BIAC requires 'Cambridge', that isn't true. The director of supplies cannot just announce he wants 'Cambridge'[-qualified workers for the course] without talking to us! ... In life people should sit down to speak about their problems. You made a good decision to come here on a Saturday morning, leaving behind your work.

It happened that, a long time back, at [the] medical records [section] there were four people who had completed Standard 7 and ten who completed 'Cambridge'. They were taken somewhere for a course, and the ones who had only completed Standard 7 passed better than the 'Cambridge' graduates! When it came for promotion (*ga go tla 'promotion'*) those who did Standard 7 were told they did not qualify because they didn't have 'Cambridge'! We'll arrange a meeting on Tuesday with the government people to make them see that they have failed to follow the agreement (*le tlodile*) here and there.

At this point different storekeepers stood up in turn to describe how they had been passed over for promotion:

Mr B.M. (from the supplies section): I was employed in 1987 as a storekeeper 1 and now I am a storekeeper [grade] 3. The supervisors said: For you to be taken to the institute [BIAC] for training (*taraina*, 'promotion') you have to stay for ten years. But we have been here for a long time and we are still in the same position; we've never been taken to the institute. A person who did 'Cambridge' can come and join us, and later he or she will be taken to BIAC and when he or she comes back, she will have computer literacy. Afterwards,

> she will be promoted to be the 'supervisor'. In BIAC they are saying we are 'failing the interview'. The director knows that the storekeepers are at school [implying that he lies].
> Mr M. (Department of Agricultural Supplies): The people employed are Standard 7, Form 2, Form 3. The 'supplies officers' go off to BIAC and one is left there doing all sorts of jobs [beyond one's job description]. I am an inspector. I do the job of an inspecting officer. We do a lot of jobs, but when it comes to going to study, it is a problem (*mathata*) [i.e. they ask people to perform high-ranking jobs but refuse to send them for training].
> Mr D. (hospital employee since 1985): I am doing the book-keeping in the hospital and district office. If the Supplies Department isn't very nice or polite to us, where should we go? We are doing everything, even jobs they [we] are not employed to do. Supplies throw us away just like rubbish (*supplies e re latlhile jaaka matlakala*).
> Mr M.: I was employed in 1998 as a storekeeper [grade] 3. When I asked why I cannot act [in this position] they said I am a junior [when people are away on training courses].

Evident here is the pain and humiliation suffered by manual workers with long years of work experience who are refused promotion because of their lack of formal educational qualifications. In his response, Johnson described the MWU as an 'ark' (that is, like Noah's ark) and asked the assembled workers to allow the officers time to discuss having the years of service and seniority taken into account. He reassured delegates that their participation in the meeting would not be held against them (by the government), and they should not be intimidated by the employer: 'People wanted to make us fail (*phatlalatsa*) but there is no one who can throw you out of work because of what you are saying here now'.

This was one of the success stories of the MWU. The leadership managed to reach an agreement with the government's director of supplies to enable storekeepers with years of experience who had not completed 'Cambridge' to attend BIAC courses. Indeed, one of the storekeepers whose story is described in Chapter 2 (MaPelotona) successfully completed the course two years later with flying colours, and was promoted.

The inflation in the number of graduates and hence also the degree required for employment in the Botswana public service has hit manual workers hard, especially when combined with PBRS schemes that also require formal qualifications. This was an issue that preoccupied the MWU officers in subsequent years.

The final meeting I attended in this early period of my research took place ten days later, in Francistown, 420 kilometres north of the capital.

Overtime Pay: The Francistown Hospital Meeting

In May 2005, union officers began a tour of the regions, with stopovers at hospitals in Pikwe, Francistown, Masunga and Bobonong. The meetings were called to explain the complex formula negotiated with the government with regard to shift pay, started in December. Some workers had been paid according to the formula while others were owed back pay. Most did not understand the new formula.

There were about 70 unionists at the Francistown Nyangagwe Hospital meeting, 55 of them women, with latecomers sitting on the floor. The shop steward and the branch chair, both women, sat at the table with two members of the union's National Executive Committee, one arriving late from Maun in the far north. The MWU officers explained at great length changes to the incredibly complicated pay structure for different shifts and overtime.[8]

The meeting drove home the challenge faced by the MWU, of conveying complex information verbally. It was not enough, clearly, to circulate a document explaining the new formula. MWU officers had to be present to answer questions, and respond to anxieties. Meanwhile, the meetings also allowed workers to air other grievances and meet union leaders. Even at NEC meetings, it was noticeable that the accounts were presented verbally, at some length. In 2005 unionists had mobile phones, and they sent each other text messages constantly. But e-mail was barely used, even in 2011. Members valued face-to-face interaction and oral communication with the leadership. The drive from Gaborone to Francistown took over five hours. The full tour of the hospitals took several days.

A Stormy Meeting: Legal Embeddedness and Union Politics

In Chapter 2, I chose to present a range of grievance cases in order to highlight the everyday embeddedness of trade unionists in Botswana in matters of the law, legal decision-making, procedural disputes and judicial processes.[9] This almost daily involvement extends to the modern urban work context a legal tradition of going to court that Batswana are familiar with in their own indigenous courts (*dikgotla*), associated with distinct modes of judicial reasoning and argumentation.[10] The description in Setswana of the MWU as a *kgotla* of the workers thus seems apt and resonant with popular experience. As in other countries, legal and procedural issues inform union affairs and politics, and the primacy of the law is signalled in unionists' willingness to take the government – and each other – to court. But alongside legal regulations, the grievance cases and disputes also pointed to the moral considerations affecting the final outcome of many cases. This is a theme I develop further in Chapter 5.

The law, morality, ethics, respect and trust were intertwined issues in the final meeting I want to consider here, part of the run of meetings during April and May 2005 described in this chapter. This was a national General Council meeting that followed a High Court victory for the official union leadership. It was followed by a meeting of the newly elected NEC on 2 May. In normal circumstances, the General Council meeting on 1 May would have been a routine affair within a calendar of prescribed official meetings by formal union elected bodies, as outlined at the start of this chapter. But this meeting was the first to bring together delegates from the regions after the rebel faction within the MWU had been defeated in the High Court. At an NEC meeting the next day, the MWU chairperson described the rebels as 'those people who thought they were clever [but] are now really and truly weeping and gnashing their teeth'. Inevitably, the general council meeting promised to be a stormy occasion.

Most members representing the rebel regions (about half the total delegates) were present at the general council meeting, sitting on the right facing the elected national chairperson and national secretary general. Representatives from the loyal regions sat on the left. The chair announced that some MWU plans had been shelved or postponed because of the factional dispute with its financial crisis. He declared, 'People, from now on we must decide that our union is here to stand for us, and not only that, but we will not allow anybody to destroy it. Not a single person!' (alluding to interfering ruling party politicians). The strength of the MWU lay in the fact that it was a non-partisan organization: 'But as you can see, our union survived, and not only that but it has survived for many years despite the fact that it has members from different political parties … [O]ur union is not some prize to be won by any political party in Botswana' – the contrast here being trade unions in neighbouring South Africa and Namibia. Because the leadership knew 'everything that goes on in every region … you can try to do your deeds concealed in dust, you can dig a hole and cover it and hide in it, it doesn't matter. We'll expose you regardless'. Once the secretary called the roll – two delegates from each region – the chair asked a delegate to play his harmonica, for 'even in church, people praise the Lord by any means they can. Some people play the drums, some play the bells'. Following this musical interlude, the secretary read out the court judgement, and a discussion ensued on disciplinary action against the rebels. So far, there appeared to be general agreement on the need to move on. But at this point the dispute broke into the open.

Delegate 1: Can the meeting discuss expelling the culprits when their identities had not been declared?
Delegate 2 (to the chair): Listen! The chair denied being rude.

By now, pandemonium had broken out.

Francistown delegate: We can't hear, with all this racket.
Chair: Mr M., please behave. Very soon you'll think I'm a bad person. Please stop insulting people, Mr M., let's continue with Item 4. People!
Second woman delegate from Francistown: What Item 4 are you talking about, when we're not even allowed to say our piece?
Johnson Motshwarakgole: People, let's please listen to each other instead of wasting time with unnecessary things. Please stop …
Chair: Hold on, Motshwarakgole. People, you are … Mr B., I can hear people telling people that they'll shit themselves [it seems that one of the MWU officers had walked past one of the delegates and whispered to her, 'You will shit!'].

> Molepolole woman delegate: Yes, he said that to me. But he's going to have to show me where exactly I'm going to shit. I know my rights, and he shouldn't say such things to me.
> Motshwarakgole (desperately trying to move on): 'Item 4 states that we should ask your permission to take both Stanbic Bank and Barclays Bank to court for giving those people money illegally. We therefore require a mandate from the council, giving us permission to take both these banks to court.

Increasing chaos reigned just as a BTV crew arrived to film the uproar. The chair nevertheless stuck to his guns, put the motion to a vote, which was passed by the majority sitting on the right, and the meeting proceeded, with the rebels calming down. Later, on BTV news, the chaos was shown but the slant given was dictated by the chair and general secretary of the MWU, who expressed their views that the cause of the dispute was government interference. BTV then interviewed a Botswana Democratic Party (BDP) government minister who called the MWU 'rotten through and through' (a smear based on misinformation and never proven); before long this would be apparent, she warned, thus in effect confirming the allegations that the government was interfering in MWU affairs. Later, I discuss the politics of BDP infiltration in more detail (see Chapter 6). Here I want to convey some of the challenges meetings such as these could produce.

During a coffee break, delegates from the rebel group told me some of their complaints: the election of the NEC was illegal, a chair should be neutral, in a *kgotla* in Botswana people should be allowed to speak, there is a saying in Setswana that in court you can just talk (without being interrupted), the chair thought he owned the MWU, the office of the elected national chair should be restricted to two terms, the people running the union are illiterate. This was an accusation repeated by several rebels and their supporters. One delegate who had been sitting in the front, smartly dressed in a tie and brown suit, said to me, 'How can they deal with permanent secretaries and people with education?'

By the time Item 10 had been reached, everyone present was exhausted. They had spoken at length on transfers, packages and exit packages, BURS, PBRS, incremental promotions, as well as the thorny issue of what do about the Botswana Federation of Trade Unions (BFTU). The BFTU had suspended the MWU at a time when it knew that the union's funds were frozen by the bank following a court order, despite the fact that it was the MWU that had saved the BFTU from bankruptcy. One further contentious issue raised was the need to account for money raised by members in the regions, supposedly in the name of the MWU, and given to the rebels. Despite the early acrimony, the meeting ended with a prayer.

The newly elected NEC meeting the following day was by comparison a relatively harmonious, benign event, with delegates reflecting back on the rowdiness and insults of the council meeting the previous day. What distinguished this meeting was the heart-searching that officers publicly engaged in about the possible causes of the MWU rift. The new executive was warned not to 'point their finger at others', spread rumours or let out confidential information. The chair pointed out that the MWU had 22 million pula in assets, which needed to be managed, and explained that MWU officers' salaries had been raised following a review of the pay structure by an expert consultant hired by the MWU. About this, Motshwarakgole, himself a salaried officer, reminded the delegates that the MWU had decided to employ its own officers in 1980 to ensure that those negotiating on its behalf could not be victimised by the government and would be free to perform their duties 'without fear'.

The two salaried officers then reflected on why the rebel faction had accused them of 'dominating', of acting as a united front, 'of one mind'. The reality was that the officers spent long hours dissecting meetings with the government and discussing the affairs of the MWU democratically, until they reached a common position. 'The harmony among myself, Mr Molaodi, Mrs Botsalano and Mr Phokontsi', Johnson Motshwarakgole said, 'is because they love their work ... [O]ne is from Kgatleng, the other is from Kgalagadi, myself I am from Molepolole. Because they are Batswana and they love the Manual Workers' [Union]' – in short, that is what enables them to work together. He told delegates that he had devoted his life to the union and did not want to leave it when it was disunited. But now he was willing to resign, if they so wished (his offer was not taken up).

The chair warned that there was still much unfinished business relating to the dispute, and the government was still interfering in MWU affairs, and he once again warned against spreading misleading information that could lead to false or malicious rumours. The secretary commented:

> Leadership is not an easy task. There are challenges we encounter day and night. You might take a decision which might put the committee in prison. In any committee, consultation (*merero*) is an important thing. Know that you work with others.

He warned people not to 'talk', adding, 'As a Committee we deserve privacy'. When information about the executive's decisions is given, it should be disseminated to all 32 regions simultaneously, he warned. He went on to explain that the executive 'dictates policy':

> We are the board of directors. The office manages day-to-day activities. They are the management team and it is my role as general secretary to protect them as long as they fulfil their jobs. Only through mutual understanding can the committee guard against enemies within and without.

Conclusion

Meetings are the life and blood of trade unions like the Manual Workers' Union. I have shown in this chapter the rational argumentation and emotional intensity of meetings typically convened by the union, in which matters of policy, law and workers' interests are deliberated. Within the space of less than three weeks, between 20 April and 10 May, the MWU held a whole range of different kinds of meetings, all on topics of major concern for manual workers. Some discussed nitty-gritty matters of pay, others principled matters of equity or mutual understanding and cooperation among unionists. It has to be remembered too that the General Council and NEC meetings in the capital required logistical planning by the union's salaried officers and national leadership: food for delegates, payment of travel and *per diem* allowances, booking hotel or hostel accommodation, the preparation and printing of minutes and agendas in multiple copies. Apart from the meetings described here, MWU officers also attended a further range of meetings at which I was not present, with the Ministry of Finance, BURS and other government bodies. There were, in addition, numerous grievance cases to settle of the type we saw in the previous chapter. There were constant meetings with lawyers, auditors and bank officials. When they were not in a meeting, union officers and delegates were on their mobiles, sorting out affairs, preparing for the next meeting. Workers travelled many hours and hundreds of kilometres to attend meetings. The meetings were lengthy and sometimes painful and tense, as officers and delegates reflected back on disruptive events or their own personal problems.

In all these meetings, respect (*tlotlo*) was an underlying theme. Comrades should treat each other with trust (*boikanyego*) and respect. As Johnson put it, he expects to be able to speak 'openly, directly, freely'. 'Know only that you are people who respect one another (*batho ba le tlotlanang*) and support this request of mine'.

Underlying all MWU activities was the problem of a living wage for low-paid manual workers in government service. The struggle for a living wage was at the centre of the 1991 strike and the court cases that followed it, and it is this to which I turn next.

CHAPTER FIVE

'Legitmate Expectations': Ethics, Law and Labour Justice in the 1991 Strike

African Trade Unions and the Law

When it comes to the law – the statutes and regulations governing labour relations – trade unionists everywhere are experts. Negotiation, litigation, mediation and dispute management are everywhere essential aspects of trade union activity. In the case of the Manual Workers' Union of Botswana, such litigation involves industrial-class workers suing or bargaining with their employers, the Botswana government, local government and parastatals.

Knowledge and expertise in negotiating on behalf of members of the Manual Workers' Union is a source of great pride among the union's shop-floor activists and leaders. In a country where formal educational qualifications are regarded as a *sine qua non* for competence and ability, they have over the years gained a reputation as formidable negotiators despite their lack of formal education, and despite being, in many cases, women. They often boasted to me about their success in saving jobs, negotiating training and promotions or bargaining on exit packages, after government began to devolve and privatise departments such as Customs and Excise or (most recently) cleaning.

Three salient types of dispute management have characterised the legal history of the MWU: judicial review, in which the union has challenged the government in the Industrial Court, High Court and Court of Appeal; internal factional disputes, also heard in the High Court; and ordinary, day-to-day individual dispute mediation and settlement cases, some local or regional, some heard in the Industrial Court or before permanent secretaries of particular government ministries. Added to these formal forums of dispute management, the MWU is also engaged in ongoing negotiations on wages, overtime and other matters in negotiating bodies such as, most recently, the National Bargaining Council, the National Joint Industrial Coordinating Council (NJICC) or its equivalents at local levels, branches of government and local workplaces, over matters specifically affecting the rights and duties of employees.

The historiography of trade unions in Africa, as elsewhere, is often a narrative of successive strikes – in mines, railways, docks, hospitals or manufacturing firms. Strikes are frequently analysed as pivotal moments of mobilisation, political conflict and consciousness-raising. They appear to encapsulate in a single event the encounter between a wide range of social forces. Mogalakwe argues, citing Peter Waterman (1976: 331), that 'throughout industrial history, and across the contemporary world, the strike has been the most dramatic expression of wage protest' (Mogalakwe 1997: 128). Strikes arise from 'accumulated grievances', 'aggravated by the intransigence of the state and capital. When the workers deliberately break the law of the land, thus expressing their disrespect for the state which is the upholder of such law, the conflict becomes political as well' (ibid.: 127–8). But equally important, though less recognised in the anthropological literature, are the court cases that often precede and follow strikes.

The 1991 MWU national strike was the second in the union's short history, the first being a minor strike in 1968, following which government reinstated workers with all their benefits (ibid.: 119–20). Against that, in 1991 the government refused to reappoint some of the strikers or to reinstate their benefits. This was a central issue in the litigation that followed. The strike lasted for only five days and was thus clearly a 'protest' or 'demonstration' strike (ibid.: 116). Nevertheless, it was a pivotal moment, and particularly so because litigation and public political argument over the cause of the strike – the minimum 'living' wage needed to support a family of six in Botswana – continued for ten years after it ended.

It is a familiar if somewhat ironic feature of trade union activism that broad principles of social justice and equity, such as those enshrined in ILO Covenant 102 of 1952, are objectified, implemented and translated into bitter union negotiations over apparently trivial, petty items and goods, from the price of tea and bread (or sorghum flour in the case of Botswana) to the cost of a pair of shoes or a bar of soap. The landmark strike of the MWU was occasioned by a dispute with the government over the basic cost of an essential basket of goods representing a minimum 'living wage'. The union's calculations and the government's counter-calculations were tabulated in minute detail in a series of elaborate tables, listing every conceivable essential item needed by a family, from a reel of thread to a box of matches (Makgala et al. 2007: 76–81). The rejection of these calculations by the Ministry of Finance and Economic Development, despite agreement with the NJICC (ibid.: 81), underscored in workers' eyes the inhumanity of the government and its unwillingness to acknowledge its responsibilities towards its lowest-paid workforce.

Workers' struggles for fair working conditions and wages are often conducted against huge odds, and failures are intensely felt as deep injustices, since they affect the very livelihood and dignity of workers. As one critical-legal theorist argues, 'Working people have indelibly imprinted the law of labour relations with their aspirations, values, and struggles, both in victory and anguishing defeat' (Klare 1982: 546). This is true in Botswana, where the government, with its immense authority and financial clout, has repeatedly refused to recognise the validity of public manual workers' claims to a living wage. In an article mostly critical of the way the courts have favoured employers over employees – even in the face of legal reform – Klare points to the *moral* underpinnings of labour relations. Notions of fairness and unfairness permeate relations with employers, and hence also litigation and negotiation in labour disputes. Increasingly, judges – especially in the High Court and Court of Appeal, as I show below – are cognisant that disputes cannot be settled merely on factual grounds, just as labour rules cannot be applied mechanically. The area of legal indeterminacy concerns standards of fairness, reasonableness and ethical conduct that should govern labour relations as overarching principles.

Legal Indeterminacy, Morality and the Law

The fundamental notion of *tshiamo*, of 'fairness' and 'justice', still used by Tswana customary-court judges in the modern, postcolonial era, is an everyday concept pervasive in all areas of social life. A sense of unfairness undoubtedly drove the members of the MWU to seek justice in the courts against their government, despite acknowledging that their strike was technically unlawful. So too, in their considered verdicts, judges in Botswana's High Court and Court of Appeal invoked 'fairness', 'reasonableness' and 'legitimate expectations', notions that reflect the fundamental indeterminacy of the law – the fact that judges ultimately must use their sense of what is morally and ethically at stake in reaching a decision. This insight is important for broader debates in legal anthropology: despite a renewed interest in ethics in anthropology generally,[1] one has to go back to the work of Max Gluckman on judicial decision-making among the Barotse of Northern Rhodesia (now Zambia) to find a foundational legal anthropological analysis of the moral and ethical dimensions of the judicial process. Gluckman's discussion is relevant here for an understanding of modern courts too, since he drew on broader theories of legal theoretical debate regarding the indeterminacy of the law.

Hence, although he did not identify himself explicitly with any school of thought, Gluckman's analysis makes evident that he is a post-legal-realist critic,[2] who anticipated discussions of morality and law in the works of Ronald Dworkin and others. He accepts the legal realists' view that the law allows, indeed requires, wide latitude for interpretation. For any case, facts must be assembled and judged as they occur in particular social situations, in accordance with a variety of sometimes conflicting rules. In deploying notions of reasonable behaviour or the 'reasonable man', Gluckman says, 'the law aims at justice, and the idea of a reasonable man implies an upright man' (Gluckman 1963a: 192).

The essential 'indeterminacy' of the law allows for 'judicial discretion', a starting point for Gluckman's analysis, as it was for the legal realists (see Gluckman 1964). Indeterminacy implies, as the American Appeal Court Judge Cardozo argued, that law is a malleable instrument that allows judges to mould amorphous words like 'reasonable care', 'unreasonable restraint of trade' and 'due process' to justify any outcome they desire (Cardozo 1921). To avoid the potential this implies for legal arbitrariness, legal realists such as Cardozo advocated that all judges must interpret the law to advance the welfare of society: the law should serve the interests of society's most fragile members, enacting legislation to protect certain vulnerable classes of employees, particularly women and children, from harsh working conditions. This strand of legal realism came to be known as 'sociological jurisprudence', according to which judges used their own sense of fairness and ethical sensibility in passing judgement.[3]

As Gluckman acknowledges, Barotse judges' notions of reasonableness were inevitably influenced by their biases, stereotypes and prejudices, rooted in their day-to-day experiences. Nevertheless, the important point he makes is that, in passing judgement, judges drew on notions of equity, fairness and reasonableness. They saw their task as a moral or ethical one – 'so-and-so did this, and it was immoral' (Gluckman 1967: 196). Necessarily, therefore, Gluckman says, 'the *kuta* [Barotse court] ends up by trying to protect the ethical code, *even if it is against the application of the letter of the law*' (ibid.: 196–7, emphasis added). Referring to Cardozo, Gluckman proposes that Barotse judges, too,

> Employ his so-called 'method of sociology' by which they import equity, social welfare and public policy, into their applications of the law. They are able to do so because the main certainty of the law consists in certain general principles whose constituent concepts are 'flexible' – as is law itself, right and duty, good evidence, negligence, reasonableness. (ibid.: 24)[4]

In their judgements, Barotse courts are dominated by ideas of ethics, justice and equity (ibid.: 256–67). These ideas 'influence their total evaluation of evidence' (Gluckman 1963a: 197). They call these principles 'laws of God', the equivalent of English natural justice (ibid.). Hence, Barotse courts of law are also courts of morality (ibid.: 194). Although they do not enforce very high ethical standards, beyond the legal demand for reasonableness, they proclaim these higher standards publicly, in their judgements (ibid.: 192).

Where Gluckman parts with Cardozo is regarding the sources of legal indeterminacy. Indeterminacy stems not merely from legal gaps or contradictions, he contends, but from the intrinsically flexible nature of certain overarching concepts such as fairness (Gluckman 1967: 337–8). Drawing on legal semantic theory, he suggests that, 'The most important legal concepts have to cover the widest range of rules and processes' (ibid.: 341), and therefore legal concepts and ethical principles should be conceived of as arranged hierarchically. This allows them to 'absorb, and be permeated by, the ever varied and changing exigencies of life' (ibid.: 355). While this is not highlighted in *The Judicial Process among the Barotse*, a key building block of legal realism was the attention to social 'situations' (Tamanaha 2009: 754), which itself became a central concept in Gluckman's extensive oeuvre.[5]

Against claims of ethnocentrism by Bohannan (1957, 1969) and others (e.g. Conley & O'Barr 2004: 209–12), a major strength of *The Judicial Process* is the attention it devotes to indigenous concepts of justice, fairness and equity. Among these, the notion of 'rights' (*Liswanelo*) matches the cognate Tswana notion of *Ditshwanelo*, meaning both rights and obligations (Gluckman 1967: 166; Schapera 1938: 35–6), a legal concept regularly invoked by trade unionists in Botswana.[6]

Gluckman's analysis was thus part of a major jurisprudential, intellectual legal movement which questioned the certainty of law, and introduced into legal anthropology as a discipline questions of ethics, everyday life and historical change. Innovative and bold as the analysis was, however, it was never fully taken up by fellow anthropologists. It certainly did not lay the foundation for an anthropology of ethics and morality. Instead, his analysis was dismissed as Anglocentric and vague, and much of the legal anthropology that followed stressed not morality but manipulation, individual strategising and the notion that, pragmatically, in most societies studied by anthropologists, power trumps law (see Moore 2001) – although this of course begs the question of why people bother with the law at all. Moore defends Gluckman on the grounds that, in the colonial context, with its racist assumptions about primitive irrationality, his aim was 'political': 'Gluckman wanted to show that indigenous African legal systems and practices were as rational in the Weberian sense as Western ones' (ibid.: 98). But she fails to acknowledge that in addition to being rational, Gluckman aimed, equally, to show that 'African legal systems and practices' were morally and ethically grounded much like their Western counterparts. Indeed, for the Barotse, he argued, morality and rationality were inextricably linked.

The 'reasonable man' and the whole edifice of ethics and morality associated with the concept and other concepts like it (fairness, equity, justice, uprightness) thus virtually vanished from anthropology, having been greeted with scepticism, never fully understood, and often taken as a substantive description of a type of person rather than a principle of practical ethical judgement.[7] As Epstein admits, 'it is plain that the notion of the reasonable man has not had the impact that Gluckman clearly hoped it would have' (Epstein 1973: 644). To rescue the term, Epstein suggests it needs to be located in the opposition between rules and standards. In legal theory, standards are much wider and more indeterminate than rules, and require judges to use their discretion in deciding whether an act is reasonable and thus acceptable (see Kaplow 1992; Korobkin 2000). Cases concerning standards are often unpredictable as a result. Epstein echoes Gluckman in arguing that the value of the 'reasonable man' concept lies in explaining how judges adapt the law in changing circumstances (Epstein 1973: 654–5). This is, however, only a partial reading of Gluckman; beyond referring to 'normative' standards, there is little in Epstein's critical evaluation that reveals that at issue is not merely judges' practical evaluation of reasonable behaviour or expectation, but the wider issue of interpersonal ethics and morality in highly politicised contexts. Conservative readings and an inability or unwillingness to raise comparison to a more abstract level, or to consider the complex intangibles of ethics in social context, have thus arguably led generations of legal anthropologists into a sterile cul-de-sac.[8]

Moving beyond legal realist insights, strikes and litigation have been considered from a critical-legal studies' perspective – a post-legal-realist approach that interrogates the way the 'formal' edifice of labour law both generates and legitimises class and labour inequalities while dialectically being subverted, from a critical, anti-formalist perspective, by the very same economic and political forces, as well as – paradoxically – by progressive judicial decisions, employer lobbying and labour activism. In the New Deal and post-war era, in response to American popular worker struggles to 'humanize and democratise work'

(Klare 1982: 563), the USA introduced a raft of new liberal, progressive labour laws protecting workers' rights. But worker freedoms, including the freedom to strike, have paradoxically been restricted by the very collective bargaining agreements intended to protect their rights. As Klare argues, this inherent contradiction often favours the employer because in such liberal labour regimes employers retain the right to make crucial managerial and strategic decisions and thus ultimately to dominate labour,[9] while the courts often interpret the law in support of employers' claims.[10]

From Protest and Strike to Judicial Review

There was little disagreement among the various actors, including officials of the Manual Workers' Union, over the fact that the 1991 strike was, seen from a strictly legal point of view, illegal.[11] But was the strike justified on moral grounds, and was the response of the government reasonable, moral and fair? Moreover, to the extent that the strike was *not* legal, could morality trump legality in court?

The litigation that followed the strike highlighted the complex intersections of politics, law and morality in the Botswana context. The strike was a postcolonial moment when a hitherto presumed ethos of government paternalism and care was cast in doubt. In the early period of post-independence Botswana, even marginal citizens on the periphery could still believe that, as loyal citizens, their appeal to the country's rulers would rescue them from oppression; in the words of a local headman in the Tswapong village studied by Richard Werbner, the president would undoubtedly 'realise that his people are being reduced in cooking like grilled caterpillars' – or, to put the matter more abstractly, that 'consent rather than coercion was the basis of government' (R. Werbner 1977: 38). In the Tswapong case, the claims of district chiefs and local government councillors to have the right to shift Tswapong villagers from their homes into a centralised village were ultimately exposed as illegal when villagers appealed to central government; it was then revealed that, since independence, new laws meant that no one could be moved against their will. Analysing the complex intersections of politics, law and moral claims in this case study, Werbner cites Schapera's perception that among Tswana, 'the more powerful a government becomes, the more numerous and elaborate are the devices by means of which subjects can protect themselves against misrule and oppression' (Schapera 1956: 220).

I cite this general faith in Botswana among ordinary citizens that government 'misrule' can be countered because the same faith evidently moved the MWU to seek justice in the courts against a government they judged to be uncaring, oppressive and exploitative, even though the government appeared to hold all the cards. In the case discussed here, the union appealed through judicial review, first to the High Court and then the Court of Appeal, to undo what they deemed was an arbitrary administrative decision that constituted a betrayal of trust.

Seen through the lens of the courts' judgements, the main subject of this chapter, the various activities during the year preceding the strike – the all-night vigils, exhausting long-distance driving to remote parts of the country, the seemingly endless meetings, exhilarating rallies and protests, moments of deep disappointment, of broken promises and a sense of betrayal; in other words, the blood, sweat and tears of a year-long struggle that led to the strike – were virtually irrelevant. This inattention to felt experience is a recognised feature of legal argumentation which takes into consideration only legally relevant facts, stripping away much of what are, for participants, emotionally compelling and highly significant details (see Englund 2006; Tate 2007; Wilson 2001).

The struggle was for a 'living' wage, a wage that would allow workers, in the words of the MWU information officer, Sam Molaudi, to 'provide their families with sufficient and wholesome food, to live in good homes, and to dress as other people do and not like beggars'.[12] How such a wage was to be calculated became a central issue of contention between the union and the government's Ministry of Finance. Before going on to address the judgements themselves, it is worth reviewing briefly the events that preceded the court cases.

The impetus for the strike on 4 November 1991 came earlier, in 1990, with a government decision to 'decompress' top civil servant salaries (Botswana Government 1990), a policy much praised by the World Bank (Kiragu et al. 2004). Decompression entailed allowing discretionary salary payments at the top of the civil service outside the fixed salary scale for specially qualified persons. Despite 5 per cent devaluations of the Botswana pula in 1990 and 1991, there had also been two pay increases of 11 and 12 per cent in April and November 1991 for all government workers (Molosiwa 2007: 72). In other circumstances, this may have seemed satisfactory, but the move to raise top civil servants' pay generated deep resentment among manual workers, whose minimum pay at the time was 236.72 pula a month (less than £60 in 1991). In Samuel Molaudi's summary of the events leading to the strike, he comments bitterly that 'the salary of a Permanent Secretary could pay 28 cleaners having decompressed the car allowance and maintenance allowance' (Molaudi 1992: 4); the 'Government cannot afford [it] when it comes to the lowly paid worker but when it is the highly paid, [it] ... can even afford to buy a Mercedes Benz which are (sic!) now used to take members of the ruling class from one eating room to the other'.[13]

Following deregulation, the MWU had commissioned a study of the minimum wage, based on a 'basket of goods' for a family of six. In the light of this study, its representatives argued that the minimum wage should be raised from 236 pula to over 600 pula, a 154 per cent increase. This figure became the basis for negotiations between the MWU and the government in what the union regarded as 'the highest negotiating body', the NJICC, a joint committee established in 1975, composed of representatives of government and the MWU, and chaired by the head of the Directorate of Public Service Management (DPSM) (Mogalakwe 1997: 124).

The strike was a test of the authority of the NJICC to determine minimum wages. The NJICC's role was to negotiate on issues of labour with the MWU. In the events leading to the strike it exceeded its brief, as it turned out, and its decisions over minimum pay, reached harmoniously and amicably in negotiation with the union after lengthy and detailed deliberations, were summarily dismissed by the all-powerful Ministry of Finance and Development Planning. The Ministry refused point blank to authorise the NJICC's jointly reached decision over minimum pay, citing a range of issues, but basically reflecting its determination not to create an inflationary wage spiral (ibid.: 124–5). This was after the NJICC had appeared to seal the agreement to the satisfaction of all parties – an agreement communicated to the union's annual delegates' conference by the head of the DPSM himself, with barely a hint that it depended on higher-level authorisation.

The establishment of viable collective bargaining instruments following this debacle became the ultimate goal for the MWU, and indeed for the whole trade union movement in Botswana. To this end a council was finally created in 2012, despite the fact that ILO Convention 98, which stipulated its establishment, had been domesticated by the Botswana parliament as early as 2005.

Once negotiations with the government finally failed, the strike began at seven sites on 4 November, joined by 22 other sites the following day, when it extended nationwide to include all 14 regions. According to Molaudi, 60,000 workers went on strike (Molaudi 1992: 12).[14] Molosiwa reports that the strike revealed a rift between the MWU and the Botswana Federation of Trade Unions (BFTU): the latter allegedly told a South African radio station that this was not an MWU strike but a 'form of insurgency' engaged in by a 'few disruptive elements' (ibid.). On 11 November, at a meeting called by the DPSM, the BFTU was alleged by Molosiwa to have said that the strike was 'illegal'.[15]

Remarkably, the Botswana independent media supported the strike. It was an exhilarating moment by all accounts (see Chapter 2). Monageng Mogalakwe, a lecturer at the University of Botswana, describes the scene he witnessed at the African Mall in Gaborone:

> The whole shopping area was like a carnival, with workers and students toyi-toying [a form of dance popularised by ANC cadres in South Africa] and singing, despite acts of provocation by units of the paramilitary Special Support Group, which deliberately drove through the chanting crowds several times. (Mogalakwe 1997: 125)

The government responded to the strike with a mass dismissal of striking workers. On 7 November, the MWU chairman wrote a letter to the strikers appealing to them to resume work on 11 November, and informing them that the union was taking their case to court (Molaudi 1992: 16–17). A letter from the Director of Public Service Management addressed to the MWU, referring to the 11 November meeting in which BFTU had participated, reiterated the government decision:

> all who had been absent from work for two or more consecutive days had their employment terminated. On re-application for employment, they would be re-engaged afresh, and would be made to fill [out] new contracts of employment, and serve a probation of two months … The exception was

> that, those who had committed criminal offences and found guilty by the [customary] courts would not be re-engaged. (ibid.: 17)

The MWU, Molaudi says, persuaded the workers 'to abide by that dirty decision noting that this new employment will be challenged in a constituted High Court of law' (ibid.). Of the 65 workers arrested while mobilising support for the strike, permissible, the MWU claimed, according to Trade Unions and Employers Organisations Act (1983), none were re-employed. Molaudi reports that: 'Twelve workers from Ramotswa got forced corporal punishment. Ten workers got four lashes or strokes each on their naked backs. They were made to lie (on the ground being naked to the waist) on their stomachs' (ibid.: 18). The memory of this humiliating punishment has rankled with the MWU ever since.

Letters of support for the dismissed strikers addressed to the government streamed in from Public Service International (PSI), the Congress of South African Trade unions (COSATU), the South African National Council of Trade Unions (NACTU), the National Union of Miners (NUM), the National Union of Public Service Workers and the South African Trade Union Coordinating Council (SATUC), which offered to send a five-man delegation to meet the minister of finance, though the offer was refused (see ibid.: 13–16). The MWU also received support from the Botswana teachers' unions, the Catholic Church, the Student Representative Council and various others (ibid.: 16).

From the government point of view, the chain of events leading up to the strike was evidently an unmitigated fiasco, yet hardly any of the intense, year-long MWU activity preceding the strike – the meetings, protests and rallies – was considered relevant by the courts. Instead, there was a conspicuous absence: ever since the initial decision to strike on 19/20 January 1991, there appeared to have been no MWU attempt to make the strike lawful, even though the union warned government repeatedly, in writing, of its intention to strike. Most probably, the union's officers believed that under the current labour laws then operating in Botswana, legally sanctioned strikes were impossible, with earlier strikes in the country all declared unlawful and ultimately defined as 'rebelliousness' against the state (Mogalakwe 1997: 127).[16] For a while, MWU negotiations with the government had also seemed to be going extremely well. When the strike did happen, almost a year later, it appeared rushed, unplanned and last minute, as though some workers simply felt that further delay would be intolerable.

The ensuing cases in the High Court and the Court of Appeal revealed areas of legal indeterminacy with regard to the legitimate government response to illegal strikes, in which judges interpreted the Trade Disputes Act (1982) quite differently, often referring to case law beyond Botswana. This indeterminacy may have been due at least in part to the shallowness of industrial relations case law in a country which had witnessed at that point only a handful of past labour disputes. The final judgement was regarded as a moral as well as legal victory for the MWU, and bore historical significance for later disputes, such as the 2012 High Court judgement following a public service strike and mass dismissal of workers in 2011, which the Botswana Federation of Public Service Unions (BOFEPUSU) won (see Chapters 10–13).

The Morality of Law: The High Court and Court of Appeal Judgements

Comparing the judgements passed by the High Court and the Court of Appeal,[17] it is evident that while Barrington-Jones, the High Court judge, set out the moral issues clearly, he made no attempt to use them to find in favour of the Manual Workers' Union. Instead, he merely appealed to the government to be generous in the conclusion to his judgement. By contrast, in true legal realist tradition, Judge Amissah in the Court of Appeal drew skilfully on a range of laws to reach a judgement that the government as employer had acted unfairly and unreasonably, at least in its response to the strike action. Both courts looked meticulously at the minutes of certain meetings, correspondence and legal statutes.

The cases make clear that Botswana's post-independence legal complexity is further complicated by the nature of the judiciary in Botswana, which includes a number of expatriate commonwealth judges, explaining perhaps the incorporation of legal doctrines such as judicial review from English administrative law. Indeed, the public law of Botswana is modelled on English law, including English administrative law, despite the fact that the country's common law is based on South Africa's Roman-Dutch law, and also encompasses customary law and statutory laws passed since independence. This legal plurality became apparent during the course of judgements in the High Court and Court of Appeal.[18]

The High Court Judgement

Judge Barrington-Jones began his judgement by reporting on the National Joint Industrial Coordinating Council (NJICC) deliberations and those of its sub-committee, established to 'justify' a 'living wage' for workers (2) 'sufficient to sustain and maintain an industrial class worker and his family' (4).[19] He criticised the terms of references of the sub-committee for being 'somewhat vague' (3) and its report somewhat unsatisfactory, with no reference to 'statistics' (4) affording an explanation of why some prices were raised in the final summary (5). Despite this, the chairman of the committee not only complimented the sub-committee 'for a good job', but said the terms of reference had been met 'very well', the 600 pula minimum wage 'had been justified', while the current 236 pula 'was historical'. The report was then 'adopted by the Council' (6). Later the NJICC chairman is recorded as admitting 'it was an oversight in drafting the Sub-Committee's terms of reference, not to have included the ability to pay, as well as relating it to the matter of productivity' (7). In his concluding remarks, the chairman had also urged the MWU 'to exercise restraint and carefulness

... taking into account that it [the agreement] had not yet been referred to the relevant authorities' (7).

Judge Barrington-Jones inferred from an earlier letter to the MWU of 21 December 1990 by the head of the DPSM that the 'relevant authorities' were the National Employment, Manpower and Incomes Council (NEMIC) and the Salaries Review Commission (7). Though the status of the NJICC was left unclear by the litigants, a speech made by the Minister of Presidential Affairs and Public Administration showed that this status derived from a 1975 Memorandum of Agreement between the MWU and the government according to which the NJICC was the 'final forum for all unresolved grievances' (8). Therefore, when the chairman of the NJICC 'expressed his satisfaction' with a minimum wage of 600 pula, Judge Barrington-Jones reasoned, 'he spoke on behalf of government' (8), though he points out again the chairman's caution of 'restraint'. This resolution was conveyed to the MWU's annual conference, when the director told delegates that at 'the full meeting of the NJICC on 11-12/07/91 ... consensus was reached and the report was adopted as presented' (9).

Nevertheless, because of the warning given in the letter of 21 December 1990 that the NJICC's decisions were subject to further discussion by other 'interested bodies', the judge found weakness in the MWU's claim: the report 'did not, in the final analysis, have the effect of "constituting a minimum wage of P600 per month for Industrial class employees" as alleged by the plaintiff' (10). But Judge Barrington-Jones also found the defendants in error. The NJICC chairman failed to report to the relevant authority, the NEMIC. Instead, he reported to the permanent secretary in the Ministry of Finance, and at the next October meeting of the NJICC four members from the Ministry and 'Statistic' were co-opted and introduced without 'any resolution' (11), but proceeded to make 'wide ranging criticisms' of the report. Thus, it was 'hardly surprising that the Union members of the Coordinating Council bitterly complained that such Ministry of Finance official[s] had been lecturing them' (11). They demanded their removal and also that the chairman tell them whether or not the government had accepted the report, which the chairman, 'very significantly, declined' (12). The judge therefore concluded that the report was 'found to be unacceptable to Government' (12). He then went on:

> If I am right in my conclusions in this regard, then my sympathies are certainly with the plaintiff Union ... I therefore consider that the aforesaid clumsy attempt to persuade the Council to revise its earlier adopted recommendation *was both improper and contrary to the accepted principles of administrative law*. (12–13, emphasis added)

The NJICC should then have rescinded the earlier resolution following a vote, which may have gone either way. The judge added that:

> unless matters placed before such bodies as the NJICC are dealt with in a regular and democratic manner, any such body will, with the effluxion

of time, lose all credence with those whose claims or grievances fail to be adjudicated. (13)

Clearly, then:

> All that transpired in the Council had sorely taxed the patience of the plaintiff Union who had clearly expected [with some justification] that the Council's adoption of a revised minimum wage would, as a matter of course, have been referred to NEMIC and/or the Salaries Review Commission; but sadly it was not. (13–14)

Having sympathised with the MWU and lambasted the government's procedural conduct, the judge nevertheless concluded that he was unable to find 'on balance of probability that the State is in breach of its Memorandum of Agreement'. The only option was to require the NJICC chairman to submit the report to NEMIC and/or the Salaries Review Commission (14).

On the 'lock out' of striking workers and their reappointment without benefits, the judge cited the argument of the MWU's counsel that workers were dismissed without a prior hearing, which conflicted with the government's own requirements for dismissals, and should, counsel argued, be judged according to the 'emerging doctrine of legitimate expectation [which] is but one aspect of the "duty to act fairly"' (15, citing Riggs 1988: 395).

Although the judge found another set of conflicting regulations, he acknowledged that absentee workers should be given an opportunity to present their defence, and they should also have the right of appeal (15). Nevertheless, because he considered, on balance, the strike was 'both unconstitutional and unlawful', since the MWU did not conduct a secret ballot as required by its own Constitution, and had rejected striking at an earlier MWU General Council meeting, he accepted it was a 'wildcat strike' (17), and hence, since negotiations had not been exhausted, the minister of finance was right to declare the strike unlawful (18–19), and the 'Government's decision to "lock out" the striking workers was not in breach of the aforesaid Memorandum of Agreement' (21).

Finally, almost as an afterthought, Judge Barrington-Jones said that while he was unable to reverse the decision to dismiss the workers:

> I do, however, believe that there are persuasive grounds, not unconnected with the clearly held widespread belief on the part of the plaintiff's members, that a minimum wage of P600 had been adopted by the NJICC; [and to strikers] inexplicably not implemented by Government ... to suggest that the State reconsider its decision to summarily dismiss all the striking workers. (22)

In the light of the confusion and 'muddled thinking', Judge Barrington-Jones said he 'believed' that the state should 'be minded to take a more liberal view'. Of course, the state was not minded to do so, and the High Court case was lost by the MWU on all six counts.

The Court of Appeal Judgement

In the Court of Appeal, the MWU's counsel, Guy Hoffman, referred to the article by Robert Riggs (1988) cited in the High Court trial. In this article, Riggs argues:

> Since the landmark decision … [of] 1963, English courts have been in the process of imposing upon administrative decision-makers a general duty to act fairly. One result of this process is a body of case law holding that private interests of a status less than legal rights may be accorded procedural protections against administrative abuse and unfairness. As these cases teach, a person whose claims falls short of legal right may nevertheless be entitled to some kind of hearing if the interest at stake rises to the level of a 'legitimate expectation'. The emerging doctrine of legitimate expectation is but one aspect of the 'duty to act fairly', but its origin and development reflect many of the concerns and difficulties accompanying the broader judicial effort to promote administrative fairness. (ibid.: 395)

Riggs proposes that 'legitimate expectation' parallels American 'due process' but is wider, in the sense that it includes both substantive and procedural expectations. In English law, the notion of legitimate expectations is grounded in the rules of natural justice and of 'reasonable expectation', all of which rely on notions of acting fairly. As cases citing legitimate expectations have increased, it has come to be defined more clearly as arising 'either from an express promise given on behalf of a public authority or from the existence of a regular practice which the claimant can reasonably expect to continue' (ibid.: 422, citing Lord Fraser). By 1988, legitimate expectation had become a doctrine widely used in English courts (ibid.: 435).

In a wide-ranging analysis, Carolan (2009) shows that as judicial review developed, English courts arrogated to themselves increasing autonomy in deciding not simply on grounds of *ultra vires* (that is, that the administrative body had exceeded its authority) or procedural grounds, but on the basis of natural justice, commonsense, reasonableness and fairness. Rather than merely interpreting parliamentary statutes and laws, the courts began to interpret the *intention* of the law makers; they did so even before the Human Rights Act (1998) had been domesticated in Britain.

The MWU's counsel at the Court of Appeal argued that given statements on different occasions by the chairman of the NJICC, a delegated spokesman, and the relevant government minister, the MWU had a 'legitimate expectation' that the decision reached by the NJICC was final, subject to formal approval through recognised channels. This was rejected in the High Court, despite acknowledging that the government's decisions were 'muddled'. The High Court failed to recognise, however, that the question was a wider one – whether the administration had acted fairly towards the MWU *throughout the dispute*.

The Court of Appeal was composed of a panel of five judges, presided over by Judge Austin Amissah, who delivered the judgement.[20] Judge Amissah was well known in Botswana as the judge who presided over the Unity Dow case in the Court of Appeal in 1992, known also as 'the citizenship case', which decreed – against an act of parliament – that Batswana women had the same rights as men to pass on their citizenship to their children (see Dow 1995; Selolwane 1998). The Court of Appeal's judgement in the MWU's case was delivered in 1995, two years after the High Court judgement and more than three years after the strike. One excuse used by the Court of Appeal's administration for the delay was that the High Court judgement needed to be 'typed up'. The MWU complained bitterly over this feeble excuse.

Judge Amissah's reasoning was important in two regards: first, he weighed the argument in favour of the employer, even expanding on the judgement of the High Court in this matter; second, he shifted the weight of argument in favour of the MWU.

Judge Amissah outlined in great detail the meeting minutes, ministerial letters and relevant clauses in the 1975 Memorandum of Agreement between the MWU and the NJICC, as underpinned by the Trade Disputes Act (1969), based on the documents submitted to the Court and agreed by both sides. He included in his review such items as a secret cabinet information note (5), an interview on Radio Botswana (10–11) and ministerial speeches previously unmentioned. On the basis of these documents, he concluded that the government's behaviour had not been inconsistent and muddled. At every stage, he showed, the Minister of Presidential Affairs and Public Administration, representatives of the Ministry of Finance and the head of the DPSM had made clear that the grounds for deciding a pay rise were productivity and affordability, and, at the very least, that decisions made by the NJICC needed to be approved by 'relevant authorities'. Judge Amissah thus found against the MWU, stating that it knew from the start and throughout that the agreement reached by the NJICC was not 'binding'.[21] According to Judge Amissah, the union's awareness that the decision was not binding was also indicated by its demand that it be represented alongside the council chairman (the head of the DPSM, who was a member of the government) in representing the NJICC's joint decision to the government (19, 25, 29–30).

Against evidence presented by MWU witnesses, Judge Amissah argued that the minutes recorded at the time had a 'ring of truth' (19) and were well documented (21). Referring to the law of contract, he concluded that the decision of the National Joint Industrial Coordinating Council constituted a 'conditional agreement'. The government had not delegated its power to the NJICC, or ever intended to delegate it, to reach a final agreement on industrial workers' wages (24). This was the first time the NJICC had dealt with wages and, 'right from the very beginning', Judge Amissah argued, 'the union side was made aware of the position of Government' (25). The NJICC was a 'technical body' intended to 'assist' the government (27). The Director of Public Service Management may have been, according to the Regulations for Industrial Employees, the official authorised to 'approve changes in the rates of pay and allowances', but in this case he was 'acting in his capacity as chairman of the NJICC' whose 'mandate' did not extend to setting the wages of industrial workers (31). Judge Amissah went on to say, 'It is not for this Court to say whether a wage of P236 or P600 was adequate to sustain a family for an industrial worker in this country' (32). In other words, the Court of Appeal cannot judge on substantive issues, only procedural ones.

So far, more than halfway through the judgement, the learned judge seemed merely to be vindicating the government with little sympathy for the MWU's case. But Judge Amissah did concede in concluding this part of his judgement that:

> The strike appears to have taken place as a result of the workers' belief that Government had resiled from its undertaking ... There must have been some misunderstanding about the powers of the NJICC ... [T]hough wrong, it does not mean that the view determined by the erroneous interpretation was not strongly held. And it did require some delicate handling to bring both parties back to the right course. Labour relations are always likely to raise strong emotions. The mere fact that news had spread about some agreement or consensus with the NJICC that a wage of P600 was justified could have led workers to believe that this was to be the legally binding minimum wage. (33)

The judge stressed the 'sensitivity' of the situation, and the obvious need for 'delicate' handling because of workers' 'strong emotions'. Four months had passed, he pointed out, from the NJICC's decision in July until the strike in November, during which, with no positive news, 'disappointment and frustration must have increased with each passing day', the judge commented. This final statement gives us a hint of where Judge Amissah's sympathies lay.

In further denying the legality of the mass dismissal of workers, the judge appealed to the law and natural justice. On 5 November 1991, the Minister of Labour and Home Affairs, the DPSM and various ministries had:

> summarily dismissed all striking workers and ordered the forfeiture of all their benefits; these summary dismissals were in breach of the Regulations for Industrial Employees as well as the Memorandum of Agreement; *all striking workers have an inherent natural right to a hearing in respect of the substantive allegations leading to their dismissal*, but no hearing was given them; the Minister of Labour and Home Affairs made an order declaring the strike illegal in terms of section 34 of the Trade Disputes Act (Cap. 48: 02), but as the order was made without giving a hearing to the striking workers, it was null and void. (34, emphasis added)

Judge Amissah thus disagreed with the High Court judge's verdict that, because the minister had acted correctly in declaring the strike unlawful, the strikers were not entitled to a hearing. Indeed, the chronology of events that he then went on to meticulously reconstruct showed that from the start the government was abusing its 'considerable power' to deny the workers the legitimate expectation to be heard. He thus invoked the *audi alteram partum* principle, 'hear the other side too', the basic principle of natural justice and equity, as pertinent to the dismissal of striking workers, even in a strike deemed illegal.

The sequence of events revealed the government's bad faith: on Sunday 3 November 1991, the day before the strike was due to begin, a savingram from the DPSM was issued to all government permanent secretaries, heads of department and district commissioners, declaring the strike illegal and advising them 'to dismiss summarily Industrial Class Workers who did not report to work at 13.45 on 4th November 1991' (35–6). A specimen letter of dismissal was also circulated which gave workers four days from the date of the letter to answer the charge of absenteeism, either orally or in writing (36). But, as the judge pointed out, at this time there had been no declaration by the minister responsible that the strike was illegal, no press release advising industrial-class workers to be at work at 13.45, and certainly four days had not elapsed from the date on the warning letter for them to answer charges. This would have allowed workers until 9 November, but by then the letters of dismissal had been written and in most cases delivered!

The government's letters of dismissal referred to Section 8.29 of the Regulations for Industrial Employees, which stipulates that an employee 'shall be given the opportunity to present his defence and to be represented in an atmosphere free from emotion'. Judge Amissah commented, 'It seems to me unlikely that in the highly charged atmosphere of an ongoing strike, and with the speed with which an answer to the charge was required, a hearing "in an atmosphere free from emotion" was possible' (38).

In the same letter, the judge remarked, reference was made to Section 8.19 of the Regulations for Industrial Employees, which stipulates, 'An employee may be considered to have left his employment if he takes two consecutive days absence without leave and without a satisfactory explanation' (38). The timing throughout was suspect: a letter dated 4 May may not have reached the president of the union on time (39). The press release issued on the evening of 5 November could not possibly have reached workers on time. A specimen letter of dismissal dated 5 November dismissed workers on grounds they did not turn up to work between '4th to 8th November'! (41–2). Even more tellingly, while it was true that the MWU had not reported a trade dispute to the commissioner of labour as required (40), it was equally true that the government was also required to make such a report, which it had signally failed to do (41). Thus, the judge commented:

> I am, therefore, constrained to ask what effort the Government side made to report the dispute to the Commissioner. Government, it seems to me, was engaged in a flurry of activity directed at dismissing the workers at the earliest possible time … It is difficult, therefore, to avoid the conclusion that Government did not wish to invite the mediating or conciliatory intervention of the Commissioner of Labour which the Act called for. (41)

Slips in dating were 'consistent with the interpretation that the decision had been taken to dismiss the workers even before the strike began'. The letter also indicated, the Judge said, 'a shift from reliance on breach of the Trade Disputes Act, as a reason for dismissal' (42). The minister of labour and home affairs had only made a declaration in an extraordinary gazette that the strike was unlawful on 6 November, two days after the strike began, to be in effect from midnight (realistically speaking), from the 7 November (43). By this time the letters of dismissal had been issued. A 'notice of appeal' to return to work was issued by the MWU to all striking workers on that day, alongside a letter to the secretary of the NJICC calling for an urgent meeting. When the workers turned up to work the following Monday (11 November), they were dismissed. Those who reapplied were not reinstated but employed anew, losing their gratuities and any other accumulated privileges, and required to sign new contracts and go on probation for two months (44). If this was correct procedure, the judge commented, no worker would 'dare' to join industrial action involving absence of more than two days (45). But is that what the Trade Disputes Act says about the settlement of trade disputes? The minister was entitled to declare the strike unlawful on the grounds that 'all practical means of reaching a settlement of the trade dispute' had not been exhausted. But none of the machinery for trade disputes had been utilised (46–7).

Judge Amissah thus first tracks with detective-like tenacity the timing of the dismissal letters in order to expose the fact that they were produced in bad faith. Only then does he introduce a landmark ruling regarding the legitimate response to an illegal strike. In a novel interpretation of the law, one which neither the High Court nor the appellant had recognised, he judges that even if the order declaring the strike illegal was valid, *it did not automatically follow that the dismissals would also be upheld* (47). The point of principle is:

> The Act is specially designed to ensure that trade disputes are, as far as possible, settled peacefully and amicably ... It is not, in my view, made to enable one side with the power to settle a dispute to its advantage. In any case, the Act does not contemplate wholesale dismissal of workers who take part in an illegal strike. The sanction it imposes ... is in the form of criminal penalties. (48)

The judge notes that later in the dispute no mention was made by the government of the Trades Disputes Act, and he concludes, the 'Government must have appreciated the weakness of their case on the Act' (48).

The Rules of Natural Justice, Fairness and Legitimate Expectations

'Those placed in authority should in the exercise of their discretionary powers act fairly. This requirement of the law is one of the manifestations of the rules of natural justice' (48). The Court of Appeal showed that the government had clearly acted in bad faith throughout the dispute, and, Judge Amissah pointed out, part of this was the fact that the real issue – why workers were on strike – 'was not a matter the employer was prepared to consider'. 'Acting fairly is not, however, limited to going through formal motions to justify a decision which has already been taken', he said (49); and he asked, further: 'Who has legitimate expectation?' As in an earlier case he presided over, which he cited, Judge Amissah said he preferred to use 'legitimate expectation', rather than 'reasonable expectation', 'in order thereby to indicate that it has consequences to which effect will be given in public law' (50).

In this case, workers had a legitimate expectation that strikes should be settled in accordance with the Trade Disputes Act. Otherwise 'the worker is entitled to some rational explanation for abandoning the course charted by the Act' (50). In an English case, Lord Taylor had argued that, 'the doctrine of legitimate expectation in essence imposes a duty to act fairly' (51). Hence, Judge Amissah concluded:

> The essence of the rule of natural justice, therefore, may not always be a matter of giving a hearing but of *acting fairly* in the exercise of discretionary power ... A strike situation seems to me to be a good example, where an ordinary hearing or showing cause on an individual basis may not lead to a just result. That, I believe, is the reason why *special provisions* are made by the Trade Disputes Act and through collective bargaining agreements for the resolution of industrial disputes. (51, emphasis added)

The government was aware that this was not an ordinary case of workers absenting themselves from work for no discernable reason. They should have called the MWU for a discussion to explore the possibility of an amicable settlement or, alternatively, gone through the processes set up by the Trade Disputes Act. They did neither. The fact that no ballot on whether to strike or not was held by the MWU, an issue mentioned by the High Court, was irrelevant, since it was apparent that the union continued to recognise its responsibility towards workers throughout the dispute. The government had acted with 'undue haste' to exercise its 'power to dismiss workers' (53). If that was permissible, 'The Trade Disputes Act would be unnecessary and of little value'. The Judge thus makes a declaratory order in favour of the MWU:

> the dismissal of the striking workers was unlawful. The consequence is that they are entitled to reinstatement, not re-employment by Government. This is especially so as the majority of the workers was in any case taken back, and no prejudice would in the main be suffered by third parties by such reinstatement. (53–4)

The verdict was a triumph for the union, a landmark victory to be remembered in its annals of struggle with the government, its employer. But it was only a partial victory. It highlighted the limitations of wage negotiations when employers withhold relevant managerial information, as Klare (1982) argues. Even after the court verdict, questions remained: Why did the government allow expectations to be raised, to the extent of agreeing that no person could live on 236 pula a month? Why did the government embark upon and encourage the consultation process when, as it turned out, it had no intention of raising wages, and all the investigations were a complete waste of people's valuable time? Clearly, the terms set for the NJICC's sub-committee were wrong and basically irrelevant. The judgements in both the High Court and Court of Appeal recognised this, but the judges were unable to impose any penalties on government for instigating a false procedure. Nor did they feel able to define the expectations generated by the process of investigating a 'living wage' as 'legitimate' or 'fair'. The establishment of a false and wasteful consultation could well have been construed as 'arbitrary' and a 'breach of ... legitimate expectation' (Carolan 2009: 208). It can be said, however, that issues of administrative fairness in the way the government had used or abused its discretionary power on labour matters were nevertheless set out by the Court of Appeal.[22]

Even though the Court of Appeal's verdict may have been a compromise, it highlighted the limits of the government's power vis-à-vis workers. In the years that followed the strike, the government first attempted to 'convert' industrial class workers into 'permanent and pensionable' and thus part of the Civil Service, which at the time was prohibited from unionising, before being advised to reverse the decision (Molosiwa 2007: 91). But for five further years following the judgement, the government continued to refuse to recognise a minimum wage hike to 600 pula, despite calls from the then opposition, the Botswana National Front, for a 154 per cent rise (ibid.: 94).

On 19 May 1999, the National Joint Industrial Coordinating Council adopted the 600 pula wage increase and referred it to the president's office, but once again to no avail. In response, the MWU wrote a letter to the president's office stating its intention to hold a nationwide strike, with copies sent to the DPSM, the commissioner of labour and others. At this point the DPSM recommended to the government that, since the minimum wage now stood at 537 pula, it was time to accept 600 pula as the minimum wage, and that 'government should effectively and seriously engage in decisive dialogue with the union in the interests of peace and stability' (ibid.: 95). Despite warnings that refusal might affect the outcome of the coming elections, the government, headed by Festus Mogae, waited until *after* the elections when, on 25 January 2000, the DPSM 'informed the union of the Government's decision to award Industrial Class employees "the long-standing" P600 minimum wage effective 1 April, 2000' (ibid.).

The same year, a 6 per cent increase across the board was denied to industrial-class workers. The government argued that the 600 pula was inclusive of that award. When the commissioner of labour examined the case, however, he judged that there 'is no indication' that the 600 pula agreement had anything to do with the cost-of-living adjustment. Nevertheless, the government refused to implement the commissioner's recommendation, and its refusal was upheld in the Industrial Court (ibid.: 97), and in the Court of Appeal in late January 2005 (Chwaane 2005). Despite voices in support of the MWU from within the government, it remained intransigent, undermining in the process the authority and legitimacy of its own labour mediatory institutions. As Molaudi had concluded much earlier, in his report in 1992: 'we have to realise that Collective Bargaining with the employer, no matter how broad and sophisticated and whilst it is an essential protection, is not enough. In the end, the future of workers is in their own hands'.[23]

Legal sceptics could thus claim that the victory in court was in many ways a pyrrhic victory. The employer used its might to deny workers a living wage. Nevertheless, it may also be argued that despite the limitations of the Court of Appeal victory, it bore considerable significance: in a developing country that actively fostered ideas of national consensus and solidarity, the MWU broke ranks to highlight the plight of low-paid workers, and challenge the established wisdom that Botswana could not afford to pay them a living wage. In this sense, the victory in the Court of Appeal, like other signal victories in judicial review in Botswana, is remembered historically as a turning point that established the independence of the Botswana judiciary and the democratic right to question unfair pay inequities and abusive employer practices.

Conclusion

It is, I think, significant that in addressing their judgements to litigants and a lay audience, judges must appeal to moral values. As Simmonds argues, in the application of rules, a 'judgement must implicitly or explicitly appeal to moral or political values that can be regarded as binding or normative for the litigants' (Simmonds 2007: 136). The same tendency to articulate moral standards in passing judgement was true, we saw, of Barotse judges' judgements. They too invoked moral principles in explaining their reasoning. In both customary and modern courts, however, judicial morality must be anchored in rational, complex judicial reasoning. Both customary and modern judges must first mobilise the full intricacy of the law in rational argumentation, whatever their ethical considerations.

Despite cynical scepticism among some anthropologists about the increasing use of the law in postcolonial nations as a legitimising smokescreen (e.g. Comaroff & Comaroff 2006),[24] it is evident that the widening remit of judicial review in both the West and developing countries, intended to curb the arbitrary power of the state by appealing to notions of fairness and legitimate expectations, has enabled activists, including public service unionists, to use the law in their democratic struggles for justice and equity. Increasingly, dictatorial regimes that attempt to hide behind the façade of the law are exposed by populist movements. Undoubtedly, critical-legal theorists are right that politics, economics, morality and the law intersect in complex ways in different social situations, as the case outlined here illustrates. But this is not to deny the force of judicial morality or the power of judicial review to overturn unjust laws and administrative decisions. Just as an earlier generation of legal anthropologists dismissed Max Gluckman's analysis of the moral dimensions of Barotse legal judgements, preferring to discern 'maximising man' and brute politics behind the legal façade in the societies they studied, so too it seems that a cohort of the current generation of anthropologists is denying the impact of increasing legal understanding and sophistication among public workers and postcolonial democratic activists, utilised as a tool to control the arbitrary power of the postcolonial state.

Despite their lack of formal education, members of the Manual Workers' Union had a life-long acquaintance with judicial reasoning in customary courts, as well as being successful negotiators in worker–employer arbitration tribunals. This led them to believe, as the cases outlined here indicate, that if they persisted in their struggle for 'fairness' and equity, ultimately justice would prevail even in the less familiar arena of Botswana's modern state courts. This faith, in the possibility of a fair judicial process, can thus be said to permeate the whole legally plural landscape, moving workers to appeal against what they regarded as a blatantly unjust decision by their employers, the government of Botswana.

CHAPTER SIX

The Politics of Infiltration: Factionalism and Party Politics

The extent to which workers adopt oppositional, radical labour politics is a central question in the study of African trade unions. In the present chapter I trace a shift in the Manual Workers' Union away from its widely recognised working-class oppositional ethos to a temporary accommodation with the government and the ruling party. This shift can be attributed, I argue, to two factors. Of these, one was the unanticipated consequences of the domestication of International Labour Organisation (ILO) conventions in Botswana in 2006 which, though meant to enhance rights to freedom of association, initially enabled the ruling party to intervene far more deeply in union affairs than in the past, when Botswana only allowed one trade union per industry. A further consequence of the legislation was, initially, competition among public sector unions over the right to collective bargaining, which had thrown previous understandings of divisions between workers into disarray.

The second cause of the (temporary) ideological and political abandonment of oppositional politics in the public sector union was the outcome of a bitter internal factional dispute, which exposed the MWU to outside interference. I trace the social processes that led to the development of this factional conflict within the MWU between 2002 and 2006, though the conflict extended beyond this period.

Factional conflicts are not new in Botswana, even in rural areas. My initial stay in Botswana in 1972/73, when I accompanied my husband on a year's field trip to a small Tswapong village, was dominated by factional conflicts over the village headmanship, which allowed the government to interfere in the affairs of the village (R. Werbner 1977). Such conflicts are endemic in village communities, as indeed they are in trade union and party politics in Botswana and elsewhere in Africa. In his history of factional politics in the Botswana National Front (BNF), the main opposition party, and the Botswana Democratic Party (BDP), the ruling party, John Makgala describes the 'emergence of bitterly opposed factions in the BDP' (Makgala 2006: 173).[1] Normally, such conflicts have followed the predictable pattern of a social drama outlined by Victor Turner: of schism and continuity (Turner 1957). The change that occurred in the MWU's factional politics after the introduction of the ILO legal reforms was that schisms no longer required internal resolution as they did in the past.

In *Schism and Continuity*, Victor Turner (ibid.) famously identified four phases in what he called a social drama: breach, crisis, redressive action, and either reintegration or recognition of schism. He argued that, following a breach in regular social relations, 'a phase of mounting crisis supervenes, during which, unless the conflict can be sealed off quickly ... *there is a tendency for the breach to widen and extend until it becomes co-extensive with some dominant cleavage* in the widest set of relevant social relations to which the conflicting parties belong' (ibid.: 91, emphasis added). 'The phase of crisis', he says, 'exposes the pattern of current factional struggle within the relevant social group ... and beneath it there becomes visible the less plastic, more durable, but nevertheless gradually changing basic social structure' (ibid.). In the present chapter I illustrate this process by examining the development of a factional conflict within the MWU from 2002 to 2005, with ramifications over future years. I trace the extension of the conflict into the national political arena, beyond the union itself, to the widest cleavage in society. The conflict enabled the BDP to 'infiltrate' the union, leading to an irreparable split in the years that followed. In place of the redressive rituals in Turner's schema, litigation in the High Court and commissions of enquiry were used in an attempt to resolve the crisis and reintegrate the MWU, but the dispute ended in schism and realignments, allowed by the newly introduced ILO legislation. In the course of the dispute, the MWU seemed to gradually abandon its militant independence.

Factional Splits and Political Infiltration

Botswana is a small country, with a population of about 1.5 million and a formal sector workforce of 281,915 in 2003 (FES 2004: 38). Figures for MWU membership thus need to be understood in the light of this baseline. In 1991, the union's membership was about 5,500, but by 1997 this figure had risen to 30,000, and then to a high of almost 55,000 in 2003 (that is, some 20 per cent of the total workforce), before declining to 37,000 in 2004 and 34,000 in 2005.[2] In 2003, the heyday of MWU membership, income from subscriptions was 3.45 million pula a year – close to £500,000, a substantial figure, especially so considering that the monthly subscription fee was 5 pula (55 pence), or 60 pula annually (about £7.50 or, in 2007, £6). From 2001 onwards, the union embarked on a major investment scheme, creating a portfolio of fixed assets worth over £1 million, and investing in shares amounting to £500,000 by 2005 (nearly 4.8 million pula). But the union's wealth created new tensions. The image of a 'rich' union, representing some of the poorest-paid workers in the country, generated contradictions which lay, perhaps, at the heart of the factional dispute.

The conflict within the MWU was first revealed to me shortly after I arrived in Botswana in March 2005. At first, the union leadership were reluctant to allow my research. Their anxiety hinted at a world of dark suspicions. It took a fortnight before one of the union's salaried officers whom I had interviewed in 2001 let drop that a major 'factional' dispute had split the MWU since we had last met, which amounted to an attempted coup by some members of the National Executive Committee (NEC). The elected vice chairman, vice secretary and national treasurer were the ringleaders, she said. There had been a series of court cases, but despite a High Court judgement in August 2004 that entirely vindicated the official MWU leadership, on 29 November the court froze the union's bank account while an appeal by the so-called 'rebels' was considered. As a result, none of the staff at the union's headquarters had been paid their salaries for the previous four months (December 2004 to March 2005). I later learnt that they had also been physically excluded from the union's offices, and unable to perform their duties. Moreover, my union friend's position in the Botswana branch of Public Service International (PSI), an international trade union, was challenged by two other Botswana public sector associations; she had been publicly humiliated and excluded from local PSI meetings, despite being the elected PSI 'titular' for the whole of English-speaking Africa and the Middle East, a position of considerable status.

When I arrived at the end of March 2005, none of these matters had yet been settled. At the same time, neither I nor the MWU officers themselves could foresee that the factional battles started in 2002 would continue right up to 2008 and beyond, amidst seemingly endless litigation and power struggles, with no sign of closure.

I am not certain why the MWU officers decided ultimately to trust me as a researcher, at least for a while. I was invited to a meeting at the union's offices in early April. In the presence of all the executive officers and union staff, I explained about my planned research, responded to questions and was given a full account of the MWU dispute, its origins, main protagonists and the officers' suspicion, nay conviction, of political infiltration. 'Infiltration' is the term commonly used in Botswana for the government or ruling party secretly meddling in the affairs of civil society actors. Those present explained that the pending case before the High Court to unfreeze the union's funds had been delayed because of an inexplicable change of judges and time pressures on the court during the period leading up to Christmas. This meant that bank accounts had remained frozen for a further two months, the MWU could not pay its running expenses and bills, could not tour the regions to help settle disputes, and that all the salaried officers, including even the lowly office secretary and cleaner, had not been paid for four months. I realised that beneath their façade of cheerful business-as-usual there was a deep sense of anxiety. Not long after our meeting, the MWU sued the High Court to expedite the hearing of the case. A date was set for 22 April 2005. By that time, the union's workers had not been paid for almost five months. During our first meeting, Johnson Motshwarakgole, the salaried national organising secretary, told me:

> These people [the rebels] are being used by the government. They went back to the High Court, having lost their case, and demanded that it freeze the union's account. This happened four months ago. Though we are unskilled people but as a movement we know what we want, we plan our own things. And we are now rich – so much so that we are a threat to the government.

In a country where most actors in civil society depend on international aid or government donations and handouts, the MWU is among the very few unions which have the capacity to act autonomously, in opposition to the government. The assembled officers were frank about the involvement of politicians from the ruling party in the factional dispute. Having first named a very prominent politician, one of the officers continued:

> Are there others apart from [him]? The other ministers are N. and M.[3] We even saw N. giving them [the rebels] money. He did it in front of parliament and we just happened to be there. E. [one of the union's officers] was with me. We even went and confronted him. N. would not deny it. He told us: 'Yes, and I will continue giving them'. They are basically financing their [the rebels'] legal claim. The litigation is very expensive.

The elected national general secretary, a short stocky man who comes from Serowe, the tribal base of the then vice-president, Ian Khama,[4] continued: 'Z. [a very high-ranking politician] thinks he has a lot of power ... But the Manual Workers' Union is a strong union. We cannot be intimidated'. The organising secretary expressed the general sentiment when he said:

> What is causing the delay in deciding on the bank account? Our suspicion is that because we are not getting paid, the government is deliberately causing the delay in the hope that we will crumble; even though the case was marked as an 'emergency application'.

He continued:

> We hear on Radio Mall [i.e. the rumour mill] that [the judge presiding over the case] is a close friend of Z. It is an emergency application but there have still been delays. We reported the matter to the police. But the police can't do anything because he [the top politician] is involved.

The assembled unionists concluded gloomily:

> During Ian Khama's [future anticipated] regime's rule, forget about democracy ... The way things are going, Botswana will be ruled Zimbabwe-style. Ian Khama once told us that if he was the president, he wouldn't allow trade unions. 'What's the use of trade unions?' he said. We don't expect the government to love us, but we do expect respect.

In an interview in 2013, Motshwarakgole recalled that once, at Maun, when Khama was still vice-president, 'Khama blatantly told him [Motshwarakgole] that he does not wants to see him upon taking the presidency' (Matumo & Pheage 2013: A1).[5] MWU officers believed, however, that the MWU would triumph:

> The problem is, remember what we told you, blue-collar workers as you [the British] call them are the only ones to stand up to government. The white-collar worker unions are a group of beggars [by this he means that they

> are cowardly and lack corporate resources]. Most think [about us that] because we are not educated, we don't know what we want. But they are making a serious mistake. Most people we represent are getting peanuts, 800 pula a month, surviving hardship. Only the union can negotiate. The union has 12 million pula in assets [£1.5 million] in terms of property. The government wonders how labourers can have so much property?

It was evident that MWU executive officers, both salaried and elected, saw things at the time in terms of a big conspiratorial picture: the government, top politicians, the BDP, bribery and corruption. This meant that the deeper reasons for the internal rift in the elected National Executive Committee (NEC) were not spelled out clearly. Although I was sceptical for a time about the alleged involvement of government ministers, the judiciary and the police in conspiracies to undermine the MWU leadership, I came to accept that the ruling party's leadership in 2005 was fearful of losing its hold on power, and that some of these rumours may have had some basis.[6] I also began to understand the passion felt by the newly elected and appointed rebel leaders of the faction opposed to the union's salaried and elected long-serving officers, and their genuine sense of injustice and suspicion of what they saw as an entrenched union leadership. And it became clear also that rather than a simple opposition between factions, there were wheels within wheels, factions within factions. One of the challenges of studying the MWU was thus to unravel some of the underlying dynamics that led to the factional rift and locate it historically within the shifting political landscape of modern-day Botswana.

Ironically, it was the adoption and domestication of key ILO conventions, long sought by the unions in Botswana, which enabled different members of the ruling party to intervene behind the scenes in union affairs. But alongside this was also the fact that the MWU had overreached itself in its ambitions to become financially self-sufficient, and had taken some risky investment decisions which depended for their long-term fruition on the income generated by a large membership. This financial risk-taking undermined earlier economic achievements, though not irreversibly. At the beginning of my research, however, none of this was yet evident. Victory in the court appeared to be all that would be needed to spell the final crushing of the rebel faction and a return to normal work relations in the office, before the conflict erupted.

The Processual Development of the Dispute: Accusations and Suspicions

Piecing together the history of the factional conflict, it seemed that it first started in 2002, shortly after the election of the new NEC. Two of the elected officers, the national vice-secretary and vice-chair, enlisted the support of the national treasurer and, along with her, nine other members of the 18-member NEC (making a majority of the NEC's 18 members, two of them co-opted) against the established union leadership.[7] In a succession of meetings, the officers expressed their opinion that the paid staff, and in particular Johnson Motshwarakgole, the national organising secretary, were enriching themselves from MWU coffers.

Some of the allegations arose out of misunderstandings over the way accounts were managed and the formula deployed for gratuity payments.[8] The MWU's finances had become increasingly complex. Ironically, the only person who seemed to fully understand the system was Johnson, and he was the main target of accusations. Suspicions of corruption partly arose from the increasingly affluent lifestyle of the union's salaried officers. All three had working spouses in pensionable jobs or in business, and they were also entitled to union loans, much like civil servants. While they had all been industrial-class workers before their appointment as salaried officers – manual labourers, like the present cohort of national elected representatives – their perceived affluence, owning several cars, houses and other properties, sending their children to private schools, were all seen as indicators of middle-class aspirations and embourgeoisement. Their salaries, though modest by civil service standards, were a multiple of four or five times those of the average industrial-class worker, and had just been raised substantially following the recommendation of a consultancy firm employed by the MWU, which was asked to fix officers' salaries on a scale which took cognisance of their duties and responsibilities.

A key event in the unfolding crisis was the Tlokweng Oasis Motel 'emergency NEC meeting' in 2004. The NEC took the decision to exclude the elected national secretary from Serowe on the grounds that he had failed to pay his dues, a claim subsequently dismissed by the High Court. The Tlokweng meeting also decided (unconstitutionally, according to the court) to sack the national organising secretary and the two other workers along with the nationally elected general secretary and national chairman, and to replace both the latter with their deputies (who had convened the so-called emergency meeting). The aborted 'coup' followed the December 2004 'emergency' national delegates conference in Kang, called by the official MWU's elected officers a year earlier than it was due. In an atmosphere of threatened violence, the police, allegedly on the side of the rebel union workers (according to both the official union leaders and lecturers from the University of Botswana invited to monitor the elections), wanted to disperse the 3500 delegates, but were persuaded by the elected national chairman from Molepolole to allow the conference to continue. Shouting erupted in the hall, but once calm was restored the elections eventually went ahead with regions loyal to the official leadership voting for a new NEC. The rebel union workers boycotted the vote.

Fears and Suspicions of Occult Attacks

After the rebel meeting in Tlokweng that 'suspended' the elected general secretary and Johnson Motshwarakgole, the national organising secretary, around June 2004, members of the rebel faction were emboldened by a sense that their side was winning. One morning in the capital, Johnson and the other union staff arrived at the office to find the rebels occupying the building. They had brought with them a *ngaka*, a 'traditional doctor', who was 'treating' the premises. The implication was clear: the rebels suspected sorcery directed against them by the MWU salaried officers. They remained in occupation of the office for several weeks until the High Court judgement by Judge Sapire found in favour of the official MWU, in August 2004. Did the rebels use counter-medicine? I was told that one was not supposed to say that (that is, to make witchcraft and sorcery accusations, illegal in Botswana), but that they must indeed have used their own 'traditional doctors'. While in the office, the rebels removed the account books and signed cheques left by the national general secretary. They used the cheques to withdraw money from the MWU's bank account and open another bank account in the union's name. All these acts were clearly illegal, and in some instances fraudulent, but it took many years before the perpetrators were called to account.

Victory

Shortly after my first meeting with union representatives, a date was set for the case to be heard, challenging the freezing of the union's bank accounts. The trip to the High Court in Lobatse, some 67 kilometres south-west of the capital, was my first chance to meet a wider range of elected MWU officers from the regions. The following account of the event is taken from my fieldnotes.

We set off at 7.45 AM to Lobatse to hear the judgement at the High Court. A large crowd of people had assembled at the MWU offices and I gave a lift in my Toyota to five union women, mainly branch or regional elected officers, with six others crowding uncomfortably into the back of the vehicle. The case was heard in Court No. 6. It was a rainy day. Some members of the opposing faction were there, sitting together on the right, including the rebel ex-national treasurer, looking plump and cheerful, wearing a straw hat. Several people arrived from Kanye and Molepolole (nearby towns in southern Botswana). There was a representative from a sister local authority white-collar association, BULGSA. The atmosphere was tense. The newly elected MWU national treasurer sitting beside me confessed to feeling nervous. Finally the judge entered and, following the usual ceremonials, settled in his chair and uttered the hoped-for decision briefly: 'dismissed'. The rebels' appeal had been dismissed! Astonishingly, the case was over in five minutes. Johnson, the national organising secretary, stood up, followed by all the others. People embraced each other. It was a joyful moment. It was still raining hard so everyone crowded back into the vehicles. On the way back to the capital, the treasurer led the victorious singing:

> Motshwarakgole had a dream,
> The dream needs a *sangoma*,[9]
> The *sangoma* are the union,
> They can translate the dream.

She explained to me that the rebel group had mocked Johnson at the recent delegates' conference at Kang, saying that he could 'dream of winning' but it would never come true. Now the dream had come true. She said: 'How can they attack Johnson, hurl all those terrible accusations against him, he who has suffered for so many years for the union, who has dedicated his life to the union?' A thin man shouted 'Viva', the MWU cry, evoking Latin American struggles for freedom. The secretary of the Princess Marina Hospital branch of the MWU, a Mormon, said she had not been at all afraid. She always knows that if she prays and then feels peaceful everything is going to be okay.

We arrived, singing, the women now shifting to church hymns. About 20 of us crowded into the largest MWU office. Perhaps inspired by the earlier song, a woman from Molepolole told the assembled group of a dream she had had. It was a strange dream. In it men from the various regional branches were coming to Molepolole to see her retired aunt, who used to be a member of the branch executive in Molepolole. But when they got there they behaved very oddly. She thought they would greet her, but they just turned their backs away from her, as though they were confused. They were just dumbstruck, silenced. Her interpretation of the dream was that this was exactly what had happened in the court to the rebel group.

This episode was followed by a prayer led by one of the MWU staff, a keen preacher. He said he thought about the journey to Lobatse and how God had saved them. People, he said, should not forget God even when they have no problems. Next the elected general secretary from Serowe spoke of the need to remain vigilant. There were challenges ahead and the struggle must continue, especially in the smaller regions. The need is to tell everyone that now the union is strong and to enlist new members after the long period of inactivity.

Now it was the turn of Johnson, the national organising secretary. He told the gathering:

> There is a misunderstanding – people think the union supports the opposition [parties]. But the union is a movement that includes within it people who support all the different parties, it is multi-party. We have already met with the BNF. Now we have to arrange a meeting with the BDP.

He mentioned that there was a need now to re-register the new NEC and sue for the money owed to the MWU by the rebel group. After standing to pray, the congregation sang a church song in parting: 'We heard them gossiping about us yesterday, / Thank you, God, we met them (we were the winners)'. This was an uplifting moment of hope for the future, of faith that rationality would triumph and justice prevail; that the MWU would be strong again.

Matters, however, did not rest there. Litigation dragged on since the rebels had confiscated a large sum of money from the MWU bank accounts and from subscription fees sent in by registered mail (300,000 pula; most fees are deducted directly, in the workplace),[10] and the MWU had also been awarded litigation costs plus legal charges (of 50,000 pula). Despite repeated appeals to the High

Court, the money was only finally paid back in 2010/11, six years later. Much of it had been used, it emerged later, for the clandestine and semi-public meetings held by the rebels in Tlokweng and elsewhere during 2004, and they had also opened an office staffed by one employee. As a result, the MWU felt it had to pay its own lawyer his legal costs. Attempts to sue the rebel treasurer for a loan she allegedly borrowed illegally from the MWU also dragged on through the courts. She claimed a cheque presented as evidence had been forged.[11] Most of the time, so it seemed to me, the MWU did not even try to retrieve the money owed, knowing realistically that much of it had been spent and that the rebel treasurer, a cleaner in the Department of Building and Engineering Services in Kanye, was broke. More serious, however, was the fact that the rebels still held sway in at least 14 of the 32 MWU regions. The problem, in other words, was political: how to convince regional and branch elected officers of the honesty, probity and integrity of the union's salaried and elected national officers; and how to persuade them to return to the fold, thus isolating the rebels?

Throughout the conflict there were also allegations of 'rudeness', in Botswana a euphemism for anger, and not a light accusation since angry vibes are believed to possibly have a real physical effect on the victim, and are often linked to witchcraft. The national chairman was said to have been 'rude', and members of the NEC could be excluded for being 'rude'. In 2006, Lilian MaMoshe the elected national vice-chair, a feisty woman, was finally excluded from the NEC on the alleged grounds that she had been 'rude' about the national organising secretary behind his back and then refused to apologise. A former colleague had maligned her, she claimed. Beneath the surface of such 'rude' exchanges there were, of course, deeper structural causes, but they were often articulated in the idiom of rudeness, a euphemism for darker suspicions. Both the recruitment of the *ngaka* (doctor) and the salt-on-the-chairs episode during the grand tour of Botswana discussed in the next chapter, point to the depth of suspicions and sense of victimhood that the dispute had generated.

Schism

Following the High Court victory, it seemed that the rebels' attempted putsch had failed, yet in the long run it resulted in a permanent split in the Manual Workers' Union. The rebel union decided to abandon litigation when they finally realised they were never going to win their case, since the courts had repeatedly judged them to have breached the MWU Constitution. Instead, they decided to create a new union, a strategic move that drew its legitimacy from the newly domesticated ILO legislation. In the past, Botswana law allowed only one union per industry, effectively making each one a closed shop. This meant that disputes had to be settled and reconciliation sought. The newly introduced ILO legislation set no limits on the number of unions per industry, nor did it limit members of unions to a single industry. Here was an entirely new ball game which enabled unions, firstly, to pay their elected representatives salaries for the duration of their term in office; second, it enabled unions to go on strike legally, which was a virtual impossibility under the previous legal regime; and third, it enabled civil servants to unionise, where before in many cases they could only form associations or were barred from forming a union by the one-union-per-industry rule. But at the same time, the legislation also provided the government with the chance to use manipulative divide-and-rule strategies, to 'infiltrate' the unions, since the possibility of a plurality of unions in the same industry encouraged fragmentation and new alliances. The result was something of a north/south divide, with rebel strongholds in the north of Botswana and, exceptionally, in some regions in the south (such as Lobatse) and in the Central District (Mahalapye and Palapye), that supported the rebel faction or were split down the middle.[12]

Structural Causes of the Factional Conflict

The conflict within the National Executive Committee of the Manual Workers' Union followed a predictable and recurrent pattern. It was, I suggest, the outcome of structural ambiguities related to the absence of clear-cut roles for the union's elected national vice-chairman and vice-secretary which put them on a collision course with the union's permanent salaried staff and those perceived to be under their influence. None of the national elected officers of the MWU are paid; their union activities are voluntary, and they continue to work virtually full time at their usual jobs, receiving the usual low, industrial-class wages the jobs entail. This relates to the fact that until the 2005/6 domestication of ILO conventions 87, 98, 144 and 151, the rule in Botswana was that elected officers must be actual workers in their industries, a rule that clearly made them vulnerable to victimisation by employers in the case of industrial action. The government had a record of repeatedly firing union leaders on one pretext or another. To overcome this, the MWU had decided to employ its own salaried officers who could not be intimidated by the government as it could not fire union leaders on some flimsy excuse since the leadership was employed by the MWU itself. Until ILO legislation allowed elected union leaders to be seconded with pay, this was the only arrangement possible.[13]

The presence of permanent salaried staff made the MWU strong, able to withstand government pressure – the government being the employer – but it also created its own contradictions. The appointed long-term salaried officers of the MWU, and particularly Johnson Motshwarakgole, the union's iconic 'boss', were, perhaps ironically, perceived by the public, the employer and many union members to be *the* union's 'leaders', even though they had never been elected to office. To the members they represented, however, these officers were paid much higher salaries and were based full-time at the MWU headquarters in the capital, Gaborone, which also had the largest concentration of union members working in various government ministries and parastatals.

Differentials in both power and pay marked relations between MWU salaried staff and the elected leadership, who were officially their employers. The salaried staff such as Johnson Motshwarakgole, the national organising secretary, or

Elsinah Botsalano, the accounts officer, had virtual control, for example, over international travel. This was a sought-after perk among NEC members since it covered travel costs, a work break and a generous *per diem* allowance. The salaried officers could – and did – use their position to reward favoured workers, though Johnson himself hardly ever travelled. In addition to travel, Johnson was also a key decision-maker in appointing members to national negotiating bodies, while Elsinah nominated members to the women's wings of the MWU and Public Service International.[14] Such appointments accorded prestige to workers, and they too came with generous *per diem* allowances.

One of the grievances of the newly appointed salaried education officer, who had previously been the elected national secretary but was now under the supervision of the national organising secretary, was that he was denied these entitlements. Similar resentment was expressed to me subsequently by the newly elected vice-chair of the NEC after 2005, who also felt she was denied the small perks of elected office, as well as being excluded from the consultation process. Like her, of the three individuals who spearheaded the rebellion, the vice-chair and the vice-secretary had both previously held elected leadership positions in the regions before being elected to the NEC, only to find that at the *national* level most of the day-to-day affairs of the MWU were conducted by the salaried staff and that they were being sidelined. All complained of being marginalised (MWU 2007: 25). Losing regional status in order to hold an elected national office thus turned out in practice to be a demotion, a loss of decision-making power and authority. The elected national chairman had remained in his seat for the past 20 years with support from the salaried officers, and only the general secretary and the treasurer were new appointments in 2005. As an expert on the affairs of the MWU, most day-to-day decisions were made and new policies initiated by Johnson, the national organising secretary, as a longstanding veteran salaried officer, though always in consultation, especially with the veteran elected national chairman who worked in Gaborone, and with key salaried senior staff in the office. The union's elected general secretary at that time lived in Serowe, quite a distance from the capital.

So, although there was an explicit ethos of consultation, reporting and transparency – and this certainly applied to the union's formal meetings, in which delegates were given details of the MWU accounts and asked to endorse MWU initiatives and strategies – informally, there was an inner cabal that set agendas and made most of the decisions in advance of these meetings. In the absence of the widespread use of e-mail, face-to-face consultations were the predominant *modus operandi* of all decision-making in the union. Mobile phones were an increasing presence, but nothing substituted for actual physical co-presence. Johnson, the national organising secretary, often implicitly conveyed his falling out with this or that colleague or regional branch secretary by failing to return their calls (as one elected officer in Palapye complained to me).

The elected representatives of the MWU – the general secretary and the elected treasurer – though living outside Gaborone (in Serowe and Kanye respectively), did have to be consulted by Johnson and the other salaried officers on some matters because they were the ones who co-signed cheques and, in the case of the secretary, signed official letters, invited members to NEC or General Council meetings, and dealt with all the other correspondence, both internally and externally. No such responsibilities were held by the elected vice-chair or vice-secretary, and they could easily be marginalised.

In retrospect, then, it seems clear that the gap between elected MWU worker representatives and salaried MWU officers had come to be perceived by some as too wide and too publicly evident, despite the inspiring rhetoric of labour and equality articulated in public speeches by the national organising secretary and his colleagues. In addition, there was the matter of the back pay and gratuities paid to employees as lump sums following the recommendations of the consultancy firm hired by the MWU. These, which took account of Johnson's long years of service in particular, added up to a vast sum by ordinary members' standards: 138,000 pula as a gratuity (about £17,000), a figure bound to cause resentment and anxiety among most industrial-class workers. This was especially so, as I found out, because no one seemed able to explain how the sum was calculated (given that it included backdated pay as well, and that the gratuities formula was complex and technical). Nor could anybody explain why it was paid after three rather than five years, though in reality this makes little difference.[15] Various other allegations of corruption were subsequently investigated and found to be groundless, or easily resolved, by a special independent committee of enquiry composed of highly respected ex-senior civil servants commissioned by the MWU. The committee did not investigate the gratuities, however, and the rebels complained that hearings had been limited to the capital and that the committee did not tour the regions to hear their objections. The view that thus emerged was that the committee's report was a stitch-up, and so the suspicions lingered.[16]

Factions within Factions: The Breach Widens

During the two years after 2005, the new breakaway rebel faction succeeded in registering as a union, though for some time it failed to achieve the crucial stage of recognition, which entails proving that a union has at least a third of the industrial-class government workforce as members. Recognition was finally achieved, presumably with government backing, in 2008 (it was later lost in the High Court after a successful challenge by the official MWU). In a further minor dispute, the newly elected vice-chair of the MWU was excluded in 2006 from the union's NEC for allegedly badmouthing the national organising secretary, an allegation she vehemently denied. A front page montage in the *Monitor* placed her picture and that of Johnson's opposite one another with the headline, 'MWU at War Again'.[17] She joined the opposition union for a while, before joining Botswana Land Board and Local Authorities Workers' Union. From being a very strong supporter of the MWU and its leaders, she had become disillusioned since being elected vice-chair.[18]

Clearly, the new legislation allowed for more choice, competition and flexibility within and among unions, but at the expense of the unity, solidarity and strength that can come with single-industry unions. Given the new circumstances, the old MWU had to fight for its continued dominance and for membership. It had expended a vast fortune on litigation, as the new national treasurer informed me when I saw her again in 2007. It had paid consultants large sums and changed its constitution, entailing even further compensation to the salaried staff. But all its attempts to block the recognition of the rival union failed, for a while. At the same time, while union registration was controlled by the Ministry of Labour and Home Affairs, recognition was controlled by the office of the president, and by the Directorate of Public Service Management (DPSM). When I asked in 2007 why its recognition was being delayed, I was told by a member of the rebel union that it was blocked by a minister in the president's office who was, I was assured, Johnson's 'cousin' from Molepolole. Initially, I was sceptical – as I had been originally of the earlier allegations that ministers N. and M. had bribed the rebels. After all, Johnson was a self-declared strong supporter of the opposition party, the BNF. It was true, nevertheless, that this minister had repeatedly been the guest of honour at the MWU delegates' conference.[19] Despite these allegations, the breakaway union formed by the rebel union did eventually succeed, as mentioned, in gaining recognition, a move that led to further litigation in the courts by the MWU.

Reflecting back on the events of 2005/6, some moves that had puzzled me at that time began to make possible sense in the light of this alleged 'kinship' connection. The widening of the breach was clearly hinted at by the elected national chairman at that first, very stormy meeting of the newly elected General Council early in May 2005, much of it held in front of Botswana Television (BTV) cameras, described in Chapter 4. The national chairman, speaking Setswana, said: 'People, from now on we must decide that our MWU is here to stand for us, and not only that, but we will not allow anybody to destroy it! Not a single person!'. He went on to say that all that had happened provided 'a lot of insight into the inner workings of our country'. It showed that the ruling party was trying to 'gain access' to the union; that the rebels had approached them, and that suggestions were made that the union was allied with the BNF opposition party. In particular, two ministers from the BDP were involved, he said. But when they approached the BDP chairman, he denied his involvement in the unrest, while confirming that the rebels had indeed gone to the BDP, and started rumours about 'our affiliations with the BNF'. He continued:

> But I would like to inform you that we are not just sitting and doing nothing. We are not the kind of people who engage in petty, back-and-forth bickering. We take no pleasure in gossiping or in mentioning people's names in newspapers. We have no intention of doing that. We only care to do what's in the best interest of the union.

Having confirmed that the BDP chairman was telling the truth, the MWU approached the BDP committee to request that the two ministers retract their allegations about the MWU. They were assured that this would be taken to the BDP central committee, and that there would be no more interference in the MWU by the BDP. The national chairman continued:

as you can see, our union has survived, and not only that but it has survived for many years despite the fact that it has members from different political parties. There are members from the BNF, BCP [Botswana Congress Party], members from the BDP and BPP [Botswana People's Party] … [E]very party in Botswana has members in our union. So when members start bringing politics to the union, it only ends up causing trouble.

The national chairman asserted the independence of the MWU:

I would like to stress that our union is not some prize to be won by any political party in Botswana. We are the Manual Workers' Union, and we are an independent organisation! Unions in our neighbouring countries, on the other hand, were prizes for political parties, for example in South Africa.

He went on to explain that during the liberation struggle, groups like the Congress of South African Trade Unions helped the ANC 'hiding out in the bush' stay in touch with events in South Africa, and similarly, the Pan African Congress was affiliated to the Public Workers' Union of South Africa. In Namibia too, he said, the National Union of Namibian Workers was the 'prize' for SWAPO (the ruling party, the South-West Africa People's Organisation). At this juncture he was thus rejecting the kind of alliances between political parties and trade union federations that occurred in neighbouring countries. Later, after the meeting, the Minister M. appeared on BTV to reiterate her view publicly that the MWU was 'rotten through and through'. She threatened that 'before long' this would become apparent.

At a subsequent meeting of the NEC in July 2005, an MWU employee said:

Let us not forget that there have been some disputes in the union, and these were caused primarily by [ministers] N. and M. These two people used our colleagues to do some truly amazing things … During our trip across the country, the workers told us that they had some of their meetings at the minister's actual home. They discussed our union, and how it wasn't being run rightly. Apparently, he [the minister] then wanted the workers to find ways of ensuring that the union was run the right way [this said with heavy sarcasm]. I can also tell you that my colleagues here and I saw him bribe some people with money. They spread rumours and all kinds of talk that the union had now allied itself with the BNF – which is when they decided that they too were going to make BDP influential in the union as well.

These remarks were followed by a speech by Motshwarakgole, the national organising secretary. Rather than taking the offending ministers to court, he suggested that the MWU should 'destroy' them politically (he used the English word), just as they had 'destroyed' a prominent minister's political ambitions after he had clashed with the union in a prior labour dispute.[20] The two ministers 'would never again dare play around with the union', he warned. They would tell everyone about who they really were, issue a press release, publish cartoons showing them as animals – a donkey and a dog with a wart on the nose – make sure they were not elected at the forthcoming BDP congress meeting in Serowe, and ensure that M. never became secretary-general of the party.[21]

In the course of his passionate speech, Johnson promised they would take out the castrating knife (*bardizo*) and use it on the minister. This kind of body language was widely deployed in Botswana as a weapon with which to lambaste political opponents. Another woman minister from the BDP, MaSerema, was quoted at the NEC meeting as saying, 'I am a bull with large testicles' – by contrast to male politicians who are *mesutsa*, impotent. I was told that on another occasion Minister N. had allegedly said about a fellow parliamentarian and member of the BDP that he should stick his buttocks out of the window.

The Widening Circles of Factional Conflict

The debate at the meeting was cast in the idiom of the BDP versus the MWU. Had I been a keener political observer of Botswana politics, I would have realised immediately that the national organising secretary was alluding not to the *whole* BDP but to a bitter factional split *within* the BDP itself, with the Merafhe faction, known as the A Team, which included the ministers said to have bankrolled the rebel faction, opposed to the Kwelagobe faction, the B Team, headed by Johnson's alleged 'cousin' and political patron from Molepolole, the influential minister in the president's office who had denied recognition to the rebel breakaway union.

We see here both the widening circles incorporated into the internal factional conflict within the union, and its insertion into national factional politics within the ruling party, with each faction in the MWU aligned with an opposed BDP faction. At the same time, most members of both factions continued to claim loyalty to the opposition party, the BNF. The contours of the alignments across union and party began to emerge, thus:

Manual Workers' Union	*Botswana Democratic Party*
Rebel Faction	Faction A (the Merafhe-led 'A team')
MWU Leadership	Faction B (the Kwelagobe-led 'B team')[22]

By the time the breakaway rebel union was being denied recognition, it had become unclear whether it was the dog wagging the tail or the tail wagging the dog; or – to use another metaphor – whether the barking dog, namely the MWU and its national organising secretary, was merely defending its owner within Faction B of the BDP, rather than fighting for the good of the MWU. The official MWU had become beholden to the ruling party and dependent on it to stave off the threat from the breakaway rebel faction; but so too, the breakaway faction was equally dependent on the ruling party. Each faction had its parallel faction within the BDP. Both seemed to have in effect abandoned their earlier support for the opposition parties, and with it any vision of radical reform.

True to their word, following the meeting, the MWU office produced two cartoons or caricatures which were widely circulated. One cartoon showed

Minister N. with the body of a dog, and Minister M. with the body of a donkey. The captions beneath the cartoons made quite explicit the ministers' meddling in the affairs of the union and their incompetence in running their ministries. In the case of M., the cartoon also alluded to her inability to manage her own family (hence the allegation of being an impotent man). The cartoons evoked a strong reaction from the two ministers, as reported in the *Botswana Gazette*.[23] In retrospect, once I realised the realignments between the MWU and BDP party factions, my naivety seemed astounding.

The striking feature of the MWU's factional battles and alliances with the ruling party was the extent to which all parties appeared to know what was discussed in the inner circles of their opponents' closed meetings. This was partly because Botswana is a small country in which networks of relatives, workmates, members of the same political party, neighbours in town, co-villagers and church members interpenetrate, allowing for gossip and information gathering: my friend in the rebel faction of the MWU works with the wife of an MWU employee; the national organising secretary is a 'relative' of the then secretary-general of the BDP. This evident capacity to access secret information generates a sense of pervasive suspicion, of spies and undercover agents, a distrust of outsiders, which can further exacerbate personal and factional conflicts.

New Alliances

I did not probe the MWU leaders on the state of the union in 2007, but there were many signs that the union had lost some members, had cashed in some of its accumulated shares and other assets, and was fighting for its numerical and financial survival as a major force in the expanding field of public sector unions. This followed moves by civil service and local authority public employee 'associations' to unionise, gain recognition and begin to establish collective bargaining rights following the domestication of the ILO legislation. Johnson had continued his battles, still immersed in litigation, most recently suing the *Botswana Gazette* for damages for defamation of character caused by a long-forgotten article which appeared in 2004. He complained, according to the newspaper, that 'the story had lowered his reputation in the eyes of the MWU members and some members of the public who [had] held him in high esteem'.[24] This admission of loss of reputation by an all-powerful union boss, adored and venerated by rank-and-file union members as someone who could do no wrong, seemed to demonstrate the overall fall in the union's fortunes.

The ex-vice-chair excluded from the NEC, who for a time joined the rival union, had been the national organising secretary's close comrade for many years before he emerged as her personal enemy for a while (she later renewed her friendship with him). She never tired of telling me that 'Johnson's *seriti* (dignity, charisma) has gone down, down, down'. The MWU was also threatening to sue the Botswana Teachers' Union (BTU) for allegedly joining (and gaining the presidency) of the Botswana Federation of Trade Unions (BFTU) without seeking prior approval at its annual congress. BTU was another union whose leadership was alleged to be strong supporters of the BNF. Falling membership numbers and a tendency towards creating larger confederations have been a noticeable trend in Britain (Waddington 2003: 222–24), and the same processes of fragmentation and alliance had become evident in Botswana.

In their battle with the BFTU, the MWU initiated the formation of the Botswana Federation of Public Service Unions (BOFEPUSU). This was the other side of the ILO liberalisation of union membership. If the government was able for a time to fragment and split the MWU, it was unable to enforce the prior principle of a single overarching Botswana Federation of Trade Unions. Initial fragmentation thus created the impetus, dialectically, to greater unity. This powerful emergence of public sector trade union unity is the subject of the latter half of this book.

Conclusion

Factional politics in the Manual Workers' Union followed the tendency identified by Victor Turner 'for the breach to widen and extend until it becomes co-extensive with some dominant cleavage in the widest set of relevant social relations to which the conflicting parties belong' (Turner 1957: 91). This is a recurrent process in Botswana: factional cleavages in the opposition BNF, and the ruling BDP's youth and women's wings, all expanded to encompass the factional opposition in the ruling party, as Makgala (2006) shows. In his analysis of the four phases of a social drama – breach, crisis, redressive active, reintegration – Turner highlights the way that Ndembu villagers' repeated attempts at reintegration ultimately fail, ending in permanent schisms once villages grow too large. In the present chapter I have argued that while attempts at redressive action were taken by the union through the courts and, as we shall see in the next chapter, countrywide tours and public assemblies, this time – unlike in the past – these failed, leading to a permanent schism.

In my very first meeting with Johnson, the official union's national organising secretary, he lamented that having fought and won so many hard struggles with outsiders, and above all the government, the present dispute, which he suspected had been brewing 'underground', came as a shock. 'Perhaps we made the mistake', he said, 'for a long time I didn't expect that in my life … We were always planning a war from outside, I didn't expect [it to take place] inside'. In fact, there had been past internal breaches, but the union had survived them, grown and prospered. I have tried to show in this chapter that a particular historical constellation of factors – the growing wealth of the MWU and its complex financial portfolio, the embourgeoisement of its employed officers, changes in labour legislation, the limited success of Botswana's opposition parties, and internal divisions within the ruling party – combined to create an enduring split within the union in a dispute that ramified well beyond its local beginnings. In attempting to win the battle, the MWU faced the spectre of abandoning its sacred working-class ethos, built in the course of the constant defence of workers' rights.

CHAPTER SEVEN

This Land is Our Land: The 2005 Manual Workers' Union Grand Tour of Botswana

A major trend in legal scholarship has cast doubt on the capacity of courts and the law in itself to effect social change (Rosenberg 1991). This sceptical approach, adopted by some critical-legal studies theorists, can be countered by the argument that to have an impact, court litigation has to be fought in tandem with wider political struggles (McCann 1994). Against the sceptical view, I argued in Chapter 5 for the need to recognise that judicial review has become in recent years an increasingly powerful tool limiting the arbitrary power of the state and bureaucracy. In Chapter 8, I consider the 2005 mobilisation of all Botswana's unions, calling for new legislation in response to the dismissal of 461 miners following a failed strike. It took several years after the ILO conventions were incorporated into domestic law before their full implications were played out, as Chapter 6 and subsequent chapters highlight.

In the factional dispute within the Manual Workers' Union described in the previous chapter, what was evident throughout was that legal victories in court that were perceived by the rebels to be 'unjust' were simply ignored by their factional supporters, given their political strength in the regions. Leaders of the rebel faction continued to act politically despite and against the decision of the High Court and the findings of the commission of enquiry into MWU affairs. This presented the official union leadership with a dilemma: how to rebuild the MWU when almost ten of the regions, among them major regions such as Francistown, had supported the rebels and were now refusing to accept the court decision, which in their view was based on a constitutional technicality? Initially, the leadership believed that victory in the High Court on April 22 2005 was sufficient, but the subsequent fracas during the General Council meeting on 2 May, with shouting and swearing by factional opponents, and the continuing refusal of some regions to respect the court verdict, underlined what had been evident throughout the dispute, namely, that legal verdicts can and often are ignored (MWU 2007), and hence that the political is as powerful, if not more powerful, than the legal. Or so it appeared for a time. Ultimately, the victorious official union was compelled to use all its constitutional powers to crush the rebellion.

After the General Council and subsequent national Executive Committee (NEC) meetings had taken place, it still took some time for the MWU to re-register and take full command of its finances. It was thus only in June 2005 that the union leadership embarked on a tour of the regions. During the whole period of the dispute, while funds were frozen and officers excluded for several months from the union's central office, usual union activities had been suspended. In addition to individual grievance cases left unattended, there were major issues preoccupying the MWU that the leadership felt it needed to consult the regions about, or which needed explaining. There were new policies like retrenchment and the shift from state employment to employment by private corporations or parastatals; the introduction of performance-based remuneration schemes (PBRS), which included new criteria for training and promotion; and changes regarding overtime and night shifts that affected hospital workers in particular. The union leadership also wanted to explain to members in the regions about the court verdict and – as it turned out – to test the loyalty of rebel regions.

The years 2004 and 2005 were perhaps the nadir of the MWU, in the sense that the leadership had to suffer humiliation and bullying, unfair allegations and at times near-violent confrontations. By 2011, when the unified public sector strike took place, these events had been left far behind, though a residue of bitterness persisted. But it is important to remind ourselves, as this chapter graphically does, of the suffering that union leaders often have to endure. These emotional dimensions of union activism, while repeatedly hinted at, are often not made fully explicit in the literature on labour relations.

The tour of the regions was a gruelling effort, and in some places extremely painful and humiliating. Five union elected officers – the national chairman, national vice-chair, national general secretary, vice-secretary and national treasurer, two of them women, and two salaried officers, Sam Molaudi, the administration officer, and Mosala Phokontsi, organiser and driver – were to travel throughout Botswana, to the far north, west and south-west, a journey of some 2500 to 3000 kilometres (2000 miles), carrying the MWU message to remote regions of the country. The capital and southern regions nearby were visited separately. On 8 June 2005, seven trade unionists crowded into the MWU's bright red, somewhat battered Land Cruiser with all their belongings. I accompanied them as far as Palapye and Serowe, met them in Francistown and then, again, in Mabutsane on the edge of the Kalahari, on their way home at the end of June (see Figure 7.1).

The Palapye Meeting

Palapye, one of the first stops on the tour, signalled the hardships yet to come and the impossible agenda the delegation had set itself. In the factional struggle within the MWU, Palapye was a rebel region; it had collected contributions for the rebel leaders' legal fees, participated in the Tlokweng Oasis Motel meeting, and refused to participate in the elections in Kang. In addition, the local executive committee's secretary and the national secretary, from nearby Serowe, did not get along. Palapye was not, however, as it turned out, a breakaway region, but it nevertheless needed to be re-established as a solid part of the MWU structure. The co-opted regional vice-chair appeared to support the

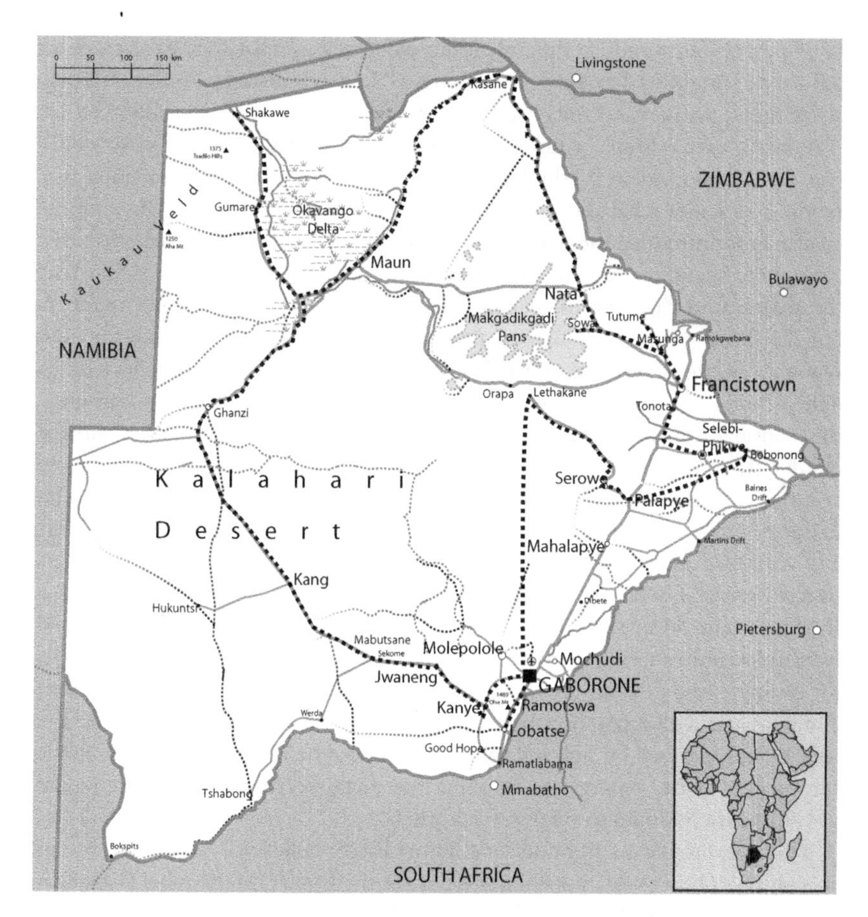

Figure 7.1 Map of the Manual Workers' Union's grand tour of Botswana (map by Peter Blore).

official national leadership. The ambivalence felt by the union delegation was expressed in the somewhat chaotic mixture in the Palapye meeting of harangues interspersed with attempts to explain current issues, such as the newly created PBRS, a somewhat illogical demand from the audience for feedback on these schemes which they were only just learning about, the announcement of the High Court judgement and defensive responses to accusations of corruption in relation to it, and a hodgepodge of other issues. In order to prevent the rebels from mobilising, the delegation had only announced it was coming that morning, at 11 AM, just before the unionists left the capital. The 5 PM meeting of about 70 persons had been scrambled together by the committee at short notice, possibly also broadcast using their loudspeaker by the MWU Land Cruiser travelling around the town.

I recorded the meeting and present a detailed account, drawing on my transcript, to give a sense of the topics and contentious issues which the meeting covered. Like all MWU meetings, this one opened with a prayer – 'Jehovah, I say, open up our minds so that when our elders tell us what they have come to tell us we should understand' – and songs – 'Unity is power, workers,/ Unity at all times, workers,/ Unity throughout the country, workers', followed by 'We work in hardship', a union favourite. A sign of the confusion to come was the announcement by the local chairperson at the start of the meeting that he did not know what the agenda was. Despite this, he called on the national chairman to introduce the delegation before introducing the regional executive committee members present. The first issue, repeatedly returned to, was that the majority in the regional executive committee were not elected members but had been co-opted at various times. There was therefore a need for new regional elections. Of the office holders, only the treasurer was elected. In light of this, after extended further rambling about there being no committee, the national general secretary suggested that the union's national chairman conduct the meeting. This was greeted, however, by a member of the audience accusing him of denying them 'freedom' and 'trampling' (*gata*) on them. The national chairman attempted to defuse the situation, saying that the past year had witnessed many disputes (*dipuo tse dintsi*) which had confused members (*re tlhakantse maloko ditlhogo*). The aim of the meeting was to address these issues so that the organisation of the MWU would be revived, ceasing to be undermined by slander and rumour, to the extent of neglecting workers' needs. Last year, for example, the government had devalued the pula but workers had not been compensated with a pay rise. Instead of dealing with this matter, however, the MWU was 'delayed by fighting' over who should be chair or secretary, 'while the owners of the powers are finishing the employees at work' – that is, the government continues to oppress its workers.

This plea to cease fighting was immediately followed, however, by an accusation: 'Didn't you contribute money for the lawyer [of the rebel faction] at Palapye?' Members' dues intended for the MWU were confiscated by the rebels 'in the name of the union', money they would need to account for, if necessary in court. The speaker then levelled another accusation: the region had made an arrangement with the mobile phone company Mascom 'in the name of the union', without the consent of the NEC. He likened this transgression to the pole placed as a warning outside the hut of a nursing mother (*Motsese*) that it was taboo (*moila*) to enter.

Having launched a dual attack, the national chairman then changed tack and began to 'inform' the region and 'report' on union activities: he spoke about early exit packages, giving an elaborate and highly convoluted explanation of the problems this entailed, especially for those who had worked less than five years. He particularly highlighted the efforts being made by the MWU to renegotiate the package with government. The union's General Council had been asked to elicit feedback in their regions, he said. From there he moved somewhat confusingly to the issue of PBRS, and the stipulation that progression was tied to formal educational qualifications which most manual workers lacked. The next subject he tackled was the privatisation of the Botswana Unified Revenue Services (BURS), and the fact that some workers had signed government 'letters' prematurely, before a deal with the MWU had been finalised (see Chapter 4).

Mr Molaudi added ironically that the 'whole world' had advised the government of the need to slim down the workforce. The MWU had successfully negotiated exit packages for Water Utilities, the Botswana Agricultural Marketing Board, the Botswana Postal Services and the Botswana Housing Corporation. He described the bargaining process as like a game of *morabaraba* (a traditional board game), stressing that since union members were the 'owners', they needed to be consulted and their opinion represented. But government negotiators were refusing to cooperate. He then went on to speak of promotion problems facing storekeepers and machine operators, and the transfer to government of community junior secondary schools. He said the MWU office was always full of people, 'like a hospital' and stressed the office 'is yours'.

Mr Molaudi then moved back into an accusatory mode: since the 'structures' had been 'left to collapse', people are now complaining that the 'trade union is dead'. But you are the trade union! It is you who are responsible, who are 'lazy' and don't come to committee meetings but instead 'whisper and shout'; who give in to pressure, give relatives jobs. 'Are you bewitched?' he asked. 'Then you shout at the leaders'. But you should know that if your time comes to be retrenched, 'notice' should be taken that 'you had worked for the nation for long and lost strength [doing so]. You should be respected and retrenched properly!' Against allegations spread by the government, the reason the MWU refused to recommend workers accept gratuities when junior colleges were nationalised was because the government in fact intended to retrench the workers, offering gratuities while telling them to reapply for their jobs because 'the employer had changed', then cunningly appointing their own relatives to replace them. In other words, the MWU was determined to 'protect' the jobs of employees. The government also tried to exclude non-pensioned workers like bursars and secretaries, but the union insisted that they too were MWU members. Though originally, these workers had derided (*sotla*) the MWU, they should be forgiven.

Having informed the meeting of current MWU activities and concerns, the national deputy chairwoman lectured the meeting on the need to build union branches and local works committees – these were the 'roots', the foundation on which the MWU was built. These works committees must guard against corrupting pressures from the employer, and fight for workers' rights. The region is 'kept alive' by local works committees, according to the union's constitution. Rather than blaming the centre, 'know that you are the ones killing the union if the local works committees are dead'.

The national general secretary commented that structures 'had collapsed everywhere; it is not Palapye only'. There was an urgent need 'to rebuild our structures'. He then moved on to talk about the High Court judgement:

> We have come to let [you] know that the disturbances which have been occurring within the union have come to an end. With our [present] faith [in the fact] that [what has been done has been] ... conducted according to the law of the country of Botswana ... we take it that ... they are finished [resolved]. The law finished [resolved] them. There is no one who is above the law!

He went on to explain the High Court judgement in some detail, including the fact that the rebels were instructed to return all the files taken from the office, all the money they withdrew ('bundles and bundles', a 'huge amount') and to pay legal costs. The Kang conference had decreed that 'even though Palapye did not attend', Palapye is a member of the MWU and must abide by the judgement. Kang, in other words, had given the new NEC a mandate. Even local Palapye office holders had agreed that no one should be allowed to get 'out of control'.

At this point the national general secretary expressed his own sense of offence: he had come to Palapye on union business but had been denied an audience because, it was said, he was no longer a union member (according to the rebels he had not paid his dues and had become an employee of Penrich). But 'whether you love me or hate me, you appointed me, to be a dumping pit (*ke thotobolo*) for all your grievances', he said.

Attempting to defuse the tension, the national chairman then opened the question of night-duty pay in hospitals (see Chapter 4), but there was no time to explain it. A speaker from the floor raised the issue of PBRS and commented that the government was oppressing the workers with international backing, favouring only the educated. Experience (*kitso*) is ignored: 'Work is by hand [i.e. manual] … a pen does not do anything'. He expressed some doubt about who 'the workers' of the MWU were, and said somewhat enigmatically that secrets will inevitably out. He concluded, 'I am in pain'. Another speaker also spoke enigmatically about the need to stop challenging other people's objectives (*maikutlo*), especially because the employer was oppressing them.

The discussion then moved to the union's constitution and the procedures for holding elections for a new regional committee in Palapye, with the national chairman stressing that this was a local responsibility. One speaker from the floor objected to the union regional committee being dissolved, which would compel workers to go Serowe. He also commented that if workers in Gaborone had made the mistake of signing the letters, this was a sign that the failure was not solely that of workers in Palapye. Another speaker asked for the judgement to be photocopied and circulated to all members. He raised doubts about whether 'the conduct of the money in the proper manner' had been dealt with; he 'doubted' the 'transparency' of the commission of enquiry's report, or that all the matters about which people were 'anxious' (*tlhobaela*) were addressed in the judgement. In response, the national secretary claimed that the national General Council has been informed of the judgement and report, and these should have been widely disseminated. The speaker then responded that they should have realised when they were provoking one another in the capital, 'we too tied up the shoes' (*re ne ra bofa ditlhako*), that is, were implicated. He defended the outgoing rebel national treasurer, saying that 'squeezing' her 'pained' him. She only wanted to 'correct' things. People were elected, he said (presumably at Kang), to 'keep quiet'. He then suggested that the delegation 'leave the region' and they would vote 'with no hurry', mobilising the whole region, rather than being hurried by headquarters, adding, somewhat ironically, 'we are ordinary people who, when you speak, we will bow our heads and see that God has descended from heaven to earth'. The national general secretary responded in a conciliatory tone, saying he did not mean to crow about the court victory. When interviewed by a journalist who asked him if he was happy to have won the case, he responded, 'It is unfortunate to be said that I have won the case in which I was sued by my parents'. The employer was the one who was happy, seeing the union divided.

The national vice-chairwoman then recalled that she and the acting regional secretary had together joined hands to try to calm the rebels, who were acting like 'children'. The fight was all about petty ambitions for office, she said. While she and the national general secretary were attempting to restore peace, they heard that the union paid officers had been taken to court. The rebels were moulding a 'clay cow' in order to make it 'moo'; that is, they were inventing a case. They had no evidence. It disappointed her to hear unfounded accusations that 'someone had spoiled' – that is, cheated the union. The national chairman echoed her words, saying that one needs to distinguish truth from falsehood. He denied rumours that 230,000 pula and 22,000 pula were taken by officers. There were invoices and receipts which the court had seen. He denied accusations of 'insulting' people, and again asked the regional secretary: 'Did you not go to Tlokweng [i.e. to the Oasis Motel meeting, where the rebels spent a good deal of money]?' He said that the money the union was accused of confiscating was spent on educating the regions on the union's Constitution. He admonished those present, telling them 'to look at the truth', even if they felt sorry for those now legally obliged to pay back the money they took.

The administration officer then tacked away from these fraught issues to the question of why BURS workers in Gaborone had signed the letters of transfer to the new authority. He spoke at length about doubting Thomases and Noah, the man of faith. They, the executive, had warned the workers not to sign. He ended by warning workers to cooperate with their elected leaders.

By this time the meeting had been going on for more than two hours, and outside it was already dark. But still questions came thick and fast from the floor. One woman pleaded with the leaders to visit the hospital to explain the new overtime pay system. Another woman asked about mobile phones: were they only for people working for local government? A third woman echoed her query. A fourth woman, from BURS, admitted to signing the government letter in the belief that this was MWU policy. Now the workers are encountering 'problems' – of promised payments unpaid, being 'cut' from housing, unclear pay structures. She elaborated at some length before deviating to speculate why the judgements had not been photocopied and why Mascom mobile phones were not universally available, conveying her sense of confusion.

For some reason, these apparently innocent questions raised an aggressive response from the administration officer. He seemed to blame the local leaders of the union for not informing members of relevant matters, saying this proved that the local union had 'died'. He called on them to 'talk the truth of what is happening'. He warned persons 'mixing up things' (*a tlhakatlhakanya dilo*) that they should go outside and speak there. He asked people not to 'hide' words, to speak frankly since 'we are alone', but without 'deriding each other', since people have a right to respect (*tlotlo*). He seemed very angry. BURS workers were 'prevented' from coming to a meeting. A delegation had come to them wanting to form a union, but they had persuaded them to join the MWU. He then spoke briefly about the domestication of ILO conventions, mentioned by someone earlier.

Questions continued, with non-attendance at meetings raised by the national chairman, saying, 'I am a tortoise who withdraws into its shell when attacked'. He raised once again the problem of trust: 'Committees will never be two, the committee is one', implying his suspicion that some unionists in Palapye would like to split from the MWU. Once again, he called for new elections.

It was at this point that the meeting erupted into a shouting match. A woman who had originally led the singing appeared to find the patronising tone and constant reiteration of the failures of the Palapye region too much. Raising her voice she shouted:

> We are people too! I mean that we are subscribing 5 pula [the monthly union subscription fee], we are supposed to comment. I have been in this movement ... for 24 years. I was once the secretary in this union ... Even Molaudi is younger than me in the union.

She went over the factional dispute, insisting: 'The [Kang] conference was not free and fair ... Those things stirred up our feelings'. The only letter they had received, she said, came from the rebel committee, alleging that MWU money had been 'eaten'. No letter came from the union's central office. 'When you pay your membership fee of 5 pula, it is your right to know the things of your union'. Meetings, she said, perhaps referring obliquely to one of the rebel meetings, can also be held at night. One such meeting, she recalled, was with Motshwarakgole and Minister Kedikilwe at Selibe Phikwe.

The penultimate speaker tried to be conciliatory, while pointing out that a promised 'booklet' had never arrived, and saying that even co-opted members of the Palapye regional committee perform their duties and should be given respect. At this point the earlier women speaker bellowed: 'Keep quiet ... You are making noise as if you are not elders!'

Finally, the Palapye chair spoke. He defended himself, saying the local committee had run around, using their own petrol, calling people to the meeting. There was no one who had thanked them. He promised to begin organising the elections for a new regional committee the very next day, but denied that Palapye had not been at Kang. Its delegation was there, but refused to vote. He pointed to further confusions: this was not an emergency meeting – the schedule of the tour was pinned at the Vocational Training Centre. Motshwarakgole had promised to inform them when the delegation would arrive, but no one ever saw the schedule. It went somewhere else. They intended to prepare for the meeting with the national general secretary, but when he finally came it was like it was a secret. At this point my tape ran out so I rely on my notes to describe the final round of shouting and complaints.

The meeting had started well with the audience responsive, singing and joking. The discussion proceeded *kgotla* style. Each person stood up to make their speech, with oratorical flourishes and pauses for emphasis. But as the discussion moved to sums of money linked to allegations of corruption, payments, Motshwarakgole driving around in a fancy car, Kgaogang not being a member, tempers flared. Referring to Motshwarakgole, the final woman speaker lost her cool completely, shouting. 'I can even shoot him!' – clicking and pointing her finger in the air at the chair (who may have insulted her). Others shouted at her to sit down. Some began to leave. 'I have the right!' she shouted, walking out. 'I will be there!' she went off, murmuring, but then sat down again. The meeting ended with an impassioned prayer by the national general secretary.

Chatting with the unionists as we ate our evening meal at the local hotel after the meeting, the national vice-chairwoman said that she thought that the national chairman and general secretary should not have responded to the accusations levelled against them, they should have left it to people like herself who were objective outsiders and not involved in the earlier dispute to respond. Both she and the national treasurer agreed that there should have been a much clearer, tighter agenda. The treasurer said she thought that Palapye was trying to get the executive to forgive the debts of the leaders of the rebel faction. The national general secretary expressed the view that meetings everywhere were being deliberately sabotaged, with union officials in the rebel areas warning members not to attend. This may have happened at Lethakeng, where attendance had been very poor. The national general secretary admitted that he was very depressed. To my surprise, he said he had not expected trouble.

Francistown, Maun and Other Tribulations

So began the *via dolorosa* of the Manual Workers' Union as its delegation attempted to establish its authority in the regions, touring the length and breadth of Botswana. Palapye, as it turned out, had not been too bad: elections were held there at the beginning of August 2005, and a new regional executive committee loyal to the official MWU elected. But the Palapye meeting made eminently evident that, despite being unequivocal, neither the commission of enquiry's report nor the court judgement could dispel suspicions and allegations about greed, corruption and autocratic decision-making afflicting at least some of the union's salaried officers in the capital. The union's wealth along with these officers' perceived affluent lifestyles created a gulf between some leaders and ordinary workers. It made the workers easily susceptible to gossip and innuendo. While some activists were resigned to putting aside the allegations for the sake of unity, clearly, while the law had spoken, its verdict was not accepted by all.

The Serowe meeting, which I attended, passed uneventfully. Serowe was one of the loyal regions. I heard about the rest of the tour when I met the delegation in Mabutsane three weeks later, on its way home. Over lunch the national treasurer and vice-chairwoman filled me in on the trials and tribulations of the journey. At first, their story had little detail but as they warmed to their tale, it began to flow. It was a tale of delays, disturbances and downright obstructions in many places, interspersed with moments of solidarity. In Lethakane, where the tour started on 6 June, the meeting was 'disturbed', the district commissioner and council secretary were 'not well informed'. In Serowe, people were 'few'. Bobonong, after Palapye, was 'very enjoyable. They were singing'. The local executive committee was 'well prepared'.

Then came Selibe Phikwe and Francistown, rebel strongholds. In Selibe Phikwe no venue had been prepared for the meeting, so it was held in a park, amidst charges of corruption. As the national chairman reported later in vivid detail to the NEC:

> as the meeting commenced, this old man with the ZCC [Zionist Christian Church] badge starting yelling all kinds of accusations at us. He accused us of stealing the union's money and so on and so forth. And then I asked him how he would feel if we took him to court, just for blindly making such accusations, without proof, which his colleagues couldn't even produce in a court of law? I told him that the wise thing for him to do would be to hear both sides, before reaching a conclusion. L. then got up and backed me. So he had no choice but to go back on his words. But they were obviously still very excited because of the 'incriminating evidence' they thought they had against us.

Among other things, a rumour had started that Motshwarakgole had stolen 48,000 pula from the union. But despite the chaos, 'People stood up, and pleaded with us to schedule a meeting with them; they had a lot of concerns they wished to air'. These were regarding personal work issues, hospital overtime pay and the absence of a local committee. Braving the barrage of accusations, the union delegates:

> continued to address the people's concerns, and answer their questions. Ultimately, we left Z. defeated in the dust. So because people were afraid of possible friction, as soon as they got their answers, they would leave. This went on for a while. When there were about 20 people left, Mrs E. was asked to make closing remarks. She said: '[National] Executive Committee, we are pleased that you could be here today. We've been attending these meetings without comprehending a thing, but now we finally understand. And the thing is that these people have turned us into liars. They are always so passionate about their beliefs, and yet today, they are completely silent'.

At this point, exhausted, the delegation decided to go home for the weekend. Then, on Monday, they went to Francistown. In Francistown the harassment reached new levels. First, there was a claim of 'confusion'. As the vice-chair reported:

> They were confusing themselves. The fax about our arrival showed a blurred date [they claimed] – [they said] we only received the fax on Friday, we couldn't prepare anything on time for the meeting. We would have organised everything, even the hall. The regional chairman, the secretary, were delaying. Then we said: 'Let's go book our own hall', but they went to the owner of

> the hall that we were trying to book and cancelled it, and when we applied for a permit they cancelled that too. They were five. Basically, they did not want the union to talk. The city council secretary told us, 'We are not the ones who locked the hall, it's your own people'.

Even after the delegates managed to book an alternative hall for a meeting, they found it locked. The very same people who had claimed that they didn't know anything had locked them out, as the hall owners informed them the next day.

Johnson Motshwarakgole, the union's national organising secretary, and Elsinah Botsalano, the acounts officer and coordinator of the Women's Wing, joined the delegation at the Tapama Lodge in Francistown. The next morning, in Tutume, just north of Francistown, one of the rebels, R., fought with Johnson and hit him. Johnson himself told me they were having a meeting with the school headmaster, just four of them, when R., a member of the regional executive committee, made threatening gestures as he moved towards him, but was stopped by the headmaster. 'The man took him by the throat', the national vice-chairwoman and national treasurer said. 'Elsinah was there'. Despite this, 'the region was wonderful. Rancholo did not want us to address the hospital meeting'.

From there, the delegation moved on to Suwa, a small settlement on the way north and with a large hospital. The meeting at Suwa was 'very well organised'. From there they travelled to Kasane, where there was another well organised meeting. 'We slept in a big hotel, Mwana Lodge. A wonderful hotel'. On Saturday the delegation travelled from Kasane to Maun, another rebel stronghold. They left in the morning at 9 AM and arrived at Maun: 'That was the big battle'. As I was told: 'On Sunday Neo [the national treasurer] and Martin [the national deputy-secretary] went to church. We were in the hotel … We were sleeping. The rebels called us from reception to say, "We are waiting for you"'. They were invited to the Rural Administration Centre (the place of the meeting), where they found the regional chairman and secretary. They saw one local leader 'hiding, driving a green Hilux'. Kaboda Phillip – the rebel ringleader who was the previous national vice-chair – had come from Gumare. 'There were about ten of them'. As Lydia, the newly elected national vice-chairwoman, reported to the NEC:

> When he was done, Phillip pointed at me, and said, 'This one? What's her name? Isn't she Lydia Tlhong, the chairperson in Kanye [i.e. not the elected national vice-chair]? This one is Kgaoganang, he works for Penrich [i.e. no longer a member of the MWU]. He is Molaudi, you are an employee of *mine.* People are talking of PBRS and PMS [performance management systems], but you are more concerned with running around all over the place. Who is doing all the work at the office while you are here? All four of you, I want you out of my sight! None of you have the right to talk to me. The only one who can do that is the chairman'.

They were told unequivocally that they would not be allowed to convene a meeting:

> As we were leaving, they screamed at us that they prayed that, wherever we go, we would be given the cold shoulder. Go! We ignored them, and went about our exit. Molaudi kept nice [and quiet]. They said: 'Have a good journey, we'll pray for you so everywhere you won't succeed'.

These repeated confrontations in rebel strongholds reveal the intensity of the rebels' antagonism, and their willingness to transgress the boundaries of public civility. The union delegates from the centre were helpless in the face of such obstructionist tactics, underlining the relative autonomy of each region, with its own power base.

At the Maun meeting, the travelling delegates noticed that salt had been strewn on their chairs. Lydia, the national vice-chair, refused to sit down, but the Maun committee members kept insisting they sit, so the national chairman, Tsalaile, said, 'Okay, let's sit down'. Lydia explained that salt is a traditional medicine given for witchcraft (*go loa*). If you notice it, it is no longer powerful. I asked if they had treated themselves against it by going to their own (traditional) doctor? She said that since they were in Maun they could not do that, so they just washed with a drop of Jeyes fluid cleaner (which apparently counteracts the witchcraft). The salt sent a message that the rebels regarded the official MWU officers and employees as powerful witches. It may be recalled, as the vice-chair told me, that the rebels, led by the former national treasurer, had brought in a *ngaka* (traditional doctor) to 'treat' the MWU offices after invading them.

Maun was the region where the rebel ex-national general secretary came from. He was later employed as a union officer, and it was he who had first stirred matters up in the office, making allegations against Motshwarakgole, the national organising secretary. Maun was another one of the places where the travelling delegation struggled to find a hall. Although they had written a letter, they kept being moved from one office to another, then another. Luckily, the chairman reported:

> Mrs Tlhong ran into someone she knew and told the person that we were still waiting for a permit. The person then informed us that the councillor for the area had gone in there and told the employees to deny us a permit at all costs. It was N., though we didn't know that at the time. They didn't want to tell us who exactly had made such an order, but they dropped hints; they asked us whether we didn't have a councillor as one of our members? Anyway, subsequently we got to this employee, who couldn't stop making faces at us. We told her why we were there, and she told us the same story, that we were not allowed a permit.

Ultimately, the delegates met the council secretary and persuaded him and his staff to grant them a permit, though he warned that the council 'couldn't involve themselves in the internal feuding of our union'.

> It turns out that from the Maun council headquarters, the rebels had gone to the police, also telling them to deny us a permit. So the chairman and Mrs Tlhong had to fight to get permits from all sides. The police chief then told us to wait for him, as he had to go to a meeting. He also instructed us to go call Mr N., and Mr Molaudi started dashing all over town, and finally found a hall in a junior community school. We paid for it and invited people using our [loud]speakers.

It was then that the delegation discovered that the rebel union had called a rival meeting: 'It was packed with workers'. When they finally convened their own meeting, one young man spoke to them in such a manner that it left the chair feeling 'cold with shame'.

After Maun, the delegation went to Gumare, the rebel leader Phillip's base. They expected the worst, but the meeting instead attacked Philip, as the national treasurer reported:

> During the meeting, the whole time, Phillip was trying to take over the floor, but these two ladies from the hospital, they didn't give him the slightest chance. They kept on his case, asking him to sit down and to stop trying to lie about the fact that they stole the union's money. When he tried to resist, the other elderly man joined in, and finally forced him off the stage. The meeting proceeded with no interruptions from Phillip. When the meeting concluded, the regional chairman told the crowd of Phillip's desire to address them. They expressed no interest in the matter, simply stating that if he allowed Phillip to take the floor, they would just leave the building.

The difficulties they encountered again and again took their toll on the delegates, as Lydia, the national vice-chair, explained:

> Even in Phikwe, even though we managed to hold the meeting [there], it wasn't easy, just because, I mean, we held the meeting and the workers understood us, but the chairman there was trying with all his might to impede our work. So we were on his case, ensuring that we didn't allow him any opportunity to use [something] against us [by making a mistake]. He tried to make excuses, saying that it was Friday, and that no one would come or whatever, but we insisted on getting the permit and inviting people over anyway. And the workers came, and they did listen to us. But what I'm trying to say is that regions like these were not easy to handle because the regional chairs didn't make things easy. But we tried our level best to get things done nonetheless.

From Gumare the expedition went to Shakawe, on the Namibian border. They left their car on the other side of the Okavango River and crossed by boat. By this time they had a clear division of labour in the meetings, so each meeting only lasted two-and-a-half hours.

Even though Maun had been a 'disaster' in the national treasurer's words, the meeting in Gumare, where Phillip was kept in the dark and laughed out of court, was an important lesson. As she explained to the NEC:

> They simply laughed at him, and it was pretty clear that these people did not have the same agenda that this man had; which therefore suggests to me that we shouldn't just generalise as to what people are thinking based on what region they are in. Those who are open-minded, we should feed them the truth. But even those who are lost, we should guide them back to the right path.

Other places in the south and south-east, close to the capital, were visited separately. They too sometimes presented problems. In Ramotswa, the regional chair's view was that 'it would be a miracle' if people actually showed up. Apparently one of the regional officers had told everybody not to attend this meeting, 'according to her own instruction and that of the regional chairman. We were still able to go about our meeting though, but with the utmost difficulty'. Despite attempts to reason with the chair, he

> responded quite angrily, but the crowd managed to douse his fury. As soon as he was gone, people opened their arms and ears to us, pleading with us to keep them updated. It was very clear that these people had been waiting, and had been starved of information and of a way out [of the impasse]. They listened to us with no problem, asked questions, and seemed to be really enjoying themselves. They even invited us back to Ramotswa two weeks later, and guaranteed that provided we make arrangements early, the hall would be filled to capacity with workers. So that's how it was.

Unlike Ramotswa, the visit to Lobatse was another 'disaster'. I tried to attend the meeting there but had been given the wrong address. When I got back to the capital, Johnson told me that they had not been allowed to speak. There was quite a full hall, he said, about 50 had gathered, but they refused to let him and the national chairman talk. They were singing and toyi-toying (dancing) on the stage. He complained that that was not the right thing – people should be allowed to speak and be listened to. The national chairman put a more positive gloss on the meeting:

> It was Mr Motshwarakgole, Mr Kgaoganang and myself. Mr M. [from the NEC] had struggled very hard to get that meeting organised. And not only that, but the people themselves showed up in large numbers, and were very keen to hear what we had to say. Mr Y. [of the rebel faction] had brought some posters, which he tried to use to lure people away from the meeting. They [the rebels] tried desperately to prevent people from entering the halls, but to no avail. When the people themselves had finally filled the hall, they [the rebels] started dancing, and every time Mr Motshwarakgole tried to say a word, they would cut him off by dancing even harder. Things seemed to

> be getting out of control at one point. My colleagues even had to warn me when I tried to slap one of the people who was dancing. But I only did that out of sheer frustration. I actually thought about calling the police once or twice, and on one occasion, I even consulted with Mr Motshwarakgole that perhaps we should call the police just to get tough with these people. They were simply getting out of control.

Whether or not the people at Lobatse were keen to hear the delegation, they clearly made it impossible for anyone to speak. As the national chairman summed up the tour:

> Constantly, we had to deal with very hostile and aggressive police people, which on a number of occasions almost caused me to abandon all self-control. You see, they knew that, as we were running around looking for permits and going to different departments, that we were organising a meeting that was going to be held outside, like a rally. So therefore they knew that in order to stage this rally, we had to have a permit. So, every time we went to the police to ask for them [the permits], we were given a hard time. That's when we told them that, in all fairness, they should call both parties to their police stations and hear both sides of the story, instead of just going with what the rogues were saying.

In Maun, he added:

> Mr Molaudi had invited the police to the meeting, the special branch forces, so they were there too. There was this young man who had been sent there by the rebels. As soon as we started the meeting, he came from the back and started yelling all kinds of profanities at me. When the police started to ask him to calm himself down, he exclaimed again, claiming that we had now brought the police to do our dirty work. So, I mean, people, these are the things that we had to deal with on that trip.

By the time I met the delegation in Mabutsane, the last stop on their way home, they had been carrying the union cross for three weeks. By contrast to some of the other meetings, however, the one in Mabutsane was joyous. The two choirs both sang, welcoming the union delegation. Many of the songs glorified Motshwarakgole, the national organising secretary:

> Workers of today, stand up,
> And build our union.
> Mr Motshwarakgole,
> We thank the Lord,
> That you have led our union for this long time,
> You have given many a great inheritance,
> To bring about the light,
> The light of close friendship.

I have a child, Iyelele,
His name is Motshwarakgole.

Motshwarakgole, our man is being disrespected,
He is being belittled.
It is not right this thing, it is not right.

The choir danced as it sang. After the opening prayer, members of the delegation were introduced with shouts of 'Viva', amidst a good deal of joking. One got the feeling that here was the union at peace with itself. As I was leaving, accompanied by my research assistant, a rather drunk man accosted us: 'But where is Motshwarakgole?' Clearly, the presence of the father of the union in the flesh was much desired.

Even at Mabutsane, however, there were darker themes, as reported by the national chairman to the NEC:

> When we started with the meeting, there was a group of women sitting at a table, babbling about all the rumours they had heard. One of these rumours was that Mr Motshwarakgole was buying his children expensive mobile phones with union money. So, I mean, not only were we surprised, but the people of Mabutsane were surprised too by these women, and were also wondering just where they came from exactly. So we initially just assumed that they were a bunch of rogues who had not organised themselves properly, but it occurred to us later that they had come all the way from Jwaneng [another rebel region]. But anyway, we managed to crush them, and even got them to leave our meeting.

It was clear, he said, that the rebels were attending the meetings, determined to disrupt the tour.

Dissolving the Regions

Altogether, out of 32 regions there had been eleven dissenting regions that constituted the rebel strongholds: Francistown, Maun, Ghanzi, Lobatse, Mahalapye, Jwaneng and Tutume, and to a lesser extent Selibe Phikwe, Lethakane, Masunga and Palapye. In the aftermath of the national tour of the regions, the union executive decided to call new elections in these regions, first dismissing ten of the regional executive members who constituted the rebel core. These ringleaders were to be called for a hearing and given the chance to explain themselves, even though it was thought that they would not attend.

There was thus a multi-pronged strategy to deal with the fallout from the internal factional dispute: first, dismiss rebels from the union after an internal disciplinary hearing; next, dissolve union branches, works and regional committees; and finally, call new elections in the dissenting regions, having dismissed obstructive members from the MWU. The first regions to be dissolved would be Francistown, Maun, Ghanzi and Lobatse. The union thus reacted with all the might of the law behind it, in accordance with its Constitution, against members who refused to accept the High Court judgement.

In the long run the law was effective, but only once the MWU had elected a new leadership, re-registered itself and re-established full control of its finances did it regain the political clout to crush the opposition. In the face of this decisive defeat, the rebel faction decided, as we saw in Chapter 6, to secede from the MWU and form their own union. They did, however, succeed in siphoning off disaffected MWU members and, with government backing, they also managed to register and even gain recognition for their new union in subsequent years, until this was finally withdrawn in August 2011 by a judge in the High Court. Despite this, the rebel faction formed a relatively small and insignificant union. Nevertheless, as the next chapter shows, they remained a significant foe that still needed to be fully crushed and liquidated in the eyes of the MWU leadership, a perception that affected the union's future strategies.

Conclusion

This chapter has highlighted the fact stressed at the outset of this book: that public sector unions, and even more so the Manual Workers' Union, reach the whole nation, wherever there is a government outpost, pump, clinic, school, hospital, local authority or agricultural station. Botswana is a large country, 602,957 square kilometres, larger than France and almost the size of Texas, but the capital where the union's headquarters are located is at the country's south-eastern extreme. The size of the country, its heat, dust, bumpy roads and out-of-the-way places were inscribed on the very bodies of union leaders during the 2005 regional tour. But on a smaller scale this is true of all union activity. I was constantly amazed by the distances union officers travelled almost at the drop of hat, setting off at 2 AM in order to reach distant destinations for a meeting at 10 AM. The union's oral culture meant that face-to-face interactions remained the preferred mode of communication, and internal air travel, though not particularly expensive, was regarded as risking members' wrath, as if manual workers' leaders were mimicking the lifestyles of government ministers or top civil servants. Despite being often opposed to the government, in traversing the land and connecting distant places, the Manual Workers' Union was engaged, in effect, in nation-building among some of the lowest-earning, least-educated citizens of the country.

A second aspect underlined by the union's grand tour was how acutely painful and distressing internal union politics often are. Despite their desire to act rationally, according to the law and the union's Constitution, unionists were constantly confronted by the feelings of members and their own feelings. The politics of the union were thus a passionate politics, catching up the aspirations, ambitions, sense of honour and dignity of protagonists who, in their struggles for the sake of the union, risked humiliation and sometimes even physical attack. Both the official MWU and the rebels were convinced they had right on their side.

Finally, the grand tour underscored the practical limitations of court judgements and commissions of enquiry in themselves to effect change or right a wrong without determined political mobilisation. The internal factional dispute had decimated the MWU's structures. In many places it had 'killed the union'. Mutual trust, essential for building effective structures, was a victim of the internal fighting. The union national executive faced the problem of respecting local autonomy, while behind the scenes attempting to ensure that loyalists were voted in. It was important not to antagonise local leaders while persuading them that the good of the union demanded that they abandon the dispute. As this chapter demonstrated, treading a fine line between admonishing local unionists for the state of their region and encouraging them to rebuild it was extremely difficult for leaders, and sometimes they failed.

CHAPTER EIGHT

Solidarity Forever: Mobilising the Trade Union Movement in Prayer and Protest

Throughout 2005, unions in Botswana agitated to have the ratified ILO conventions domesticated and implemented, and the Public Service Act with its provisions for collective bargaining passed. There were, however, unanticipated consequences to this new legislation. For one thing, as we have seen, it allowed for unions within a single industry to split, and thus also for government intervention in the internal affairs of unions. This was evident for both the Manual Workers' Union and for the Botswana Mine Workers' Union (BMWU), as this chapter discloses. But in the long run the new legislation also facilitated alliances between unions. My fieldwork in Botswana in 2005 coincided with a period of intense mobilisation, alliance building among unions and public protest, as well as factional in-fighting and schisms.

Background to the Protests: The 2004 Debswana Miners' Strike

In 2005, the Botswana Federation of Trade Unions (BFTU) mobilised to protest against the dismissal of 461 miners by Debswana, the Botswana diamond company, following a strike in 2004 deemed by the courts to be illegal. The dismissed miners were said by Debswana to have been essential service workers, even though many worked in jobs that, on the face of it, could hardly be described as 'essential'. A further matter that created the impetus for mobilisation of the wider trade union movement was the dismissal of two trade union leaders among the miners, and apparent interference by the government in the internal affairs of the BMWU, with the old executive committee in some of the mines refusing to recognise the newly elected committee, or to transfer the BMWU's funds to it. Even in 2007, several ongoing court cases remained unsettled, while a complaint lodged in 2006 at the ILO offices in Geneva was being considered by the ILO's governing body at its 2007 meeting (ILO 2007: 67–81).[1]

Whatever the technicalities of their legal right to strike, the grievance felt by workers, and the sense that they had been treated grossly unfairly, was genuine. In 2003, Debswana had awarded a generous bonus to employees in recognition of their hard work for the company. Below, I quote directly from the Industrial Court case heard on 30 July 2004.[2] An affidavit presented by the miners' union (the respondents) describes the memorandum sent to the miners by the managing director of Debswana on 13 March 2003. Under the heading 'Subject: Special Bonus for 2003', the first two paragraphs of the memo, addressed to 'all employees of Debswana in the C band and below', reads as follows:

> Debswana had another record year in terms of diamond production and sales. The growth and development of Debswana have been evident in many ways. The success of the Company was without doubt due to the hard work of our employees and the support they have given management. We extend our gratitude for all your contributions and look forward to even greater challenges in the years to come. To show management's appreciation for the contributions that resulted in the Company's success I have decided to award a one-off *ex gratia* special bonus equivalent to P2,500 after tax. Current permanent employees, secondees and fixed term contractors in the C band and below who were in the Company's employment on or before 1 October 2002, will qualify for the payment of the bonus. Payments will be pro-rated for service with the Company of between three and twelve months during 2002.
>
> The court reports that,
>
> This '*ex gratia* special bonus' of P2,500 was paid to all the aforesaid employees [around 6000 miners] on 31 March 2003. When the payment was made, the parties [Debswana and the BMWU] were already locked in negotiations regarding salaries and conditions of employment in respect of bargaining unit employees for the period 1 April 2003 to 31 March 2004. On 23 March 2003 [just before the bonus was paid] the parties, after much negotiation, concluded an agreement, which provided for matters concerning the percentage of salary increases, the payment of a merit award, funeral assistance, teachers' special leave, maternity allowance and payment of a housing allowance. The penultimate paragraph of this agreement reads as follows: 'This Agreement constitutes full and final settlement of the 2003/2004 negotiations concerning improvement to wages and conditions of employment of employees who fall within the bargaining unit, whether such conditions of employment are written or verbal or both written and verbal. The Company and the BMWU intend this Agreement to be legally binding on them'.

Having signed a binding agreement on 31 March, the next day, 1 April, the workers at one of the mines discovered that, whereas they had been offered a bonus of 2500 pula, unbeknownst to them, members of the Debswana management had received bonuses in the region of 95,000 pula each (ILO 2007: 69). In response, they demanded that their bonus be upped to 15,000 pula per miner, a demand later increased to 25,000 pula. In other words, the BMWU discovered that Debswana had paid a much larger total bonus to its employees, but that the lion's share of the bonus payment went to management. Against this interpretation, Debswana argued, however, that the bonus payments to managers were performance related, based on an earlier agreement reached with them, whereas the miners had refused to sign a performance-related scheme. Second, that the BMWU had signed a binding agreement for that year and the matter of the *ex gratia* payments was unrelated to it. For their part, the BMWU argued that in the previous year, 2002, an equal bonus had been paid to *all* mine workers, including management, and this created a 'legitimate expectation' that a similar distribution would occur the subsequent year. The Industrial Court, however, found in favour of the mining company, arguing that 'one year' did not constitute a 'regular' practice that created the grounds for a claim of legitimate expectation.[3]

Both issues revealed the severe limitations of the miners' collective bargaining terms with the employer, which had allowed the company to keep secret the relevant financial information from the BMWU. Public sector unions in Botswana have argued for the need for 'transparency' (Modikwa 2008). An ILO report for Southern Africa on collective bargaining states that 'Disclosure' by the employer of 'all the relevant information' is 'an essential element of good faith bargaining' (ILO 2007: 8). The Botswana Public Service Act (2008) states that, subject to the provisions (2) to (5) protecting individual employees' privacy and confidentiality, 'The employer shall, on request, disclose all relevant information to a recognised trade union that is reasonably required to allow the trade union to consult or bargain collectively'.[4] In the case of the miners' dispute, it cannot be said that Debswana negotiated 'in good faith', since the large bonuses management paid itself were disclosed to the BMWU only *after* the collective agreements for 2003 were signed and sealed. Clearly, the virus afflicting the West had travelled south to infect the culture of upper management in Botswana too.

The perennial issue of interpreting who constitutes 'essential' services signally affected the outcome of the 2004 miners' strike, as it did the 2011 public sector union strike discussed in Chapters 10 to 12. According to the BMWU, 'The employer submitted a list of essential services comprising almost all of the departments, including cleaners and gardeners' (ILO 2007: 63). In its response the government argued in defence of Debswana that

> Clause 11 of the Memorandum of Agreement concluded between BMWU and Debswana classifies several services as essential, and which must continue to operate in the event of a strike – including those related to hospitals, schools, security, refuse disposal, power, water supply and sanitation, firefighting, mine safety and transport. The classification of these services as essential recognises the fact that Debswana's mining operations are located in remote areas and that the company is responsible for the provision of the above services to the communities in those areas, rather than the local authorities. (ibid.: 68–9)

In effect, this meant that virtually all the services at the mines were classed as essential.

Without going into the details of the strike, which went ahead despite being declared illegal after the employers served the BMWU with a court interdiction (ibid.: 67–8), the matter of the 461 fired miners refused to go away. When the then BMWU leaders decided to return to work, the membership elected a new leadership that supported the illegal strike, leading to a factional division (ibid.: 66–7) that was all too painfully reminiscent of the one in the MWU described in previous chapters. In an interview I conducted with Golekanye Mokeng, president of the BMWU, he commented on the breakaway union, said to be sponsored by Debswana:

> It's there, it has been registered, but they are still unable to recommence because apparently people know that the union has been formed by the employers. What benefit can they derive from such a union, when they are fighting against the employer? There is a lot of interference from government. The government doesn't want unions to grow.

Even though the established union won against the breakaway union in court and 'those people went to prison for six months, when they came back they had Debswana waiting for them!' Employers, he said, 'apparently sponsor people to cause trouble in the unions, they fire the union leadership'. He himself had been a victim of this. 'I was fired merely for being a leader of the union'. Moreover, 'there is no law that protects workers against retrenchment', which the employer can choose to implement at will. In addition, the 'enforcement of labour laws is weak', while the industrial court has a three-year backlog for no good reason. 'There is just a hell of a problem in this so-called shining example of democracy in Africa. The laws could be there, they are not being enforced'. The law requires holding a ballot before a strike, but the company can intimidate workers and prevent them from attending the ballot meeting. There were a lot of security personnel 'infiltrating organisations, infiltrating conferences'. 'Any rally, any rally, particularly opposition protests, are filmed by the police'. Then you have to wait 30 days [to strike legally] but '[b]y the time you reach 30 days people are disillusioned and the union is toothless'. Mokeng spoke nostalgically during the interview of ex-President Masire's support for the unions and legal reform, and complained that the government-led ILO delegation to Geneva had included the president of the Industrial Court: 'How can you expect judges to be impartial if they have to go and represent the government at the ILO?'[5]

In addition to firing the 461 strikers, most (but not all) deemed to be essential services, Debswana dismissed four union leaders on 9 June 2004 for allegedly 'divulging confidential information' about the mine's finances and salaries (ILO 2007: 70). This was after the BMWU, had 'commissioned a consultant to conduct research on the wage structure of the BCL Mine workforce', which had exposed the exorbitantly high incomes of mine managers (ibid.: 64). In January 2009, well after the 2005 mobilisations described below, the BMWU took Debswana to the Court of Appeal regarding the Industrial Court's refusal to condone a late appeal in 2005.[6] The appeal was deemed to be 'out of time' by the Industrial Court, mainly on technical grounds, refusing to accept the miners' reasons for the lateness of the referral linked to their factional dispute. The Court of Appeal upheld the Industrial Court's decision that the delay was 'unreasonable', even though it acknowledged the plight of the dismissed workers; it supported the lower court, however, in partly 'blaming' the dismissed workers for relying on their union rather than taking the matter individually into their own hands.

A significant 'substantive' judgement of the Court of Appeal in upholding the lower court's decision was that dismissed workers were not entitled to a hearing, perversely citing the apparent authority of the judgement of Judge Amissah in 1995 in *National Amalgamated* v. *Attorney General* (1995) that 'an ordinary hearing in a strike situation may not lead to a just result'.[7] The 2009 decision of the Court of Appeal, following the Industrial Court, appeared to imply that in Botswana, the *audi alteram partem* rule ('hear the other side'), a fundamental principle of natural justice, did not apply to the dismissal of workers in a strike deemed to be illegal. But this citation, taken out of context, entirely distorts Judge Amissah's argument in *National Amalgamated* v. *Attorney General* (1995) (on which, see Chapter 5). The judge had made clear, as we saw, that:

> Those placed in authority should in the exercise of their discretionary powers act fairly. This requirement of the law is one of the manifestations of the rules of natural justice. A manifestation which in some cases is described as the *audi alteram partem* rule.[8]

This was summed up in the judge's statement that:

> A strike situation seems to me to be a good example, where an ordinary hearing or showing cause on an individual basis, may not lead to a just result. That, I believe, is the reason why special provisions are made by the Trade Disputes Act and through collective bargain agreements for the resolution of industrial disputes.[9]

As we shall see, this distortion by the Court of Appeal in 2009 of Judge Amissah's 1995 judgement led the government to believe it was entitled to ignore the *audi* principle and dismiss workers *en masse* without a hearing in future strikes deemed illegal.

Mobilising the Labour Movement for Protest

Some of these disputes were still making their way through the courts when members of the BFTU and other non-affiliated unions took a decision to mobilise and protest against the dismissal of the miners and their leaders. The BFTU leaders I interviewed in 2007 all spoke about the financial straits the BFTU was in at the time. But between May and July 2005, trade unionists across the spectrum, including the MWU, despite still being at loggerheads with the BFTU, acted in solidarity with the miners. Johnson Motshwarakgole told me that this was the very first time that all the unions and associations had come together for joint action. He said: 'I thank God that, if it was not for Debswana, this kind of a meeting would never take place. The BFTU never did this [i.e. convened a meeting of all the unions]. It's just dead wood'. The mobilisation of all the unions was initiated, it seems, by leaders of the teachers' unions, and there was a large range of representation from other unions.

I attended a series of meetings to discuss handing in a petition to the mining company and then the president of Botswana, holding a demonstration and a march to the president's office and appointing a delegation to meet him. Participants discussed the nitty-gritty of demonstration costs, from the questions of whether to distribute T-shirts for free or sell them, and how to produce placards, to the route of the march and the need for police permits. The meeting agonised collectively over the wording of the petition. Who would the signatories be? The draft presented was wordy and pretentious. The Botswana Banking Union representatives complained that the petition was not ready: 'We must delegate to prepare the petition'. There was a letter from the president's office saying that an official would receive the petition at 8 AM, which was a problem since the march would only arrive at the president's office at 9.30. An intelligent young woman trade union delegate from Palapye, representing the Botswana Power Corporation, alerted the meeting to the limitations of the petition: 'There should be something on deadlines to be met, a message to the president'. The principal demands should be: reinstatement; the corporate government report to be published; the right to strike legalised; an independent commission of enquiry; no work, no pay (according to the ILO convention) rather than dismissal. If the demands were not met there would be no option but to 'go international'. The decision taken by the meeting was to work on the petition and meet at 5.30 the next day: 'We are wasting time'.

The meeting then turned to debate how to inform and mobilise people for the demonstration, and whether there should be a single national demonstration or coordinated, simultaneous regional demonstrations. How should transport be arranged? It was an open forum of invited union representatives resolved to listen to all those present. Altogether in one meeting I attended there were 17 union representatives present. They sat around tables arranged in a rectangle and covered with silver covers imprinted with the BFTU slogan, 'We educate'. None of the better-paid civil servants attended.

The BMWU representatives were extremely bitter. The new chair of the BMWU told me that their union had investigated and found that miners in Botswana were paid well below the regional average wage, despite Botswana being hugely wealthy in diamonds. One of the strikers who had been fired, a woman from the mine's accounts department, was unable to comprehend why she was classed as essential services, commenting that the unions could 'dirty Botswana's pure reputation in the world'. Clearly, a connection was being made between the workers' predicament and the deposed academic Kenneth Good's case (going through the court at the time), the Basarwa case, and the 'blood diamonds' allegations by Survival International.[10] The representatives stressed repeatedly that Botswana goes all over the world emphasising what a wonderful democracy it is, sending delegates to all the international meetings and signing charters, but people don't know what's actually going on at home.

There was a series of larger union meetings and press conferences, one at the President Hotel, another at the Gaborone Hotel. In all of these meetings, the MWU's Johnson Motshwarakgole was a very prominent speaker. Clearly, within the wider trade union movement in Botswana, he was a highly respected figure.

He spared the time to come to meetings even though he was still immersed in sorting out the fallout from the MWU's own internal factional dispute.

The first solidarity demonstration was held jointly by all seven public service unions. It took place on 25 May after a series of postponements linked to Debswana's refusal to accept a petition from the unions. The intention was also to carry the petition to the president, but he was away in India. In the end, the demonstrators marched around the Central Mall and then back again to Gaborone Secondary School. They had been refused permission to deposit the petition at the Debswana offices (in the Central Mall). A bigger rally was planned for 4 June. The first rally was supposed to mobilise all the public service unions in the Gaborone region, but turnout was rather poor. There were some 150 unionists, mostly from the MWU, carrying large banners, with one relatively small banner brought by the Botswana Teachers' Union (BTU), despite the fact that it had been the driving force behind the mobilisation. Red T-shirts were sold at 20 pula each by various unions, emblazoned with 'Reinstate 461 Debswana Workers! An injury to one is an injury to all!' The backs of the shirts listed all seven participating unions.

There was a good deal of dancing and singing by MWU members, with strong women's participation. The union's red Land Cruiser had toured that morning, announcing the rally on its loudspeaker. It followed the procession, led by a police car and videoed by the police. Altogether the rally was filmed by three government video cameras, a practice that seemed to be taken for granted by the unionists. A young man kept up a stream of noisy commentary throughout on the loudspeaker. Returning to the grounds of Gaborone Secondary School there

Figure 8.1 Assembling for the demonstration.

were speeches. A woman from the BTU made a fiery speech about the injustice suffered by the miners, followed by an even more fiery speech by the deposed chairman of the BMWU who – in rhetoric unusual in Botswana – accused Debswana's management of being white racists who extracted the wealth of Botswana from black people. Motshwarakgole spoke last, with good humour, listing all the participating unions. His call to the police to come closer since they were fellow workers was greeted with laughter.

At a dinner party at his house later that evening, it was agreed that the rally was successful despite the low attendance, which had mostly consisted of MWU members. Lydia, the vice-chair, said, 'We are teaching them'. Neo, the treasurer, said about the civil servants, at the time members of the Botswana Civil Servants' Association: 'those people think they can't dirty their new shoes [by marching] but we too have new shoes [in other words, they look down on us but we're all in the same boat]'.

Petitioning the President and Praying to God

The second demonstration, convened to carry the petition to the president, was larger. I counted about 300 unionists, most wearing T-shirts and carrying placards bearing the slogan 'Re-instate the 461 Miners' (see Figure 8.1). It started more or less on time, at 7.30 AM, but people kept arriving and running to join the main procession until about 8 AM. We walked from the BFTU's new headquarters in the African Mall, as yet unfurnished, to the president's offices opposite parliament, down Kaunda Drive, Khama Crescent and then into the government enclave. It was a colourful procession of marchers wearing union shirts of different colours and designs. The rally opened with a song led by Motshwarakgole: 'Our Master, Save Our Nation', followed by shouts of 'Viva workers, viva! Down oppressors, down! Forward, ever forward! Backward, never backward!' and later, after the petition was read, 'Viva, working-class power, viva!' First, the petition was read out by the secretary general of the BFTU for the press and the assembled unionists, standing in front of the closed gates of the president's office.

The Petition

> We demand the unconditional reinstatement of the union leadership recently dismissed at both BCL and Debswana mines. Government must immediately call upon Debswana to stop the ongoing disciplinary hearings, which are characterised by intimidation and victimisation of workers. We demand that government expeditiously set up an independent commission of inquiry to investigate the breakdown of labour relations at BCL/Debswana, which caused disharmony. This is legitimate, arising out of expectations by society for the government to intervene the same way it did when there was a crisis at Air Botswana.
>
> For purposes of transparency, we demand the release and publication of the audited report on Debswana's Corporate Governance. The workers of

Botswana are united in their belief that democracy will never be meaningful as long as citizens are expected to cast their votes and then withdraw from the process [of democratic participation] for the next five years. Workers' organisations are committed to stand in solidarity against all forms of injustice and oppression.

We recognise and call to your attention the deteriorating standards of labour practices in Botswana. It is equally important that government ensures that international labour standards and practices, especially the ones to which Botswana is a signatory, are adhered to. We strongly believe in the freedom of workers to demand their rights without fear of retribution. We also believe in the right of the union leadership to act in the best interests of their constituents and demand that these should not be curtailed.

It is clear that there is a tense labour environment in the country. Instead of adopting the no work, no pay principle, Debswana decided to dismiss workers who collectively participated in a strike without affording them a hearing. It is totally against the principles of natural law and justice. As if that was not enough, Debswana management continues to persecute and harass the trade union leadership. The dismissal of four union leaders at BCL and two at Debswana is a clear indication of hostile relations between management and the labour movement in Botswana. This attitude is totally unacceptable and cannot remain unchallenged.

We wish to draw Your Excellency's attention to the psychological trauma and inhuman life-threatening negligence with which Debswana evicted the dismissed workers from their houses, threw students out from mine schools mid-term and threatened the lives of those living with HIV/AIDS by cutting them off from anti-retroviral therapy. In the midst of all this, government has remained silent. We find this attitude unacceptable and abhorrent from a government and employers who preach team work, good industrial relations and now and then remind us that we are a tripartite partnership. We call on the government to take heed of our concerns and make rapid progress to meet the demands in the petition.[11]

The Speech

Next, the MWU's Elsinah Botsalano led an uplifting hymn, which was followed by Motshwarakgole's speech. He began by calling all the union leaders to the front. 'These handsome men are the presidents of the trade unions of the country of Botswana. They are being led by the mother body (*Mma MaKgotla*), BFTU'. He said they had come in faith, because they trusted Botswana's president to mediate their problems. 'It won't help anyone to have a president who knows nothing about what is happening at the bottom. That is to sit on top of the adder's hole (*go nna masima wa phika far godimo*)'. He expressed the hope that the president would call the unions to him for discussion. 'We do not want to be led into temptation (*tlhaelo*) to end up saying the diamonds of Botswana are for murder (*polao*), because we are the ones who have been protecting them while others despise (*kgôbôtla*) them'. He went on to criticise the top echelons of the civil service. 'Now, when we are in this for rights, there are some civil servants (*badirela puso*) who forget that when we are in trouble we are supposed to unite for these problems. They are not the government'. He continued: 'We should close with a prayer. Do not worry. God has power to do things. God asked that we do not open with a prayer but we will close with a prayer from His house. He put it to take it to bless this work, coming straight from Jesus. People of my home (*bagaetsho*), let us bow our heads and close our eyes ... Let us have deep silence'. The political prayer that followed was enunciated by Pelothsweo Baeng, at the time president of the Botswana Unified Local Government Service Association.

The Prayer

God our Father, the Son and the Holy Spirit. We thank you, Jehovah, to have counselled us, sent us a prayer which is blessed, the Holy King. We received the prayer. I am here, the Holy King. We are bowing our heads, all of us here. We are workers, the Holy King. Regardless of whether you wear an overall or you wear a tie when at work, the heavenly King, [whether] you have a high salary or lower salary, the Holy King, we are all workers. God who is full of patience, in the name of Jesus Christ we say, 'look at what is happening in the land of Botswana'.

However, even though you, the Holy King, you have created all these minerals, everything in the earth, and made them so that those who are yours living in the land of Botswana should share them equally, the Holy King, there are a small group of people who are cowards (*mabina go tsholwa*), who grab this wealth, extortionately (*ikgaga pelelang*). You created for all, the Holy King. We beg you Jehovah, we beg you to accept our feelings so that we do not curse the country, the Holy King. God, you are the one who knows everything, the Holy King. You know these extortionate grabbers (*baikgagapeledi*); their father, Satan, tempted them to come and lead. They end up taking control just like Pharaoh did. They are the grabbers.

However, they were being sent by Satan, Holy King. We are sending you, Jehovah. We are beseeching you, Jehovah. We send your voice, Holy King. Push away their bad soul inside their hearts and empty thoughts, Holy King. Go to them, the Lord, full of patience. When the Israelites were refused by the Egyptians, Holy King, you sent frogs, you sent darkness, you sent boils, Holy King. We say, go to the offices of Debswana and the employers who grab the wealth of the country of Botswana more than it is fair. Just do that because your duties are of good purpose, Holy King.

If you have beaten, Holy King, you know how to heal. We say, beat, Holy King. We say we feel pain. We beseech you, Holy King, take care of the president of our country wherever he is. However, there is an obstacle which has started, Our Lord. There are grabbers who are not like our forefathers who were acting justly, Holy King. We say, even before he arrives, give him the wisdom of Solomon, Holy King, to come and read our thoughts, Holy King, and reply, Holy King.

But we know, God above, that there are some people who are cruel (*dilalonye*), they are looking at the workers and tomorrow they will say [that] we are in politics, parties of the opposition, Holy King. But we say, Holy King, reproach those people, before they speak, stop their voices. God, we talk of our thoughts, we talk of the life we are living, day in, day out. Our bread we eat day by day, Holy King.

It is what we are saying: the politics of the workers, of bread and butter, Holy King. God who is full of holiness, we thank the leaders who are here, and those who are the representatives of the president. They are holding a diamond. They are holding our groom (*monyadi*) to take him to the president. He should receive him [i.e. the petition]. Take care of them until he arrives, give them strength to advise him in a right manner, Holy King. God, who is merciful, we do not want to pray to you at length, but we cannot but pray for the mutual cooperation of the trade unions of Botswana. God, we agree that democracy is not to go for elections after five years, Holy King, and just stop there, waiting for another five years to come, Holy King. This is another thing happening in Botswana. Let it finish at this moment because it has given the grabbers the opportunity to do as they like, Holy King. Merciful God, give us power. Change the country of Botswana so we all share in the affairs of our nation. We have beseeched you, Holy King, in the name of Jesus Christ and all those left out. Include them, Holy King, in the name of Jesus. Unity of the workers! Amen.

Later, Johnson praised the unionist who led this highly political and moral prayer, saying he 'liked that young man very much'. It was uncertain whether the president would ever hear either the speech or the prayer, since Botswana TV did not even bother to turn up, and the president, it emerged later, was in New York receiving an award.

What was noticeable about the demonstration was the high level of civility and mutual respect in the way the president's delegate received the petition, with handshakes all round. Although the police provided virtually no escort except two cars, at the front and back of the march, there were no incidents and much cheerful amity, singing, praying and shouting of 'Viva!'

Despite this optimism and civility, at the end of August 2005 it was announced that the government had rejected the key demands of the unions as spelled out in the petition. A letter supposedly endorsed by the president, informed unions of the government's refusal to set up a commission of inquiry or to publish the report on the corporate climate in Debswana. To do so would be to 'disrespect the principle of the rule of law' (Morula 2005: 4). The government 'had already put in place laws that provide for "internationally accepted governance processes" to resolve industrial disputes' (ibid.). The unions responded in '"disgust" to the government's audacity in referring them back to the courts of law when it knew full well the laws guiding those courts were anti-worker' (ibid.). Instead of settling their differences, the government was colluding shamefully with the employers in infiltrating workers' unions in order to destabilise them (ibid.).

The Botswana Labour Movement at Prayer

Harold Wilson, the British prime minister, once said that the Labour movement owes more to Methodism than Marx (McIntyre 2010). Indeed, as Eric Hobsbawm (1959: 140–1) and E.P. Thompson (1963: 395–400) have shown, English workers' lay preaching in Methodist chapels combined faith, labour and politics, so much so that many early labour leaders and trade unionists had their roots in the Methodist Church. Hobsbawm proposed that in the transition to the new industrial world that had emerged in nineteenth-century England, fervent worship in the new protestant sects appealed to the 'newest and the rawest' proletarians (Hobsbawm 1959: 130–1; see also Gutman 1966: 79). So too in Botswana: the struggle for worker rights drew 'spiritual' legitimacy from biblical truths learnt in the myriad churches workers in Botswana regularly attend. The Christian God justified and sanctioned workers' claims for their rights. It 'ennobled' labour (Gutman 1966: 82). As the political prayer recorded here reveals so dramatically, Christian faith and current politics are interwoven into a seamless whole, as God is beseeched to protect workers from greedy employers who rob the workers of their fair share, and – at best – the cold indifference of the government. As Gutman argues in his masterly account of 'Gilded Age' first-generation workers and trade unionists within the American labour movement in the nineteenth century,

> Here, then, was a religious faith that justified labor organization and agitation, encouraged workers to challenge industrial power, and compelled criticism of 'natural' economic laws, the crude optimism of social Darwinism, and even the conformist Christianity of most respectable clergymen. (ibid.: 81)

Against a Protestantism 'tainted with the money and morality of capitalism', 'Christian morality became a contested terrain' in Philadelphia in the nineteenth century (Fones-Wolf 1989: 63), as many churches began advocating the Social Gospel (ibid.: 94 *et passim*). In the twenty-first century USA, the national Living Wage Movement drew together a coalition of progressive churches, other faith groups and trade unions, to fight against excessively low wages that led to 'working poverty' among full-time workers (Snarr 2011). They appealed to divine notions of public justice, responsibility, interdependency and equity to 'frame' the movement morally; they listened to testimonials of low-paid workers, and encouraged them to be active agents across divisions of race and gender; they mobilised economic data, helped build coalitions and used symbolic religious tactics to publicise the movement's cause. They argued that 'the inclusive love of God requires that preference be given to the needs of the marginalized, dominated, silenced and oppressed' (ibid.: 91).

The question could be asked, however: with the majority of the population in Botswana being church goers, is there anything distinctively working-class about trade union piety? In England, a contrast was drawn between the Anglican Church, the 'Tory Party in prayer', and the non-conformist Methodist Church that extolled the Protestant view of labour as a divine calling or vocation, and provided a platform for lay preachers, capturing the imagination of workers (Thompson 1963). Not so in Botswana, where workers, particularly public sector workers, belong to a wide range of churches, including the established Catholic, Anglican and Congregationalist churches. Nor has Botswana been influenced greatly by liberation theology. Nevertheless, the divine sanctification of labour rights in the prayers and speeches of trade unionists in Botswana creates a hybrid discourse which is distinctively both local-vernacular and working class. Many other excluded and oppressed groups struggling for their rights, most famously African Americans in the USA, have also fused Christian faith with their claims to freedom, equal civil rights and dignity.

From Solidarity to Schism: The Breach Widens

The solidarity achieved during the protests in 2005 was short lived. Two years later, the BFTU was threatened with a split, linked to their historic fallout during the factional conflict within the MWU in 2004/5 (see Chapter 6). The MWU bitterly resented the fact that at the height of the dispute, when the MWU's bank accounts were frozen, the BFTU suspended the MWU's membership on the grounds that it had 'not paid its membership fee'. Despite this, the MWU, as we have seen, celebrated the solidarity achieved across the trade union movement during the 2005 demonstrations. But it could not forgive the fact that once the breakaway Botswana Government Workers' Union (BOGOWU) was formed and registered after the factional dispute within the MWU described in Chapter 6, the BFTU accepted it as a member. On both counts, but especially the latter, the BFTU had put itself beyond the pale.

We saw in Chapter 7 that, as Turner theorised for the social drama, at the height of the MWU factional dispute, the breach within the MWU widened and extended to encompass prior factional divisions within the ruling party. It also came to coincide with an emergent schism within the BFTU. This happened gradually. As public service associations converted into unions during 2006 and 2007, they initially augmented the numerical and financial strength of the BFTU. Pelotsweo Baeng, president of the newly formed Botswana Land Board and Local Authority Workers' Union (BLLAWU), was optimistic that the BFTU could regain its former glory, create an educational programme and formulate policies that would address national issues such as universal national insurance or school fees. He told me:

> In the past there was at least the presence of a labour movement. The past leaders were able to maintain the presence of the labour movement. That is commendable. It was not dead. And labour in the past, at least it was able to pressurise government to sign the ILO conventions, and then the public sector to unionise. Yeah, labour liberated us.[12]

Most of the unionists I interviewed were strongly critical of the rise of a privileged managerial elite. Golekanye Mokeng, president of the BMWU, expressed a pervasive view:

> The one thing we see is that the wealth of this country is centralised in a very small clique of citizens, a very small clique. Those people must have [links to] civil servants or politicians in government. You know why? Because they have inside information that they can manipulate for themselves.[13]

He then listed a number of known 'magnates' who had enormous wealth: 'People are keeping [their wealth] to themselves. If they're rich, it's my wealth. Nobody should share it with me. Everybody wants to get rich. Because this country is rich and the majority of its citizens are poor'. Even workers in the city, he said, are indifferent to the plight of people in the rural areas. Meanwhile, the president of BLLAWU told me: 'There is a lot of money – it is a matter of the policies that the government has adopted, it emphasises an unequal distribution of wealth. How can you tax people for school fees when they are poor?' Unions had the right to participate in politics, he said:

> Politicians don't have the moral right to determine which class has the right to take part on this particular issue. The moral right. It's a matter of managing our state. Meeting the challenges. They will get used to that, because they are not used to that [i.e. civil society making political pronouncements]. They complain and try to convince us that it is not part of our mandate. But it is our mandate! The [trade union] movement is not restricted to speaking about salaries and conditions of service only. They [the unions] have to be concerned also about issues of national interest. Because we are the tax payers. We are the voters. We are a class on our own ... They [the government, the ruling party] think we have to be told what is good for us. That the rich are able to take care of the country efficiently and effectively. They are the ones to employ other people. They know how to save money, that's why they are rich. Those are some of the explanations, justifications and philosophy.

Gadzani Mhotsha, secretary general of the BFTU and president of the Non-academic Staff Union at the University of Botswana, told me there had been a problem of 'leadership' in the BFTU, but that their belief 'now is that we have a leadership in place though we are still struggling ... [W]e have drafted some policies, they have gone through the council ... financial policies, how do we handle our staff'.[14] The BFTU was financially challenged, Mhotsha confided, and on top of that the affiliates were not paying their dues, but he was hopeful that with the new public service unions joining, this too could be resolved.

> And the other advantage that we had, we had two big unions, actually staff associations, the former BTU and the Botswana Secondary School Teachers' Union (BOSETU), affiliated to BFTU. The Botswana Secondary Schools [Union], they've got about 8000 plus members, BTU has got 11,000 plus, so they are big. And actually this helps our finances. Their monthly subscription stands around 100,000 pula.

The president of the BTU, who had been fired by the government on flimsy grounds following his criticism of the introduction of school fees, was elected president of the BFTU. Mhotsha explained that the MWU, another big union, was suspended for not paying its dues. I asked, 'Why not?' He replied:

> Ey, they are difficult comrades. There's a rumour that they want to form another federation. There is a union, the government employee workers' union, it's a new union also, it numbers also quite a number of people because it's from the government side [i.e. they are government workers]. The former BCSA, now BOPEU [Botswana Public Employees' Union] – so the two, MWU and BOPEU – there is a rumour that they want to form a federation. Of course, we have made it very clear that that won't be the right way to go. If there are issues, let us sit down and resolve them. We are a small population. We can't afford two federations ... They [the MWU] haven't actually even disaffiliated. They are still our member. So this is a challenge, we have taken a decision as a federation that we are going to sit down with the two of them, separately of course, to try and make them aware that what they are trying to do won't work for the labour movement in the country.

He acknowledged that the affiliation of BOGOWU, formed by the MWU rebel faction, with the BFTU had created a breach, but criticised the MWU for being

> led by the employees, not by the political leaders [referring to salaried union officers such as Motshwarakgole, as against elected union leaders]. But they will not agree with us, not agree with our advice that – look, you are political leaders, you are elected to lead. These are employees, they have to take instructions from you. But with them it's not like that. Even them, I found, if I called the secretary general, he will tell me to talk to the organising secretary who is an employee in the office. And that's one of the reasons why we've failed to meet with them. We don't want to meet the employees, we want to meet the leaders. So those are some of the challenges, but we believe we will overcome.

Including the new public service unions, he said, 'the total membership goes up by 25,000, which is more or less what [the] BFTU used to have, not including manual workers – if they were to come in, we'd probably be 100,000 members'. Mhotsha talked about the future, of trade union education and empowerment:

> Our political ideology is very clear. We believe in the workers, in a socialist inclined political system able to take care of the disadvantaged. We are aware that our government sometimes says, 'We are a socialist government because this is a country where most of the amenities are provided by the state', but the problem is they are busy redoing that. Because of that, labour may be viewed as being anti-government.

The Creation of BOFEPUSU: The New Federation

Gadzani Mhotsha radically underestimated the resentment felt towards the BFTU for excluding the MWU in 2004, officially because the MWU had not paid its dues, despite the federation being fully aware that the court had frozen the union's bank account. The animosity was compounded by the BFTU's acceptance of the union formed by the breakaway rebels, BOGOWU. The MWU officers complained to me that it was they who had bankrolled the BFTU and helped finance its new premises. Mhotsha also underestimated the political influence of the MWU. By 2008, all the public service unions, including the teachers' unions and the local government union (BLLAWU) had left the BFTU and joined with the MWU and the Botswana Public Employment Union (BOPEU), formerly the civil servants' association, to form a single new federation, the Botswana Federation of Public Service Unions (BOFEPUSU, henceforth also 'the federation'). Theoretically, they could have still remained affiliated to the BFTU, but in practice they chose not to be.

BOFEPUSU was formed to create a strong, unified coalition which could negotiate on behalf of public sector workers in the new bargaining council being set up by the government following the domestication of the Public Service Act in 2005. Ironically, in the past the MWU had always treated the civil servants with the utmost disdain; they were seen as a bunch of 'beggars' and government stooges.

In September 2007 I interviewed Andrew Motsamai, the president of the newly formed civil servants' union, BOPEU, when the federation was still at the planning stage. An intelligent, soft-spoken man with a mellifluous voice and evidently supreme Southern Tswana negotiating skills, he made clear that in his opinion the likely future for the MWU was within the umbrella of *his* union, now that the law allowed government workers to be unionised while being 'permanent and pensionable'. For manual workers, this would be a departure from the earlier gratuity system of the five-yearly lump-sum payments prevailing hitherto. He expected MWU members to join the ranks of the civil servants, with all the perks attached to that in terms of government-funded pensions,[15] private health insurance and loans. These were public service workers' rights, negotiated by highly paid government civil servants, he stressed, even without a formal union. As we were speaking, he told me, the MWU was still haemorrhaging members, partly due to retrenchment policies. He even envisaged the future inclusion of the MWU's rebel faction, the BOGOWU, within the fold, a suggestion which would have been anathema to his new allies. His mandarin inclinations and anti-radicalism seemed to me evident at the time in everything he said. He even explained to me that the MWU had 'never been a union really', since they did not sit on the national salary negotiating committee and did not have collective bargaining rights (which was a feature of earlier legislation).[16]

Was an alliance with white-collar workers, previously disdained, likely to be the future of the largest working-class union in Botswana, with its roots in radical international labour traditions of solidarity and defence of the poor? At the time of the interview I wondered whether the MWU, with its numerical superiority, proven negotiating skills and national democratic organisation, would be able to dominate a joint public service union? It seemed doubtful that a full merger was feasible, if only because of the view expressed by BOPEU's president that public sector manual workers in Botswana are 'paid very well, comparatively speaking'! According to him, it was they, the civil servants, who were 'underpaid'.

While he criticised the teachers' unions and appeared to support school fees, Motsamai nevertheless confessed his admiration and liking for the MWU leaders:

> I respect quite a number of them, especially in terms of experience and exposure. There is quite a lot that they can offer – they are a bit fast at picking up some things, but probably not good at articulating their position, so they get lazy in the process. They've also been able to build their experience among [only] a few people, not among a diverse group.[17]

Speaking of Johnson Motshwarakgole, I commented that MWU members thought he had a 'magic' touch. In response, he said:

> But he's also very good. As an orator, when he has to talk about some of the things, you would really admire him. But I think it's partly because of his experience. He's been in the business for quite some time. But I'm a great fan of his, especially him and Molaudi. That's why I'm probably the only person who has decided that I can work with these people and we can actually forge a relationship together, and these are the people who can actually make the rest of the group appreciate that we are not a big brother, but we are willing to work with them.

Ironically, in the light of events to follow in 2011, Mr Motsamai still had great faith in 2007 in the capacity of BOPEU to affect government policy 'from the inside':

> We have always had a relationship with the employer which has been good. It's important to build a relationship ... [W]e have always believed that we should bring the employer to the table. And discuss things out ... [The government] readily understand our issues because, generally, it is the same industry that they are [in themselves – i.e. the civil service – so they are] actually used to it. So, consequently it has made us appear to them [the MWU] like that we are not that militant. But we are not militant because we go to government, sit with government at the table and convince them.

It was difficult to imagine at the time of the interview that this apparently conservative mandarin would prove to be a flaming radical four years later. In 2007 it still appeared that the MWU détente with the previously derided civil servants' union was indicative of the way the internal factional conflict had pushed the MWU to seek alliances with groups, whether the BDP or BOPEU, likely to compromise its radical working-class ethos. This appeared to be signalled at the MWU's annual delegates' conference in December 2007, at which the same NEC and elected officers were re-elected unopposed.[18] The invited guest speaker, Daniel Kwelagobe, from the ruling BDP, a key gatekeeper responsible as Minister of Presidential Affairs for the Directorate of Public Service Management's capacity to grant or deny union recognition, appeared to reflect the MWU's shift away from its radical dissenting roots. Not surprisingly, the inaugural congress of the civil servants' union, BOPEU, was hosted, according to Botswana's *Sunday Standard*, by then Vice-President Ian Khama and other high ranking government officials, while the extensive press coverage was said to reflect the union's 'preferential treatment' by government (Ganetsang 2007a, 2007b).

By April 2008, the clash between the newly formed BOFEPUSU (an alliance of the MWU and BOPEU) and the BFTU had come to light with a public attack on BOFEPUSU by the president of another public service union at that time still affiliated to the BFTU, the Botswana Land Board and Local Authorities Workers' Union (BLLAWU):

> [U]nionists are the only ones who can rescue themselves from the chains of oppression and exploitation at the workplace ... [However, with the formation of the rival federation] the labour movement in Botswana is dividing itself to death ... These people have unnecessarily weakened the labour movement in the country without any justification ... We need to have a strong voice as public sector unions.[19]

In the meantime, BLLAWU had been vigorously and openly recruiting members both from the MWU,[20] and from the rival rebel union, BOGOWU. Its drive appeared to have been motivated by the need to gain recognition itself.

Nevertheless, despite its president's grandiose pronouncements, BLLAWU too ultimately joined the public sector federation. After I left Botswana in October 2008, BOFEPUSU was officially formed amidst legal challenges from the BFTU regarding its legitimacy, claiming exclusive collective bargaining rights on behalf of public sector workers (see Mhotsha 2008). Once again, the battle lines were drawn and complex trade union legislation, along with accusations of undue government interference, invoked. By March 2010, however, when the new Public Service Act came into being, BOFEPUSU had gained the affiliation of all the five major public sector unions who announced their future merger, but without the rival BOGOWU (Baputaki 2010).

Conclusion

The dismissal of the 461 miners in 2004 refused to go away. As late as 2011, President Khama promised the mine workers that the case of the 461 dismissed miners would be reopened. This chapter has traced the broader mobilisation of the entire labour movement in Botswana in response to this mass dismissal. It underscored the centrality of notions of fairness and a just distribution of resources by the employer in the conduct of union affairs. In the miners' dispute, the courts were seen to side unfairly with the diamond company management, who had failed to divulge company finances and 'cheated' workers with impunity, hiding behind technicalities to 'grab' the nation's wealth for themselves.

But the chapter also highlighted the schisms and cleavages that soon developed within the broader Botswana trade union movement. The moment of solidarity uniting the movement was brief, and soon lost in the politics of factionalism. The achievement of the MWU, one highlighted in the following chapter, was to persuade virtually all public sector workers to join a united federation – not a single amalgamated union – and together to seek recognition for the federation to become the sole negotiator in representing public sector workers on the envisioned new bargaining council, an achievement that had to be fought through the courts despite repeated setbacks.

CHAPTER NINE

Winning Against the Odds: Speaking Truth to Power and Dilemmas of Charismatic Leadership

Beyond the Problem of Agency

In his theorisation of 'working-class organic intellectuals', Antonio Gramsci emphasised that the organic intellectuals of the working class combined emotional passion with rationality, and were 'organically' embedded 'from within' in the working class, hence knowledgeable about the challenges it faced (Fischman & McLaren 2005: 434–5). For Gramsci, the working-class organic intellectual was not an intellectual *prior* to her or his activism, but an activist who 'fulfils an *intellectual function*' (ibid., citing Laclau 1990).

The conundrums raised by poststructuralist critiques, sceptical of Gramsci's somewhat utopian valorisation of working-class leaders as the vanguard of change, make it illuminating to consider a single life narrative, in this case of a charismatic leader of a manual workers' union in Botswana. A singular biographical focus may, I suggest, disentangle the articulations of class, education, leadership and counter-hegemonic ideology in the life of a prominent unionist. In Chapter 3, it will be recalled, I argued that 'hard times' moved women trade unionists to public activism and led to their expanding ethical and cosmopolitan outlook. At times of transition, I proposed, individual agency is the product of both subjection *and* creativity, co-existing historically in dialectical tension. Like the women union leaders in the Manual Workers' Union discussed there, the subject of the present chapter became a union leader in the face of 'hard times'. Like many other unionists, he endeavoured to manage his conflicting positions of being at once in the vanguard of working-class counter-hegemonic resistance to the state as employer, while being at the same time increasingly subject to powerful pressures towards consumption and bourgeois living in modern Botswana. This chapter considers the grounds of his evidently powerful charisma in the light of these contradictory forces.

Education versus Charisma

In Botswana, as in most postcolonial African states, formal education is often seen as the *sine qua non* of status and urban honour (Fumanti 2007, in press; Lentz 1994; P. Werbner 2010b: 136). To be educated is to be an expert, a knowledgeable actor, a person worthy of dignity, skilled at manoeuvring in the worlds of bureaucratic governance, regulation and law. A lack of education is widely equated with ignorance and carries with it the stigma of backwardness – of a doomed incapacity to act effectively in a modern environment. While the countryside is romanticised by urban Batswana as a place of idyllic rural peace, at the same time traditional ways of living and doing politics are *not* seen to confer skills transferable to the city.

Reflecting these biases, the Botswana government introduced a performance-based remuneration scheme (PBRS) into the public service in 2005. This stipulated criteria for training and promotion that took little account, as we have seen, of long years of experience and excluded workers without formal university or senior-high-school qualifications from promotional ladders – in other words, the scheme discriminated against the majority of industrial-class workers in the public service. As we saw in Chapter 4, the battle against these new criteria was bitterly fought by the MWU.

In the light of this widespread, taken-for-granted assumption that formal education implies innate knowledge and wisdom, it may seem at first glance paradoxical that the uncrowned king of the labour movement in Botswana is an uneducated manual worker, anointed supreme labour spokesman by the press and media and, increasingly, also by the majority of his more educated comrades within the broader labour movement. Johnson Motshwarakgole, the national organising secretary of the MWU, is, as we have seen throughout this book, without doubt a hugely charismatic figure. Short and broad-shouldered, with his greying beard and dark-rimmed spectacles he cuts the figure of a working-class intellectual, a typical union boss, outspoken and earthy. During union rallies he usually wears a dark cloth cap and sports jacket, his shirt or jumper tucked into his trousers over a somewhat bulging belly, one hand casually in his pocket while the other gestures to emphasise a point, in every way the captain of his ship (see Figure 9.1). His reputation for possessing an almost mythic capacity to win battles against the odds follows him everywhere. As I witnessed repeatedly during my fieldwork, his entry electrifies a room. When he rises to the podium, assembled crowds fall silent in anticipation. They await his arrival. His photograph constantly adorns articles in the press about Botswana labour and trade union issues. His forthright condemnation of government, in a country where most people watch their words, is legendary. While he boasts of his humble origins, he is at the same time a man who exudes self-confidence and mingles convivially with Botswana's elites, from MPs and ministers to chiefs, respected members of civil society and opposition party leaders. He describes many of them as his 'friends'. He 'knows' everyone and everyone knows him. At the same time, he is like a magnet – he draws blame to himself whenever things go wrong, he is envied, accused of selfish motives, his very success a source of jealousy and suspicion.

What has made Johnson so powerfully charismatic? In the present chapter I attempt to uncover the possible sources of his charisma and its significance for understanding the complex relationship between spoken and unspoken cultural assumptions in modern Botswana.

Figure 9.1 Johnson Motshwarakgole addressing the strikers (photograph by the author).

Early Years

I begin by presenting Johnson's early years in his own words, taken from an interview with me recorded at the MWU's headquarters in 2011, in the presence of several other officers, following a public sector strike.

> J.M.: I was born in Molepolole in May 1954 and grew up there – it's my home village. And, of course, I didn't go to school because I was from a poor family, a very poor family.
> P.W.: What did your father do?
> J.M.: My father was a worker, but during those days [he was] working for nothing! I was from a family of eight. And then I came to Gaborone, in 1969. I worked as a gardener. Somewhere, the house is still there, in the village. There was one British woman who lived there by the name of Thompson. Miss Thompson was a secretary to the permanent secretary of home affairs. In those days, you see, the typists who were secretaries – I think their salary was

better than it is today because during those days, the secretary of the permanent secretary, a typist if you like [must have earned a lot]. I was the gardener of a typist! And there was also one white man by the name of Fanseyo, he was a Boer, he was staying not far [away], he also had a gardener. And at one stage the gardener kicked Fanseyo's dog, and he was fired for that. Because we are from different cultures. Because in Setswana culture we can beat a dog and just say *footsek* (scram). And he was fired for that. And he reported the matter to [the trade union]. Because during those days it was when the trade unions of Botswana were starting in this country – because we wished to go to *letlapa la babereki* ('rock of the workers') where there were films, a bioscope [cinema], with a projector.

We used to go there and see how the trade unions worked in eastern Europe, because in those days, the gentlemen who came with trade union knowledge were gentlemen from eastern Europe, the Soviet Union, Yugoslavia – they were schooling there.[1] When they came [back] to Botswana, they didn't even get employment from [the] government, because in those days, the main employer [in the country] was the Botswana government. Now, because they were from Eastern Europe they used to call them 'communists'. It was difficult for you to get a job in [the] government when you were from the Soviet Union, Yugoslavia, communist China. One gentleman I remember very well. He's still alive, he is a chief now in Palapye by the name of Rre Motshidisi.[2] … They used to teach us, you know, how a trade union works, show us the films. Because, you know what? Television is a good teacher. If you see physically what is happening.

The day after I was employed by the veterinary department as a labourer – in 1970 May, as a labourer – that lady, Miss Thompson, told me that, 'Yes, to work in the government is a good thing; if you want to come back, don't hesitate, come back'. She was my friend.

Then I went to Maun [in the far north-west]. I was employed, like, [from] today, and tomorrow [the following day] we were on a trip to Maun. It was my first time even to see Mochudi [40 kilometres from the capital and about 60 kilometres from his natal village]. To have to travel to Maun, you could see that I was in trouble! We spent the whole day on the journey. We slept in Francistown; the whole of the next day [we travelled], [then] we slept at Maun. The whole day [we travelled], the third day, we arrived at Shakawe [at the northern tip of Botswana]. The roads were rough. And my first salary was 6 rand [about £1.75 at 1970 rates]. My subsistence allowance was 1 rand 50 per week, which is 5 thebe per night [about 40 pence]. My first salary, I sent my mother the whole salary, I remained with 1 rand 50. It was a lot of money to me.[3] The second month, the second month's salary I bought myself clothing. You know, it was a nice something in which you could look presentable, which I liked very much. A safari suit. During those days, the safari suit was Kaunda's fashion. President Kaunda's fashion.[4] Kaunda did not put on a tie, even up to now. He used to wear safari suits.

So I bought myself a safari suit and I was … then, that's when I started a trade union movement. Because the conditions were tough then in the public service and I was – fortunately, two, three months later I was elected shop steward. I didn't even know what a shop steward was! Even in the committee, nobody knew what a shop steward was. Even trade unions – we only knew the name 'trade union', and only knew that usually in a trade union, always, you should be together. And a trade union is formed for the strike: if you form a trade union the intention is to strike! The intention is to be together always [in solidarity]. Even if you are cut [dismissed], your partner, even if your colleagues talk nonsense. Because you are in a union together. You should agree with each other! That's how I started. Yes, I was in Shakawe, it is far from here, it is 11 kilometres from Namibia. Bangwan, there was a big camp there at that time of the South African army. Remember, it was during those days when South-West Africa was still colonised.

P.W.: What were you doing in the veterinary department?

J.M.: Fences. Yes. Then, we were making [putting] fences on the border with South-West Africa, up to Monyan [with a click] area. Then I became a shop steward, like I said. I liked the union. Three, four years later, there was now a national centre, there was a Botswana Trade Union Education Centre which was assisted financially by the Africa–America Labour Centre, they were helping with money for training. In the 1970s, I attended the seminars of the trade union [there], which helped me a lot. I can assure you that if you can attend classes, basic courses about the labour movement, that can help. Those seminars, I attended them. Then, in the early eighties or late seventies, I was in the [National] Executive Committee of the MWU; [I was there] for a long time.

P.W.: When you joined the Ministry of Agriculture, at that time did the MWU exist?

J.M.: Yes. It existed. Remember, during those days it was only a name, without people, without education. In the late seventies I was elected to the [National] Executive [Committee] of the MWU. I still remember, I was elected in Mahalapye. As an additional member of the Executive. I was just a member. And I served as a member of the National Executive Committee of the Manual Workers' [Union] for a long time. I was elected, even unopposed, all the time. By then I was in Gaborone. I was still in the Ministry of Agriculture. Until 1980 or '81.

I was then working for the CTO department, a government department of transport. And I was fired because they were saying I was a ringleader, that I was poisoning people. There was a meeting of the [National] Executive Committee in 1981 in Gaborone, when I was fired. The Executive Committee took a decision that I must become a full-time employee of the Manual Workers' [Union]. That was in 1981. Before that at one stage I had been national vice-chair, but for a very short time. [The other MWU salaried officer] was Rre Manale, he's still alive, living in Tlokweng. He was the admin. secretary. He was employed [by the MWU] in 1980. I was employed as an organiser in 1981.

I was the one who influenced Manale's employment. When he was employed he was the national chairman of the Manual Workers' [Union], a very clever old man. I was a member of the [National] Executive Committee.

So we took a resolution – in 1980, one year prior to my own appointment – that it's better that we employ somebody on a full-time basis who could represent us *without fear*. Because then, if you were an activist, you used to be fired because of that. So we decided that the best place to look for somebody who is clever, who is honest, who can represent us, and to pay him so that he represents us without fear [was in the National Executive Committee]. He can represent us without fear that he will be fired.

That was 1980. Then I was fired, and [at] the [National] Executive Committee meeting of, I think it was 1981 August, they took the resolution. I was at the meeting. They asked me to go out. I went outside without knowing; then they called me later, they told me that you are being offered employment as a national organising secretary, to go and organise members. I didn't have a salary because there was no money. They said, 'If you go and organise you'll get your money from the members. You are employed, but there's no money to pay you. Go and organise first, then you'll get a salary'. So that is what I did. I organised and got a salary. My salary was 130 pula a month. The subscription [for MWU membership] then was 25 thebe. And there was no check off system [i.e. centralised deduction of MWU dues by government]. Each and every member had to come to the union [offices] and pay [their monthly subscription]. It was very difficult to come on a monthly basis, to come and pay, 25 [thebe], 25. And a year later, MaBotsalano was also employed.

Since Johnson was obviously highly literate, and an outstanding orator who also spoke reasonably good English, I wondered about his narrative of himself as never having gone to school:

P.W.: You say you come from a poor family of eight. But you must have gone to school for some time?

J.M.: For a short time, about Standard 2 or 3.

P.W.: You learned to read and write?

J.M.: Yes.

P.W.: So where did you acquire your English?

J.M.: No, English is a language. I don't think you need to go to school to acquire it. I'm not sure even whether I speak English properly. But remember, I told you: I was a gardener. We [he and his employer] used to communicate [laughs]. If you are a gardener, a gardener of a British white lady, you should communicate. You are forced to communicate. Because she was my friend, a very close friend.

P.W.: Were you self-taught? There is a lot of bias in Botswana against people who haven't had formal schooling. They even think you [i.e. such people] don't know your rights. Of course this is nonsense.

J.M.: That's why I enjoy, most of the time, I enjoy working with educated people. Because if you are with them, intellectual educated people, if you are with them they think you are not clever; they think you are stupid. And I enjoy working with them because most of them, I know how to handle them. And I have handled them for some time. Yes. And I will continue handling them.

At this point Johnson introduces into our discussion the formation of the Botswana Federation of Public Service Unions (BOFEPUSU) in 2009. By 2010, BOFEPUSU included five public service unions (two teachers' unions, the civil servants' union, BOPEU, and the local authorities workers' union, BLLAWU, in addition to the MWU). His interview reflects events that took place in 2011, long after the factional disputes discussed in Chapters 6 and 7. I include his remarks here in order to underline the dilemmas experienced by MWU leaders arising from being uneducated in a world where formal education is regarded as the primary criterion of knowledge and wisdom.

P.W.: You exploit their misperception?
J.M.: Yes, that's right.
P.W.: In order to get the best of them? Because they are not on their guard? So for you it's a kind of battle of wits? A battle of minds that you enjoy because you can see that they think that you are not as educated as they are, and therefore it will be easy for them ...
J.M.: To do anything they like. I know that they are wrong. And I used to tell ... just like that, I used to tell them [his colleagues in the MWU], 'Don't worry about educated people'. As far as I know, educated people are not clever. Even right now [June 2011], most of the unions in this country, they don't know what a union is. They are learning from the Manual Workers' [Union]. And they don't want to show anybody that they are learning from us.
P.W.: I saw in the newspapers that they were talking of other unions learning from the experience of the Manual Workers' [Union] – and that was the first time it was acknowledged publicly that this was possible. You are dealing here with four other public service unions in which at least three of them regard themselves as, you know, as people with education. Many of them have had four years of university [i.e. a Bachelor's degree], plus maybe they've also done a Master's degree. Some are doctors. And they come from this country where there is [a] deep bias [in favour of the educated]. It should open doors for you, and in fact, what they were upset about [during the 2011 strike] is that they were not being treated with respect [by the government]. Especially in the case [of] BOPEU [the civil servants' union]. The teachers are used to it by now. So how is it possible for you and all the manual workers to cope with this situation?
J.M.: It's just a very, very difficult situation, I must say [...] [The] Manual Workers' [Union], it's a blessed movement, I must tell you. You see these colleagues of mine, sometimes I laugh alone. I admire them. We [the MWU] decided, deliberately so, that we should group the labour movement of Botswana [the public sector unions], we should group these educated people. We should group these intellectual people. They think they know what they don't know. We should group them and make one BOFEPUSU [the federation of Botswana's public service unions]. The BOFEPUSU idea is from this office, by the way. Clever people know that. We decided, deliberately so, that – you know what? These clever people, these educated people, in order to group them under one name, one strong labour movement, let's

give them positions of leadership, don't contest for any positions of leadership. It started from this office! Let's grant them to be president, they like to be called president; let's form a federation. They agreed with us. We told them that, because we are not clever, lead it! We cannot afford to lead it. They said, 'Okay, we will lead it – *wena* you are president, *wena* you are secretary general, *wena*'. Then they ask us, 'No, can't you offer one of you to become vice-president?' And we said, 'Yes, we can. If you can help us to help him, we can give you [one officer]. Can't you come to be secretary for labour [referring to his own position in BOFEPUSU]?' At one stage, MaBotsalano was on the committee, MaBotsalano, Neo, they were on the committee of BOFEPUSU. Our aim was to win them [over], and we won them [over] by respecting them, by assuring them that their thinking is better than our thinking. We assured them that they are cleverer than us. That's the way BOFEPUSU started.

P.W.: But aren't you afraid that they will make bad decisions?

J.M.: No, no, no, no. They have realised on the way, after we have done so, they have realised on the way that they can't make decisions without these people [i.e. the MWU]. Even if we are here [i.e. in the office], they cannot make decisions usually. They will call us. They will ask us, 'Is this correct or what?' They will ask us. They cannot make anything.

P.W.: And why is that?

J.M.: That's so because I think they've realised they make so many mistakes. And when we come we help them ... [A]fter helping them, the popularity remains with them. And we have no problems of popularity.

P.W.: But can they help the industrial-class workers?

J.M.: They cannot help them [i.e. us]. They cannot help, and we know that, even my colleagues, all of us, we know that, that they cannot help the industrial class. They are the ones who have enjoyed assisting the oppression of the industrial class. Even now, most of them, sometimes they forget that we are together, we are colleagues, they forget sometimes.

P.W.: And how do they express this? Give me an example.

J.M.: For instance, even right now, when the strike was called off right now. They are saying [that] we [the MWU] called the strike off; it's not them, it's us. Or it's me who called the strike off. Some of them are thinking I called the strike off because I don't understand the issues. Because I'm not educated, which is not the case. So sometimes they forget.

P.W.: And why do they think it was called off? Because, after all, they are the president and general secretary of the federation.

J.M.: No, no, no. The issue here, within this class, there is division also. Those who are the president, there are those within the very same group who want to take the leadership away from those who are in. That's the difference from the Manual Workers' [Union]. The Manual Workers' [Union], we don't have much problem with the struggle to lead. That's the difference. Not at the moment [responding to my comment].

P.W.: Without putting names on it, it seems to me that X. is a very straight person.

J.M.: Yeah, X. is a straightforward person, but she still lacks the trade unionism culture.
G. (another union officer): She has to learn. If you want to learn, wholeheartedly, she has said to herself that trade unionism can be taught by the Manual Workers' [Union].
P.W.: And she makes mistakes! Hugging Masisi! [the minister of presidential affairs, an incident discussed in the following chapter].
J.M.: You saw her yesterday. She wanted to go with me to Yarona FM [a local radio station]. I didn't want to go because sometimes, you know, I'm uncomfortable. I'll do anything with my colleagues. So sometimes I become nervous. Not because I am undermining myself. You know, the way they understand issues, it's different! From the way we understand the issues.
Elsinah Botsalano (E.B.): Like yesterday when we were interviewing, teleconferencing [with PSI in France], she talked for almost 45 minutes alone [excluding Elsinah, who was in fact the PSI representative for Botswana], so I was just writing [notes for her] because I knew, always, she would like to speak alone. So I had to put some notes and give it to her. But she did appreciate it. Because *hakiri* [isn't it?] we knew, [even] if she speaks for a long time, she will leave out some of the things. So she would see that she is humble, to have those notes.
J.M.: And shocked! And shocked!
P.W.: That's not very good. That's not good leadership.
E.B.: *Important* notes [laughing].
J.M.: Sometimes they [the educated civil servant trade unionists] do that. Not deliberately.
G.: I think we are understanding them, knowing their weaknesses. We have to know the weaknesses of the people we are working with, so we can accommodate them.
P.W.: But what I'm asking is: is it a strength? I can see that BOFEPUSU has certain strengths, because it is big and [the] government can't ignore it the way they can ignore the Manual Workers' [Union] on their own, so that's a great strength. But I can also think of it as a kind of weakness.
J.M.: No, I think I know what you are saying. What we should do as a way forward, we should go along with them. We should keep [our] union to represent the interests of the manual workers.
P.W.: Not have an amalgamation?
J.M.: No, no, no! And to be spokespersons of the marginalised workers. We should leave BOPEU as the spokespersons of the middle class. We should also create something within BOFEPUSU where doctors, where engineers, where teachers, you know, could represent themselves and bring whatever we want to force [the] government to do in the federation together. *Bone* ['they', i.e. those people in the other public service unions], they are making a serious mistake. They think they can organise the manual workers to join BOPEU, or they think they can organise manual workers to join BLLAWU.
P.W.: Really?
J.M.: Yes. They are trying to do that even now.

P.W.: At the same time that they are organising the federation [BOFEPUSU]?
J.M.: Yes, at the same time. You can see that that is ignoring people, already ignoring people [that is, manual workers' interests]. Only a fool can do that. You cannot organise a manual worker to become a member of BOPEU. They will ignore him, they will discriminate against him. The culture is different.

Tricksters and Experts

Implicit in this interview extract is a familiar trope, that of the trickster. The poor, the marginalised and the uneducated have always used their trickster powers to gain the upper hand by disguising their superior knowledge. Like classic tricksters, Johnson and his fellow MWU leaders were willing to underplay their evident expertise in all matters of trade union conduct, government perfidy, strikes, labour law and the rights of workers, proven by the fact that they won case after case against the government, in order to bring their fellow public service trade unionists on board. They exploited these educated unionists' evident ambitions and biases, their assumption that education made them superior, to flatter them into believing that they were the decision-makers when, in reality, it was the MWU's much longer and deeper experience of conducting labour affairs that repeatedly compelled these others to defer to their greater knowledge.

Being a trickster is often associated with charisma, perhaps because it lends the persona of charismatic leaders a sense of mystery and unpredictability. Trickster irony energised the aura of playfulness and humour fostered by Johnson, and strengthened his ability to attract elites and ordinary folk alike. At the same time followers were aware that beneath his humour lay a tough determination and immense authority; in other words, that the trickster is always liable to flip. But unlike some eminent public figures, Johnson made a point of being approachable to comrades and friends. He exuded a physical presence, an overflowing paternal warmth, generosity and kindness. With his ready, broad smile, he reached out to fellow men and women, holding their hands in communion, throwing an affectionate or comforting arm around their shoulders, greeting new arrivals with welcoming bear hugs. This sense of intimacy conveyed his trust in and love for his loyal followers. His deep belly laugh, jokiness and easy camaraderie did not, however, disguise his powerful leadership qualities; in particular, his forthright public outspokenness about government mendacity or other rival unionists' betrayal; his clarity of exposition, much appreciated by the press and ordinary workers; and a decisiveness that lent him immense authority. Johnson's word was his command. He made an effort to consult his colleagues, but there was no questioning his authority. His permission was necessary before any initiative could be taken.

Another strategy favoured by Johnson to overcome the perceived liabilities associated with a lack of education was to use the growing wealth of the MWU to employ experts as consultants. Virtually all the appointed employees working in the MWU's offices were, as a matter of principle, former manual workers with minimal education. Union officers were, nevertheless, careful administrators and sticklers for legal and bureaucratic procedures, who kept meticulous accounts and were genuine experts in all matters of labour law. But in Botswana, a land of consultants, there was no reason why the MWU, the largest union in Botswana, should not employ the services of experts with doctorates or professional qualifications, from lawyers to accountants, to 'advise' the union on a range of matters – from pay structures to internal conflicts. Even writing the gloried history of the MWU was entrusted to university academics employed as consultants. As in any consultancy, the final reports submitted were subject to union control and approval. Such consultancies were not cheap, but the fact that the MWU could afford to pay all these highly educated, learned individuals highlighted the status of manual workers: they were the superiors, able to employ others who had to follow their remit. And having such educated consultants afforded them public legitimacy.

Somewhat similar was the way Johnson and the MWU deployed the courts to assert their equal worth and, at times, as Chapter 5 in particular highlighted, to win against the odds. Here too the union used its wealth to prove its standing and dignity, its *seriti*, by employing attorneys and even at times well known advocates brought in from South Africa to serve their cause. They repeatedly proved that apparently uneducated, lowly manual workers could and would challenge arbitrary government decisions and call the state to account through judicial review. Quite often, several court cases were being handled by the MWU simultaneously, as the following chapters highlight. Defeats were costly, but as long as union dues continued to flow in, they were affordable.

Rhetoric and Oratory

Johnson loved using aphorisms and sayings in his addresses to meetings and union rallies. He often compared the plight of low-paid manual workers and their union to the exodus of the Children of Israel from Egypt, their crossing of the Red Sea and their wanderings in the desert for 40 years as they struggled to reach the Promised Land. In a meeting at Customs and Excise early on in my research in 2005, I was struck by the number of proverbs and biblical references he made in quick succession. He began with a warning to government: 'Those people cut by a razor are the very ones being shaved by it' (*ba ongwa ka legare ba bo ba beolwa ka lone*) – that is, those people (government representatives) who have threatened workers will find themselves in trouble of their own making. He went on to say 'We found the Bible existing and will leave it (that is, when we die) being there still'. In other words, negotiations with the government are always tricky, nothing ever changes. During the next two weeks, he warned the assembled workers, 'Your wisdom tooth should not be loosened' (*le seka la repa motlhagare*) – that is, don't let your guard down. And he continued, 'a river is crossed by a bridge' (*dinoka di tolwa ka borogo*) – that is, we can arrive at a satisfactory 'package' only through the 'bridge' of negotiations.

He described the MWU as an 'ark', 'like Noah's' ark. 'If you have seen yourself here' (at the meeting), he said, 'that means that your "parents" (*batsadi*) are the MWU'. 'We are "consultants" when it comes to the affairs (*merero*) of the workers'. He then quoted one of his favourite biblical verses, from the Book of Jeremiah: 'If you see it is good to go with us to Babylon, let us go, but if you see it is no good, just stay. If you refuse, just refuse. But know that bad things will come to pass'.[5] In other words, if you don't follow us, the MWU, you cannot blame us for the consequences. Ironically, this Old Testament saying is attributed to the King of Babylon's guardsman, offering the prophet Jeremiah the choice of going with the conquerors to Babylon and into exile (which Jeremiah refuses), but this is not how the saying is interpreted in Botswana. Johnson continued: 'We are crossing the Red Sea' – in other words, we shall overcome this ordeal. Finally, before departing from the meeting he concluded, 'We are walking in revelation' – that is, the MWU is divinely inspired, it will resolve the issue.

Johnson, unlike some of his fellow unionist leaders, is not a particularly devout Christian. I was told in 2011 that he had only just joined the United Congregational Church of Southern Africa (UCCSA). Nor does he use the dramatic style of many Tswana preachers. On the contrary, he is admired for the clarity of his reasoning, and he often laces his speeches with anecdotes and jokes, at times even at his own expense. How, then, are we to interpret his delight in using proverbs and biblical quotations? Clearly, he knows that his audience is well-versed in the Bible since most are church members. By deploying familiar biblical myths and narratives, Johnson elevates the MWU's battles with their employer to the status of a historic struggle for justice and redemption, in which the union is the saviour, the ark, the parents, leading the workers to the Promised Land.

This, I want to suggest, also gives a clue to a key source of his charisma. In his ebullient self-confidence, boldness and visionary hopefulness, and in his willingness to stand up to the might of the government, he seems to concentrate in his persona the aspirations of ordinary manual workers, to embody an honour from the margins, which reflects glory on them. He epitomises the capacity to achieve equality with the highest in the land, proven by his easy conviviality across status and class divisions.[6]

On the trip to Mabutsana described in Chapter 7, it will be recalled that the choir sang and danced as they greeted the MWU delegation, glorifying Motshwarakgole in particular, condemning his detractors and extolling his almost sanctified distinction:

> Workers of today, stand up
> And build our union.
> Mr Motshwarakgole,
> We thank the Lord,
> That you have led our union for a long time,
> You have given many a great inheritance,
> You bring about the light
> The light of close friendship.

And in another song:

> Iyonana, iyonanana, yonana,
> I have a child, iyelele,
> His name is Motshwarakgole.

And in a song condemning the rebels:

> Motshwarakgole, our man is being disrespected
> He is being belittled.
> It is not right this thing, it is not right.

In another song, the first stanza again refers to Motshwarakgole:

> Motshwarakgole, work,
> Work, work, work,
> Motshwarakgole, work.
> Teach the people about the union.

One of the songs during the 2011 strike singled Johnson out, calling on him to teach the government a lesson:

> Motshwarakgole who is ours, speak angrily, scold (*kgalema*),
> Those people playing games with us.

Family and Contradictions in Status

Johnson met his wife, a bank employee, while he was working for a short time as a miner in the diamond mines at Jwaneng. She was a bank teller in Jwaneng for three years before transferring to the capital, Gaborone.

> P.W.: You told me you met your wife in Jwaneng?
> J.M.: Yes, I was at Jwaneng for a very short period. And there was a big strike there. And most of the people think that I was the one who caused the strike. Do you know Peter Olfson? Peter Olfson is one gentleman, he's a consultant, a Tsabadiri consultant [Tsabadiri is a consultancy firm]. He was then – he's a British man – he was then a labour officer. Then he went to Jwaneng to go and mediate the dispute. Even now Peter Olfson thinks and is sure that I was the one who organised [the strike]. I was there as an operator of this big machine. I have knowledge of this big mine machine but I was there, then I didn't like the conditions.
> P.W.: You left government service?
> J.M.: I left government service for a very short period. I went to Jwaneng, worked on those machines. It was less than six months; I trained on the machines for three months. I worked, it was just less than six months. There

was a big strike. I was the leader of the strike, of course. It was the first strike I ever led. It was a very bitter strike. Because they were all, all the miners, were dismissed. Except *nna* [me]. Yes. And I said, I will go with them, and I went, but I was not dismissed. They dismissed all the miners.
P.W.: Why did they keep you [on], when you were the leader?
J.M.: I was informed by people, whether true or not – in the diamond mines, if they want to get rid of you, if you are a troublemaker, they will threaten you with a diamond. So that it will disqualify you, you'll be finished, you'll be doomed, not even allowed to go to work.
P.W.: They'd plant a diamond [on you]?
J.M.: I was informed that. I realised, I suspected so. That if they fired all the people and they are saying I'm the one who led the strike, and they didn't want to fire me, they must want to do something to me. Then I decided: No, no, no, sorry, thank you. I'll go with the people. They didn't fire me, you can ask them. Then I returned to government service immediately.

With his wife an educated banker, once he became a paid union officer with an NGO-equivalent salary, Johnson could be considered 'middle class' in terms of income and status. The family owned a relatively modest detached house in the Village, earlier leased from the Botswana Housing Corporation. Originally an out-of-the-way marginal suburb of Gaborone, the Village became a valuable location as the capital grew, close to the university and other public institutions, and known for the large, leafy plots that surround each house. The MWU offices were also located there, on a large plot subsequently sold in 2013.

Johnson's daughters attended Maru-a-pula, the only private high school in the capital, along with most of the children of diplomats, academics and elite civil servants and politicians. They spoke fluent English and were sophisticated young women, far removed in their daily experiences from the worlds of manual workers. Later they attended universities in Johannesburg and Cape Town.[7]

Given the enormous growth in the MWU's wealth, the apparent embourgoisement of their leader, perhaps not surprisingly, led to suspicions and sometimes accusations of 'corruption' among disaffected colleagues, as the previous chapters have documented. These were accentuated when, in 2006, the family moved out of Gaborone to a purpose-built house in Phakalane, an outer suburb, joining an exodus of the elite from the capital. In reality, however, Johnson was always meticulous in handling union finances. Not unlike other dual-income families in the capital, and with a foot on the property ladder, he simply capitalised on the family's joint earnings.

But the interview extract, like the previous chapters, also points to some of the bitter disputes Johnson had been involved in over the years. In some instances he was willing to forgive and forget. He told me, for example, that one of the government ministers who had alleged that the union was corrupt during the factional dispute in 2005, and whom the MWU had satirised in an offensive cartoon, was now his 'friend'. In fact, he said, she had 'always' been his friend. She proved this publicly with her strong support for the public service unions during their 2011 strike, going against the country's president and convening a parliamentary caucus debate during its recess. Lilian, the ex-vice chair of the union, told me she too was Johnson's 'friend', despite their bitter quarrel. The trouble between them had been stirred up by a colleague, she said, it was not his fault. But there were others Johnson was unwilling to forgive, particularly those who had betrayed the MWU and done it immense harm. He was not a person to be crushed or defeated in any battle. Thus he continued to wage war against the breakaway union, the BOGUWU, and the Botswana Federation of Trade Unions (BFTU), taking them to court repeatedly and ensuring that they were not part of the newly envisaged bargaining council. Despite his pragmatism in some contexts, he was a tenacious adversary, as others repeatedly learnt to their cost.

Against 'Tradition'

Johnson is a man who dismisses Tswana traditions and things of *bogologolo* (long ago) as often unjust and, indeed, sometimes dangerous. Once, sitting around with union officers at a restaurant in 2011, he responded to my husband's recitation of Kalanga and Tswapong praise poems, meant to entertain, by commenting that he rejected these poems. He condemned the act of praising a chief.

A year later, in 2012, when I asked unionists gathered at the union office whether 'justice' (*tshiamo*) was the same in customary and modern courts, Johnson responded by stating that he did not like customary courts. Indeed, he did not believe they achieved justice. He had sat on such courts, he said. When I argued that it seemed to me that justice was the same in both, he conceded that in the past, perhaps, participants in a customary court would express their opinions and the chief would sum up the general feeling, so that the courts were 'democratic'. But customary courts had changed: they had started to imitate modern courts and had ceased to be democratic.

When I told the assembled unionists that the Ministry of Wildlife and Tourism had taken over Moremi village's Manonye spring and gorge in the Tswapong Hills, handing it with a 20-year concession to a private company – and even charging villagers 22 pula to enter their own land, Johnson commented that he did not like 'wild animals'. This rejection of game tourism reflected his strongly held belief that the future of Botswana lay in the modern sector with its modern-day institutions, not with chiefs and wildlife who seemed merely to harm ordinary, often impoverished, citizens.

Opposition Politics: Allies and Enemies

Like virtually all the officers and employees of the Manual Workers' Union, Johnson was a keen supporter of the opposition party, the Botswana National Front (BNF). He had briefly been elected a councillor for Gaborone City Council in 1999, when, along with eleven other BNF councillors, he walked out in protest against the Council's recommendation to hike manual workers' pay by 154 per cent, rather than the 600 pula settlement the MWU demanded.[8] He then resigned. When I accompanied him around the Village in 2005, inspecting different MWU properties there, he confided to me that the BNF had asked him to stand as an MP but that he hesitated to do so. He had, apparently, been close to the outgoing leader, Kenneth Koma, but seemed equally at ease with his successor, Duma Boko.

None of Botswana's presidents escaped his sharp tongue. He castigated President Mogae for failing to recognise the contribution Botswana workers had made to creating the country's wealth (Mokotedi 2006: 2; see also Piet 2007: 4). During the 2011 strike, after Ian Khama had assumed the presidency, opposition party leaders, MPs and other public speakers were welcomed at the strike rally grounds, including those making calls for 'regime change'. Johnson addressed a three-party opposition party rally during the strike in which he spoke bitterly about the president, accusing him of being:

> so irresponsible that he goes around donating blankets to the poor and old in remote areas when there is a national crisis caused by the strike … 'Khama has a racist and colonialist mentality of the imperial powers who use compassion to patronise people so that they can look up to him as a messiah'. (Keoreng 2011a)

According to Keoreng, Johnson 'declared that workers constitute a big constituency and can use their vote to change the political landscape' (ibid.). The veteran unionist was speaking at a rally organised by the opposition parties in Gaborone to support striking civil servants. He said the labour movement intends to use its numbers to unseat politicians who do not support the workers:

> We are not politically affiliated, but *re nale konopo* (we have a large constituency), with our children, our wives brothers and sisters, we will vote for someone who is supportive of our plight … We will not vote for an MP (whether from the opposition or ruling party) who does not support us. (ibid.)[9]

As he reviewed the 2011 strike at the MWU headquarters, Johnson sighed and confessed that the end of the strike was tough. He had thought when he proposed suspending the strike that the workers were in agreement with him, that he had convinced them. Now he was once again being blamed and accused wrongly of betraying the cause. His colleagues reminisced about other, earlier such conflicts, such as one in 1987 when they had travelled all the way up to Maun for a meeting in which the leadership was accused of betrayal and removed from office. For a while there were two national executive committees, they told me, before eventually the matter was resolved. Although they laughed at the memory, it attested to the sense of predicament they felt in 2011 when the strike had ended with the press and workers accusing them of treachery.

Later, after the strike was over, Johnson, along with other leaders of BOFEPUSU, did their utmost to persuade the opposition parties to unite in an umbrella coalition. At that point, unionists were arguing: 'We cannot apologise for participating in politics. In fact we should apologise for coming in late because this has long been overdue' (Modikwa 2011b). Johnson was forthright in expressing the federation's disappointment when the talks collapsed.

> 'I find it scandalous that the parties simply locked themselves away from the people only to emerge to announce the collapse of the talks', Motshwarakgole said in interview. 'If they knew anything about democracy, they would have gone back to their respective structures and engaged other stakeholders because this project is just too big to be allowed to fail'.
>
> He added that, as workers who want a strong opposition or an alternative government, they feel betrayed by the leaders of the concerned opposition parties and would like the labour movement to put pressure on them to resume the talks. In his view, the talks failed because those involved put partisan and personal interests ahead of national interests. (Mpolokwa 2012)

In the aftermath of the strike, and even before it, there was strong government pressure for BOFEPUSU not to involve itself in national party politics. Following the collapse of the opposition umbrella talks, most members of the federation decided to back out of party politics. Johnson is quoted as saying that, 'We want a strong opposition and a strong government' (Makgapha 2012). His pragmatism is evident here. This was not a moment to risk disqualification and another court case.

If Johnson was an open supporter of the opposition, he was equally at home with some members of the government led by the Botswana Democratic Party (BDP). He confided in me several times that he 'knew what was going on' in the corridors of power. His friendship with a fellow homeboy from Molepolole, Daniel Kwelagobe, for many years an influential minister, MP and leader of the BDP, allowed him access to the government. Kwelagobe was a regular speaker at the MWU's annual delegates' conferences.

Johnson's outspokenness was legendary. Following the 2011 strike, 400 striking nurses were not reinstated. When an outbreak of diarrhoea killed babies in the Maun area, he responded with an attack on the government:

> BOFEPUSU secretary for labour, Johnson Motshwarakgole, said their investigations revealed that about 120 children succumbed countrywide. 'These are the people who were killed by the government. The government is being economic with the truth when it claims only 67 children died because of the epidemic', Motshwarakgole said.
>
> He said the government should change its hard stance and rehire all dismissed nurses. Johnson said the recent statement by President Ian Khama on Botswana TV that his government will never re-employ the dismissed nurses who had participated in the national strike earlier this year was to be regretted.
>
> Motshwarakgole declared that some clinics in the Okavango were still closed after the nurses were sent packing. He also said clinics in areas such as Phitshane, Kweneng, Kgalagadi and the north-east are operating with

> skeleton staff or with no nurses, hence the high death toll as a result of the diarrhoea outbreak. About 367 nurses were dismissed from work and the nurses who are at work are not coping with the workload; they could not disseminate information to the public about how to prevent this epidemic. 'These avoidable deaths should be blamed on president Khama. He has blood on his hands', Motshwarakgole charged. (Mosikare 2011b)

Not long after this, in December 2011, most of the nurses were reinstated (Mooketsi 2011).

Sheer Effort and Dedication

By the time I returned to Botswana in 2011, Johnson had been leading the Manual Workers' Union for 30 years, through good times and bad. He had been instrumental in building up its fortunes, but despite the leadership's huge efforts, manual-worker wages lagged behind, and the pay differential in the public service between low and high-paid employees continued to grow exponentially with every inflation-related pay rise. Many workers had lost their jobs in a continuing retrenchment of industrial-class workers whose services were being privatised. Despite this, it was above all the union officers' total dedication to the MWU, their day-in, day-out investments of time and effort, that won them the admiration and loyalty of the rank and file.

Much of Johnson's work on behalf of the union involved the sheer effort of long-distance travel to settle labour disputes, and attendance at seemingly endless meetings that often continued late into the evening. As already noted, the geographical reach of the MWU mirrors that of national and local government, presenting a major logistical challenge in administering the affairs of the union, given that almost all the national officers are based in the capital. Despite Botswana's small population, under 2 million, it is a vast country, larger than France. The headquarters of the union in the capital, Gaborone, are located in the far southern corner of the country, and although much of the population is concentrated in the south, around the capital, and in the east, along the line of rail, distances are still huge. Unlike the president, who arrives at remote villages by helicopter, or top civil servants and politicians who travel to official meetings by plane, union officers spend hours on Botswana's roads, travelling to remote schools and hospitals where members of the union work. Johnson's willingness, even as he grows older, to repeatedly go on these arduous, long-distance trips, driving himself and often setting off at 2 AM in the morning to attend the matters of lowly unionists and address workers in remote parts of Botswana, may be the ultimate source of his charisma in the perception of union members. As MaSeriti told me:

> The people who are complaining don't understand Johnson – he is carrying a lot of people on his shoulders. Everyone is always ringing him up, and

> he is always friendly. When he says he will help, he will. No one can be as effective. The government like him. He can understand your problem.

Or, as MaPelotona commented: 'They [the rebel group] can't make it because there is no one like Johnson who can stand with these people. I don't know if he's a lawyer, but we have got a lot of things through that man'.

Conclusion

As the previous chapter highlighted, Johnson was a member of a cohort of increasingly outspoken labour leaders, both within the Manual Workers' Union and beyond it. Most of these unionists were younger and more educated. Only a few had risen through the ranks, at a time when university and even high-school education were rare achievements, particularly among manual workers. In some ways he resembles Gobe Matenge, a Kalanga from the north-east whose life history is portrayed by Richard Werbner (2004), who rose to be a prominent permanent secretary and later a wealthy entrepreneur and post-civil servant dignitary, despite having completed only primary education. Matenge was a founder of the Botswana Civil Servants' Association, which defended public sector workers' rights. But Matenge came from a leading family in his village, and while he too was in some ways a radical and a maverick, he was born 30 years before Johnson, in the early 1930s, and was incorporated into the early cohort of young civil servants who built up the state, many of whom were also Kalanga like him.

Despite his ebullient self-confidence and very real optimism, Johnson was a realist and a pragmatist, all too aware of the government's power and the extent to which, when things went wrong, he was invariably blamed. He pitted his wit, experience, charm, cunning, observational powers and common-sense understanding of where to draw the line against more educated colleagues and antagonists. What kept him going, ultimately, despite his trials and tribulations, his perennial temptation to retire, was his love of his work as a unionist. Even beyond that, he was a man of vision. Talking about the camaraderie under the *morula* tree during the 2011 strike, he told me: 'That's what I've been dreaming of, for a long time, to see workers, like that, under the *morula*. Togetherness. Togetherness'.[10] The obliteration of class divisions was his greatest dream, a man who came from humble origins and yet had achieved distinction, *seriti* (dignity), *tlotlo* (respect) and a middle-class lifestyle against the odds, and who was thus able to stand tall in any company without sacrificing his integrity and outspokenness, and without denying his origins as a man of the people.

CHAPTER TEN

'The Mother of All Strikes': Popular Protest Culture and Vernacular Cosmopolitanism in the Public Service Unions' Strike, 2011

The events of the Arab Spring inspired a new sense of hope and determination among people living geographically far apart. They underscored the power of ordinary people to make a difference, their capacity to mobilise against authoritarian regimes by using social media, texting and other networks of citizens or workers to protest against drastic economic cutbacks, and to demand a rethinking of current values and priorities. The rebellions in Tunisia and Egypt, epitomised in the giant gatherings in Tahrir Square, became a symbol of protest against the odds, and of courage in the face of brute tyranny. They inspired a series of other rebellions elsewhere in the Arab world, and huge protests beyond it. In Botswana, nearly 100,000 public service trade unionists sang songs of rebellion as they gathered daily for over two months under a giant *morula* tree in the capital, and in towns throughout the country.

From Egypt to Botswana, a range of quite different countries witnessed worker, youth and middle-class rebellions against the political and capitalist status quo, the privileges of a tiny, wealthy and often corrupt elite, at a time when the majority could no longer earn a decent wage. Participants stressed the democratic, egalitarian nature of their protests, animated by a spirit of inclusiveness across religion, gender, class and ethnicity. They demanded a return to the welfare state and the egalitarian principles that underpinned it. And wherever they occurred, mass mobilisations did not simply express a politics of revolt: they were, equally, staged aesthetic and poetic performances that echoed and re-echoed similar themes in song, slogans and gestures from country to country, across the globe. Each protest was local and distinctive aesthetically, but they also borrowed from the rest, creating in each place a sited, vernacular cosmopolitanism.

Botswana had joined the global wave of protests on 18 April 2011 with a massive strike of five public service unions jointly claiming to represent 93,000 workers out of 103,000 public sector workers, in a country with a population of 1.7 million. Because Botswana is a remote and sparsely populated country in Southern Africa, the strike failed to capture the global media. Locally and nationally, however, it was perceived to open a new chapter in the country's history. Although it began as a simple labour dispute over pay, the eight-week strike escalated to become a test of fundamental values of democracy, social justice, equality, freedom of speech and the right to live in a welfare state that paid its employees a living wage. It articulated the desire for 'change' with a big C. Like the mass strike in Wisconsin in 2011, which encompassed trade unions and community groups (Collins 2012), the Botswana strike also resembled new social movements in forging a shared identity across a wide occupational spectrum and in mobilising the whole of civil society in a call for dialogue and justice. The strike's social and cultural effervescence negated the apparent decline of trade unions in the industrialised world – from being some of the earliest social movements to becoming highly sclerotic and institutionalised. In the global South, however, the Arab Spring was not only massively supported by Egyptian trade unions but followed several years of mass worker mobilisation (Alexander 2011), while in Tunisia, too, the trade union federation played a central role in the revolution of 2011 from the beginning.

Trade unions in Central and Southern Africa have historically always been, in many respects, cosmopolitan or 'international' in their orientation, aware even during the colonial period and more so since independence of the International Labour Organisation and international law, human rights and labour struggles elsewhere.[1] In his magisterial survey of the 'labour question' in French and British Africa outside South Africa, Frederick Cooper (1996) documents the emergence of an emancipatory discourse of self-governance, citizenship and labour rights, and the growing international links of African unions to international labour organisations during the period following the Second World War. There has also been a tendency within the worldwide labour movement for popular culture, songs and slogans to cross international boundaries. This internationalism has become even more marked in an age of global media and news dissemination. In this spirit, the present chapter argues that during the 2011 public service union strike in Botswana, tribal and popular cultural traditions and ideas of authority were deployed and combined with a wider cosmopolitan consciousness of protest movements elsewhere to create a shared vernacular cosmopolitan culture of protest.

The central adversary in the strike, the government-as-employer, came to be epitomised in the figure of Botswana's president, Lieutenant General Seretse Ian Khama. Khama had been commander of the Botswana Defence Forces before entering politics. Despite being democratically elected with a large majority in 2009, his authoritarianism was perceived to stem not only from his background as a soldier but from his ancestry – he is the elder son of Sir Seretse Khama, founding president of Botswana and hereditary paramount chief of the Bamangwato tribe, the largest in Botswana, an office Sir Seretse abdicated when he entered secular politics. Unlike the father, the son was crowned paramount chief (a title currently held temporarily by his brother). While his royal ancestry made him powerfully charismatic among rural folk, among workers and the intellectual elite his unwillingness to abdicate the chiefship was popularly seen as another sign of his sense of absolute entitlement, and hence of his authoritarian personality. He is head of the Botswana Democratic Party (BDP), which had ruled Botswana by winning free elections without a break since independence in 1966. For unionists, many of whom support the opposition parties, this uninterrupted stretch of 45-year rule is seen as another sign of Botswana being a *de facto* authoritarian, one-party state.

Khama was thus regarded as a highly authoritarian figure by the unions. If the strike seemed revolutionary to the media and public, it was because thus far in his presidency, President Khama had countenanced little dissent, was seen to have surrounded himself with 'yes men' (and women), and to have made a series of arbitrary decisions. Among these, and widely regarded as particularly ominous, was the establishment of the Directorate of Intelligence and Security (DIS), an internal security agency equivalent to MI5 and the FBI, an apparatus that lacked financial transparency and reported directly to the president.

Like other protest movements in 2011, the strike in Botswana was aestheticised through a process of 'citation': a fusion of images and discursive tropes from the past and from spatially distant events in North Africa and in Occupy movements elsewhere with currently invented images in new bricolages and assemblages.[2] The 'political' thus came to be powerfully inserted aesthetically by encompassing such displaced tropes, often subliminally, through performative acts of (re)iteration, 'doubling up' and mimesis, into the new context of the strike.[3] In particular, strikers and the media aestheticised the false pretensions of autocratic power and illegitimately acquired wealth while prefiguring, through performance, the just society. They appealed to a transcendental morality and Christian values.

Theorists of social movements have debated whether the state is necessarily always the main target of such movements. Missing in this debate, however, is the fact that the state is not simply an objective reality; it must be constructed culturally and aesthetically.[4] So too in Botswana. As in most chiefly societies in Central and Southern Africa, Tswana traditionally have made a distinction between the *office* of the chiefship and the *incumbent* of that office (Schapera 1956: 137, 220; Gluckman 1963b; Comaroff 1978; Gulbrandsen 1995). A good chief is one who serves his people, and they, in turn, grant him legitimacy. Schapera cites the Tswana proverb, 'A chief is chief by the grace of the people', which reminds chiefs that if they ill-treat their people the people will abandon them (Schapera 1956: 138). Historically, a good chief (*kgosi*) was expected to put the people above his private affairs, to seek good council and always 'consider the welfare and security of his people … safeguard the land and other rights of his subjects … be generous and hospitable', and, as was said of an early Southern Sotho chief, be '"kind, affable, and easy of access"' and conspicuous among his contemporaries '"for his love of peace"' (ibid.: 138–9). Good chiefs were expected to aim for peace (*kagiso*) and harmony, and to be virtuous, generous and caring (Gulbrandsen 1995: 421).

As we shall see, this popular expectation did not accord with the tough, uncompromising, monetarist policies adopted by President Ian Khama, which he defended as being aimed at bringing down the deficit, and which were much praised by a visiting delegation of the International Monetary Fund. The belt-tightening in the public service followed the global financial crisis in 2008, which hit diamond-dependent Botswana particularly hard. At one point in 2008, Botswana ceased to trade in diamonds altogether, and was haemorrhaging its accumulated reserve funds. At the same time, as unionists and opposition leaders repeated in speech after speech at the strike grounds, President Khama was widely regarded as extremely self-indulgent and personally wasteful, and his trumpeted policies towards poverty alleviation were – rightly or wrongly – rejected by workers as short-termist and idiosyncratic.[5]

President Khama's unwillingness to meet directly with the leaders of the Botswana Federation of Public Sector Unions to achieve peace (*kagiso*) rather than confrontation, was another source of wide popular condemnation. This refusal, along with his various policy decisions, had made Khama a worthy target of popular dissent, viewed somewhat hyperbolically as a potential 'dictator' who needed to be reminded that he was ruler only by the grace of the people. As one speaker at the strike grounds in Francistown was reported as saying, 'We thought we had a father [in President Khama] to whom we must show respect, but it has happened before that children stopped respecting their father when the father behaved badly' (Ngakane 2011: 36).

The different aesthetic and performative dimensions of the strike as protest culture forged, I propose, a local, vernacular working-class culture, while echoing the protests beyond Botswana. Popular culture in the strike was dramatised in multiple bodily and sentimental articulations: in the spiritual expressions of protest through prayer; satirical humour, dances, hand gestures and songs of 'rebellion' mocking politicians and civil servants. In the stunts and forays beyond the strike grounds to invade government meetings, in attending successive court hearings *en masse* while dressed in white in solidarity with nurses and doctors, in lending support to strikers in other towns, and in the speeches calling for change, including 'regime change', strikers made reference to and echoed the Arab Spring. The strike thus created a consciousness of cosmopolitan participation – for the first time Batswana were part of a wider international social movement. This fabricated not only an innovative, popular vernacular cosmopolitan culture; workers also spectacularly forged, through performance, solidarities across classes between manual workers and white-collar or professional civil servants. In many senses, this was a middle-class rebellion that encompassed manual labourers as well, but it was also a working-class protest that encompassed middle-class workers. Above all, it was youthful, humorous and ludic, signalling a generational shift among public service workers. In the next chapter I document the politics of the strike. Here I want to illuminate its popular cultural dimensions.

Initially, the strike was in support of a BOFEPUSU demand for a 16 per cent pay rise across the board, following three years of 30 per cent inflation in which public service salaries were frozen voluntarily following the temporary collapse of diamond mining in 2008. The government refused, however, to contemplate a pay hike while Botswana's economy was still in deficit and the world economy shaky, despite the rise in diamond sales during 2011. There were undoubtedly additional, political motives behind the public sector unions' decision to strike, among them the government's delay in forming a bargaining council, and the desire by union leaders to publicise the existence of the newly founded public service federation. But the radical erosion of salaries was a critical factor, especially so for industrial-class manual workers who are the main subject of this book. They in particular were barely surviving on salaries that even before the global financial crisis were well below a living wage.

Both sides, but particularly the government, dug their heels in. President Khama refused to meet with the BOFEPUSU leadership. Over time, as the strike dragged on with no resolution in sight, the federation began mobilising support among an increasingly expanding number of actors in civil society. Both the independent press and private radio stations supported the strikers from the start, but joining the voices calling for dialogue were chiefs sitting in the House of Chiefs, church leaders, former national presidents, opposition (and some government) politicians, representatives of the Botswana Confederation of Commerce, Industry and Manpower (BOCCIM), MPs and parliament, the great and the good. Support came additionally from international trade unions such as Public Service International (PSI). Before the strike ended, the whole nation had in effect mobilised to demand that President Khama meet the strikers, which he obdurately avoided doing. The scale of the strike, its national reach, was unprecedented. The unanimous support of the independent media, press and radio, created a critical public debate on matters of social justice as never before. The profound sense generated was that something fundamental had changed for the better in Botswana, that, as I was told, Botswana would never be the same again.[6]

Initially, the strike did not appear to be about social justice, but as it progressed and the chasm between the workers and the government became more and more evident, issues of social justice and equality, which affected in particular low-paid industrial-class manual workers, surfaced and became central to the negotiations.

Under the *Morula* Tree

During the whole eight-week strike, workers in the capital gathered daily under a giant *morula* tree in the grounds of Gaborone Secondary School (GSS) for the whole day. Throughout Botswana, similar trees became sites of worker assembly. Botswana is a deeply Christian country, and the first hour of each morning was devoted to prayers, hymns and sermons, often assuming the character of a revivalist meeting, with singers and preachers recruited from among the workers who stood or sat under the tree in a semi-circle around the stage.

One of the preachers, an older man with a creased forehead, gave an impassioned prayer one morning asking God, the heavenly *kgosi* (king or chief), to alleviate the workers' pain. He called on the worldly *kgosi*, Ian Khama, not to fail the workers. Political prayers are a generic feature of union piety, as we saw

Figure 10.1 Under the *morula* tree (photograph by the author).

Figure 10.2 Carrying branches from the grounds of Gaborone Secondary School (photograph by the author).

in Chapter 8. Workers have faith that God is on their side. As one speaker said on another occasion:

> And so with our prayer … being that the Lord is on our side … So we assemble under this tree every day … God himself said that if there are two or three people meeting in my name, then I am the fourth one there! So too in our case, God has been here with us. He has been walking with us and encouraging us to go on.[7]

The federation delegates' conference likewise opened with a prayer:

> Our father in heaven, we come before you this afternoon … in the name of Jesus. We are gathered here Lord as your people, in your presence … and we look upon your divine intervention.[8]

Almost from the start of the strike, the *morula* tree under which the praying, choir-singing and speeches all took place began to assume mythical, sacred dimensions, much like the centre of a pilgrimage cult (see Figure 10.1). As Johnson told the assembled workers:

> Those of us who are gifted singers and gifted poets … I know that there are some teachers here who are gifted at both. Let us now find a name that we can call this tree by. Because this is a historic *morula* tree! We have to give it a name befitting it! This tree is the one that will set us free![9]

One of the songs sung by the choir glorified the tree:

Latlhaba laba la dikela,	The sun rose and set,
BOFEPUSU e kae?	Where is BOFEPUSU?
Babereki ba kae?	Where are the workers?
Ba teng fa, mo moruleng wa rona.	They are here under our *morula* tree.

As workers began to go out on forays beyond the grounds, they carried with them green branches cut from trees in the grounds (see Figure 10.2). Although they told me the trees were merely for shade,[10] it seemed evident that the branches were also a metonymic extension of the sacralised strike grounds and the *morula* tree to other places in the land, a further sign of the tree's and ground's powerful sanctification in prayer and song. The tree became a symbolic counterpart to the grand structure of parliament, a rival *kgotla* (traditional public forum, often convened in the shade of very large trees at the centre of Tswana villages) occupied and 'owned' by the workers of Botswana.[11]

Beyond Division: Songs of Rebellion and Worker Solidarity

The strike was a major achievement in itself: the first legal strike in Botswana with clear terms agreed with the government – or so the unions believed. The link to the Arab Spring had also already been established by the press, which proclaimed that 'Botswana joins worldwide uprisings as civil servants prepare to strike' (Tshukudu 2011). The very name given to the strike, 'the mother of all strikes', ironically echoed the wars in the Middle East.

By 27 April, however, what had started as a ten-day strike had turned into a strike that was extended indefinitely, after the government broke its own strike rules. Motshwarakgole stressed the achievement of worker solidarity across class in the strike during a public speech under the tree:

> Yes, it was by intention that we founded ... BOFEPUSU. A union where you would find doctors for members, nurses and labourers for members – the likes of us [jokingly], the Motshwarakgoles of this world! Cleaners, clerical staff and teachers for members, social workers and drivers for members [again jokingly], bootlickers (*malope*) [a reference to the scabs who had not joined the strike] for members, as well as meteorologists for members! It was by intention that we founded such an organization! We deliberately set out to do that!

For Motshwarakgole, long-time leader of the lowest paid, least educated blue-collar manual workers in public service, and himself claiming to be uneducated, the fact that the strike rallies transcended divisions of class and occupation between workers fulfilled a long-held dream. Worker status distinctions were obliterated in shared performance under the tree.[12] The strike mobilised not only blue-collar and white-collar workers but highly qualified professionals – hospital doctors, lawyers from the attorney general's chambers, even revenue collecting officers, accountants by training.

As the salary gap in Botswana has continued to widen hugely, with luxury consumption accentuating class divisions, the marginalisation of industrial-class workers has become ever more evident. Johnson had worked hard to initiate and foster the formation of BOFEPUSU. It was his idea, sold to the other public service workers. The reasons were presented as pragmatic. The federation would give public service unions greater clout in their bargaining with the government. But visionary, even utopian ideals of worker solidarity were explicitly articulated during the strike. Whether this solidarity could outlive the strike or not, what was clear was that a local working-class cultural vernacular was being created through performance, one that drew on generic folk, church and traditional ritual and ceremonial shared across Botswana, and combined them with a modern worker consciousness. Motshwarakgole continued:

> But what [has] stunned me most [are] ... [t]he songs that are sung here, and the way in which they are created ... Every time I come here, I find that there is a new song release! Every time I come here I'm told that, 'they are doing a run-through of their new song, one that they just came up with!' So, truly, this is testament to the amount of talent we have in our midst here!

The grounds in the capital, where I attended the strike, had a festive quality. Dozens of food stalls sold anything from sugar cane, watermelons, mealies (corn on the cob) and large fried *burewurst* (South African-style sausages), to traditional

Figure 10.3 Parasols (photograph by the author).

Figure 10.4 Rangers choir (photograph by the author).

street-corner lunches, *seswa* (beef cooked Tswana style), lamb chops, chicken stew, curries and roasted, cooked pumpkin, beetroot, green cooked vegetables, soups and salads – all for bargain prices. Fizzy drinks and icy-cold water were on display, while peddlers sold oranges and sweets, walking around the grounds pushing supermarket trolleys. The vendors, men and women, were doing a roaring trade. This was the beginning of the strike, and workers still had money in their pockets.

Colourful clothes added to the carnivalesque atmosphere. Workers wore an assortment of multicoloured union T-shirts or boiler suits boasting union logos or past worker rallies. Young women, tall and slim, hair piled in pleated designs, chatted with young men in the crowd, immaculately dressed in the latest fashions. Other workers were dressed casually, in jeans. Standing all day under the tree in the hot sun was an exhausting experience. By 10 o'clock the grounds began to look like a beach resort, with people relaxing in cavernous folding canvas chairs, shaded from the hot sun by multi-coloured golfing umbrellas that serve as parasols in Botswana. Clusters of teachers from the same school sat together (see Figure 10.3).

The dancing and singing were repeated and elaborated day by day as dozens of new songs, dances and choir performances were invented, responding to incidents, satirising, mocking and insulting politicians and senior civil servants who were said to be oppressing the workers. The two competing choirs, Rangers and Mosquito (later renamed International), had formed during the first few days of the strike. Each had its own choir leader and its own style. Sometimes a veteran MWU leader would sing one of the old, traditional, pre-strike, union labour songs from the podium in his booming deep bass voice, but the young strikers preferred the new songs. The old songs seemed passé, of a bygone era. The audience around the tree joined in the choruses and, as the choirs danced, new recruits from the crowd entered the dancing circle, singing and clapping (see Figure 10.4).

The new songs travelled throughout the country. Many contained satirical comments on the current catastrophic state of workers' household economies, defiantly proclaiming that they would survive since they were already chronically indebted to micro-lenders:

Re tswa kgakala le machonisa,	We've come a long way with the moneylenders,
Ga re na sepe.	We don't care.
O a kgaola,	[Even if] he/it cuts, he cuts,[13]
O a tsaya otlhe,	[Even if] he/it takes it all,
Ga re na sepe.	We don't care.

In another song in the same spirit choir members, in a coordinated gesture, enacted throwing their wallets to the ground:

Ditaola di ole Makgolela,	The divining bones say, '*Makgolela*'.[14]
Tsa bolela tsa re Sepatshe,	They (the bones) say that our wallet,
Se ile ka Ian.	Was taken by Ian.[15]

Other songs attacked the Director of Public Service Management (DPSM), MaBakwena, representing the government as the employer. In the words of one very popular song:

Re biletseng MaBakwena,	We call MaBakwena to us,
Re mo tsenye mo ganong la tau ta-oo.	To put her deep in the lion's jaw.
BOFEPUSU ke mocha ochele,	BOFEPUSU goes powerfully on and on,
O kgonwa ke madi a tsenye.	It is only defeated by [lack of] money.

In one version of this song, the singers speak of Rra Boloto, sexually mocking the allegedly castrated vice-president.

MaBakwena, representing the employer, unsurprisingly came in for a good deal of flak, some with crude bodily imagery. Her confrontation with the unions was satirised in the press (see Figure 10.5).

In another 'insult' song,[16] workers attacked false rumours about them.

MaBakwena tlhobola,	MaBakwena remove your blouse,
O kgwata.	To be flogged/beaten.
Kedikilwe, tlhobola o kgwathe.	Kedikilwe, remove your shirt to be flogged.
Rona, re fedisa medumo le dikgang,	We are ending the noise and news/ chatter,
Tsa babareki.	About the workers.

MaBakwena is here portrayed as a petty criminal, to be flogged in the customary court.

As the strike progressed, the number of cartoons increased and songs surfaced about President Ian Khama, the chief target of the workers' wrath. The son of an Englishwoman and Sir Seretse Khama, Ian, a 50-year-old bachelor, was often mocked for the grammatical errors he made in Setswana. The following very popular song was one I first heard when the workers marched to hand over a petition to the Minister of Health, after he had fired hundreds of doctors and nurses.

Ga/Fa le mpotsa ke tla araba,	If you ask, I will answer you,
Ga le mpotsa ke tla ikarabela,	If you ask, I will answer for myself .
Sebatana se Mariri/se maroo,	A predator/lion with a mane/claws,
Ke tla a dirang ka sone/sona?	What can I do with it?

In one interpretation of this song, Khama is a dangerous, out-of-control lion with a mane or claws; alternatively, he appears dangerous but is really impotent. One newspaper quoted further lines (Baaitse 2011: 12), referring to Khama being a lone bachelor:

Figure 10.5 Confrontation between MaBakwena and Johnson Motshwarakgole (cartoon by Selefu, *Monitor*, 16 May 2011, p.12).

Figure 10.6 Bruising battle (cartoon by Selefu, *Monitor*, 20 June 2011, p.8).

Figure 10.7 Khama smashes a car (cartoon by Billie Chiepe, *Monitor*, 16 May 2011, p.6).

Ian ke tau e e tsofetseng, ga ena meno,	Ian is a toothless old lion,
Ga e na ngwana, ga e na 'cheri'.	He has no child, he has no 'darling'.
Sebatana se Mariri.	A hairy predator/lion with a lion's mane.
Ke tla dirang ka sone/sona?	What can I do with it?

Meanwhile, in newspaper cartoons, Khama is depicted as angry, oppressive or trapped (see Figures 10.7, 10.8 and 10.9).

Even more 'insulting' was a song sung in the last days of the strike, that compares Khama with Mugabe and Gaddafi, again signalling the international consciousness of the workers:[17]

Ka ntate, re ka mpa ra tsena ka dikgolegelo,	By my father, we would rather go to prison
Ruri, re ya ikana,	Truly, we swear.
Ka ntate, re ka mpa ra buswa ke Mugabe,	By my father, we'd rather be ruled by Mugabe,
Go na le Khama.	Than by Khama,
Ruri, re ya ikana.	Truly, we swear.
Ka ntate, re ka mpa ra buswa ke Gaddafi,	By my father, we'd rather be ruled by Gaddafi,
Ruri, re ya ikana,	Truly, we swear,
Go na le Khama,	Than by Khama.

Several of the songs mocked the *malope*, the so-called 'bootlickers' or union scabs, who had not gone on strike but spent their time instead currying favour with the government, including government officials and ministers:

MmaBakwena lesa bolope,	MaBakwena leave bootlicking,
Iyelele.	[a cry].
Ka re, ga se maloba,	We say, isn't it just the other day,
O re neela chenchi?	That you gave us small change?
Ga se maloba?	Isn't it the other day?
Kare, wena, Masisi,	We say, you, Masisi,
Lesa Bolope.	Abandon bootlicking
Kare, wena Matambo,	We say, you, Matambo
Lesa Bolope.	Abandon bootlicking
Kare, wena, Ian,	We say, you, Ian,
Lesa bogoma.	Abandon your arrogance.[18]

In a contemporary cartoon (Figure 10.10), Masisi is satirised as a thug. Another bootlicker song criticised Khama for hiding from the workers while going around villages distributing charitable handouts such as blankets in front of BTV's cameras (see Figure 10.14).

Figure 10.8 Khama: 'I'm gonna squeeze 'em' (cartoon by Billie Chiepe, *Monitor*, 6 June 2011, p.6).

Figure 10.9 Khama tied to a tree (cartoon by Selefu, *Mmegi*, 17 May 2011, p.8).

Figure 10.10 Masisi (cartoon by Albert Lekgaba, *Weekend Post*, 4–10 June 2011, p.10).

Fela ga ba re bona,	When they see us,
Ga ba re bona ba iphitha ka batho.	They hide among people.
Heela, malope ba ithaya, ba re.	Hey, the bootlickers think, they say,
Heela, Ian o ithaya ba re bo a ratiwa ke batho,	Hey, Ian thinks he will be liked by people,
O ba phakisa mapai.	[When] He gives them a blanket.

Some songs drew on expressions from other Southern African languages:

Phanzi madoda, re dula re thabile.	Relax guys, we live to be happy.
Ya re MmaBakwena a betwa ke pelo,	When MaBakwena lost her temper,
A kgaola makgabe,	She cut her skirt fringe [she was overwhelmed],
A ntse a re o batlana le badiri.	When searching for the workers.[19]

At the grounds, the choirs entered the circle in a long line, two or three persons deep. Many of the dances were adaptations of widely practised traditional folk, drinking or wedding dances. Having danced round in a circle blowing penny whistles and vuvuzelas, the singers formed a semi-circle, with the onlookers clapping or joining in. But singing was equally an important part of forays beyond the grounds. Some of the songs were borrowed from neighbouring countries, just as some early union songs were translations of worker songs from Europe. I first heard the following song during a march to the Ministry of Health, but it was said to have been first sung when Nelson Mandela was taken to prison, and, I was told, had also been sung at the earlier, 1991 MWU strike:

Rona re saya,	We are being taken away,
Re saya kgolegolong.	Taken away to prison.
Lona lo sale lo lwela,	You remain to struggle for,
Ditshwanelo.	Our rights.
Lefa re sule,	Even if I die,
Re lwela ditshwanelo,	We fought for our rights.
Lona lo sale,	You remain,
Lo lwela ditshwanelo.	To fight for our rights.

After a petition was handed to the minister of health at Civic Hall, unionists streamed out of the gates and, apparently spontaneously, danced down Independence Avenue opposite the main Gaborone shopping mall, blocking the traffic (see Figure 10.11). They formed two blocks, singing favourite insult songs, blowing soccer referee whistles and vuvuzelas and waving the green branches they carried from the strike grounds at GSS. The police stood by impassively. At this point the strike was still very peaceful.

Figure 10.11 Dancing outside the mall (photograph by the author).

I talked to some teachers at the grounds about 'insult' songs (*dipina tse di roganang*). They immediately denied that the songs were insulting. What about the MaBakwena song, I asked. The MWU is the lion, that's not an insult, I was told. What about the song that says that Khama has no child, no sweetheart? That's just a fact – he *is* a predator, a lion; chiefs are lions (but, they added, he is an old lion). What about the song saying that people would prefer Mugabe or Gaddafi to rule them? That's not an insult either. What about *malope* (bootlickers)? That's not an insult, just a statement of fact.

The implication was that the songs were in a Tswana tradition according to which 'a song contains no insult' (*Pina ga e na morogano*).[20] Many old Tswana songs have insults, I was told, but people just tell you that it's from *bogologolo*, long ago. In Botswana, where to insult someone is said to be against the law, these responses point to the roots of union 'insult' songs in the licence accorded traditional songs of rebellion widely sung by commoners against chiefs on ritual occasions throughout Southern Africa (Gluckman 1963b). Even though the songs were spontaneously produced without, it seems, consciously drawing on the past, they were understood in terms of that genre, as indeed are popular local rap songs. Despite this tradition, 'insult' songs did provoke anger from politicians, and later the police.

Notwithstanding this ancient licence, some persons targeted by the songs threatened to sue the singers. I was at the BOFEPUSU offices when a letter arrived from a lawyer, written on behalf of a school headmistress threatening to sue the federation for 200,000 pula unless she received a public apology for 'insulting' songs alleging she was a turncoat and a coward sung by unionists on the occasion of handing her a petition. Head teachers were under immense pressure during the strike since pupils were coming to empty classrooms, which led to rioting and the destruction of property. Despite the fact that in Botswana verbal insults are illegal, Motshwarakgole, who was in the office when the lawyer's letter arrived, expressed his opinion that this did not apply to these 'insult' songs. The federation would consult its lawyers. The songs attached to the letter were, I thought, indeed quite 'insulting':

Kae MaKumela wa lelope wa l egatlapa,	MaKumela is a bootlicker and a coward,
O tshabile go tla go tsaya petition,	She is afraid to take the petition
Gatwe o tsene ka fa tlase go bolao,	It is said she is hiding under the bed.
Selo seo se makgakga,	That thing is rude/disrespectful/vulgar.
Re tsile go mo ruta batho.	We are going to fix her, teach her a lesson.
O batla go kabololwa di tshoka.	She needs to remove the wax from her ears [to listen].
MaKumela o itshekologile.	MaKumela has become polluted/unclean.
O batla go tlhatswiwa ka,	She wants/needs to wash herself with the,
Madi a konyana.	Blood of the lamb.[21]
Bagaetsho, a re rapediseng MaKumela	People, let us pray for MaKumela
MaKumela wa lelope,	MaKumela is a bootlicker,
O re rekisitse.	She has sold us out.
MaKumela o apere dangari,	MaKumela wears dungarees,
O ntshitse letsogo la yone,	With one arm missing.[22]
School head wa mokaloba!	The school head is a giant!

The last of these three songs seemed to be mocking the head's appearance. The words of the songs were attached to the solicitor's letter.

The songs were noticed by the Botswana independent media that followed the strike from day to day, providing reams of commentaries, reports, thought pieces, op-eds and cartoons. A local journalist, Gothataone Moeng, describes the strikers as appropriating 'popular folk songs and hymns – demanding, cajoling, mocking, defying and subverting' (Moeng 2011a: 12). The singers 'lampoon the wealthy upper crust for living it up while the workers do not have money to buy basic essentials' (ibid.). Gospel songs, he continued, had been converted by the workers into 'defiant lyrics' ('We don't want 2 per cent, we want 16 per cent'). He concludes that, while such music was 'common in other Southern African nations that struggled for independence', it was new in Botswana, a nation which had had a 'largely peaceful transition to independence'. Now, however, 'the workers have given birth' to 'an essentially protest music' (see also Baaitse 2011).

The songs represent the more exhilarating moments of fun the strike generated. They were embodied, performative moments of collective creativity and affective solidarity that built up a sense of camaraderie and comradeship across divisions of class, occupation, gender and regional origin. In other respects, however, the strike exacted a heavy toll on workers, especially as it dragged on for eight weeks without resolution, and moved to a confrontational stage when strikers were fired or denied their salaries.

Court Cases and Early Forays beyond the Strike Meeting Grounds

From the start, as the cartoons highlight, the independent media in Botswana, including both the press and radio, supported the strikers, while South African TV news provided regular bulletins. In contrast, the government-controlled national media, the *Botswana Daily News* and Botswana Television (BTV), ignored the strike, as though it was not happening. This news blackout was satirised by the independent press (see Figures 10.12 and 10.13). But despite the official blackout, the strike was clearly regarded in Botswana as the only news in town. Instead of meeting the Unions directly, Khama chose to speak about the strike on his visits to rural areas, broadcast on BTV (see Figure 10.14).

The strike was characterised by forays, incursions and invasions beyond the meeting grounds at GSS. The lengthy court cases between the unions and the government were dramatic events which lasted late into the night and, in one case, into the early hours of the next day. They brought workers together bodily as they sang their way to court or sat for hours on end, packed like sardines into the court's exceedingly hot, limited space, while they listened to complex, technical legal arguments. During the second court case, on 6 May, BOFEPUSU members from all over the country converged on the capital. The crowds at the grounds were vast, a sea of white in sympathy with striking doctors and nurses (see Figure 10.16).

Though Facebook and the internet are not yet universally used in Botswana everyone owns a mobile phone, and texting is constant. Strikers could assemble instantly at the Industrial Court, mobilised by SMS messages sent by union officials, as in one case that began at 7.30 PM and ended at 3.30 in the morning, having lasted most of the night (see Figure 10.15). Workers streamed out of the court house, dressed in white, and danced around the front court plaza and car park, singing the MaBakwena song. There were still at least 100 workers present.

This was a case won by the federation. The fourth (and final) court case in this series was, however, a blow to the unions: the presiding judge confirmed his earlier interdiction, ordering all essential workers back to work, including manual workers who were non-medical staff. The press responded to this back and forth with its own brand of humour. This led to the second phase of the strike.

Figure 10.12 Government news blackout (cartoon by Billie Chiepe, *Monitor*, 30 May 2011, p.6).

Figure 10.13 State-owned media poodles of government (cartoon by Selefu, *Mmegi*, 24 June 2011, p.46).

Figure 10.14 President Khama at a village campfire (*Botswana Guardian*, 13 May 2011, p.12).

Figure 10.15 Advocate Chilisa at the Industrial Court (photograph by the author).

Figure 10.16 Unionists at the Industrial Court (photograph by the author).

The Second Phase of the Strike: Political Confrontation and Cosmopolitan Iterations

On May 3, in announcing a five-day extension of the strike, Johnson Motshwarakgole invoked the Arab Spring explicitly:

> People, let us not forget that now, as never before, nations of North Africa are freeing themselves from the chains that once bound them. The Egyptians and the Libyans are setting themselves free ... [T]hey are setting themselves free, especially taking into account that over there, people get killed for that. But over here, no one can be killed. Our arrangements are in accordance with the law. We deliberately extended this strike by five days.[23]

Speaker after speaker under the *morula* tree reiterated that the law had been subverted by the Industrial Court. The hardening mood was signalled by the workers' refusal to sing the national anthem, which they had touchingly sung a few days earlier during the May Day rally. In the escalating confrontation, doctors and nurses along with many other essential service workers ignored the court order to go back to work (see Figures 10.17, 10.18 and 10.19).

One of the doctors addressed the crowds at the grounds:

> We never used to break the law ... But the courts of law have taught us to break it [i.e. the court's judgement was itself not according to the law]. They showed us how to go about breaking the law! So we are going to follow their example. Like we just finished saying, we came from Marina [the hospital]. We went there to ask the respectable government employees ... who do respectable work ... to come and sit under this tree ...
>
> So we are not to be given instructions, we are too grown [up] for that! A person should sit with us and talk to us ... so that we show him reason, and he shows us reason. Only then will it be a discussion! We can then decide the way forward from there! So we are still going to be under the shade of this tree waiting to be spoken to. A lot of Judases were still at Marina [i.e. doctors who chose not to strike or returned to work at the hospital] ... We reminded them of the hardships they are confronting ... the hardships they have continued to struggle against even as they are still reporting to work ... [A]nd [we] made them appreciate the fact that nobody was going to fix them [i.e., the issues confronting the doctors] for them ... that only they could fix these hardships! Even the nurses at Marina ... we assembled them and told them that they were going to struggle until the road gets bare ... if you do not go to the tree ... so that we force our employer to start to listen to us and talk to us like adults! ... So people, we are not children ... you do not tell us [bedtime] stories. Our case is straight ... [W]e are doctors, and we are going to stay here until ... – if we have to die here, then we will die here. The graveyard isn't full yet!

According to the *Echo*, reporting from Francistown, the number of doctors on strike had doubled since the court verdict (Majube 2011).

Figure 10.17 The Industrial Court orders workers back to work (*Mmegi*, 28 April 2011, p.8).

Figure 10.18 Doctor bins court order (*Telegraph*, 18 May 2011, p.8).

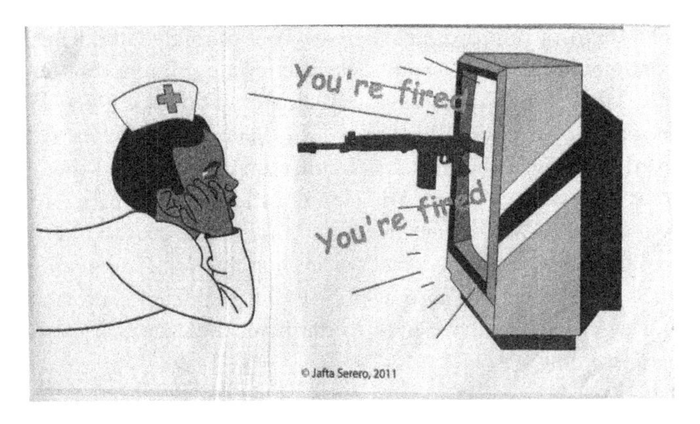

Figure 10.19 Nurse, You're fired! (cartoon by Jafta Serero, *Weekend Post*, 11–17 June 2011, p.10).

Protests elsewhere in the world were echoed in gestures borrowed internationally, though some had undergone a metamorphosis. Thus, for example, every time speakers talked about 'regime change', workers rolled their hands in a wheel motion to indicate change. This gesture took off and became a great source of enjoyment. The word for change, *fetola*, is apparently used for marinating meat on a spit while the spit rotates. In the original UK Uncut protests,[24] however, the same gesture was used to mean, 'I'm bored, get to the point', a meaning adopted in the Israeli protests in the summer of 2011. Workers shouted their appreciation using the old MWU cry, '*Viva babereki* [workers], *viva!*', answered with 'Viva the spirit of no surrender!'. The South American and Cuban roots of 'viva' and 'hula' still echo among trade unionists as these rallying cries travel globally. 'Regime change' too was a concept that had travelled – from debates about the aim of the war in Iraq, to the Arab Spring's removal of long-serving dictators – to be adopted in Botswana, a democratic country where unionists felt strongly that the ruling party had been entrenched in power for too long, and where the president was too autocratic, with a tendency to disregard parliament, and who might be inclined, they feared, to continue in office after his maximum two five-year terms ended. The ambiguity in using the call for regime change – was the call for an immediate revolution or simply a hope of future electoral political change? – gave ammunition to the government during the second phase of the strike.

On 17 May 2011, a week after the final court case, the government fired all striking essential-services workers, including 80 doctors, as well as more than 1000 nurses, cleaners and groundsmen. The news was announced on radio and TV.[25] True to its warning, the government also did not pay the monthly salaries of more than 50,000 workers on strike (Gaotlhobogwe 2011).[26] For Manual Workers' Union members in particular, this was a terminal blow (see Figure 10.21). Given all their loans, mortgages and other commitments, it was questionable whether they could continue to strike, an implication one cartoonist graphically summed up (see Figure 10.20). This cartoon refers to the middle-class lifestyles of workers in the capital, as well as their endemic indebtedness. The press reported that micro-lenders were refusing to lend money to strikers, who were trying to postpone their normal monthly payments on mortgages, car loans, pensions, funeral insurance, utility bills and so forth.

The final phase of the strike began at this point, with BOFEPUSU offering a compromise, and mobilising the nation in support of a negotiated settlement. This was the phase in which issues of morality and social justice beyond the law became significant as the federation reached out to make alliances.

Social Justice Unionism: From Spectacular Forays to Mobilising the Nation

Botswana is a small country. Most people in public positions know each other, and networks are widely ramifying. The strike affected everyone. Many had visited the strike grounds in their respective towns, children had been rioting

Figure 10.20 When disaster 'strikes' (cartoon by Albert Lekgaba, *Weekend Post*, 28 May–3 June 2011, p.10).

Figure 10.21 Thin and fat men before and after the strike (cartoon by Albert Lekgaba, *Weekend Post*, 14–20 May 2011, p.10).

Figure 10.22 Ministerial flight (*Telegraph*, 18 May 2011).

at schools, hospitals were struggling to cope, businesses were not being paid, relatives of strikers were feeling the pinch, welfare recipients had not received their benefits. Day after day, for more than six weeks, the media had been dominated by reports and analyses of the strike and its implications. As it became increasingly evident that President Khama would not bend, that MaBakwena lacked the authority to negotiate, and that the courts had failed to deliver, so too BOFEPUSU turned to mobilise a whole range of civil-society actors.

In a sense, from the start the strike had had the 'feel' of a social movement. It was culturally creative, and its participants constantly reflected upon themselves, working collectively to forge a shared identity that would unite their different unions and suppress divisions between them. If both the leadership and ordinary workers made huge efforts to achieve unity, their *modi operandi* differed radically. The workers at the strike grounds drew inspiration from traditional performance genres, and fused them spontaneously into a new, shared, worker ethos. They drew on international worker and protest movements in gestures, slogans and songs, and made these their own. As the strike progressed, there was a heightening sense that this was truly a people's protest, reaching beyond fruitless negotiations in stuffy committee rooms, far removed from the corridors of power and yet tangibly 'political', a lived politics.

Could one describe the strike as an expression of social movement unionism? In the South African context, social movement unionism (SMU) arose when unions forged alliances with community-based groups, other social movements and political parties, such as the anti-apartheid democratic movement and the ANC during the transition to democracy (Adler & Webster 1999; Barchiesi 2011: 55–7), the Treatment Action Campaign (TAC) and the Anti-Privatisation Forum, a community-based movement (Barchiesi 2011: 158).[27] This was true of the 2011 Wisconsin protests as well (Collins 2012). In Botswana, in the absence of the kind of powerful civic movements present in South Africa and the USA, the federation sought other allies within civil society. Sometimes defined as 'social justice unionism' (Dibben 2007), the assumption is that such new labour movements 'espouse radical change' (Scipes 1992), workplace democracy and gender equality (Waterman 1993; Hirschsohn 1998, 2007).[28]

Writing about the 2011 strike in Botswana, Monageng Mogalakwe argues that 'Social movement unionism recognises the broadness and the interconnectedness of the interests of workers as citizens, commuters, consumers, parents, rent payers, and voters, … [it] supersedes the notion of a single class identity and interests' (Mogalakwe 2011c). The stress here is on associational networks. In all this definitional elaboration, however, I want to suggest that what is lost is the original stress in new social movement (NSM) theory, as formulated by Alberto Melucci (1989, 1996), on culture, creativity and identity. Although the Botswana 2011 public service strike was not in any simple sense post-materialist, the strike combined materialist claims with a post-materialist moral demand for social justice, an innovative symbolic and cultural reconstitution of both the state and workers-as-citizens, and widespread mobilisation of civil society associations to create a new, hybrid social movement formation.

In her masterly account of the 2011 Wisconsin protests, Jane Collins analyses the convergence in a single movement of a wide range of social actors with diverse economic and political stakes: public- and private-sector trade unions, community-action, anti-racist and anti-poverty groups, the gay movement, the interfaith coalition for social justice, and 'massive numbers of non-union community members', leading her to wonder 'what kind of alliance or amalgamated movement was emerging in this snowy square in the upper Mid-West' to occupy the Wisconsin state capitol building (Collins 2012: 2).

Such diversity highlights the futility of previous narrow theoretical approaches to the rise of social movements that stress, for example, 'post-materialist' identity politics (Melucci 1989), resource mobilisation in economic and political protest, or citizen rights mobilisations against the state (see Edelman 2001). Waterman (1999) too points to resemblances between the new 1980s labour movements in Poland or South Africa and new alternative social movements (NASM) in an age of globalisation: democratic, peace, feminist and environmental movements, all drawing on international networks.[29] The mass protests in North Africa and Wisconsin suggest that labour has once again become internationalist, insofar as it has rearticulated itself with popular democratic struggles (ibid.: 255), and promotes a broader social vision (ibid.: 258). Waterman coins the term 'New Social Unionism' to reflect the affinity within these new social movements. I prefer, however, to speak simply of 'new social movement unionism' to highlight explicitly the cultural dimensions of worker mobilisation in Botswana as they called for justice and forged a new, shared identity.

Initially, however, it was unclear whether the strike was really about social justice. President Khama, for one, accused strikers on BTV and in the press of selfishly and unpatriotically demanding a pay rise when, he claimed, more than half the population were unemployed and the country was still recovering from an unprecedented recession that had virtually brought it to its knees.[30] Vice-President Merafhe mockingly noted the vast number of 'luxury cars' filling the strike grounds at GSS (see Makgapha 2011a). Newspapers and cartoons recognised that a 16 per cent across-the-board settlement would favour high-earning civil servants, at the expense of manual workers (see Figure 10.21).

The move towards greater equality and a just redistribution of resources was first articulated in a BOFEPUSU delegates' conference, gathering together regional representatives from all the unions. The leadership put to delegates the radical proposal to redistribute the 3 per cent the government had offered, some 400 million pula, in a 'pyramid structure' so that low-paid workers would receive the lion's share of the pay rise while higher-paid employees above Grade 4 would receive nothing. The idea had originated with the Botswana Council of Churches (BCC), whose Anglican bishop offered an 'ethical solution' to the strike. It was supported by BOCCIM, the Botswana equivalent of the Confederation of British Industry. Most remarkable for me was the fact that none of the more highly paid civil servants and professionals in the federation, such as doctors, rejected the proposal, even though it would mean relinquishing the pay rise they were striking for. One of the striking doctors addressed the delegates' conference:

> The issue of salaries negotiation ... particularly the pyramid scheme ... – we agree with it with all our hearts. The doctors have sent me to tell you that although some of you under this tree may be on the smaller end of the pyramid scheme [i.e., will be awarded a lower pay settlement], we should encourage it, because in the long run it will show that selfishness is not within us, but it comes from way up there [referring to the top echelons of the government].

Despite the fact that even parliament had issued a communiqué endorsing a distribution of the increment 'on the principle of equity',[31] the government continued to object to a tiered pay settlement, insisting on an across-the-board rise since, it argued, this was a cost-of-living issue – despite, as Motsamai told the conference, the unfairness of a pay rise that meant that, 'The one who receives 45,000 pula could pay three people with his 3 per cent! So we cannot agree to that ... The preachers are praying on this!' he added.

This mobilisation of support and sympathy for the strikers across the social spectrum, from bishops to industrialists, from NGO leaders to politicians, along with the demand for a more equitable distribution of resources, a social justice vision, underscored the transformation of the strike into a social justice union movement.[32] The strike was no longer simply about pay. Pleading for a 'suspension' of the strike, which appeared to have reached a deadlock, Motshwarakgole hinted at this greater vision:

> In the beginning, we were all about sitting under a tree and demanding our 16 per cent, but now it is broader than that! ... This is proving to be the same journey that was taken by the Children of Israel, that ended up taking 40 years!

Implicitly, he was voicing the hope that, even if it was unsuccessful, the strike would lead to radical change, the toppling in the long term of the entrenched BDP establishment.

His comment that dealing with this government was like 'sitting around a bonfire with a madman' was confirmed when, on 9 June, ten days after the delegates' conference and three days after a grand prayer meeting appealing for reconciliation, an official government press release announced the suspension of all negotiations with BOFEPUSU until the strike was over, on the grounds that the strike had become 'political'.

Ministerial Escapades

Once it had suspended the negotiations, the government embarked on a countrywide information campaign to 'explain' its response, sending ministers to convene public assemblies with local 'communities'. Well informed, the federation sent workers to attend these meetings and make sure the ministers had something to answer for. Strikers who had packed a *kgotla* meeting in Tlokweng, for example, told me they asked questions the minister was unable to answer. They returned in triumph to the GSS strike grounds, waiving the green branches of *mopani* trees they had carried from the grounds, singing and dancing as they entered the grounds before forming a circle in front of the stage.

At another *kgotla* meeting at Mogoditsane, we waited and waited before eventually being informed that the minister (or was it ministers?) had 'run away', apparently fearing the multitude. Such failed meetings were reported by the local press and media, which had a field day, describing ministers running through the mud, desperately jumping into their vehicles. The captions tell it all: 'Masisi runs for dear life', 'Masisi, Rakhudu booed out of "secret meeting"', 'Ministers run for cover' and 'Ministers flee from audience' (see Figure 10.22).[33]

The flavour of these meetings can be gauged from the following report in *Mmegi*:

> Maxwell Motowane (Assistant Minister of Local Government), followed by Gaotlhaetse Matlhabaphiri, Assistant Health Minister and his boss, Health Minister Dr John Seakgosing trailing behind cut a comical picture of serious men running away from something terrible. [E]ven the police officers … stood perplexed … The race, which took a little less than two minutes nearly turned ugly as the ministers threw themselves into a government vehicle, as the driver floored the accelerator nearly colliding into another vehicle … The audience had been waiting patiently … not knowing that the dignitaries were actually watching them from the Mogoditshane Kgotla office windows. So as everyone was trying to get a better seat for the meeting, the trio bolted like a bullet out of a gun, stunning everyone. (Keoreng 2011b)

A *Botswana Guardian* reporter added:

> The only small obstacle on their way back to their vehicles was a patch of water coming from a leaking pipe but Seakgosing this time around did not mind getting dirty and ran through the water. When the *Botswana Guardian* team arrived at the Mogoditshane Kgotla, people were taking pictures of the minister's footmarks … 'This is a souvenir', declared one, taking pictures with his cell phone. (Kavahematui 2011b)

But what had the ministers feared? The assembled workers were as peaceful and good humoured as they had been throughout the strike. The stunts were fun and there was certainly no threat of violence. There was clowning and parodying of absent ministers.

The Prayer Meeting

By this time, there was no doubt that the strikers had humiliated the government publicly, and made a mockery of its venerable ministers. The workers' frustration at the government's intransigence was also becoming more tangible. It was in this context that an open prayer meeting for peace, reconciliation and dialogue assembled at the Mall end of the GSS strike grounds, called five days after the above events, on Sunday afternoon, 5 June. This was a meeting of the great, the good and the noble: three church federations, including the Botswana Council of Churches, MPs, chiefs, government ministers, and former President Masire, now in his eighties, who had been working tirelessly behind the scenes with the churches to find a settlement.

Figure 10.23 Peace meeting (photograph by the author).

The speakers emphasised that the strike was legal. They asked for peace and reconciliation for the sake of God and the country. During the closing prayers, congregants raised their arms, shutting their eyes (see Figure 10.23). Masega, the president of BOFEPUSU, sat next to Minister Masisi. In her speech, Masega called for reconciliation and asked forgiveness for the suffering the strike had caused in schools and hospitals, while stressing that the strike was legal. At the end of the meeting, she and Minister Masisi embraced, to the delight of the gathered press and BTV. These conciliatory gestures, as it turned out, were badly misjudged: both the government and the press claimed the federation had 'apologised'.

Kagiso, my lodge's manager, who attended as a member of one of the evangelical churches, was deeply moved by the event. 'It was wonderful', she said. She spoke passionately. 'No, the union hadn't lost because they had been outspoken and had shown they were not afraid! There has never been such a strike in Botswana before, and the government would know in the future that they can't just ignore the unions', she added hopefully.

The strikers were back at the tree the next day, while BOFEPUSU leaders remained locked in negotiations, apparently with the higher echelons of the government rather than the DPSM. At this point, the workers at the grounds echoed the sentiment of the prayer meeting – that the strike had been peaceful, and that Botswana was a peaceful country. Two primary schoolteachers told me about Masisi. 'Did you see how humble he was?' they asked. They had seen him on BTV. 'The government has realised', they said, 'how powerful the unions are'. 'The strike has definitely had an impact', they stressed.

A couple of youngish men complained bitterly about the pathetic pay of low-paid government workers. Government policies were a charade, they said. The Ipelegeng Project (work welfare) and so-called 'backyard gardening' were merely disguised welfare, but the money was taken from the same budget as public service salaries. Ipelegeng workers should get rights like any other worker, they added. The Ministry of Agriculture was failing, and the Botswana Meat Commission was in a state of collapse, now reduced to selling to private butchers (due to an outbreak of foot and mouth).

Why did President Khama disdain the civil servants while agreeing to meet the miners? They suggested that all these BDP ministers had private shareholding companies, and thus a greater interest in the stability of the private sector than the civil service. They were the *bahumi*, the rich, the greedy fat cats, *bomakgorwane*. They echoed the discourse of the worldwide Occupy movement: a few tycoons, bankers, financiers, privileged politicians and civil servants have enriched themselves at the expense of the people. Several teachers stressed that, beyond pay, there were many other problems to be resolved in the teachers' case, that the minister of education had, for example, been saying, falsely, that teachers get a 15 per cent housing allowance.

The general feeling was that the government had been humiliated, taught a lesson it would not easily forget. The feeling was that Khama must talk to the workers. The previous night's cabinet meeting (on a Sunday) had gone on until almost midnight. Striking workers began the morning optimistic, expecting the negotiations to be concluded quite soon. Almost six hours later, at 2.30 PM, there was still no word from the union leadership. Eventually, at about 5 PM, people gave up waiting. Later, it was learnt that the government had offered virtually nothing: it would 'allow' workers to reapply for their jobs, and it had offered 3 per cent across the board from September. That was all.

I think it was Kagiso, my lodge's manager, who said, 'Botswana is a very Christian (or religious) country'. When things get tough, the church leaders have to step in. But neither prayer nor the federation's ability to disrupt services had swayed a president determined to stick to monetarist principles at any cost in order to repay the national debt. By now, the call for the president himself to enter into dialogue with the unions personally had been elevated to a supreme value in its own right. At stake was the *seriti*, the dignity, of the federation and public service workers. President Khama had agreed to meet the miners' leaders, and even to reopen the case of the 461 miners dismissed in 2005. Yet he seemed to disdain government workers, the very people who made Botswana an orderly, transparent, functioning democracy. Three days later the government issued a press release:

> It has become clear that the strike has been diverted by the unions and opposition parties from being a dispute over public service wages to a political campaign, with a view to winning favour from those on strike and the public. As stated in earlier statements, some of these activities and utterances are unlawful and have the potential to cause public disorder and destabilize our peace-loving nation.

The press statement by the office of the president continued:

> In view of the fact that the government has made its position on the economy clear, [and in view of] the politicisation of the strike and the unlawful activities and utterances by the unions and opposition party leadership, the government has decided to suspend all wage negotiations until the strike has ended.

There was a surprising absence of commentary in the press on why the Botswana government had decided to reject the equitable 3 per cent pyramid structure, redistributing the 3 per cent offered to favour the lowest paid, a solution widely supported, even by parliamentarians. Two days before the Sunday prayer meeting, on Friday, 4 June, in a stormy seven-hour special caucus of parliament convened by Dr Margaret Nasha, speaker of the National Assembly, MPs agreed to send a delegation to President Khama urging him to support the 3 per cent salary increment distributed 'on the principle of equity'.[34] The *Botswana Gazette* reported that, out of 38 MPs attending, all except five BDP members agreed that the increase should be distributed in a pyramid form (Rantsimako 2011: 18).

President Khama refused to meet the delegation or agree to the pyramid solution. There were rumours of divisions even in cabinet (Basimanebotlhe 2011b; Kanani 2011b), though these were later denied by the office of the president. Apart from justifying the refusal on the grounds that the 3 per cent was a 'cost of living allowance', the impression left was that President Khama was determined to humiliate the unions by not giving an inch. They in turn had humiliated him and his ministers publicly. In the battle for honour and dignity, both sides came out bruised.

The End of the Strike

Despite the prayer meeting's call for peace, the strike ended in conflict. From the point of view of BOFEPUSU's leadership, the strike was unsustainable. They did not have the funds to help striking unionists who had not been paid for almost two months, though some of the other public service unions were able to give their members loans. Effectively, the government had used the strike to 'retrench' industrial-class workers, replacing those dismissed – cleaners, rubbish collectors and drivers – with employees of contract firms, without even the usual requirement to negotiate an exit package. They also threatened to replace dismissed doctors and nurses. There were signs of increasing violence, greatly exacerbated by the police's over-response to minor infringements, such as road blocks and setting fire to tyres in the very last days of the strike.

At this point, two days after the prayer meeting, the mood was sombre. At the GSS strike grounds, the young chair of the Gaborone strike committee spoke at length, invoking the figures of Mandela, Archbishop Tutu, Martin Luther King and President Obama, who had all made sacrifices, he said, for the sake of a dream that one day a black man, walking 'arm in arm with a white man', would become a national leader. It was a blustery, cold day. The trio of BOFEPUSU leaders arrived and mounted the stage. Motshwarakgole was delegated with the difficult task of persuading the strikers to suspend the strike. It was a suggestion he had made before. The response was vociferous and unanimous. Several workers took the microphone, standing beneath the stage, and spoke against ending the strike. Several of the speakers were women, and they were all adamant that the strike should go on. As one said to me, 'We have been striking for seven weeks, how can we go back to work now, with nothing?' Eventually, Motshwarakgole asked for a show of hands. Virtually all the workers present raised their hands to continue the strike. It was a dramatic moment. The leadership rushed off to a press conference. By then it was close to 4.30 PM, time to disperse. The Gaborone chair made the final speech. He told the crowd there had been tire burning in Francistown, clashes with the police in Molepolole and, it seemed, elsewhere as well.

Next day in Gaborone the police responded disproportionately, with tear gas and rubber bullets. This contrasted with the previous eight weeks of the strike, when the police were remarkably invisible at the rallies. Now, however, they encircled the perimeter fence of the strike grounds, three or four policemen standing together, in full riot gear, with shields, batons and helmets (see Figure 10.25). One policeman filmed the assembled workers.

It was early morning prayers, 9 June. In one of the prayers, the workers turned away from the stage towards the periphery fence, facing the police, arms lifted upwards and palms open, their eyes closed (see Figure 10.24). Later, when I asked them if they were gesturing towards the police to leave the grounds, they said no, they were just praying. Several of the preachers were women (it was a Thursday, women's preaching day). One of them said, 'We are now in prison' – a reference to being surrounded by police. The prayers went on for much longer than usual, until after 10 AM. At about 10.30, the federation leadership arrived once again. Motshwarakgole made yet another speech explaining why the strike should be suspended – not ended – citing the experience of the 1991 MWU strike in which the union successfully sued the government in the Court of Appeal, and all striking workers who had been dismissed were fully reinstated and compensated.

This time the call for suspension seemed to hold, unlike the other day. But when I arrived at the grounds about noon the following day, 10 June, I found the workers caucusing in circles, each union in its own huddle. Some carried banners, declaring 'Regime Change: Ian Must Go'. The caucuses echoed Tswana *moreros*, village caucuses or moots, and as with these, workers appeared to be extremely well versed in deliberative democracy. I witnessed the MWU caucus group as it was conducting its discussion. After a while the workers

Figure 10.24 Facing the police (photograph by the author).

Figure 10.25 Police in riot gear (photograph by the author).

divided into two blocks – on the left were the majority, the nay-sayers who wanted the strike to continue (*tswelelo*), and on the right, a relatively large group in favour of suspension.

After they dispersed, I chatted with a young man both about his opinions – he favoured returning to work – and about the violence of the previous day. He said it was the police who started it. The workers were dancing around the periphery singing, mocking them, when the police began lobbing canisters of teargas into the grounds. Two 'insult' songs in particular appeared to have incensed the police:

Majelathoke ke lona, *Le loilwe ke mang?*	You, eaters on the side [i.e., sell-outs], Who bewitched you?
Mpimpi tsa ba abuse, *Sokela koo rona!* *Re a tsamaela.*	Traitors/stooges of the ruler,[35] Away with you! We are going forward.

The young man had crossed the road and been shot with a rubber bullet in the upper leg. He wasn't doing anything. An employee of the Department of Forestry, he was, after eight years, still only paid 1300 pula a month. It was impossible to get ahead, he said. He had a girlfriend expecting his baby who worked in IT. She had found a better paying job than his, then left him because he wasn't earning enough.

We discussed the huge pay gap in Botswana, and the fact that, according to him, all the top ministers and MPs owned shares and land gained with insider knowledge. His example was a minister who had bought a farm in the Ghanzi area in 1991, knowing a road was planned through it, then demanded millions of pula in compensation, and finally parcelled out the land into plots for more millions. He said he liked his job and was trained for it, but the pay was so abysmally low – he paid 550 pula rent in Tlokweng, plus insurance, food and medical insurance, and sent money to his parents. After that there was nothing left. He received no pay last month.

He told me that top civil servants like Molelo, the permanent secretary to the president, earn around 50,000 pula a month. When they go to the ATM, he said, they never take out less than 2000 pula (about £200) at a time, but they pay their servants derisory wages. He mentioned that certain lawyers had offered their services free to the federation.

Others I spoke with favoured continuing the strike. One was a young man from the Land Registry Office who said he was a key worker, so the office couldn't function without him. Out of 200 plus workers in his office, 78 were on strike, just over a third.

At about 2.30 PM the unions reconvened under the tree and reported back on their caucusing. All five unions recommended continuing with the strike. One man I met, from the teachers' union BOSETU, commented that he did not know why the leaders had made the decision to suspend the strike in such a hurry, not giving workers an opportunity to express their opinions. In addition to the decision to continue the strike, the workers condemned all violence and, it appeared, the central leadership as well. The minutes were written in English but presented in Setswana, with some rapporteurs struggling to find the right Setswana words. The crowd, however, kept insisting: Setswana, Setswana! The demand for Setswana only highlighted the indigenous, popular roots of the strike. The vote to reject the suspension of the strike was unanimous. In other places, the press reported that workers had accused the leadership of being sell-outs.

We waited and waited for the leadership to appear as promised. In the meantime, speakers entertained the crowd. Finally, we dispersed, frustrated. It was Friday afternoon. The chair of the GSS strike grounds said a prayer in Kalanga, and told workers to reconvene as usual under the tree on Monday morning. Meanwhile, the press reported that other regions were extremely angry at the decision to suspend the strike, with Francistown accusing the leadership of not being 'genuine' and being 'bribed' by the BDP (Kologwe 2011: 2). The leadership was caught in a dilemma: only a total strike of the whole workforce could have defeated the government, but that had not happened and some workers were drifting back to work. Many had lost their jobs.

Federation officers went round the country trying to convince the strikers that suspending the strike was the right decision. The MWU national treasurer went up north, to Francistown, Masunga and other centres in the north-east. Everywhere, she told me, she encountered huge opposition. Two officers toured the Kgalagadi, one went to Maun. Everywhere, according to the local newspapers, the strikers objected to suspending the strike, arguing that the proper consultation process had not been followed. In Francistown they said that the BOFEPUSU leadership should resign. Exceptionally, in Kanye strikers approved the suspension.

The Gaborone strikers had agreed to reconvene as usual on Monday morning. When I arrived at the grounds, however, later than usual, I found the whole place deserted. There were no cars and no strikers, only pieces of paper fluttering in the wind. I later learnt that about 200 strikers had stayed at the grounds until 2 PM, when the police arrived in full riot gear carrying a giant red (!) banner declaring:

> All persons assembled here are commanded in the name of the PRESIDENT of the Republic of Botswana to disperse peacefully and go to their homes or work. Persons who disobey this order will be dispersed by force, which may include RIFLE FIRE. All persons remaining here after this order are liable to arrest and imprisonment.

After holding up the banner, the police advanced on the strikers brandishing guns and baseball bats (see Figure 10.26). At this point the workers dispersed, running to the civic hall, the Central Mall and the Anglican church. Giving chase, the police arrested some 30 people randomly at the civic hall. They were later released. Dumo Buko, leader of the opposition BNF and a human rights lawyer, who was at the GSS grounds, accused the police of acting illegally. A police spokesman claimed, however, that 'according to the law eight or more

Figure 10.26 Police banner (*Midweek Sun*, 15 June 2011, front page).

people gathering together without a licence amount to an illegal gathering' (Galeitse 2011: 3). The jury is still out on this matter.

The shocking belligerence of the banner, threatening to use gun fire against a relatively small, peaceful assembly gathered in the middle of a vast, empty football field, has to be considered alongside the terrified response by the government ministers to the crowds of peaceful strikers attending their meetings. No wonder one of the MWU leaders commented to me mournfully that 'We live in a military dictatorship!'

The police threat of violence points to a yawning social gap between the government and its own respectable, educated and hard-working civil servants. Rather than recognising that the strikers are 'one of us', and the strike a peaceful, mostly middle-class rebellion, the government seemed to have convinced itself that the strikers were a rampaging mob, out of control like the rioting school pupils.

The rejection of the federation leadership's call to suspend the strike points clearly to the new social movement dynamic of the strike, to the autonomy, self-empowerment and democratic tradition that the strike rallies had produced. In their caucusing and open democratic debate, strikers were in effect '"prefiguring" the just society they hoped to create' (Armstrong & Bernstein 2008: 79; Graeber 2009). While the leadership recognised pragmatically that it was urgent to reach an agreement with the government regarding the dismissed workers, striking unionists could not be blamed for feeling that to return to work would be to admit defeat.

Conclusion

This chapter has analysed what I have termed 'new social movement unionism', Botswana style: the collective creation of a shared worker identity and ethos, drawing on local popular culture and ritual, traditional modes of celebration, and echoing cosmopolitan themes from protest movements elsewhere in the world in the aftermath of the Arab Spring. In particular, it showed, newly invented 'insult' songs called politicians to account and reminded them that, from the president downwards, 'the chief is chief only by the grace of the people'. The emergent protest movement that the workers shaped collectively was not only exhilarating: it endowed strikers with a sense of empowerment, dignity and autonomy, and united them across divisions of class, occupation, gender, education and income. But unlike the familiar old labour movement with its international political roots expressed in rousing songs of protest, solidarity, hardship and struggle, this protest was youthful, humorous, satirical and self-consciously part of a global movement, reflecting a radical generational and political shift.

Despite being largely a middle class rebellion, the strikers' courageous willingness to stand up and be counted, to resist what was widely seen to be an unjust, authoritarian government endorsing the growing gap between rich and poor, emerged spontaneously, and over time it swept the whole of Botswana in its wake, from priests and chiefs to parliamentarians and ordinary folk. The values invoked in the public domain were those of fairness, justice and a return to the welfare state. Although the strike seemed, on the face of it, to fail in its stated objectives, confronted by a powerful government determined to pursue prudent monetary policies and eliminate the national deficit before the next elections, scheduled for 2014, and although some workers lost their jobs and most were not paid for over two months, the events of April to June 2011 were nevertheless a watershed in the history of Botswana. During the eight weeks of the strike, strikers forged a new national and workers' consciousness, and gave notice that ordinary citizens were determined to protect Botswana's 45-year-old tradition of democracy, freedom of speech and egalitarian values.

In Egypt, the popular uprising followed mass strikes by labour unions, and was supported by them once the protests began (Alexander 2011). In Botswana, the felt experience of owning the 'political', and the obliteration of the usual social divisions between workers, did not occur in what Benjamin called 'homogeneous, empty time' (Benjamin 1968: 261). It was grasped by workers as a significant moment in history in which, as Benjamin put it, 'time stands still' (ibid.: 262); a time in which prior visions of authority were reworked, extended and revitalised in rhetoric and popular culture. As Sertag Manoukian has argued with regard to the 2009 Iranian post-election protests, the experience of 'suspended time' linked the Iranian protestors to earlier historical moments when people took to the streets, and in which political subjectivity was 'remolded and reconstituted' (Manoukian 2010, 2011; see also Nugent 2012). In Botswana, where past mass protests were few, protestors linked themselves, in time, to ritual traditional local protest genres and, in space, to world protests elsewhere, in Southern Africa and the Middle East.

CHAPTER ELEVEN

The Political and Moral Economy of the 2011 Strike: Public Rhetoric, Conflict and Policy

Throughout the strike a range of public actors debated its significance for Botswana as a democratic country. They included trade unionists, opposition and ruling party leaders and parliamentarians, journalists, academics, business leaders, student activists and ministers of religion. Framing the debate were six issues: first, the call for Botswana's president, Ian Khama, to enter into 'dialogue'; second, in the face of his obdurate refusal, the constitutional limits of his executive power and accountability to parliament; third, the current state of Botswana's labour laws, following industrial court decisions reached during the strike; fourth, the need for an independent broadcasting authority following the news blackout regarding the strike by the government-controlled Botswana TV (BTV) and the *Botswana Daily News*; fifth, the evolving power relations between the unions and the government, dramatised in their political and legal manoeuvrings and counter-manoeuvrings during the strike and its aftermath. Linked to this, the sixth issue – the outcome of the strike – concerned the government's unqualified refusal to reach a pay settlement, and its decision not to reinstate some 750 dismissed essential-service workers. In response, the Manual Workers' Union began appealing multiple cases that had been lost during the strike in the Industrial Court and High Court, thus initiating a further round of litigation discussed fully in Chapter 12.

Winning legal battles, as we saw in Chapter 7, does not guarantee winning the war without a concerted political struggle. In this chapter I proceed, first, to consider the build-up of the conflict; and second, to outline the moral disagreements about policy priorities between the government and the public sector unions; and, finally, related to both these issues, the negative adversarial rhetoric targeting President Khama's persona that reached a crescendo during and after the strike.

Politics and the Build-Up to the Strike

The 2011 strike marked a watershed: it was the first legal strike (barring one diamond sorters' strike) in the history of Botswana.[1] It tested the newly domesticated International Labour Organisation conventions. The unfolding events came to be seen as experimental, testing the limits of both parties' power and the law itself. Botswana's industrial relations were, and still are, at a formative stage in which each conflict is also a learning experience (Mogalakwe 2011a, 2011b).

The strike responded to multiple grievances: rising inflation, privatisation, forced early retirement of high-level civil servants and the delaying of the new National Public Service Bargaining Council (NPSBC), due partly to government procrastination. Its demand that unions gain recognition afresh was challenged by the Botswana Federation of Public Sector Unions in an urgent application to the High Court, after the labour commissioner refused to recognise the federation as a single bargaining party within the envisaged bargaining council. The delay was also due to wrangling among public sector unions, arising from prior conflict between the MWU and its breakaway union, the Botswana Government Workers' Union (BOGOWU) the latter a member of the federation's rival organisation, the Botswana Federation of Trade Unions (BFTU). There were also challenges from the Trainers' and Allied Workers' Union (TAWU), another BFTU member. Both these small public sector unions challenged BOFEPUSU in the Industrial Court, arguing that each of the seven recognised public sector unions should be equally represented in the bargaining council. The case was heard in the Industrial Court on 29 April 2011, some ten days after the strike started, leading to a further postponement in the creation of the new council.[2]

For their part, the government and President Khama as head of the ruling Botswana Democratic Party (BDP) rejected claims by public sector unions that they had the right to a say in national politics. This may have been a response to the MWU's support for Faction B of the BDP, as we saw in Chapter 6. According to one journalist:

> In the last general elections [i.e. 2009], the trade union movement, this time represented by the Manual Workers' Union, launched a campaign known as 'The Enemies of Democracy'. The union campaigned to have most of the BDP's A-Team candidates rejected by the voters. The union circulated leaflets and posters depicting MPs such as Jacob Nkate, Mompati Merafhe and Phandu Skelemani as enemies of democracy. There are various accounts as to what effect that campaign had on the actual voting, but a majority of observers have argued that the losses of such candidates as Nkate in Ngami and the dramatic slashing of leads [that] such figures as Skelemani carried from the 2004 General Elections had a lot to do with the campaign. (Motlogelwa 2011)

Interference in the elections themselves was preceded by interference in the BDP Kanye convention. Justin Hunyepa suggests that the replacement of Minister of Presidential Affairs Daniel Kwelagobe, the unions' friend and supporter, by Margaret Nasha, may have been one cause of the delay in the implementation of the Public Service Act: the unions' 'open political party campaigns ... has infuriated government' (Hunyepa 2009).

Even before the strike began, leaders of BOFEPUSU had asserted their right to make political interventions. Section 5(5) of the Public Service Act (2008) makes explicit that government employees 'shall not ... publicly speak or demonstrate for or against any politician or political party'.[3] Although Motshwarakgole was not a government employee, his fellow leaders in the federation were, having been temporarily seconded from their jobs. While the government argued that 'public servants are obliged to remain politically neutral', so that 'uttering political statements is a direct breach of the conditions of their employment', federation leaders countered that they were acting as *union* representatives, not individual government employees, and that 'unions are governed by the Trade Unions' and Employers' Organisations Act (TUEOA); [thus] the provisions of the Public Service Act do not apply to them'. Federation leaders further promised to 'challenge the act that bars them from engaging in active politics' (Makgapha 2011c).

President Khama had been advised by the attorney general to stay out of the government's negotiations with BOFEPUSU during the strike. But he was undoubtedly already hostile to the federation because of its political interference in the affairs of the BDP and its attempts to influence the outcome of the national elections. This may explain his refusal to accord BOFEPUSU the respect of engaging with it in direct dialogue. This disrespect, and the refusal to consider their demand for a pay rise, merely exacerbated the mutual hostility between the government and the unions, in a schismogenetic process that continued to escalate.

In November 2011, the government suspended Goretetse Kekgonegile, president of the Botswana Land Board and Local Authorities Workers' Union (BLLAWU), who was also the publicity officer of BOFEPUSU, from his job as principal social welfare officer in the North-West District Council on the grounds that he had breached his conditions of employment, apparently for intervening in the opposition's umbrella talks.[4] Kekgonegile had personally delivered a solidarity message at the Botswana Congress Party's (BCP) tenth national conference in October 2011. On 16 December, an e-mail attachment to a letter from the Director of Public Service Management (DPSM) to the secretary general of BOFEPUSU complained of 'unpalatable and provocative language', sometimes 'hostile, with political overtones', used by delegates in their 'comments, songs and speeches' against government ministers present at the annual general convention of the Botswana Public Employees' Union (BOPEU). The letter quotes Sections 36 and 37 of the Public Service Act, which state, among others things, that any act is a misconduct that 'tends to bring the public service into disrepute', and that it is a misconduct for an employee 'to engage in any activity outside his or her official duties which is likely to involve him or her in political controversy' or 'otherwise conduct himself or herself in a disgraceful, improper or unbecoming manner or, while on duty, is grossly discourteous to members of the public or any person'.[5] Evidently, the federation members' songs of rebellion had found their target.

The delay in signing the Public Service Act, apart from postponing the establishment of the NPSBC, had also allowed the government to 'retire' 17 senior public servants from the Ministry of Works and Transport before the age of 50, thus putting it on a collision course with BOPEU. The new Public Service Act, according to one journalist, outlawed 'the appointing authority's power to retire a public officer, at his discretion' (Modise 2010).[6] Section 28a of the Public Service Act states clearly that, barring exceptional circumstances, 'an employee shall retire from the public service on attaining the age of 60 years'.[7] BOPEU sued the government in January 2010, but lost its case, heard by the newly appointed chief justice, Maruping Dibotelo, in November 2010, and then in the Court of Appeal (Kavahematui 2011c).[8] The dismissal, in May 2009, thus set the government on a collision course with BOPEU.

The BOFEPUSU leadership also resented the fact that it was not consulted about the national budget before its announcement in February 2011. The government felt that most civil servants (excluding industrial-class workers!) had been awarded a *de facto* pay rise of 10 per cent in 2010, applied retrospectively from May that year. This followed the implementation of the Public Service Act, which raised the number of days per month they officially worked.[9] Here was another reason for President Khama to refuse to engage with the federation.

Finally, in a privatisation move threatening industrial-class workers and the MWU in particular, the budget announced the government's intention to 'embark on a mandatory Public Service Outsourcing Programme (PSOP), where all Ministries will be required to outsource office cleaning, grounds maintenance and landscaping, and security services. These services are considered non-core and if outsourced, will relieve the government of the administrative burden of providing them'.[10] MWU leaders commented that this would lead to a massive rise in unemployment (Kavahematui 2011a).

The advice given to the government by the Bank of Botswana and the International Monetary Fund (IMF) was that it should 'slim down' the civil service so that it could pay higher salaries to those who remained. The argument was that the public sector annual bill of 12 billion pula was untenable: it was higher than the development bill (10 billion pula), disproportionate to Botswana's GDP, and it skewed the public–private sector ratio (see Konopo 2011). In reality, even the private sector was heavily dependent on the government, generating a crisis when, during the strike, private firms were not paid.

Against the advice of the Bank of Botswana and IMF, the government had decided to defend public sector jobs. In a nationally televised address during the strike, President Khama told a business audience that, unlike many other countries burdened with budget deficits, Botswana had taken a 'deliberate decision to avoid at all possible costs reducing the size of the public service, let alone cutting salaries to save money'. He 'regretted' that the government's willingness to go to the extreme of borrowing money from the African Development Bank in order to save public sector jobs had not been 'appreciated' by public officers (Khunwane 2011: 1–2). The fact that President Khama chose to speak in the forum of the High Level Consultative Council (HLCC), rather than to union leaders directly, indicates that what rankled deeply with him was the fact that he had gone out of his way, against financial advice, to protect public service employees' jobs, and thus to avoid swelling the ranks of the unemployed; and yet federation leaders, knowing this, and knowing that the country was operating with a budget deficit, had nevertheless decided to strike for a pay rise.[11]

The solution he offered, however, failed to appreciate that the lowest-paid industrial-class workers – who had *not* been awarded a 10 per cent rise – were, after a three-year pay freeze, quite unable to meet their basic living costs in the face of a 30 per cent rise in the price of goods, food, housing, fuel and transport, which included a rise in VAT. The government was in effect denying the obvious truth of government manual workers' working poverty.[12] Raising their salaries would have made virtually no dent in the public service bill, but despite this the government rejected a selective public pay settlement.

The Economic Crisis and the Morality of Policy

Khama had assumed the presidency in 2008, just as the global financial crisis hit Botswana's diamond sales. The government was forced to tap into its huge foreign reserves, shut down a number of diamond mines for several months and borrow $1.5 billion from the African Development Bank. Since the downturn, government workers had their salaries frozen despite rising inflation for three years in succession.

Although the sale of diamonds picked up considerably in 2011, Botswana still had a 7 billion pula (£700 million) deficit at the time of the strike, while the world economy remained shaky. President Khama had vowed to make good the deficit before he left office. He also declared his commitment to meet Botswana's 2016 Millennium Development Goals on the eradication of poverty.[13] To fulfil the unions' demand for a 16 per cent pay rise would have increased the deficit by another 2 billion pula (£200 million). He was determined that this was not going to happen on his watch.

His declared aim was to reform both the country and, it seems, the civil service. He introduced the Road Traffic Amendment Bill, which imposed much higher fines on traffic offences (Piet 2008), and slapped a 30 per cent levy on alcohol, proclaiming drink a national scourge that undermined productivity and the nation's youth. His monetary policies mimicked international trends, but Botswana remained committed to largely free health and education, and increased its spending on poverty alleviation despite the negative trade balance. The government had, however, been tough on its public sector workers.

Like most workers in the West, government workers in Botswana live on credit, with high mortgages and hire-purchase arrangements for cars and other acquisitions. The country's 30 per cent inflation, with much higher fuel and utilities costs, hit hard. As the deputy permanent secretary in the Ministry of Finance and Development, a friend of mine, commented ironically to me, the appearance of development in Botswana – the malls, the cars, the roads, the houses – was an illusion. Botswana was ranked as a middle-income country, but people were living on borrowed money. The whole economy was dependent, indeed over-dependent, on diamonds. What would happen in 2020 when diamond deposits started to run out? It really scared him, he said. This was also the problem with drawing on the reserves, he explained: during the credit crunch, the reserves were being depleted at a frightening rate. Because the economy was not sufficiently diversified – like, for example, the British economy – Botswana could not afford *not* to have foreign reserves to cover it for about a year and a half. Even in the tourist industry, most of the profits were made by outsider companies in South Africa and Zimbabwe.

Botswana had for many years been trying to diversify its economy, moving away from its heavy reliance on diamonds, but, despite attractive terms and loans offered to foreign and local investors, most projects had failed, my friend lamented. The government had believed in manufacturing, but it hadn't worked, he concluded gloomily. Now he thought the real answer was in agriculture. Botswana had plenty of land, and all that was needed was water. But experimental subsidies for ploughing and sowing introduced by President Khama proved disappointing due to repeated droughts.[14] One of the president's schemes, backyard gardens, intended to establish some 12,800 plots for vulnerable people while countering the huge trade deficit in vegetables and fruit from South Africa, was regarded with scepticism by public sector workers and much of the press.[15]

President Khama was consistently mocked by speakers and the press for his poverty alleviation schemes: the Ipelegeng Project (*ipelegeng* means 'self help') paid workers a meagre 20 pula a day in 2011, or 400 pula a month, to carry out 'essential development projects'.[16] Grants allocated to support youth constituency sports leagues and the Presidential Housing Appeal, which raised donations to build homes for destitutes, were all seen as wasted money or personalised schemes intended to glorify the president himself.

Yet poverty *was* a major national challenge. The 2011 budget speech noted that according to the last Household Income and Expenditure Survey (HIES), poverty in Botswana was estimated at 30.6 per cent, a figure 'not acceptable by any standard'. There were said to be 45,000 Batswana who live in extreme poverty (see note 6). In December 2011, the Botswana Core Welfare Indicators Survey (BCWIS) found that 21 per cent of rural households sometimes go for a day without food.[17] Anti-poverty programmes included Ipelegeng, Destitute Housing, the Self Help Housing Agency (SHHA) programme, the Integrated Support Programme for Arable Agriculture (ISPAAD), various youth programmes, support to NGOs, community development programmes, the Livestock Management and Infrastructure Development (LIMID) programme, backyard gardening and livestock support for remote areas. To fund these, the budget allocated some 730 million pula,[18] including 100 million pula from the Alcohol Levy Fund.[19] Added to this, 230 million pula went to old-age and Second World War veteran pensions.

One of the most derided schemes the government had initiated, according to the *Botswana Gazette*, was the charitable distribution of blankets and hampers by the president to villagers, donated by local philanthropists.[20] The distribution was shown on BTV, with the president and his entourage greeted with ululations by elderly women who swept the ground at his feet with their shawls in a traditional show of respect for a chief. If President Khama had declared his commitment to tackle poverty in Botswana before raising wages, many complained that he was simply applying a band aid to plaster over a huge problem. The need was, they argued, for real job creation (though what this might be in practice remained unanswered). Meanwhile, public sector workers, with vast numbers of dependents – a huge, invisible number of rural beneficiaries – were being squeezed and denied a fair wage.

Despite the recession, the government was financing major infrastructural projects, including a new international airport, a major new coal-fired power station, roads and railway projects. It was supporting the 'down-streaming' of diamonds, expanding from the mining of raw diamonds into polishing and cutting, a policy which aimed in the long run to develop jewellery manufacturing, banking and trading, thus making Botswana a major 'diamond hub' in Africa. The country had also invested in an undersea fibre-optic cable system along the East and West African coasts, to support high-speed internet. Botswana was ranked highest in Africa for transparency and had retained a high credit rating despite the recession.[21] It was against this economic, moral and political background that the 2011 public sector strike took place.

The Rhetoric of the Strike: Calls for Regime Change and Constitutional Reform

With workers bitter, the strike grounds open to speakers from opposition parties, students and preachers, and the dead weight of the continuous, seemingly interminable, 45-year rule of the BDP, there were calls for 'regime change' – even if the explicit rhetorical target was President Khama himself. It was not that anyone denied that the BDP had been elected legitimately, most recently in 2009, in fair and transparent elections; it was that Khama's intransigence, his unwillingness to even meet the strikers, was seen as a sign of the arrogance and complacency afflicting the country's political establishment. His refusal was regarded as striking at deeply held national values of *buisana* and *rerisana* (mutual negotiation and dialogue) that had always guided Botswana as a peaceful nation living in *kagiso*, harmony.

One journalist commented that, 'The endless gladiatorial court battles, late-night judgements, early morning appeals, and mid-morning counter appeals have now precipitated a more interesting development – a make or break political end-game' (Motlogelwa 2011). In a series of newspaper articles, Monageng Mogalakwe argued that President Khama could not claim a 'monopoly on patriotism' or ignore the fact that workers were also voters. Instead, Mogalakwe suggested that he enter into a 'national dialogue' with unions and opposition parties who, after all, accounted for 47 per cent of the popular vote.[22] This would not be seen as a 'sign of weakness', suggested Mogalakwe, 'but of statesmanship'. Genuine dialogue included full disclosure by the employer, in this case the government, of financial information (Mogalakwe 2011c).

The calls for 'regime change' echoing protests elsewhere, targeted President Khama's person: his moral character, his questionable policy initiatives, his inscrutable personality, his personal life. Indeed, the strike's discursive rhetoric was dominated by moral questions: the ethics of the strike itself, the ethos of Botswana as a nation and the questionable morality and suspect wealth of some of its established politicians and civil servants. The president became, for speakers, the personification of a new authoritarianism threatening Botswana's established democratic traditions, its institutions, rights and freedoms. Speakers seized on the fact that he was the first son of the founding president of Botswana, a traditional chief and an army brigadier-general to boot. He was perceived to pose a potential risk to democracy, backed as he was by an entrenched, privileged elite. It was seen as ominous that he had appointed cousins, nephews, affines and ex-army comrades to key political positions, including the minister of defence and security and the head of the Directorate of Intelligence Services (DIS), a new body under his direct control.[23] The shooting in 2009 of an unarmed criminal, John Kalafatis, in controversial circumstances, seemed to point to the imminent rise of a police state.[24]

Internationally, Khama was a publicly committed democrat who had consistently boycotted illegitimate African leaders (in Zimbabwe, Sudan and Côte d'Ivoire) and endorsed UN resolutions against Gaddafi, often in the face of other African countries' prevarications. He had also spoken out against a tendency among African leaders to reject election results and seek power-sharing arrangements, as in Kenya. Nevertheless, his background and governance style created a sense of unease. His decision not to enter into a direct dialogue with the unions or authorise debate about the strike on government media, particularly BTV, were miscalculations that backfired. Especially galling were his rural tours, filmed by the media and BTV, where he made pronouncements beamed to the nation around village campfires, saying he would 'never agree to settle even if the strike lasted five years!'

The result of this was that rather than the merits and demerits of the strike itself being subject to public scrutiny, the president's intransigence, his unwillingness to listen or talk to the unions, became the main focus of public debate.[25] There was virtual unanimity across the nation that President Khama was at fault for not agreeing to 'dialogue'. As outlined above, he may well have resented union interference in BDP and electoral politics and their ingratitude towards him, despite refusing expert advice to defend their jobs. These matters were never publicly raised by his critics. Instead, both orators at the strike grounds and publicists in the print media accused him openly of being a 'failed' president, of being 'weak' and incompetent, lacking leadership, or alternatively of being arrogant and authoritarian, a soldier determined to get his way and win the battle at all costs. It was insinuated by the opposition that he was not truly a Motswana, proven by his poor command of Setswana and the fact of having being born in England to a white mother and privileged father. His efforts to alleviate poverty were dismissed as populist ventures to boost his rural image. Rather than bringing back prosperity, it was alleged he self-indulgently spent money on luxury projects and unnecessary security. Botswana was, after all, a peaceful country with no discernable enemies. Who needed a secret service when a financial crisis denied workers their rightful pay? Press headlines such as 'The Silent March of the Dictatorship', 'Attributes of a Dictator', 'We Have a Monumental Ego for a President', 'Regime Change Now' and 'This Government Is a Big Joke' were not unusual.[26]

Rank-and-file union members felt exploited. Whatever the national interest, they expected, by right, to earn a fair wage for their labour. Against this reasonable expectation they set the president's apparent wastefulness, repeatedly listed in detail by union orators and other speakers at the grounds. Dr Thapelo Otlogetswe, a senior lecturer in the Department of English at the University of Botswana, summed up the litany of alleged presidential offences:

> On economic management, since April 2008 there have been many reckless expenses by his [Khama's] government: the government black Mercedes Benzes were replaced by BMWs 7 series [a luxury car]. Then right in the middle of a recession there was massive spending which was not budgeted for to establish the DIS with at least P26 million at the beginning and more millions following.[27] Then in 2009 a presidential jet was purchased. Then there was the P300,000 spent on one minister's furniture. Then the story of the purchase of a P46,000 fridge rocked the government. Then about P81 million of taxpayers' money was used to construct 16 houses for cabinet ministers. It was also revealed that the government spends P1.24 million annually paying the maids, guards and gardeners for the 16 ministerial homes. (Otlogetswe 2011)

Otlogetswe went on to describe Ipelegeng and backyard gardens as 'useless projects', the latter a 'pitiable strategy to reduce poverty with onions, sickly carrots and cabbages the size of a man's fist'. 'Mountains of money' were spent on the 'President's constituency (football) leagues'. Furthermore, 'Additionally, P20 million was spent on renovating the state house and an estimated P7 million spent on the construction of the barracks in the state house. This is just the tip of a giant iceberg'. His critique continued: 'The strategy is to attract attention to the President so that he appears as a kind and generous man', and 'Many people in the top echelons of the party are today scared to speak their minds because of the stature of Khama'; they are mere 'bootlickers'. Parliament pushed through a 'draconian media law which the Press Council of Botswana feared was crafted to limit media freedom and muzzle freedom of expression' (ibid.).

Some of the accusations were manifestly unfair. In particular, the presidential jet was decided upon by Khama's predecessor at a time of plenty, before he took office, while the act creating the DIS was passed in 2007 and implemented on 1 April 2008, the day the president assumed office, just as the economic recession hit Botswana, too late to cancel. In any case, their aggregate cost, with the exception of the poverty alleviation programmes, amounted to far less than the cost to the national coffers of even a modest rise in the public sector bill.

Such counter-arguments in defence of the president and the government were, however, rarely raised. Instead, the same examples of wastefulness on unnecessary luxury items were repeatedly cited as evidence of the government's profligacy, wastefulness and selfish desire for luxury consumer goods. The long list of items convinced workers that it was they who occupied the moral high ground. The ethics of the strike were thus spelled out by the union federation in terms of the hypocrisy of the government's claims that a pay rise was simply unaffordable. If the government was not tightening its belt, the workers reasoned, why should they be expected to do so?

Despite Botswana being ranked first for transparency in Africa, there were persistent rumours among the workers of cronyism and corruption in high places, proven when top officials were involved in financial scandals.[28] The pay differential was huge: according to Keith Jeffries, former deputy governor of the Bank of Botswana, 'income distribution [in Botswana] is very unequal, with the richest 20 per cent of households earning around 70 per cent of total household income' (Jeffries 2011).

Khama's perceived autocracy created renewed calls in the private media, the opposition and at the strike grounds for constitutional change. In practice, the incoming president is selected by the outgoing president resigning in mid-term, in so-called 'automatic succession', and the selection is then approved by parliament. Only later does he (or she) have to contest elections, as head of the ruling party. The president is not required to have a constituency or be an MP. Apart from opening parliament and presiding over the budget, it was repeatedly noted that Khama showed little interest in parliamentary affairs. The only limitation on the president's executive independence is that his (or her) removal is possible, following a parliament motion of no confidence.

Most parliamentarians and commentators appeared to feel that direct presidential elections would be preferable, making the president more accountable. In a thoughtful article, however, which appeared during the strike, Zibani Maundeni of the University of Botswana rejected this view, arguing that Botswana 'runs a hybrid system, combining parliamentary and presidential elements' (Maundeni 2011: 9).[29] Rather than direct presidential elections which would 'empower the presidential side of the equation', he favoured strengthening parliament:

> constitutional reform needs to resuscitate [the legislature], to demand that the President be the leader of the House and to field questions in Parliament. The President should be the Leader of the House, and should face a question time where he should be required to answer questions directly. This is one reform that could strengthen the parliamentary side of the hybrid system as it would make the President more accountable to Parliament. (ibid.)

He also advocated that 'the President should have a constituency just like any other MP', noting that 'Seretse Khama [Botswana's first president, and Ian Khama's father] actually had a constituency and was voted twice in that regard'. Further:

> If cabinet ministers can play a double role of being minister and MP, so too can the president. If the President lost his constituency, then he could not become President. This would allow Parliament to directly elect the President. (ibid.)

Finally, in the case of a vote of no confidence, he suggests, the president would be required to resign but should not have the right to dissolve parliament. The striking involvement of Batswana university academics in the debates that took place in the public sphere during the strike underscored the extent to which the strike came to encompass the whole of civil society. Debaters were passionate and spoke at length, to audience applause. But beyond that, the strike also raised serious issues about freedom of speech, of the media, the nature of the Constitution, the safeguards to democracy, transparency and a vision of justice and equity. The outcome of the strike was, however, deeply disappointing for the strikers at the strike grounds. In the end, it was the workers who blinked first, while the government remained recalcitrant.

What Went Wrong?

The strike was planned as a ten-day affair. While unionists may have hoped it would lead to a pay settlement, it was assumed all along that salaries would ultimately be negotiated once the new bargaining council, the NPSBC, came into existence. The strike was therefore above all a test of the very possibility of holding a legal strike. Secondly, it aimed to solidify the unity of the BOFEPUSU leadership, its capacity to coordinate, mobilise and act together in joint negotiations, while bringing together rank-and-file members from all the five unions across the country organisationally in a spectacular operation. Third, it aimed to publicise the very existence of the federation as a major organisation to be reckoned with. Related to this, a fourth aim, especially for the MWU, was to crush BOGOWU, the rival breakaway union, by proving the Manual Workers' Union's radical credentials as leader of the labour movement and champion of workers' rights. Fifthly, the strike was intended to register the anger of the unions at not being consulted before the 2011 budget was announced, and at the delay in establishing the bargaining council. Finally, the federation wished to proclaim loud and clear that public service workers now found themselves in dire financial straits after three years without a pay increase.

The government misread the strike completely, with disastrous consequences. However 'prudent' its management of the economy was, when it came to handling the strike its conduct was remarkably careless and even irrational, given that its central objectives must undoubtedly have been to ensure the least damage to the economy, a minimum disruption of services and a speedy return to work. From the start, the DPSM subverted the rules and agreements she had herself entered into, causing the strike to escalate well beyond its intended limits as the federation was compelled to retaliate. On the federation's side, although the legal planning of the strike was meticulous, the mobilisation of workers for the strike – particularly of civil servants in the capital's government enclave – was less than total. This weakened the unions' bargaining position considerably, and caused it to rely heavily on the impact of the withdrawal of essential services, particularly of health workers, doctors and nurses, once the strike was prolonged.

BOFEPUSU's five unions between them controlled a labour force of some 90,000, out of a total of 110,000 public sector workers. If all 90,000 unionised members had joined the strike, even with the agreed 30 per cent of essential services continuing to work, the government would have been totally paralysed. But this did not happen. The unions involved had canvassed their members for support of the strike, but the majority, apart from the MWU, had not balloted members, and none had held a universal secret ballot, which is not required by law in Botswana. The two teachers' unions and the MWU had experience of prior strikes and were more established organisations. Their members turned out for the strike in very high numbers, as did local authority members of BLLAWU. Despite the column inches written about the strike, none of the newspapers or media attempted to gather accurate statistics. The government claimed, without providing any evidence, that only half the workforce was on strike. The unions denied this but themselves did not provide exact figures, referring merely to the ballpark figure of 90,000.

There appeared to be broad agreement among strikers at the grounds, however, that some ministries, like the Ministry of Labour in the capital, had continued to function fully, with virtually no workers on strike. There were nevertheless pockets where the strike was effective. The strike in the Department of Accounts, for example, seemed to impact strongly on private businesses, which reported a total absence of orders, and outstanding invoices were left unpaid, causing havoc to the economy. The Department of Maps and Surveys was also paralysed, as were some departments in the Ministry of Agriculture. The massive number of teachers on strike meant pupils came to empty classrooms, resulting in violent riots in which school youngsters clashed with police and vandalised school buildings. The minister of education finally had to admit defeat and closed schools temporarily. Later, retired and voluntary teachers were recruited to stand in for the strikers.

The DPSM broke the strike rules it had agreed with BOFEPUSU on two counts. First, it did not submit, as the agreement specified, a list of essential workers required to report for work. Instead, the Ministry of Health unhelpfully supplied a list of all the worker categories in service. The agreement was that 30 per cent of all essential workers, covering a wide range of government ministries, would continue working during the strike. The figure was suggested by the government itself, who could have set a higher bar. Without a specific, named list, it was unclear which essential workers should report for work. The figure agreed for non-essential workers was 20 per cent.

The second rule broken by the DPSM – having announced to the media that the strike was having no impact on hospital and clinical services – was to begin recruiting external workers to replace the strikers. This infringed the legal requirement of non-replacement of labour during the first 14 days of a strike. In response, the federation took the DPSM to the Industrial Court on 23 April, and won an injunction requiring the employer to cease employing external labour.

This happened on the fifth day of a planned ten-day 'demonstration' strike. In retaliation, on 26 April, eight days into the strike, the DPSM took the unions to the Industrial Court to call for an urgent rule nisi requiring essential services to return to work. In retaliation, the federation extended the strike for a further ten days. On 29 April, eleven days into the strike, it then sued the government in a counter-move. The court's judgement in favour of the employer, the government, was that the strike of essential services was illegal and thus unprotected, based on several sections of the Trade Disputes Act (2004), the judges concurring with the DPSM's legal counsels, basing its reasoning on the absence of an actually signed agreement, even though neither party – the government nor the unions – disputed the 30 per cent agreement they had reached in the case of essential services. The judgement appeared to mean that, henceforth, essential services in Botswana were prohibited from striking altogether, and that any disputes involving them should be referred to arbitration. This obviously did not accord with other sections of the Trade Disputes Act, with the spirit of the ILO conventions on which the Trade Disputes Act was based, or with the agreement reached between the unions and the government as the employer prior to the start of the strike.

I discuss the court cases further in Chapter 12. What needs to be pointed out here is that the the unions called a legal strike in good faith, following all the rules and procedures specified for declaring such a strike legal. The government had domesticated ILO conventions that expanded the range of workers entitled to unionise, and instituted for the first time a process allowing for legal strikes. In this it also appeared to be acting in good faith. When it came to practice, however, once it became evident that the strike was effective, the government subverted its own laws, rules and agreements to render the strike of essential services illegal. After the strike was suspended, it further expanded the schedule list of services defined as illegal.[30] When this amendment failed to be approved by parliament, it resubmitted it again, this time gaining approval.[31]

From the perspective of the unions, for whom laws and regulations are sacrosanct, the bread and butter of their daily activities, the government riding roughshod over its own laws, regulations and agreements left a legal quagmire to which the only response was a continuation of the strike, legally or illegally. This revealed a further careless mistake on the part of the DPSM: MaBakwena, the director, admitted that she had assumed the strike was for ten days only and had not realised the agreement was for an 'indefinite' strike. Thus, to sum up, the government broke the strike rules from the start in not providing lists; it further broke the rules in recruiting outside labour on the fifth day of the strike; finally, it tore up agreements made in good faith by the unions before the strike started, and declared the strike by essential services illegal. It used its influence on the court, primarily because as manager it could claim authoritatively that 'people are dying' in the hospitals, to sway the judges, whether or not members of the bench had other, more personal, considerations for deciding in favour of the government, as unions suspected.

Members of the MWU had told me they 'never take cases' to the Industrial Court. Leaders of BOPEU were inexperienced, they said. To this they added that they did not trust the High Court in Lobatse and preferred the one in Francistown. They complained that rather than lawyers from the attorney general's chambers, the government had chosen to be represented by Collins,

Newman and Co., a private law firm used both by Khama himself and the BDP, allegedly at the cost of 3.5 million pula in legal fees (Tsimane 2011: 2). This proved, in their view, that the real battle was not with the government but with Khama and his party. One of the lawyers representing the government, Parks Tafa, was reported in to be dismissive of the attorney general, Dr Athaliah Molokomme (ibid.). The other lawyer, Vigil Vergeer, had recently been appointed a judge in the Industrial Court, though this had not yet taken effect. Tafa was chosen once again to represent the government at the appeal of the case in the Lobatse High Court in May 2012 (Ganetsang 2011) and in the Court of Appeal in 2013. It seemed to unionists that the government was thus willing to pack the judiciary with loyal, conservative judges.

On 16 May, six days after the temporary injunction for essential services to return to work was confirmed, the government dismissed some 2000 workers (see Chapter 10).[32] Since the judgement was given at 9.30 PM on Tuesday 10 May, the government's claim to have given due notice to all essential workers to return to work was dubious. A press release could not have been issued before Thursday 12 May. Notices of dismissal for Monday 16 May, must have been prepared on Friday, one day after the press release. Indeed, many people who were *not* on strike also received letters of dismissal. The government's precipitous move seemed almost like a re-run of the 1991 strike – though in that strike dismissal letters were issued even *prior* to workers being given notice (see Chapter 5). By mid May the government had also implemented the 'no work, no pay' policy, with much confusion as to who had or had not been at work.

Clearly, the government was determined to clobber the unions with all its might, however lacking in due process this was and whatever the national cost, much as Margaret Thatcher, the British prime minister, had been determined to 'destroy the power of the unions for almost a generation' after the 1984 coal miners' strike.[33] The irony was that the Botswana government had only just liberalised the country's labour laws to allow legal strikes in accordance with ILO conventions.

During the strike, the MWU and other unions had continued to recruit nurses and other workers both in Gaborone and outside the capital who had never unionised before. With the law in tatters, metaphorically speaking, after the 10 May court case, essential-service workers, doctors and nurses felt justified in continuing to strike. Their dismissal came as a shock and led to even more health personnel joining their colleagues at the strike grounds.

By this time a sense of crisis had enveloped the whole country. There appeared to be no end to the strike: patients were being turned away from hospitals, pregnant women were giving birth unattended, firms were not being paid, the economy was tottering on the brink, court cases were piling up, welfare recipients were not receiving their benefits and school children were rioting. If the government suspected and unions were aware that attrition had set in among some workers who had not been paid for close to two months, this was not evident to the public. With its mismanagement of the strike, the government had driven itself and the unions into a cul-de-sac since it still refused to make a reasonable pay offer.

Publicly and behind the scenes, union leaders were reaching out to anyone who might intervene to find an honourable way out of the deadlock: chiefs, parliamentarians, church leaders, the Botswana Association of Local Authorities (BALA), even the private sector through the Botswana Confederation of Commerce, Industry and Manpower (BOCCIM). It was at this point that the ethics of the strike came under renewed scrutiny. The government, and some members of the public,[34] had accused doctors and nurses of irresponsibly abandoning their patients to die; teachers were accused of leaving their pupils unprepared for final examinations, and veterinary workers of abandoning their posts during a foot-and-mouth disease outbreak, which threatened the cattle industry. The unions were said to be unpatriotic, selfishly demanding a pay rise when Botswana still faced a huge deficit.

As we have seen, the extension of the strike was largely due to government bungling of the strike negotiations. Nevertheless, the impasse was evidently causing a national crisis, and it needed some kind of honourable exit strategy. In his sermon at the Gaborone Anglican Cathedral of the Holy Cross on Sunday 22 May, the bishop of Botswana, Dr Musonda T.S. Mwamba, reflected on the implications of the strike.[35] At the most obvious level, he said, 'the simple equation is that the unions want a public salary increase and the government's position is that it cannot afford this increase at the moment as it is grappling with a budget deficit'. Nevertheless, he proposed, echoing the general view, this truth 'needs to be communicated directly to the unions in person'. Not only that. The strike, he continued, was also a 'story' about 'ethics': materialism, the Hippocratic oath, the limits of politics and 'working together'. It is this fourth ethical dimension that led him to make a bold suggestion: that rather than across the board, the government target the salary increase at those 'public servants most in need ... The rationale is that it is those most in need who deserve wage adjustments'. The (total) amount offered to the lowest grades of workers would be 'equivalent to the government offer [to all workers] of 3 per cent unconditionally using across-the-board criteria'. The bishop's bold economic resolution to the impasse was justified ethically since: 'Profoundly in this story of working together our focus is on God because life is more than the possessions we have. In this holy space we are lifted to higher values that transcend our ordinary existence and challenges'.

This suggestion became the basis for BOFEPUSU's acceptance of the 3 per cent offer, as we saw in Chapter 10. I witnessed Motshwarakgole explaining the so-called 'pyramid structure' to a caucus of MWU delegates before the federation special general meeting called at the end of May. It provided moral justification for his call – unheeded at that point by the other unions – for a suspension of the strike. At the meeting, the general secretary, Andrew Motsamai, supported the compromise, reporting that the pay gap in Botswana was 'higher than in Brazil'. It was unanimously agreed upon, even by the higher-paid unionists who stood to lose most.

The equity-based compromise was also supported by many BDP MPs in a special meeting called the following day. Ten days later, on 3 June, in a special general assembly called by the speaker of the house, Margaret Nasha, MPs agreed that the 'aggregate increment of the wage bill by 3% be distributed on the principle of equity, without undue distortion of the current salary structures'.[36] It was said that out of the 38 MPs gathered, only five BDP members objected to the proposed pyramid pay settlement (Rantsimako 2011: 18; see also Basimanebotlhe 2011b). The suggestion went, however, against the uniform system of grading in Botswana, which followed the integrated Paterson grading system widely used throughout Southern Africa (see Jordan et al. 1992). This had been introduced in 1988 and modified only by so-called 'parallel progression' and 'scarce skills' allowances. Subverting it was a major policy change, and thus the attempt to reach a compromise based on the principle of equity was refused by the government, and the deadlock continued.

Why did the government refuse the compromise? No cogent explanation was ever offered. One suspects that the government feared that if it accepted the pyramid structure pay deal, this would be widely construed as a sign that the strike had succeeded: that the unions – especially the reviled MWU – had triumphed. Beyond that, the government may also have feared that a 10 per cent pay increase for low-paid manual workers would generate pressure towards similar pay settlements in the private sector, leading to an inflationary spiral. Whatever the reasons, no justification for the blank refusal was ever given. With the refusal, the government lost the moral battle.

As the strike continued, two BDP MPs left the party along with several local councillors, while members of the BDP youth wing resigned (Motlhabane & Ntibinyane 2011). The government began hiring overseas doctors and nurses, and private refuse collectors, cleaners and retired teachers, as well as outsourcing manual workers' jobs in large numbers. At the same time, the government accused unions of politicising the strike, and suspended the talks. The headlines shouted 'Government Takes War to the Unions' (Lute 2011a).

The strike had been very peaceful for the first six weeks, but the government's hard-line tactics and the continuing deadlock inevitably led to some minor violence as it entered its final phase, especially as the police began overreacting to minor violations of the law. One leader of BLLAWU was accused of inciting strikers to make petrol bombs, though he was later acquitted for lack of evidence (Gabathuse 2011). The same unionist, along with some others, was charged with assaulting a military intelligence officer (Ontebetse 2011), an accusation again found to be without foundation. The Sunday prayer meeting described in Chapter 10 failed to persuade the government to attenuate its intransigence. Quite the opposite: it responded by announcing the cessation of all negotiations on the grounds the strike had been politicised. Minor outbreaks of violence with disproportionate police response – teargas and rubber bullets – began to surface in some towns, and this persuaded the union leadership finally to suspend the strike.

I described strikers' opposition to the end of the strike in Chapter 10, as well as the government's disproportionate response. In the end, the hoped-for 'revolution' did not materialise. Strikers returned to work disheartened, dejected and demoralised, with nothing to show for eight weeks at the strike grounds except empty pockets. Many accused the leadership of selling out. The strike had been crushed and there seemed no prospect of repeating it, despite the leadership's announcement that it had merely been suspended. By September 2011, some 2000 dismissed essential-services workers had not been rehired, including 300 nurses, cleaners, cooks, drivers and porters.[37] The strike had given the government an excuse to 'slim down' the public service by outsourcing cleaning, refuse collection, laundry and other manual worker services to private companies, undoubtedly at lower wages and with fewer pension rights. In addition, it seemed that workers over the age of 50 had not been rehired. For many workers the situation was dire. BOFEPUSU, however, still believed it could win its case in court against what it perceived to be unfair dismissals. As Motshwarakgole argued, if the government wished to retrench workers, it should first have reinstated them in order to negotiate an orderly exit package. By October 2011, the federation had no less than six court cases pending against the government (Makgapha 2011c). A complaint on the change in the schedule and the conduct of the strike had also been lodged by the federation with the ILO.

At the height of the strike, some workers had seriously dreamt of 'revolution', of immediate regime change. They perceived the strike as 'evolving into a different object altogether – a nationwide struggle of the "Tahrir Square" type' (Kelebonye 2011: 22). Following the defeat in the Industrial Court, the journalist Kelebonye suggested that 'the three-week walkout might just be the beginning – a new chapter, an important turning point in Botswana's history – a herald of the class struggle where the workers could soon be calling the shots' (ibid.). The strike, he argued, responded to the Arab spring:

> The great zest with which workers have approached the matter owes its source to the revolutionary events in North Africa and the Middle East. From the time Tunisia's Mohammad Al Bouazizi doused himself in petrol and lit a match in front of a government building after a policeman shut down his innovative but illegal attempts to sell fruit on the street, a new, determined consciousness has been ignited among workers and youth around the world. That little match flicker has become a worldwide bonfire amid shouts of 'change!' It's a call for change of the current political order and ideologies that have left the unemployed and working classes exasperated. (ibid.)

'Botswana', he continued, 'splendidly connected to the global village, finds itself with a workforce that shares the same interests as workers in Egypt, Tunisia, Libya, Yemen and Syria. And closer to home, South Africa and Swaziland' (ibid.). He pointed out further that 'people who ordinarily are sympathetic to different political parties', including the ruling BDP, were dining together 'in the spirit of labour' (ibid.). In the end, no revolution took place, while the popular protests turned out to be little more than 'rituals of rebellion'.

But was the strike a total defeat for BOFEPUSU? As he reflected back on the strike in June 2011, Motshwarakgole told me that, whatever else, seeing workers from different classes, doctors and cleaners, come together was the fulfilment of a vision he had 'dreamt' of his whole life. No divisions, no classes. These people, he said, who are looked down upon by everyone, ignored and rejected, had participated together as equals with some of the most educated workers in society. He still believed that all the workers dismissed would be reinstated when the federation won its cases against the government in the High Court. This indeed did happen, as Chapter 12 details, though the verdict was overturned in the Court of Appeal. Internationally, some 3000 unions had signed a petition to the Botswana government, and they had the full support of Public Service International. The opposition parties had been given notice that they must unite if they wanted workers' votes in 2014. Labour and its interests were now firmly on the national agenda. Regime change would be achieved, Motshwarakgole believed, through the ballot box.

A major achievement of the strike was the consolidation of the BOFEPUSU leadership team and its test under fire. Federation leaders met daily in the rather grand office of the federation's secretary general, Andrew Motsamai, to discuss their plan of action for that day and future campaigns and strategies. They gauged each other's strengths and developed a clear division of labour. They managed relations with the police, the press and the media, MPs and a range of civil-society actors. Workers on the ground needed to be given regular reports, speeches needed to be made across the country and new campaigns had to be invented, if only to keep strikers occupied. The organisational logistics of the strike, which extended over the whole country, were a huge challenge, and so too was the management of the different court cases. The public relations impact of the court cases and the strike more generally were evidently massive, but the strike's potentially negative impact also needed to be averted. If the federation seemed to sail close to the wind at times in allowing opposition parties a platform from which to attack the government, this was partly because the strike grounds were open to all speakers with little supervision and no censorship. The aim of the speeches was to fill the long days under the *morula* tree and entertain the strikers. The strike enabled new young leaders to emerge, like the union chair of the Gaborone Secondary School strike grounds, who managed to keep strikers calm and on course with his daily speeches, even in the absence of representatives from the federation executive. When I asked him what gave him the confidence to lead the mass of strikers, he told me he thought he gained that confidence being left as a young boy at his uncle's cattle post to fend for himself as he herded the cattle! His comment reveals the profound roots of strikers in the countryside, where most had grown up.

Conclusion

This chapter has outlined the competing moralities of the dispute between public sector unions in Botswana and their government. It disclosed the divergent ethical premises and priorities that motivated actors and impacted on the political and moral economy of the country. Each of the sides, from their perspective, believed in the righteousness of their cause and mobilised the law, political alliances and supporters against the other. Seen in strategic terms, the chapter also argued that initial misperceptions by the government of the unions' intentions and priorities led the government as employer to repeatedly break its agreements with the unions in the early stages of the strike, and undermine the very labour laws it had recently legislated for, with the consequence that the conflict escalated to the point of creating a perceived national crisis. Although the government defeated the unions' specific claim to an equitable cost-of-living wage increase to compensate for high inflation and a three-year pay freeze, this came at a heavy political cost. The government was seen by the wider public as intransigent and immoral, failing to live by the national values of dialogue and *kagiso*, (peace and harmony), and failing to recognise the plight of the low paid, despite its claims to *botho*, humanity, expressed in its efforts on behalf of the poor and the unemployed during a devastating economic recession.

CHAPTER TWELVE

Legal Mobilisation, Legal Scepticism and the Politics of Public Sector Unions

The 'Carnival' of Law

Court cases are popularly perceived to be dramatic events. In reality, however, much of the argumentation about labour disputes in court is often dry, technical and arcane, with lengthy affidavits on what happened rather than adversarial interrogation of witnesses or grandiloquent appeals to the jury and gallery. Whatever the confrontations between workers and employers that led them to court, hearings about labour conflicts seem to consist mainly in legal counsels on both sides citing unfamiliar legal precedents, or arguing in abstruse detail about possible inconsistencies between different acts promulgated by the state, or between those acts and international conventions.

Even in the case of more sensational criminal cases, however, the drama of legal debates in courts has seldom been framed by scholars in terms of embodied popular cultural experience during mass mobilisation. These disattended aspects of the law are centrally significant, however, in locating legal contestation within wider struggles for legal reform and social justice. My argument here joins legal scholars who reject a sceptical reading of the 'myth of law' (Lobel 2007: 941) – of theories contesting the long-term impact of progressive litigation. Against that, the new critical scholars advocate restoring 'critical optimism' in the legal field (ibid.: 987): the view that legal mobilisation, as McCann (1994) proposed in his classic study, must be evaluated within the context of wider social movements for reform or social justice in which legal battles are invariably embedded.

This issue, of legal mobilisation, was reflected in the 2011 'mother of all strikes' in effervescent, carnival-like performances of legal contestation during the strike and its aftermath. Movements back and forth to the Industrial Court set the scene for other forays and invasions from the strike grounds. The court cases were dramatic events lasting late into the night, even in one case into the early hours of the next day. They brought workers together bodily as they sang their way to court or sat for hours on end, packed into its exceedingly hot, limited space, listening to complex, technical legal arguments.

The First Court Case

The cases took place in Court Number 1 of the Industrial Court, a magnificent new building opposite the newly constructed Southern African Development Community headquarters. This first case began at 9.30 AM with people standing up to honour the presiding judge, Tebogo Maruping. The case lasted some 12 hours, with several adjournments of an hour or more. By the end of the day the court room was stifling hot and there were literally hundreds of unionists in attendance. The adjacent Court Number 2 had to be opened up to accommodate the numbers. Many had come from the Gaborone Secondary School (GSS) strike grounds at the end of the day, though some members of the Mosquito choir had arrived much earlier, dancing and singing during intervals in the plaza in front of the building.

The Botswana Federation of Public Service Unions had brought a top labour advocate from South Africa to represent their case. Alec Freund, senior counsel and member of the Cape Bar, argued forcefully, at length and with great subtlety, citing South African and international law, the ILO, the Botswana Constitution, the Trade Disputes Act and legal principles of interpretation, but to no avail. The interdict requiring essential services to go back to work was confirmed, inevitably perhaps as the government prosecutor repeatedly spoke in tragic tones of 'people dying' in hospitals for lack of medical staff. The government as appellant presented the court with 500 names of alleged essential workers striking illegally. After the case ended, there was dancing and singing in the front plaza, with dancers raising their arms in the air and then flinging an imaginary wallet down to the ground. Someone made a speech shouting *Hula!* and *Viva!* to cheers from the crowds. A spokesman for the federation reminded people of May Day, two days hence, and announced marches to the strike grounds from the BBS mall and the railway station, starting at 7 AM. I took the Mosquito choirmaster and two other women back to the GSS grounds. Some spectators had not eaten all day.

The Second Court Case

Forays to the Industrial Court in the capital ultimately reached across the whole country. A week later, on Friday 6 May, a second court hearing took place to decide whether the interdict on essential workers striking would be made permanent, which was attended by crowds of workers who had travelled to the capital from the far reaches of the country. Seen as a popular cultural event, workers arrived dressed in white to signal solidarity with hospital staff, some elegantly dressed in beautiful white dresses and hats.[1]

Coaches and large mini-buses came from the north and south, each greeted with loud cheers from the expanding crowd, as their provenance was announced: Masunga, Francistown, Phikwe, Tonota, Serowe (Bamangwato, two coaches) in the north; Mochudi, Tlokweng and others from the south. With the whole country converged on the capital, this led to dramatic moments.

Workers abandoned their place under the *morula* tree to form a solid phalanx in the grounds, at least 50 metres wide and about ten people deep, dancing and singing towards the new arrivals. They sang their favourite MaBakwena song. The visitors descending from the coach, all in white, and formed their own group, dancing and singing towards the welcoming party. As they met, the welcoming singers parted, forming two parallel walls with the newcomers dancing through the middle. It all seems so practised, I reflected, despite being spontaneous, no doubt echoing other traditional events, perhaps the wedding *gorosa* (the procession bringing bridewealth cattle and gifts by the groom's party).

The crowds were vast, a sea of white. The Gaborone district chair, a youngish officer with the Botswana Land Board and Local Authorities Workers' Union (BLLAWU) attired in his usual red overalls, spoke authoritatively, followed by two women, one a new arrival. The Rangers and International choirs entertained the gathering masses. International, whose numbers had swelled, all dressed in white, sang in harmony, by now a skilled choir. The federation had been refused the right to march to the Industrial Court by the police, so the decision was taken to walk to the court, with instructions not to sing or shout, which could be construed as a demonstration, and whenever possible to avoid roads and cut across the 'bush'. The marchers set off, arriving at the court in record time.

By the time I arrived, masses of workers were gathered in the court plaza, an ocean of white (see Figure 10.16). The judgement was postponed to 4.00 or 4.30 PM, but by 2.30 Court Number 1 was packed, with floor space only. The lawyers representing the two parties had arrived and took their seats in a row in front of the bench. Legal representations were followed by the ruling that the strike by essential-services employees was 'illegal and unprotected', and strikers were ordered to go back to work. The general feeling was that the judgement was biased and unfair; the judge was undoubtedly in the government's pocket, workers told me.

We returned to the GSS grounds. This time I gave a lift to three young women social workers who expressed concern about their clients, deprived of support during the strike. But they were committed to continuing with the strike. The buying power of their never-high salaries had been drastically cut, they told me. The federation president, Masego Mogwera, announced the federation had lodged an immediate appeal against the interdict meaning that the judgement was on hold, and the strikers could return to the 30 per cent essential services agreement – this was known as a 'stay of execution'.[2] The audience roared its approval. Other speeches followed. Motshwarakgole reminded workers of the earlier victorious judgement in *National Amalgamated* v. *Attorney General* (1995), the Court of Appeal case after which dismissed MWU workers were ultimately reinstated (see Chapter 5). As dusk fell, the federation secretary general, Andrew Motsamai, rose to the podium and shouted 'revolution'. Perhaps he is more radical than I originally thought, I reflected.

The following day Elsinah told me that the leaders were 'pushed' to continue with the strike by the workers. But what about those who didn't want to continue, the silent ones? I wondered. 'They should speak up', she said.

The Third Court Case

Two days later, on Sunday 8 May, Elsinah called at about 7.15 PM. A court case was proceeding 'now' at the Industrial Court. When I arrived, the trial was already in full swing in the enlarged Courts 1 and 2, crammed with workers mobilised by text messages, sitting in any available space, down the aisles, two to a chair. I managed to squeeze in on the floor as workers made space for me. In this particular case the appellant was the government, appealing the federation's request for a stay of execution of the judgement delivered on 6 May. The federation's lawyers argued that an appeal to the Botswana Court of Appeal had been lodged directly after the judgement, automatically suspending the execution of the Industrial Court's interdict for essential services to return to work until after the appeal had been heard, which might not be for several months, a ploy the lawyers were clearly proud of.

In response, the government had lodged an urgent counter-appeal. Now the respondent (the federation) asked for a postponement. This was granted for two hours only, from 8.30 PM until 10.30 PM – on a Sunday night! Those present included most BOFEPUSU officers, a DPSM representative and scores of workers. The same judge was presiding, and it was hard to imagine, I reflected, that he would approve a stay of execution of his own judgement. We mingled and chatted while unionists entertained themselves, joking, dancing and singing in the court's front plaza.

The advocate for the government, Vergeer, claimed that he had read in *Echo,* a weekly tabloid, about the federation's plan to appeal and thus stay the judgement. Motshwarakgole then rang him up on Saturday afternoon to let him know that the appeal had been lodged. Vergeer now invoked once again earlier government arguments about the danger to life that the essential services' strike posed, proposing that the Industrial Court had even greater authority than the High Court (where a stay of execution pending an appeal did not apply) since it was a court of equity and settlement. The federation's advocate responded that, on the contrary, the stay was authoritative with no exceptions.

I found a seat among the unions' representatives, this time sitting next to the federation treasurer and president of the Secondary School Teachers' Union, (BOSETU), Shandukani Thubu Hlabano. An English literature teacher with a Master's from Nottingham University, he told me that his father was the famous Kalanga diviner, Thubu.[3]

The court reconvened at 11 PM. Much of the argument contested the jurisdiction and authority of the Industrial Court. Finally, the judge announced: 'We need time to come to a sensible resolution. Let us reconvene on Thursday, 12 May, 2.30 PM'. After pleas by both counsels, he decided to bring this forward two days. 'In the meantime, the 30 per cent essential services' agreement is acceptable!'

This was a major triumph for the federation. The terms agreed with the government before the strike commenced had now been reinstated, albeit temporarily. In fact, in the ensuing period the government continued to ignore the injunction to hand over to the federation the list of workers it deemed essential within the 30 per cent terms of the agreement.

By now it was 3.30 AM on Monday morning. There were still a few union leaders in the court. As we began to disperse, workers described Mboki Chilisa, the federation's young lawyer, as 'brilliant'; his performance had indeed been very impressive. We streamed out of the court house. International, led by their choir master, formed a group and danced around the front court plaza and into the car park, singing the MaBakwena song, which had become the strike anthem (though I was told it 'belonged' to Rangers). There were still at least 100 workers present. I went to bed at 4.15 AM.

The Fourth Court Case

Two days later, on 10 May, came yet another marathon court case. As before, the court room was jam-packed. People were sitting in the aisles, on every inch of floor space. I arrived late and squeezed into the front aisle of Court Number 2, among a press of workers who kindly made room for me on the floor. As Chilisa, the federation's young lawyer, entered the courtroom, the women around me swooned, shouted and clapped. They clearly adored this young man. Overnight, he had become a celebrity, a star. He smiled shyly. He looked very young, about 26 or 27 (born 1985 according to my neighbours on the floor), a recent graduate from the University of Botswana, he was said to be 'so brilliant he terrified the lecturers'. When he spoke, the audience in the court hung on every word. I was sitting besides a nurse from Old Naledi and an immigration officer from Lobatse. Both had been to the first two court cases on 29 April and 6 May. They told me that the two parties should have 'dialogued' and not gone to court; that many nurses and immigration officers were still working, even though they were union members; that Botswana was a peaceful country. Even if they go back, they said, they will insist on working to rule and not perform doctors' duties at present assigned to nurses throughout Botswana.

The federation's lawyers' demanded that the judge recuse himself from the case because he was likely to be biased in deciding on the appeal, and furthermore that the rule nisi issued on 6 May be suspended pending the appeal at the Court of Appeal. The judge had first to decide if he – and the court – could judge the case. Unsurprisingly, perhaps, he decided against the recusal. His final decision was to reimpose the interdiction for all essential services to go back to work and to impose court costs on the federation. Both decisions were clear signals of his displeasure, and came despite the magnificent performance of Chilisa.

People streamed out of the courtroom, deflated. It was 9.30 PM by now – another marathon day in court, with the judge seemingly willing to go on for as long as it took. During the break, I spoke with one of the federation's officers who was convinced that the judge was in the government's pocket. Not only had he been employed at one time by the legal firm representing the government; my interlocutor had heard that he was hoping to be nominated president of the Industrial Court to replace the present incumbent.[4] The federation's president announced that the strike would reconvene at the *morula* tree the following morning.

Legal Participation

Throughout the agony and the ecstasy of the court cases – their moments of elation and despair, high expectations and dashed hopes, exhaustion and fun, comradeship and exhilarating collective activism, one feature of workers' participation was particularly striking: their active intellectual engagement with the complexities of legal argumentation and judicial reasoning, much of it procedural. This was true even of the relatively uneducated manual workers in court. Botswana is a litigious society, with highly developed customary as well as modern court traditions, and this was manifest in the workers' willingness to listen to hour after hour of lengthy, often obscure and highly technical deliberations. I often felt that I was the least informed person present.

What was striking in the post-case deliberations was the widespread suspicion of the possibility, even inevitability, of corruption-linked cronyism, reflecting the widening income and social gap between workers and top civil servants, politicians and private business managers in banking, insurance, large scale retailing, housing and the stock market. In this sense, Botswana had joined the rest of the world in becoming more middle class, while recognising that a small minority had become multi-millionaires.

Initially the federation was still optimistic that the ploy of going to the Court of Appeal would be sufficient to stay the execution of the essential services interdict. Motshwarakgole expressed as much when he addressed the gathering under the *morula* tree:

> So if you know that God is on your side, and you know that you are doing everything according to the word of the law, then of course, everything should pan out in our favour, no matter what. Whatever the outcome on Friday [in the court case], it will be in our favour. Why? Because if on Friday [6 May], we are lucky enough to lose – did you hear me? I said *lucky* enough to lose – well then we will appeal it [the verdict] at the Court of Appeal. And the rules of the Industrial Court dictate that in so doing, the judgement of the Industrial Court is put in abeyance while we await the verdict from the Court of Appeal. Do you understand what I am saying to you? So, if that happens, then we are going to recall our fellows from the essential services, because there'll be nothing barring them from joining us. On the other hand, if we are unlucky enough to win it – understand me now, because really, in this instance, to win would ironically not be as lucky for us as to lose. Because should we win at court, then 70 per cent of us would have to remain behind and keep with the strike, while 30 per cent have to report back to work. I mean it's lucky, but it doesn't compare.

Motshwarakgole went on to encourage compliance with the law: 'If we ... make the economy run on only 30 per cent capacity – well, then the employer will have no choice but to give us what we want'.

The period after the Industrial Court debacle was followed by several other court cases. Several federation leaders were arrested (and later acquitted) for allegedly threatening real violence in a public speech reported extensively in the press. Legal costs mounted, with 224,000 pula spent on legal fees – one South African attorney, Freund, alone had cost 96,000 pula (Basimanebotlhe 2011a), and with no resolution in sight the federation increasingly tried to explore more 'political' forms of mobilisation. These included a whole range of stunts, as we have seen, from handing out petitions to ministers and chiefs to the invasion of ministerial meetings.

One of the court cases I missed concerned the BLLAWU officer accused of incitement to violence and later acquitted. When granted bail:

> [he] was received like a hero by the multitude of striking workers who were in court to hear the case. When he made his first step out of the court, he was grabbed by the workers who held him aloft as they sang liberation songs. The police were at the receiving end of the songs formulated to ridicule them. (Morewagae 2011a)

The unionist then appeared before cheering crowds at the GSS grounds. Many workers 'shed tears', the journalist reports, when he talked about his encounter with the law (ibid.).

Legal Scepticism and the Politics of Law

These mobilisation events showed repeatedly that workers' identities in Botswana are deeply embedded in the law, conceived of as a complex of ideas, dramatic performances and institutions. This is hardly surprising. Trade unions are inherently litigious organisations, and Batswana are used to 'living their lives in courts', with customary moots and hearings central to village life. The belief in the right to go to court and the rightness of going to court to defend one's rights is thus taken for granted by most Batswana.

The importance of the law in Botswana is signified by the magnificent edifices built in the capital to house it. The Industrial Court is an imposing ochre structure, its central broad flight of steps rising from a large courtyard flanked by two hanging walkways which lead to a two-storey-high oval glass entrance, framed by four 30-foot columns. The new High Court and adjacent Court of Appeal, inaugurated in December 2012, is a huge, diamond-shaped building with high, cathedral-like glass foyers and more than one hundred 60-foot high rectangular columns flanking an external walkway that surrounds the whole building, its roof capped by twin silver domes with a statue of the goddess Justinia at the apex (see Figure 12.1). A statue of the 'three chiefs' who, in Botswana's foundation myth, travelled to England to negotiate the Protectorate with Queen Victoria, is set apart on a circle, separating the two courts.

When, on my return visit in 2012/13, I tried to suggest, acting devil's advocate, that perhaps litigation was a waste of time and money, given the advantageous position of the employer, not a single Motswana agreed with me. It was inconceivable to my interlocutors across the board, from MPs to civil servants, academics and trade unionists, that workers would *not* claim their rights in court.

Figure 12.1 The new High Court and Court of Appeal (photograph by the author).

At the MWU offices, when I said that scholars suggest court cases are a waste of time and money since the courts are unable to ensure the implementation of their judgements, the response was unanimous. Motshwarakgole said that 'these intellectuals in Botswana don't know anything, they don't come to talk to us, and they are afraid of the government'. Molaudi said, 'we have won 90 per cent of our cases so far', referring to the federation's appeals in the High Court in 2012, which it had won. For Motshwarakgole, the matter was simple:

> After the strike the workers were tired, they needed time, so we had to go forward with the struggle in another way. The court cases were a way of going forward, continuing with the struggle. They were part of the struggle. The money [i.e. the costs] was not the main thing.

He added that it was also important internationally, with the International Labour Organisation (ILO), to fight and win cases in Botswana. The government was a member of the ILO and wished to retain its good standing as an employer.

This determined belief in the value of going to court has been questioned, however, by a range of legal scholars on various grounds. The sceptics argue that legal victories in court, and even progressive legislation, represented in the New Deal or Civil Rights legislation, depress protest while leading to co-optation and the illusion of social change. In reality, they legitimise persistent structural inequalities, particularly economic dominance, and disguise employers' continued capacity to subvert the law. Legal reforms thus mask, critics argue, social containment, continued discrimination and persistent deprivation, whether in the workplace or in contested fields such as race or gender.[5] The same scepticism regarding the futility of the law and legal challenges in court (or 'lawfare'), with the implication that fighting causes through the courts merely mystifies continuing injustice, inequality and domination, is expressed, albeit somewhat obliquely, in the argument of pervasive 'legal fetishism' in postcolonial societies (Comaroff & Comaroff 2006). In some of these societies, though not Botswana, the futility of the law may be further aggravated by the evident lack of an independent judiciary.

The most far-reaching response to this type of radical critique remains Michael W. McCann's classic theory of legal mobilisation in his study of the pay equity reform movement in the USA (McCann 1994). Legal mobilisation theory is grounded in the empirical fact that although the struggle for legal reform and social justice cannot be fought exclusively through the courts, legal challenges in court act as crucial catalysts in movement mobilisation – energising, publicising, raising awareness and conscientising a wide range of potential supporters. According to this view, legal activism supports building a movement, leveraging negotiations, forcing implementation, developing policy and compelling policy concessions (ibid.: 278 *et passim*, esp. 292). More even than grassroots activism, strikes and other spectacular events staged by a social movement, court battles are widely publicised in the press and media, reaching diverse audiences, including legislators, politicians and other public actors, as well as ordinary workers. To paraphrase McCann in my own terms, press releases, judges' statements and media articulations frame discourses, symbols and workers' moral narratives, give voice to their aspirations and their sense of entitlement, and build new vocabularies of rights. These challenge the transparency and taken-for-granted assumptions of established hegemonic discourses. Drawing on Marc Galanter (1983), McCann argues thus for the need to recognise the *catalytic* role of legal activism arising from the courts' capacity to 'radiate' effects well beyond the narrow audience or issue at stake in any particular trial.

As a theory, legal mobilisation is thus a dialectical approach that – while recognising that legal reform is a highly politicised process chequered with setbacks – rejects theories of the law-as-mystification, of the 'mystifying "lure of litigation"' (McCann 1994: 294) or the organisational costs of litigation, arguing instead that legal tactics can generate as well as consume financial resources by attracting support from middle-class and corporate contributors (ibid.). In sum, the central insight of legal mobilisation theory is the embeddedness of legal activism within broader social movements. These can and do deploy a whole range of other tactics and long-term strategies in addition to challenging the employer or government in the courts.

Like McCann, Orly Lobel (2007) rejects the fundamental assumptions of the legal sceptics, and particularly their espousal of extra-legal struggles within civil society as an alternative to litigation in court. In a wide-ranging critique, Lobel demonstrates cogently that grassroots mobilisation and legal education beyond the court are equally liable to co-optation. The fact that the original ideals of a movement are not always fulfilled, she argues, cannot deny the reach of the law or the interpenetration of state and civil society. Hence, ironically, she says:

> The rejected 'myth of the law' is replaced by a 'myth of activism' or a 'myth of exit', romanticizing a distinct sphere that can better solve social conflict. Yet these myths, like other myths, come complete with their own perpetual perils. The myth of exit exemplifies the myriad concerns of cooptation. (ibid.: 974)

One possibility, she suggest, echoing McCann perhaps, is to recognise 'the need to diversify modes of activism' (ibid.: 982), 'embrace a multiplicity of forms and practices' (ibid.: 983), avoid 'the dangers of absolute reliance on one system', and develop 'multiple courses of action' (ibid.: 988). Hence, she concludes, despite its weakness:

> Law is an optimistic discipline. It operates both in the present and in the future. Order without law is often the privilege of the strong. Marginalized groups have used legal reform precisely because they lacked power. Despite limitations, these groups have often successfully secured their interests through legislative and judicial victories. Rather than experiencing a disabling disenchantment with the legal system, we can learn from both the successes and failures of past models, with the aim of constantly redefining the boundaries of legal reform and making visible law's broad reach. (ibid.: 988)

In responding to Lobel's rejection of the sceptical view 'that the law often brings more harm than good to social movements that rely on legal strategies to advance their goals' (Cummings 2007: 63), Scott Cummings begins by recognising that, 'Whether reforms are hard or soft ... the product of lawyer-led litigation campaigns or broad-based social movements, they are always vulnerable to strategic reinterpretation, deliberate nonenforcement, and political backlash' (ibid.: 67). Nevertheless, this does not imply the wholesale refusal of legal activism as a route to reform, but a recognition that 'social change strategies by definition are ongoing and complex' (ibid.). Much movement litigation, in other words, comes *after* progressive legislation has been enacted, and is concerned, McCann recognises, with enforcing what has been gained, creating legal precedents and challenging policies that contravene the new legal reform. To consolidate change often requires further litigation to 'change law on the books' (ibid.: 68). Hence, while recognising the law's limits, legal activism 'seeks to exploit law's opportunities to advance transformative goals' (ibid.: 70).

Both the tendency to go to court and the need to defend achievements were evident in union legal activism in Botswana. At one point, the federation had five major cases and innumerable minor ones going through the courts. The cost of these cases was huge; each High Court or Court of Appeal case involved not only employing local law firms but bringing over senior counsels (the equivalent of silks in the British system) possessing detailed labour expertise from Johannesburg and Cape Town. These advocates, as they are known in Botswana, were paid hundreds of thousands of pula for representing the unions at the High Court and Court of Appeal.

It may seem paradoxical that despite their deep faith in the law, Batswana frequently disregard court decisions or retaliate when they lose. An example of the power of government to punish workers after a court victory was its five-year delay in raising workers' salaries after the victorious judgement in *National Amalgamated* v. *Attorney General* (1995), as we saw in Chapter 5. After the 2011 strike, the government proceeded to retrench industrial-class workers in cleaning, portering, laundry and refuse-collecting services. A more blatant disregard for court decisions by one party to a dispute was the response of the rebel faction of the MWU to the established union's victory in the High Court in 2005. As we saw in Chapters 6 and 7, repeated failure in court did not prevent the rebels from refusing to reimburse the MWU or ultimately forming a rival union, with government support. It was only in August 2011, seven years after the start of the dispute, that the High Court ruled in favour of the MWU against the Directorate of Public Service Management (DPSM), withdrawing recognition from the rebels' newly founded union on the grounds that it did not represent, as the law required, a third of the 28,838 industrial-class workers employed by government.[6] This legal achievement had taken over two years of litigation.

Beyond labour law, the government of Botswana has repeatedly been shown to undermine, *post hoc*, San victories in the Court of Appeal regarding their rights in the Central Kalahari Game Reserve (CKGR). After their first victory, the attorney general announced that only the one hundred named litigants would be allowed back into the reserve, but without water rights and services such as health and schools, or any means of livelihood. After the second victory, the government conceded the right for the San in the CKGR to use a water borehole it had blocked, but refused hunting permits or rights to other means of livelihood. Since then, San men have been subjected to violent intimidation, searches, harassment and imprisonment, and fined extortionate sums for being caught hunting. In other words, after each defeat in court, the government has shifted the goal posts with the consistent aim of preventing the San community from claiming its birthright in the CKGR. At the time of writing, the government may well be taken to court by the San yet again, supported by Survival International – though in its submission in 2013 to the United Nations Human Rights Council, the government appeared to change tack and appealed to the Council for 'help' in advising it on how to protect the rights of Basarwa (San), among other issues (Bosaletswe 2013).[7]

The futility of the law seemed most evident during the 2011 strike when the DPSM seemed intent on undermining the reforms to labour law the government had itself navigated through the National Assembly: the amended Trade Disputes Act (2004) and the Public Service Act (2008) were both intended to liberalise labour law in accord with ILO conventions. During the first few days of the strike, acknowledged as legal by the government in a press release, the DPSM broke several rules agreed upon with BOFEPUSU during the pre-strike negotiating phase, as well as a legal statute. When it argued the case in the Industrial Court, it did so by challenging the Trade Disputes Act itself.

This past record of obduracy gives some grounds for legal scepticism. So too do workers' suspicions regarding the impartiality of judges, whether in the Industrial Court, the High Court or Court of Appeal. As in the West, Judges are labelled 'liberal', 'progressive' or 'conservative', having particular political leanings, but in addition, some are known to have friendships and shared histories with those in power – the ruling party, the opposition and even the president. Thus, Ian Kirby, the president of the Court of Appeal, where three landmark essential services eventually landed in 2013, was known to be a friend and long time confidante of President Ian Khama. As attorney general he had advised Khama's father, Seretse Khama, and in private practice was legal advisor to the ruling Botswana Democratic Party (BDP). Kirby was also known to share the current president's enthusiasm for wildlife, and to have had business dealings with him or his relatives in the past (Motlogelwa 2010). On the other side, Judge Key Dingake of the High Court, regarded as a courageous, progressive judge, was the brother of the former president of the opposition Botswana Congress Party (BCP).

It is remarkable that bitter experience and current suspicions did not diminish unionists' faith in the law as an abstract ideal. After all, as Molaudi had pointed out, the MWU had won '90 per cent' of its cases. Politics simply made legal battles more complex and risky, even when unionists felt certain that the law was on their side. Backtracking by government meant that much of the litigation was not aimed at legal reform *per se* but at establishing precedents through court action to confirm progressive legislation and inscribe it unambiguously in 'the law on the books'.

Defending Natural Justice in the High Court

In the opening statement of his judgement on the dismissal by the government of thousands of essential service workers in May 2011, Judge Key Dingake in the High Court defined the case before him as a 'test case of considerable importance, the first strike case to be considered after the passage of the Public Service Act 2008 which entrenches the principles of natural justice' (2).[8] The judge made clear from the start that at stake was an issue of natural justice: 'The applicants challenge the decision of the respondent on the Administrative Law ground of breach of the principle of natural justice, more particularly, the *audi alteram partem* rule' (2). 'The key issue', the judge continued, 'is whether the respondent acted fairly in dismissing the public sector employees who participated in the illegal strike' (3), whether the 'decision to terminate the contracts of public officers constitutes an exercise of public power and is susceptible to judicial review in accordance with the well-known principles of Administrative Law' (12), and whether 'employees had a statutory right to be heard having regard to the relevant provisions of the Public Service Act 30 of 2008 and other codes' (13).

In some ways the Industrial Court, High Court and Court of Appeal cases in 2011, 2012 and 2013 were a replay of *National Amalgamated* v. *Attorney General*

(1995) (on which, see Chapter 5), with some exceptions. First, the later cases specifically concerned the legality of essential workers striking and being dismissed without a hearing.[9] Second, the dismissal of 461 miners, cursorily heard in the Court of Appeal in 2009, was used by government as a precedent allegedly questioning the *audi* principle established by the Court of Appeal in 1995 during *National Amalgamated* v. *Attorney General* (1995). As shown in Chapter 8, in the miners' case the court cited Judge Amissah's judgement that 'an ordinary hearing in a strike situation may not lead to a just result' to erroneously conclude that the *audi* principle did not apply to illegal strikers, an interpretation that clearly subverted the 1995 judgement.[10] The third important change that had occurred since 1995 was the passing by the Botswana National Assembly of an amended Trades Disputes Act (2004) and Public Service Act (2008). These were relied upon by the unions in their 2012 High Court challenge to the government's dismissal of thousands of essential workers to discredit the precedent established by the government in the 2009 case concerning the striking miners, going back instead to *National Amalgamated* v. *Attorney General* (1995), which concerned public sector workers, and to various South African labour court precedents that had established the *audi* principle unambiguously.

In other respects, however, many of the issues were the same: the dismissals were rushed, the federation and workers were given little or no notice, no attempt was made by the government as the employer to hold a hearing either with the unions or with individual workers; indeed, astonishingly, not a single meeting was attempted by the government with the federation during the whole of the period leading to the strikers' dismissal. The government operated 'from afar' through a series of five ultimatums addressed to workers (not the unions), published in the dubious government media, the *Botswana Daily News*, Radio Botswana and Botswana Television (BTV), and by repeatedly taking the federation to the Industrial Court.

A weakness in the government's case, which Judge Dingake pointed to at the start of his judgement, was a principled one: the two parties had agreed the terms of the strike, and the government only challenged the strike's legality on the eighth day of a legal strike expected initially to last ten days. Courts do not intervene lightly in a strike in favour of one side, the Judge said, once ground rules had been established and agreed upon, even if these may have been carelessly formulated.

In his judgement, Judge Dingake reviewed at length the growing stress in court decisions since the 1980s on the *audi* principle, and particularly the fact that:

> in recent years, judges have insisted on applying the principles of natural justice to promote good governance and to bridge the gap between law on the books and law in action. The result is that the applicability of the *audi* rule is a contested terrain for the simple reason that its application requires some flexibility and depends in large part on the circumstances of each case. (40)

The judge commented that in Botswana, while the High Court and Court of Appeal had recognised the *audi* rule, the Industrial Court had consistently denied the right of dismissed workers to be heard, a notorious instance being that of the dismissed 461 miners – though in that instance the court relied on labour law rather than administrative law principles. 'In Botswana', the Judge noted with oblique irony, 'the jurisprudence of the Industrial Court seems to suggest some reluctance to extending the right to be heard to striking employees, more particularly those participating in an illegal strike' (44). Against that trend, he quoted at length from *National Amalgamated* v. *Attorney General* (1995), which found in favour of the MWU and privileged the rule of *audi*, along with the principles of legitimate expectations and fairness – thus signalling that this historic case for the MWU had now also come to occupy a privileged place in the historical development of labour law in Botswana.

Moving beyond Botswana, notably to South Africa but also the USA, the judge went on to cite a range of cases through which *audi* had come to be entrenched in common law since the 1980s, implying thus that Botswana was lagging behind in the administration of basic justice for workers. He stressed that 'an ultimatum cannot replace a hearing' (60), and that a 'fair ultimatum' needs to be of 'sufficient duration' to enable applicants to consult their members and give them time to 'cool down, reflect and take a rational decision' (61). Against the government's claims, he argued that the proceedings in the Industrial Court were unrelated to the subsequent dismissal and could not be construed as a 'hearing' and, indeed, he elaborated at some length, dismissal could result in a 'grave injustice' (66), an 'ultimate punishment with disastrous consequences' (67). The High Court's final decision, delivered on 21 June 2012, was thus that 'All public officers who were dismissed by the DPSM on 16 May, 2011, are retrospectively reinstated to the posts which they were employed in, immediately prior to their dismissals' (70).

The judgement was a major triumph for the five public sector unions that made up the federation. It proved the independence of the judiciary in Botswana and clarified the legal history of its labour relations. But it was not the final chapter.

The Court of Appeal: Politics and the Law

The High Court decision was stayed by the president of the Court of Appeal until after the court's hearing, which I attended on 21 January 2013. The arguments put to the bench were to a large extent a replay of those made by the government and the unions in the earlier High Court case presided over by Judge Dingake. Little new was added, and the DPSM's attempt to claim that a meeting held with the unions on 12 May, four days prior to the mass dismissal, constituted a pre-dismissal 'hearing', sounded lame and unsubstantiated.

The international dimensions of law in Botswana were the most salient feature of the Court of Appeal hearing. The federation had mobilised four distinguished labour advocates who were senior counsels, three from South Africa and one from Botswana. Of these, Wim Trengove towered above the rest, a charismatic giant among South African barristers credited with being at the forefront of changes to the South African legal system (Beresford 2006), but the other three South African advocates (one representing the government) were also prominent in their fields. Their presence caused a buzz in the legal community in the capital and in the media, with a whole bench in the courtroom reserved for local lawyers. Kwelagobe, then current chair of the BDP and an old MWU friend was there, along with Saleshando, leader of the opposition. The Director of the DPSM was present at one of the cases, his deputy at the other. Court 8, the largest in the capital's new High Court edifice, was packed; the partition with Court 9 had been opened, but people were still sitting down the aisles and on the floor.

In addition to Trengove, Anton Myburgh and Martin Brassey, respectively advocates for the government and the federation, were members of the same chambers in Sandton, Johannesburg. The third barrister, Alec Freund, was based at the Cape Bar (see Figures 12.2 and 12.3). As this was an important case, on the bench were five judges: Ian Kirby, president of the Court of Appeal, born in South Africa and a naturalised Motswana for many years, Lord J.A. Abernethy, a distinguished Scottish judge who had been the reserve judge in the Lockerbie trial and regularly sat on Botswana Court of Appeal sessions, and John Foxcroft, formerly of the Western Cape High Court and now a judge in Swaziland's Supreme Court. The other two were Isaac Lesetedi and Steven Monamotsi Gaongalelwe, both Batswana.

It seemed remarkable to see white men from another country (only one advocate, Sidney Pilane, was from Botswana) slogging it out in court about the intricacies of law and justice in Botswana, another country, in front of a bench composed of two black and three white men, two of them foreigners. But for Batswana this is normal. The bench always includes a Scottish judge, I was told, since Scotland follows Dutch Roman law, as does South Africa. There is thus a universe of legal assumptions shared by all the key actors. Botswana has very few senior barristers, hence unionists took it as given that they should invite well-respected South African advocates. They intended to make it clear to the government that they intended to win, and to the bench that they should be treated with the utmost respect. Any colonial or racial connotations were thus entirely absent in the explanations offered by local Batswana; their attitude was pragmatic and colour-blind. Virtually all important cases in Botswana relied on South African advocates, I was told. It did seem, however, somewhat paradoxical that a foreigner was arguing for the need to privilege Botswana common law, as Myburgh, the government advocate and a South African, did in defence of the government dismissal of the workers without proper *audi*. It was this that made the MWU's victory in *National Amalgamated* v. *Attorney General* (1995), a Botswana precedent, so important.

Judgement was postponed for a later date to give the judges time to peruse the voluminous submissions handed to them. Unlike in the 2011 Industrial Court hearings, as the audience filed out the mood was sombre. Hope was mixed with despair. The young lawyer, Chilisa, his voice breaking, told me, pessimistically, it had all been useless: Ian Kirby had mentioned the 'crisis' caused by the essential-services strike several times, hinting at his real views. Several of the

Figure 12.2 Advocates at the Court of Appeal – government lawyers on the right, federation lawyers on the left (photograph by the author).

Figure 12.3 The lawyers Alec Freund and Wim Trengove in the Court of Appeal (photograph by the author).

unionists, however, were more hopeful: the Dingake judgement had been so clear and coherently argued, the president of the court had been active, asking questions that seemed to indicate some understanding and even agreement with the federation's case. Much seemed to hang on Kirby's biases. Brassey told me that the court could not take extraneous issues into account (like 'they are dying in the hospitals'). Elsinah thought the public service unions would definitely win because the government had failed to show they had consulted the federation.

Defending the Right to Strike

The second 2013 Court of Appeal case I attended, two days later, was the long-awaited appeal by BOFEPUSU against Judge Maruping's interdiction of essential workers striking in the Industrial Court in 2011, described in the opening pages of this chapter. The same advocate, Alec Freund, who had represented the unions at the time, also represented them in the Court of Appeal, in front of the same five-judge bench as the Court of Appeal case detailed immediately above, and he repeated once again the arguments he had made in the Industrial Court.

This was a case in which extra-legal appeals by the government – 'people are dying in the hospitals' – seemed to carry a good deal of weight, clouding the legal issues and even the common-sense judgement of Judge Maruping, the presiding Industrial Court judge. Stripped to its bare essentials, the argument of the government was two-fold: first, essential workers were prohibited from striking altogether, and should have been sent directly to arbitration according to Sections 9 and 42 of the Trade Disputes Act (2004); second, no strike rules had been conclusively agreed, a claim that relied on a misinterpreted affidavit by the federation's general secretary.

Against that, Freund for the unions argued that Section 45 of the Trade Disputes Act (2004), following Sections 9 and 42, while admittedly inconsistent with these earlier sections, in coming *after* them was to be read as paramount, overriding these earlier sections in accordance with Botswana's Rules of Interpretation Act (1984, amended 2010). Section 45 and the succeeding sections 46 and 47 explicitly allowed essential workers to strike without breaking their contracts as long as the procedures leading to the strike had been followed, which they had in this case. A reference in Section 45 to sub-section (4), which did not exist in the Act, though clearly a drafting or typographical error, was exploited by the government advocates to discredit Section 45 in the eyes of the judge. Another fruitless and confusing debate surrounded which workers were included in the essential-worker category: did it include hospital groundsmen, for example, or cleaners, cooks and laundry personnel?

Alec Freund, a veteran of the anti-apartheid struggle and early member of the Legal Reform Centre (LRC) in Johannesburg and Cape Town, now an advocate of the High Court of South Africa, responded to these arguments by mobilising the full authority of his legal expertise to reason with the bench and, one felt, educate the judges on the intricacies of labour law. One wondered, as he spoke rationally and persuasively, whether he or his fellow advocates felt they had a mission in Botswana, perhaps to advance its labour laws. Reminiscing about his life, he once told an LRC interviewer somewhat ruefully, 'There's only a hundred ways in which you can dismiss a worker and I've done each a hundred times' (LRC 2008: 14).

The main achievement of the government advocates was to create a confusing tangle of apparent legal contradictions, facts out of context, quasi-facts and untruths, in the shadow of an alleged national crisis. The Industrial Court judge had clearly succumbed to this sense of crisis. In reality, the facts were simple: the government and the unions had agreed on the strike rules and this was announced publicly in the press and on the radio. The Ministry of Health and other ministries that employed essential workers should have supplied the unions with a list of specific workers needed to provide a skeleton service, amounting to 30 per cent (a proportion suggested by the DPSM itself, which the unions had agreed to), and a second list of non-essential workers, amounting to 20 per cent of the public sector. This the ministries, including the Ministry of Health, had failed to do. Instead, the Ministry of Health gave a comprehensive list of categories working in it. As Freund argued, the employer is vested with the right to determine who should work. Rather than selecting the essential-service workers required, the Minister of Health first denied in the media that the strike had caused a crisis at all, then mobilised replacement labour illegally, but was prevented from employing them by the Industrial Courts following a challenge by the unions, and only then – on the eighth day of the strike – did the government seek an interdiction for all essential workers on the grounds there was a national crisis and that, mysteriously, essential workers were breaking their contracts and were actually not allowed to strike. The argument about arbitration was particularly surprising, given that the government had never offered essential services the option of arbitration in the period leading to the strike, a possibility never discussed, as Judge Kirby pointed out in the Court of Appeal.

Arguing lucidly on a series of points, Freund moved through this intricate maze of side issues, sub-issues and sub-sub-issues, responding cogently to questions from the bench. These concerned, *inter alia*, whether *all* essential services should be prohibited from striking because *some* clinics had been closed, or whether 30 per cent had been specified per facility, per ministry or over the whole public sector? Even if it was correct, Freund argued, that at some sites the full 30 per cent were not there, did this justify the Industrial Court's universal interdiction of essential services' right to strike which was abstract, total and in perpetuity? The remedy to a breach, surely, was to enforce the employer's right, but no more than that. It was not conceivable that a breach by one unit rendered the whole strike unlawful.[11]

Rather than dramatising the strike events, as government lawyers had, Freund made evident that he was wholly in command of the law of Botswana, as well as beyond it, a lawyer at the top of his profession. He accepted that the drafting of the law (both the Trade Disputes Act and Public Service Act) had been clumsy and that the parallels between the two acts were not made fully explicit – another matter discussed at length – with some significant minor additions or omissions in the later codified Public Service Act. But the bottom line was that there *had* been agreement, albeit not fully satisfactory, and it could *not* be said to be 'void for vagueness' as the government's lawyers contended. The next day Elsinah expressed her satisfaction that the unions' hard work in establishing agreed strike rules in great detail with the government had been recognised in court. She spoke passionately. The judges should have heard her, I reflected.

Seen from my non-expert perspective, the most astonishing aspect of the case was the government's subversion and denial of its own rules, and its apparent desire to discredit the two acts it had itself passed through parliament. The government had already announced that it intended to revise the Public Service Act. In the Court of Appeal, its advocate expounded at length the view that prohibiting essential workers from striking did not contravene ILO conventions, perhaps in anticipation of this envisaged legal reform.

In the mid-morning break in court proceedings, I discussed the case with three former cleaners at Marina Hospital in Gaborone who had been sitting in the audience, all of whom were dismissed and not re-employed after the strike. I asked them if they were enjoying the trial. Yes, they said. Did they understand everything? Not everything, they admitted, there were some words they did not know. But the case was about them, their lives. They had been dismissed as essential services even though they were just cleaners, and no one had told them before that they were essential services. 'Now', they said, 'we are just sitting at home. We have lost everything, lost our dignity. This is not our country'.

I asked them why they had not gone back to work after the Industrial Court interdiction. 'We didn't know', they responded, 'we didn't know we were essential. We were told the strike was legal. We went to Marina to ask, but someone there told us to go back to the grounds. The union (i.e. the federation) never told us to go back to work'. 'On the last day [when the police displayed their banner at the GSS grounds] the union [i.e. the federation leadership] was not there'. Freund had argued in court that the unions did not have a legal obligation to make its workers go back to work. A union is not a policeman.

The two cases heard in the Court of Appeal within the space of two days were clearly intertwined, and it was difficult to see how the federation could win one case without winning the other; of course, the obverse was also true. The same panel of judges sat in both cases. If the federation won, this would be a historic victory for labour law and the rights of workers in Botswana. The country's past record had been at best mixed, as indicated by Freund's comment about the case of the dismissed miners – whom he also represented at the Court of Appeal – that the judgement there had been 'crazy'.

Ultra Vires: Defending the Constitution

The judgement in the third case within the trilogy of trials heard between 2011 and 2013 was delivered by Judge Key Dingake at the High Court on 9 August 2012. A one-hundred page tome, it is a jurisprudential treaty of such wide-ranging philosophical depth and legal brilliance that it could well serve as an annex to the Constitution of Botswana.[12] The issue at stake in this third case was the peremptory extension by the Minister of Labour and Home Affairs of the schedule of essential workers, to include teaching, diamond cutting, sorting and selling, veterinary services, transport and telecommunications services, and support services of all the essential services, thus substantially increasing the scope and range of workers prohibited from striking, to include in effect virtually the whole public sector workforce.

Like the other two cases discussed earlier, this one bore all the hallmarks of the government acting in haste, unreflectively and without due process, relying on a literal reading of the law and arrogating to itself the right to disregard it with impunity, apparently moved by a mixture of panic and vindictiveness towards the unions. I was in Botswana when the minister amended the schedule in June 2011, a unilateral act whose legality I doubted. I had left by the time the unions applied to the High Court for a judicial review. The appeal by the government of the High Court judgement, described below, finally took place in January 2014, with an identical Court of Appeal bench, headed by Ian Kirby, as in the other cases. The judgement in this third case was postponed to April 2014 (see p. 251). During the interim period since 2012, BOFEPUSU had sent a delegation to report the matter to the ILO in Geneva.

In extending the schedule, government relied on Section 49 of the Trade Disputes Act, which says, quite simply, 'The Minister may, by order published in the Gazette, amend the schedule'.[13] It was the nature of the amendment, its illegitimate scope, its non-procedural conduct, its use of executive power to subvert a parliamentary decision, and its evident ulterior intentions, that led not only to the annulment of the amended schedule gazetted by the minister but to Section 49 itself being expunged from the Trade Disputes Act by the High Court on constitutional grounds, a radical decision not taken lightly.

The background to the case can be summed up briefly. On 10 June 2011, the unions suspended the public service strike. On 13 June, the labour commissioner notified the Botswana Federation of Trade Unions (BFTU), as required by law, of the minister's intention to expand the schedule. Before a scheduled meeting could take place, however, the minister of labour proceeded to gazette the amendment, on 17 June, without consultation. When it was brought to the National Assembly, however, the House voted to annul the amendment, in what constituted in effect a backbench rebellion. The minister immediately re-tabled an identical amendment, this time ensuring that the full cabinet of almost 30 MPs was present to support it. This series of acts was challenged by four public sectors unions (the Botswana Public Employees' Union, the MWU and two teachers' unions), represented once again by Alec Freund, who took the government to court.

Judge Dingake introduced his judgement by signalling its importance: '[T]he case involves fundamental questions of constitutional and administrative law. It also raises issues relating to the place of international law in the municipal law of Botswana' (3). Drawing on the writings of philosophers from Montesquieu to John Locke, and citing progressive American justices such as Brandeis and

Cardozo, Dutch-Roman legal scholar Grotius and constitutional cases from Botswana (the Unity Dow citizenship case), South Africa, Australia and the UK, Judge Dingake traces in his judgement the theoretical foundations of the doctrine of the separation of powers as it applies to countries that subscribe to the doctrine of constitutional supremacy. In these countries, the legislature, he argues, is limited with regard to which laws it may pass. Significantly, in order to guarantee the separation of powers, parliament may not delegate subsidiary legislative powers to the executive. Admittedly, there is a somewhat looser separation of powers in those countries influenced by the British parliamentary system: in these, members of the executive are very often also MPs. (This was made evident in the present case, in which the executive effectively packed the legislature in the second vote.) But this loose boundary, Dingake contends, makes the role of the judiciary all the more critical:

> The Constitution empowers the courts to declare invalid any exercise of power by any of the arms of the State that may be inconsistent with the Constitution. The Judiciary is required to carry out its task without fear or favour. It would be a travesty of the Constitution if in carrying out its functions it becomes paralysed by fear or favouritism. A manifestly independent and impartial court lies at the heart of the system of checks and balances built into the Constitution. (34)

The central argument in his judgement, therefore, is that by including Section 49 in the Trade Disputes Act, 'Parliament acted *ultra vires* the Constitution' (11) – it exceeded its legitimate authority by delegating law-making powers to the executive. This was underscored by the nature and scope of the amendment made by the minister, which clearly went well beyond mere detail, proving, if proof was needed, that Section 49 was impermissible and illegitimate. The huge expansion of the essential-service schedule also contradicted ILO conventions both on the right to strike and regarding the range of workers deemed to be 'essential'; it denied freedom of association as laid down in Botswana's own Constitution, and it infringed Section 9 of the Statutory Instruments Act of the Constitution,[14] which prohibited the executive from retabling an annulled instrument. The expansion was thus *ultra vires*, it defied legitimate expectations, was unreasonable, unlawful and contrary to the welfare of society. Judge Dingake reminds his fellow judges, 'We, the justices of this court, should never lose sight of the fact that the final cause of law is the welfare of society, of which the workers are a significant part' (89). It was Judge Benjamin Cardozo, he continues, who said:

> The final cause of law is the welfare of society. The rule that misses its aim cannot permanently justify its existence. Ethical considerations can no more be excluded from the administration of justice, which is the end and purpose of all civil laws, than one can exclude the vital air from his room and live. (89)

Defeat: Turning the Clock Back

Against this optimistic invocation, when defeat came in March 2013 it was doubly bitter, costly both in human and financial terms. It seemed to confirm the sceptical view that the law was a mere fig leaf for judicial bias. Judge Kirby, president of the Court of Appeal, framed his two judgements on the dismissal of essential workers in terms of the danger to life the strike posed.[15] This made clear where his public sympathies and values as a conservative judge lay. Repeatedly, throughout the 2013 Court of Appeal judgement, which reversed Judge Dingake's earlier High Court judgement, the president of the Court of Appeal, Judge Kirby, stressed that the strike 'posed obvious threats to the life and health of patients', and the 'authorities stepped in to address the emergency' (4). There was an 'emergency' in the health service (59, 68, 94); the strike was illegal, 'endangering the lives and welfare of members of the public' (72, 88); the strike of medical personnel caused 'a real danger to the sick and others in need of medical attention' (16). The notion of 'endangering the life, personal health and safety of the population' is taken, of course, from the law itself, and Judge Kirby cited the Public Service Act with regard to the definition of essential services. He concluded that, while the requirement for a pre-dismissal hearing may have been 'fair' where there was no 'pressing urgency', this would 'virtually never be the case where there is danger to lives and property, and decisive action is required for the protection of the public' (66). A similar stress on 'danger', repeatedly quoting the act, permeated the Maruping Court of Appeal case, also lost by BOFEPUSU.

If 'danger' was the first pillar of Judge Kirby's judgement, obedience to the law was the second. He makes a broad statement about 'Botswana' as an exemplary country: Botswana has enjoyed 'peace and stability for more than forty-five years since Independence' (52). Wage negotiations have always been 'sensible' and the civil service is 'diligent' and 'disciplined'. Most importantly:

> Botswana is also a country in which the rule of law is universally respected. Court orders are to be obeyed, promptly and without debate, as every Motswana knows. Disagreement can be debated later, in an appeal. No exceptions are made in the case of strikes or their unions. (52–3)

In such cases, he stressed, in Botswana the 'public interest will prevail over individual rights' (67). Citing a South African judge, he underlined his own belief that 'obedience of a court order is foundational to a state based on the rule of law' (61).

The third pillar of the judgement was political. His personal political sentiments are revealed when he comments on the government's predicament in negotiating a salary rise for public servants during the financial crisis:

> Public officers had not had a rise in salary for a considerable period,[16] and the cost of living had risen steadily. But this coincided with a worldwide recession from which Botswana was not immune. Diamond sales had slumped

> and there were severe budgetary constraints. This made salary negotiations extremely difficult. (53)

Echoing President Khama, he argued:

> Government must choose whether, in the light of prevailing economic circumstances it is in the public interest to increase public service salaries at the expense of competing interests such as health and social services, which support the poor and the unemployed as well. (36)

Under these circumstances, 'since it impacts upon the populace, a strike in the public service should be a rare occurrence indeed – a weapon of ultimate resort, when all else has failed and working conditions have become financially unbearable' (36–7), which he judged not to have been the case.

The fourth pillar of his verdict rested on practical or pragmatic premises of 'reasonableness' – on what can reasonably be expected of reasonable actors. Here Judge Kirby used his (undoubtedly) long knowledge of the country, or simply common sense, to refute the respondents' arguments. For example, he first condemns the instruction by the federation to striking workers not to read the *Botswana Daily News* or listen to Radio Botswana before commenting that the 'chance' of this order being obeyed was 'negligible':

> The overwhelming probability is that all the union members, to whom the strike, which affected their livelihoods, was the central issue of the day, would have continued to read, listen to or watch the Government media, while taking note of their union's scepticism. (82)

Moreover, based on a common-sense reading:

> It is also unrealistic, indeed facile, for the unions themselves to suggest, as Mr Motsamai [BOFEPUSU's president] did, that they too were unaware of the ultimata because they were honouring their own direction to boycott the Government media. It would have been totally irresponsible of any union to enter a state of self-induced ignorance of the events of the day, particularly on matters which were of such importance to their members. (82–3)

In any case, the government ultimata were reported in the private media as well as the state media. Similarly, strikers must have known about the final court interdiction, even though the federation was at fault for not recommending that they comply with the order:

> It was not proper to suggest to the strikers that they should await receipt of the court orders so that they could read and consider these before complying. The effective order was made in open court and was clear. The suspension of the earlier order was lifted, and the strikers were to return to work forthwith. Their representatives were present and received the order. (90)

Moreover, realistically speaking:

> It may be neither fair nor possible to hold such a hearing where, as in this case, some 3000 employees spread to the four corners of the country engage in collective misconduct which results in endangering the life and health of a part of the population. (31)

Judge Kirby's sentiments regarding the strike are captured by these four pillars of the Court of Appeal judgement: the strike by essential services endangered life and was thus irresponsible; it came at a time of economic crisis for the country and was thus unrealistic and selfish; in not returning to work following an unambiguous court judgement, the unions disregarded the rule of law and used patently spurious, gratuitous excuses, which no reasonable person could be expected to believe. In addition, it was unrealistic and hence unreasonable to expect a hearing to be held encompassing 'the four corners of the country'.

Nevertheless, Judge Kirby is careful in his judgement to be seen to uphold the principle of 'fairness', stressed in much of the case law he cites, as in *National Amalgamated* v. *Attorney General* (1995), which sided with the MWU, and the various acts. He concedes, 'It can never be fair if an innocent person is dismissed, even in a situation of apparent collective responsibility' (68). At this point in the judgement, the venerable judge arrives at an ingenious new legal resolution to the problem of *audi* and 'fair treatment': rather than a hearing *before* mass collective dismissal,

> fairness on an individual basis will be achieved, in my judgment, if after the emergency is past [*sic*!] there is a post-dismissal opportunity or right given to the dismissed employee to make meaningful representations as to why his dismissal should be reversed, or as to why he should be re-instated in his own particular circumstances. (68–9)

The natural justice principle of *audi* is upheld, but in cases of mass dismissal it turns out to be an *ex post facto*, post-dismissal individual appeal, which enables 'fairness' to be maintained, in the judge's view.

In legal terms, this resolution means that the judge did not have to accept as definitive *National Amalgamated* v. *Attorney General* (1995) – that a hearing is required before a collective dismissal – pointing (as indeed Judge Dingake had) to other cases in Botswana where illegally striking workers were dismissed without a hearing (including the Debswana miners' case). Dingake's view that 'administrative law' requires a higher standard than private employment is rejected by Judge Kirby on the grounds that, if anything, the Public Service Act not only allows mass dismissals 'in cases in which the employer cannot reasonably be expected to hear a disciplinary inquiry', but there is no mention, as there is in the Trade Disputes Act, of the right of essential workers to strike.[17] Hence Judge Kirby concludes – against Dingake's judgement – that the government was within its rights to dismiss the workers en masse. Workers' refusal to obey the court order amounted to 'criminal conduct' as court orders 'are to be obeyed promptly' (52).

> In Botswana, there is no room for an argument that in such a case time for reflection or for cooling down is to be allowed before that [i.e. obeying a court order] is done or for an argument that a show cause letter must be addressed to the strikers' union before the dismissal of strikers for such conduct. (67)

An ultimatum, in the opinion of Judge Kirby, suffices.

Evident here is the disparity between Judge Dingake's judgement, which stressed respect for workers' dignity and the right to be heard, and which highlighted the terrible hardships and humiliation dismissal entailed, and the conservative judge's stress on law and order. Ironically, however, despite the piety of his sentiments, the political reality was that government had used dismissal as a tactical weapon to frighten workers into calling off the strike before any pay settlement needed to be reached. If the government had really regarded the dismissals as final, the whole health service and the other essential services would have broken down entirely and irremediably. In the end, medical personnel were re-employed, though it took a while for a minority of the nurses. Most of those not re-employed were industrial-class workers whose jobs were privatised (with dire impact, it turned out, on adequate hospital cleaning, laundry and portering services).

Seen on a broader canvas, in saving the government the cost of reinstating 500 low-paid workers by absolving government from the duty even to consult the federation before mass dismissal, Judge Kirby in effect performed a great disservice to labour law in Botswana. During the strike, it was evident that the government believed (mistakenly, according to Judge Dingake) that they could dismiss workers with impunity without a hearing, while the unions for their part believed (mistakenly, according to Judge Kirby) the very opposite, basing their view on *National Amalgamated* v. *Attorney General* (1995) and other case law: that workers could *not* be dismissed without a hearing. This led to mutual incomprehension, an impasse, a stand-off, a series of ultimatums and, as it turned out, a tactical dismissal of doctors and nurses.

Commenting on Judge Kirby's judgement, Wim Trengove is quoted as saying:

> Our view is that the judgment is littered with too many political statements that were not germane to the resolution of the dispute between the parties, and which are not supported by evidence that was led by the parties, e.g. the executive's budgeting process; the economic recession; the suggestion that strikes in the public service should be a rare occurrence. There is no legal basis for the assertion that strikes in the public service should be a rare occurrence; it may be what the executive wants, but it is not supported by any legislative interventions because both the Trade Disputes Act and the Public Service Act permit public servants to resort to industrial action in furtherance of any dispute of interest. (Mosikare 2013)

Though second, the Maruping Court of Appeal judgement was judged primarily on technical grounds, once again Judge Kirby displayed his clear sympathy for the government.[18] Most strikingly, he allowed the government to make repeated mistakes without paying a judicial price. It was alright for MaBakwena to 'discover' several days into the strike that it was 'illegal' for essential-service workers to strike, despite the fact that she had agreed publicly to their going on strike (30). It was all right for the government to mistakenly provide the wrong strike form, one which mentioned only Section 7.1 of the Trade Disputes Act that referred the dispute to the labour commissioner prior to a legal strike. The unions should have known better – that they needed to raise section 45.1 as well: the fact that neither party raised the issue of essential services, either Section 9b (disputes involving essential services must be referred by the labour commissioner for arbitration) or Section 45.1 (essential services can strike), did not deter the judge from placing the onus for errors entirely on the unions.

The federation had erred in allowing an ambiguity in the strike rules agreed by the mediator – namely, that government should 'provide the trade union party with the categories and/or names of employees required to work in essential services for the effective provision of essential services to the public during the strike' (27). This ambiguity was seized on by the judge to absolve the government from providing a proper essential-services work schedule detailing those employees expected to work during the strike. Instead, government was within its rights to provide only broad categories, the minimal reading of the strike rule set by the mediator, and it remained up to the unions, according to the judge, to nominate strikers who would staff the clinics and work in the hospitals!

Similarly, it was up to the unions to seek clarification from the government regarding the dismissal ultimatums, not for the government to afford the unions a hearing. *If* the unions had reported the strike dispute to the Commissioner with reference to Section 45.1, the strike would have been legal, but they mistakenly omitted to refer to this section. Hence, the judge reasoned, the strike was illegal. On the admissibility of Section 45, he introduced a convoluted plethora of secondary laws from various acts to reach the conclusion that there were sufficient grounds to accept the Industrial Court's ruling nullifying section 45 (because it was 'not mentioned'), especially as the procedures laid down in it were not followed by the labour commissioner. That the Judge was not entirely happy with his own judgement was signalled by the fact that he did not award damages to either party, on the grounds 'that the Trade Disputes Act did contain contradictory and confusing provisions, and that the sections of the Public Service Act dealing with industrial action was also not fully aligned with the [Trade Disputes Act]' (72). Nevertheless, his verdict was that essential workers had acted illegally in going on strike, despite an agreement with government, publicly announced.

The question is: Was it worth going to court, given the huge expenses the unions incurred? As in the US Supreme Court, in Botswana too, it seems, a conservatively inclined judge can have a devastating impact on liberal law, not by fiat but by explicitly setting forth their reasoning in detail, on grounds that seem rational, logical and humane. But there is another side to this, one which favours the unions: at the political level, the extension of the strike, though illegal, enabled the unions to agree among themselves, with widespread public support, on their proposal for a 'pyramid pay structure' based on notions of equity and redistribution. Although rejected by the government, this demand for equitable pay for low-paid workers experiencing financial hardship at a time of rampant inflation *was achieved* when the National Public Service Bargaining Council subsequently allowed for a 'recession-related payment' to low-paid workers in 2013.

Seen in terms of social movement theory, the High Court and Court of Appeal judgements may or may not have strengthened the opposition's chances of winning the 2014 general election and, if they do win, of adopting a legal framework more sympathetic to labour by amending the law. In the meanwhile, the unions belonging to BOFEPUSU were faced with a huge legal bill.

Victory at Last

On 22 April, 2014, judgement in the third Dingake case concerning the unilateral ministerial extension of the essential services schedule (see pp.242–5), was finally delivered at the Court of Appeal in Lobatse.[19] The delivery, by Justice Ian Kirby, was itself something of a cliffhanger. In fine comparative and historical detail he argued that delegating to the executive the right to formulate rules and schedules was usual in parliamentary democracies, once statutes were passed by parliament. Kirby also contended, contra-Dingake, that in Botswana the right to strike is not constitutionally enshrined (p.68).

As unionists assembled in court listened to the 85-page judgement, they felt increasingly certain that government had won yet again, with dire consequences for the freedom to strike of most public sector workers. Only on p.71 did the judge announce his verdict: classifying a service as essential was an important policy matter 'to be debated in Parliament' and 'subjected to public scrutiny' (71–2), especially 'because the right to strike', was only recently 'conferred by an Act of Parliament, after full debate. To allow it thereafter to be arbitrarily cancelled by a member of the Executive would not', the judge concluded, 'pass constitutional muster' (72–3). The government had lost, with costs.

Conclusion

If legal activism is embedded in wider social struggles for justice, it is equally true, as this chapter has shown, that workers' identities are embedded in the law and in the courts, as vital to their sense of subjectivity and dignity as the air they breathe. In light of this, I believe that anthropology needs to re-examine some of its assumptions about the role of the law in postcolonial nations. It is remarkable that, even in lesser trials, locally trained Tswana attorneys representing the MWU in court cite the need to consider public welfare and morality, and invoke the Constitution alongside a myriad of statutory acts and common law precedents. Such broader issues are raised in order to challenge employers' unilateral, unexplained and apparently irrational inclination to break agreements with workers. And as in nationally significant trials, so too in lesser ones: workers pack the gallery and listen with deep concentration to abstruse legal arguments and often inaudible, impenetrable exchanges with the bench.

In 2013, the MWU challenged the Rural Industries Promotions Company (RIPCO) in the High Court over their attempt to 'repudiate' for the second time an exit package they had agreed with the union.[20] I asked some of the workers in the audience, several of whom had been dismissed without an exit package, if they were able to follow the arguments in court, surely so different from a customary *kgotla* hearing where they easily understood everything. They nodded. Why, then, had they come? They responded that the case was about 'us'. 'Although we don't quite understand it all', they admitted, 'we are learning'. One woman added that this was her 'first time', but she intended 'to come again from now on'. As they saw it, their very sense of themselves as agents justified their bodily presence in court. One worker, who had studied engineering in Leicester and completed a Master's degree in Bradford, added that, like the others, several of whom were manual workers, he too had come to court to 'learn'. 'When you learn you come out another person', he told me.

In the MWU newsletter of June 2012, the headline in large letters announced 'The Winning Month' (MWU 2012: 1). The MWU has won three cases, one against DPSM (the Dingake High Court case concerning the essential services dismissal, discussed above) and two others lesser cases, all in June. But against such successes, legal sceptics can also claim their day in court. Another front page headline, this time in the *Telegraph* in 2013, announced that public sector unions planned to launch a 'crusade' against MPs and the government for favouring themselves in a pay settlement denied workers. Having fought long and hard to have the National Public Service Bargaining Council established, it had become clear that the government was constantly disregarding its 'structure and the agreement signed between the state and labour movement' (Ontebetse 2013: 1). The aim of the government in backdating only MPs' salaries was, the BOFEPUSU spokesman claimed, 'to discredit the labour movement who were negotiating for a salary adjustment at the bargaining council'. Public sector unions, however, would be holding demonstrations to show workers 'who their real enemy is', he warned (ibid.).

The government in Botswana, as this chapter has repeatedly shown, does not hesitate to strike below the belt or to disregard its own laws and court decisions. It has many weapons in its armoury, including amending the law in parliament if it loses cases in the Court of Appeal. It is equally true, however, that unions – particularly public sectors unions – along with the private media and a few select NGOs, are uniquely placed in Botswana's civil society to stand up to government autocracy, defend the morality of public law, and demand the independence of the judiciary and legislature in the face of unbridled executive power. Unions are relatively wealthy, independent organisations, not beholden to the government, able to go to court to represent the common people in their collective struggle for worker rights and a living wage.

CHAPTER THIRTEEN

Concluding Remarks: Class Identity, Dignity and the Agency of Labour in Botswana

There are many ways of approaching identity. It may be seen as oppositional or experiential, cultural or social. Class identities have been construed, subtly, as inflected by lifestyle (following Bourdieu 1984), and theorised as intersecting with other, equally determining social identities – of gender, age, ethnicity or race. The present book has followed E.P. Thompson and other historians of class in attempting to describe the growing salience, depth and uniqueness of working-class identity in Botswana. My objective in using ethnographic methods of thick description has been to portray a nuanced picture of the various strands that constitute Batswana worker identity: steeped as it is in Christian faith and the law, mobilised in popular culture, threatened by the precariousness of regular employment and fear of job loss, rooted in 'home' villages, yet aspiring to middle-class lifestyles.

Although the very existence of a working class in Botswana is relatively new – given that class identity has been shaped among workers who grew up in a predominantly rural society – as an identity, class is nevertheless culturally compelling, embodied and entangled in powerfully felt subjective notions of honour and dignity. Working-class identity, both individually and collectively, constitutes for workers a narrative of virtue, moral commitment and self-respect, *seriti*, to be defended against those in power.[1] To lose this identity is deeply traumatising. Recall the words of workers attending the Court of Appeal hearing who had lost their jobs: 'We are just sitting at home. We have lost everything, lost our dignity. This is not our country'.

Can public anthropology as a discipline contribute to an interdisciplinary conversation on national identity in the context of modern labour relations? The making of working-class identity in Botswana has been conceived of here as a process, responsive to current predicaments and crucibles that have made it historically significant. This has been so, we have seen, particularly with regard to the development of a more enlightened, ethically grounded body of case law in Botswana. The book has traced the route of local labour law through the courts over a period of more than 20 years, from the 1991 national strike of the MWU and the cases that followed it, through the internal union factional disputes tested repeatedly in court, to the mine workers' union's failed court challenge of its members' dismissal. Despite the subsequent domestication of

International Labour Organisation (ILO) conventions, and the introduction of, in theory, more progressive labour legislation, the national strike by the Botswana Federation of Public Sector Unions exposed the hollowness of the promise of progress when, in 2011, the government dismissed thousands of workers, leading to a further round of High Court hearings. These fundamentally tested precedent law and the moral intentions of the new legislation.

The question of how to achieve social change and render the struggle for justice effective from the position of an uneducated manual worker has animated this book. There have been notable constitutional victories in court: in the Court of Appeal in 1995, and in the High Court – twice – in 2012. But the challenge of translating these victories into lasting rights for workers still remains, faced as they are with an intransigent and powerful employer willing to invoke nightmarish visions of a future Armageddon to justify low-paid government workers earning less than a living wage, even as the salary gap with top civil servants widens. This challenge, of transforming worker rights achieved through legislation and the courts into a better, more humane and just working environment, is familiar to workers throughout the industrial world.

Workers in Botswana, we have seen, even manual workers, share a cosmopolitan, international consciousness of their labour rights. They are not parochially confined by their class or the nature of their jobs. They travel to Geneva to ILO meetings. They invoke ILO conventions and landmark historical labour achievements elsewhere. They follow the news of popular protests in other countries. Their internationalism is articulated in their slogans and in their creative appropriation of union songs.

As a study of a trade union, and of union activism, this book has considered the role of a union of low-paid and relatively uneducated public service workers in the making of modern Botswana. A major actor in civil society, the MWU reaches, distinctively, to the far corners of the land, encompassing town and country, transcending ethnicity, so that even in its conflicts with the government, the employer, the union simultaneously contributes to nation-building. As a powerful dissenting voice it embodies, performatively, values of democracy and freedom of speech. As an organisation able to mobilise sufficient funds to challenge the government effectively through judicial review, it tests the independence of the judiciary. In alliance with other unions, it joins workers in solidarity across class and educational status.

When it comes to unions, politics are pervasive: in adversarial relations with the employer, with other unions and, internally, in periodic factional disputes. The legitimacy of union involvement in politics is a perennial topic of public debate in Botswana, as public sector unions try to encourage opposition parties to form an alliance in the hope of gaining a more humane employer. The internal political division that almost tore the MWU asunder in 2004 and 2005 freighted its officers with a bitter memory of suffering and left accounts still unsettled. The sedimented injustices and animosities the dispute engendered fed into wider divisions within the ruling party, and had long term consequences for later divisions and alliances within the broader trade union movement. Thus, even though the MWU was internally at peace in later years, such factional

Figure 13.1 National Executive Committee meeting in the Manual Workers' Union's new offices (photograph by the author).

divisions – which all unions seem to experience at one or another point – were analysed in depth in the book; they could not just be brushed aside as a passing moment in history.

By 2013 the MWU had grown as an institution, with its own burial and benefit schemes, a low-interest cooperative mutual saving society, financial arrangements for larger, long-term loans at a locally favourable rate, access to medical insurance, a periodic newsletter, and several new, young, IT-savvy union employees in the capital. The MWU had lost and continued to lose members because of government retrenchment, but it was modernising and computerising its membership. It had plans to expand in the future, perhaps to bring into the union ambit more low-paid private sector workers and to create an industrial bargaining council for members working in parastatals.

In February 2013, the MWU moved from the old office huts in the capital's Village quarter (see Figure 4.1), crowded with people and overflowing with files piled high on every available surface, to large, state-of-the-art, smart new offices in the most expensive area of the capital, a stone's throw from the recently inaugurated High Court (see Figure 13.1). The MWU had acquired the offices by realising some very lucrative, successful earlier investments. The Village plot it owned outright was itself worth millions of pula. But despite all this, the struggle with the employer had if anything intensified, as the Botswana government began to implement cutbacks to the civil service, starting with industrial-class workers.

In considering all these developments, how are we as public anthropologists to conceptualise the transformative agency of workers? At times, it did seem to unionists, despite their irrepressible optimism in the face of adversity, that the cards were stacked against them. At other times, they reminded me that they had 'won 90 per cent of their cases' against the government. Crucially, many of their unmentioned and unreckoned day-to-day activities were concerned with negotiating and mediating individual disputes between employer and employee. They relied on their accumulated expertise to hold the employer to account. But beyond that, the life and achievements of a major trade union also chart the life and destiny of a country. As workers struggle individually, discovering their agency in the process of overcoming hard times, so too do workers' collective struggles through their labour unions endow them with agency on a broader stage, as this book has shown. If capitalism and class antagonism cannot be abolished altogether in Botswana – and this is not wished for by workers – the lesser, more achievable aim is to contain and tame the worst inequalities and iniquities such economic systems produce, and to demand that all workers who contribute their labour share, as a right, in their country's wealth.

APPENDIX

Further Grievance Cases Settled by Lilian MaMoshe

The Case of the Reluctant Land Board Driver

This was the case of an officer employed as a storekeeper with the Supplies Department who was redeployed to be a driver by Ngwaketse Land Board. The redeployment followed a review exercise. In the new strategic plan, her post as storekeeper was not accommodated. She was shifted, unwillingly, to the post of driver. She brought the matter to me as her union shop steward. I challenged the Land Board's decision on the grounds that she was not consulted. I appealed her matter to the director of the Department of Land Board Services, requesting that he reconsider the matter. The director agreed that the consultation had not been thoroughly done.

Resolution: In favour of the storekeeper maintaining her post. The case was decided on the following grounds: the officer had held the same post for more than five years; she was denied the opportunity to choose for herself an alternative position available in the organisation, regardless of the fact that she had other academic qualifications (certificates in secretarial administration, a driver's licence, and 'Cambridge', i.e. GCSE). The management had instead re-deployed her as a driver which was below her educational standard.

The Case of the Studious Land Officer

An officer was an employee at the Ngwaketse Land Board as land registration officer. She was appointed after she had already registered with the University of Botswana to do a Master's degree part-time. The Ngwaketse Land Board advertised the post of land registration officer, and she deliberately applied for it and was offered the post. She assumed her duties at Kanye. After two months, the management notified her that the post had now moved to Maokane Sub-Land Board in a rural village. Maokane is in a remote area, far from the capital, where there is no adequate transport or telecommunications. She made an effort to negotiate with management, explaining that she was unable to move to Maokane because she was already registered for evening classes at the University of Botswana, but this was in vain.

She called me on board to represent her as union shop steward. First, I had to establish where the post was advertised by studying the staff organisation's establishment register, and the advertisement copy of the post in which it was stated that the post was in Kanye, not Maokane. The letter of appointment also stated the same. The employer had given her the option to resign or take the post at Maokane.

Resolution, on appeal: the permanent secretary of the Ministry of Lands and Housing found in favour of the officer keeping her post in Kanye, and recommended that she be allowed hours to attend classes, and, when needed, to be granted study leave.

The Case of the Underpaid Hospital Workers

The management of Kanye Seventh-Day Adventist Church Hospital had two categories of industrial-class staff, the first paid by government funds and the other paid from hospital funds. The difference was that the government workers were paid according to the required standard, while the other workers were paid below the recommended rate. I was called on board as the shop steward because the disparity led employees to call for clarity from the union. As part of my investigations, I consulted the Ministry of Health to clarify the matter, and was informed that the practice by the hospital management was totally out of line, and the Ministry of Health was not aware it.

Resolution: The hospital management paid all the industrial-class workers their appropriate wages as per government standard-of-living income scales, but failed to pay them gratuities for the number of years worked. The hospital had no funds to cover the lost benefits.

The Case of the Overworked General Duties Assistants

The Southern District Council had employees in the Clinics Department. They were engaged on an hourly basis to work long hours, including several hourly breaks with no pay (the union norm is 7 hours 45 minutes a day). The management scheduled their day duties so that they had to work three hours in between one hour breaks. This meant that they did not enjoy their working conditions, and they felt management was avoiding paying them overtime, instead opting to give them shorts breaks during their day work.

Resolution: I had a discussion with the Southern District Council secretary to at least clarify why they had not scheduled general duty assistants' working hours instead of allowing them to work their long hours. The matter was taken up with the Ministry of Local Government but in vain; there was still no clarity.

The Case of the Cooks' Gratuities

This was a case at Southern District Council. It affected the primary school cooks' gratuities. There was a misunderstanding in the Human Resources Department on the right formula for paying the gratuities of employees while on duty, and the retirement gratuity. Gratuity while on duty was calculated as follows: 5 (days) times 5 (weeks) times 5 (years) at the current rate of daily pay. The gratuity for retirement should have been calculated as follows: count all the years worked, multiply by 25, and then multiply the outcome by the worker's current rate of pay; then subtract from the total all gratuities already paid in the past to the employee, and the remaining balance goes to the employee, plus any leave days accumulated.

The Case of the Underpaid Weekend Workers

Southern District Council management was not familiar with calculating payments for weekends spent away. The correct formula was as follows: overtime worked in the duty station is not calculated in the same way as weekends spent outside the duty station. Overtime worked in the duty station at weekends should be taken as worked hours multiplied by 2. Overtime worked outside the duty station during weekends or holidays is calculated as multiplied by 2 plus 1; in monetary terms it will be the equivalent of three days for every day worked.

Resolution: A copy of the directive was circulated among all the payroll officers to familiarize them with it. Members of staff are now well conversant with the formula.

The Case of the Overworked Nightwatchmen

Southern District Council employed nightwatchmen in the primary school, and their condition was specifically long hours, short effort (they weren't paid overtime for 12-hour shifts). The council paid them for normal hours of 20 days work at the flat rate. But the correct scenario should have been calculated as follows: normal pay was 183.5 pula per day, divided by 7.75 hours, which gave their hourly rate, multiplied by the number of hours per week/month usually worked. Anything over this is overtime, and is paid at a different rate. The normal number of hours was subtracted from the accumulated number of hours they had actually worked. The result should have been treated as the overtime they had worked. The total pay should have thus been normal pay plus accumulated overtime.

Resolution: Copies of the directive clarifying the nightwatchmen's pay were circulated among all the payroll officers. The nightwatchmen were paid accordingly, and their arrears were calculated and paid. Today they are experiencing no difficulties regarding their pay.

Notes

Chapter 1

1. But see e.g. Beynon and Austrin (1989) on the Durham miners' gala.
2. 'Working poverty' has been defined as working full time for a salary that cannot meet basic needs (Snarr 2011).
3. Butler argues that there is no subject prior to discourse, so that the paradox of subjectivation is to locate 'agency as a reiterative or rearticulatory practice, immanent to power' (Butler 1993: 15). Foucault sees resistance as invoking power: 'if there was no resistance, there would be no power relations' (Foucault 1997b: 167). See also Mahmood's discussion of agency (Mahmood 2001, 2005), which draws on Foucault's notion of technologies of the self, Bourdieu, and in particular Aristotle's notion of 'habitus' as a learned, embodied ethical disposition. In stressing submission, Mahmood ignores, however, the fact that Muslim women paradoxically aspire through their submission to positions of leadership, *diyani*, more consonant with Foucault's ethical theory of leadership in his later work.
4. Foucault never fully theorises the cosmopolitanism of the Stoics and Cynics (see Foucault 1997a).
5. For a full discussion, see Garbett (1970), van Velsen (1979) and R. Werbner (1984), and contributions to Evens and Handelman (2006), particularly Kapferer (2006) and Handelman (2006).
6. See e.g. on Africa, Cheater (1986, 1988), McCracken (1988) and Simons and Simons (1969).
7. On this in Southern Rhodesia, see e.g. van Onselen (1976), who argues that, cumulatively, over time, ideologies of worker resistance came to be established, rooted in the industrial landscape despite a labour repressive system and the failure of individual strikes.
8. For a review of the events leading to the massacre of a breakaway union faction protest demonstration, see the article at: http://en.wikipedia.org/wiki/Marikana_miners'_strike (accessed 11 December 2012).
9. On ethnic minorities, see e.g. Durham and Klaits (2002), Motzafi-Haller (2002), Solway (2002) and R. Werbner (2004); on the marginalisation of the disabled, see the exemplary study of Livingstone (2005); on the intersection of gender and class, see Griffiths (1998); and for an overview, see R. Werbner (2002c) and the collection edited by Mazonde (2003).
10. Something of a north/south divide did emerge temporarily during the factional dispute, but the dispute was never defined ethnically (on this see also R. Werbner 2004).
11. On the USA, see McCann (1994) and Snarr (2011).
12. This tendency to form complex alliances and amalgamations in the face of 'modernising' trends has been apparent in Britain too: see Bach and Winchester (2003) and Waddington (2003).
13. For a comprehensive review, see Berger (1992) and Simons and Simons (1969); see also Good (2002: 175–6, 182–6).

14. I am grateful to Tom Etty for this point. The best comparative analysis of the relations between unions and political parties is Taylor (1989). On the relationship between UNISON, the British public service union, and the Labour Party, see Jones (2000) and Sawyer (2000), and more broadly on UNISON's policies and agendas, the contributors to Terry (2000). The 'dual face' of social movements refers to their populist roots on the one hand, and their instrumental or institutionalised insertion into the bureaucratic structures of state on the other (Cohen and Arato 1992: 523 *et passim*).
15. In 2003, at the height of union membership, there were 60,000 members. The numbers dropped drastically following a factional split in 2004/5, but it remained the largest union in Botswana with around 45,000 members in 2014.
16. Minutes and other official documents are, however, in English.
17. The pula is the national currency of Botswana, whose exchange rate varied throughout the research conducted for this book. Where appropriate, pula amounts are given in British pounds sterling. When quoting from official documents, amounts are sometimes given using the symbol P; thus, P500 equals 500 pula.
18. There were, however, some early strikes. On the strike in Pikwe, see Parsons et al. (1995: 320–2); on civil servants organising, see R. Werbner (2004: 168–74); on unions generally, see Molokomme (1989) and Selolwane (2000).
19. See e.g. Peace (1975) on mutual stereotypes of different classes of African workers and the sense held by factory shop-floor unionists that they were the true opposition to oppressive management. Peace (1979) argues that low-paid workers in Nigeria were far more closely embedded in and hence aligned with the peasantry and urban masses than they were with the more highly-paid salariat in Nigeria.
20. In 2011, a splinter party, the Botswana Movement for Democracy (BMD) split from the BDP. Some members have since returned to the BDP. Its electoral fortunes are yet to be tested at the time of writing.
21. Regarding Britain on this matter, see Cole (1926: 171). The leader of the BNF, K. Koma, is said to have opposed formal trade union affiliation with his party.
22. Meeting with the MWU's National Executive Committee, 1 April 2005.
23. I was told this in 2011 by a deputy permanent secretary in the Ministry of Finance and Economic Development.
24. The list was being updated with the arrival at the Palapye regional headquarters of a new, energetic and competent social worker, who was said to 'have humanity'. Some people, I was told, were just 'lying in the lands', destitute, but not applying for support.
25. See in particular Arrighi and Saul (1963: 69, 80–81, 120–21, 141–3).
26. On this, see Manoukian (2011).
27. On the power of mimesis, see Taussig (1993: 250); on hybridity as a displacement or the 'doubling up' of signs, see Bhabha (1994: 119) and P. Werbner (2001: 136).

Chapter 2

1. An earlier version of this chapter appeared in P. Werbner (2010a).
2. This thesis is republished in Arrighi and Saul (1963: esp. pp.69, 80–81, 120–21, 141–3).
3. For a masterly account of the precarious lives of non-state sector workers in post-apartheid South Africa and discourses surrounding what he terms the work-citizenship nexus, see Barchiesi (2003) and particularly (2011). Barchiesi shows how, against state normative discourses, wage labour in the casualised, contract sectors is precarious, underpaid, demeaning and insecure. See also Brewster and Wood (2007:

8) and Desai (2002) for an evocative account of the precarious lives of South Africa's poor and early mobilisation for protest.

4. The one-way linear urbanisation thesis of African workers was strongly critiqued by the Manchester School; see Mitchell (1966).
5. On Botswana, see R. Werbner (1989: 109–48, 245–98; 2004: 133–46).
6. The examples are too numerous to cite. See, for example, Larmer (2007), who focuses on the Zambian Copper Mine Union's struggle for multi-party democracy in Zambia.
7. Retirement from the civil service in Botswana can be very early. Section 15(3) of the Public Service Act (1998) gave the government authority to retire public employees who reached 45 years of age. The section was eliminated in the new Public Service Act but there were fears in 2011 that it might be reinstated after the Botswana Public Employees' Union (BOPEU) lost an appeal in the High Court to reinstate 17 directors whose jobs were terminated before they reached 50 (Kavahematui 2011). The official retirement age is 60, though retirement at 50 is quite common, despite the fact that old-age pensions are only paid to those over the age of 65 (the rate in 2011 was 220 pula a month, increased to 250 pula in 2013).
8. On the emergence of this post-civil service elite, see R. Werbner (2004).
9. For example, in May 2009 a civil service job in Botswana was advertised at scale E2, with a salary of 252,744 to 262,956 pula per annum (roughly £25,000); E1 equals £29,000. This compares with the average salary of 24,000 pula per annum of an industrial-class worker (£2180 per annum; £1 was about 11 pula at the time). The lowest-paid workers in the public sector earn 1200 pula per month (about £1320 per annum). Botswana also has a 'super scale' for very senior civil servants (S1 and S2), which is far higher. In September 2011, the salary for a permanent secretary was increased by 3 per cent from 556,896 pula (£49,000) to 573,612 pula (£50,500) a year, and that of the lowest A3 scale salary was raised from 14,448 pula (£1270) to 14,892 pula (£1309) annually. This amounted to a ratio of 1:38.5 between the lowest and highest paid (see www.gazettebw.com/index.php?option=com_content&view=article&id=11439:government-to-pay-the-3-in-october&catid=18:headlines&Itemid=2, accessed 6 October 2011). According to the World Bank country report for 2011, income inequalities in Botswana are among the highest in the world, but this includes the private sector as well (see http://web.worldbank.org/WBSITE/EXTERNAL/COUNTRIES/AFRICAEXT/BOTSWANAEXTN/0,,menuPK:322821~pagePK:141132~piPK:141107~theSitePK:322804,00.html, accessed 6 October 2011).
10. Cleaners and cooks, along with groundsmen, are among the lowest paid in the public sector. Among middle-income women workers, nurses and teachers, usually highly educated above tertiary level, earn between 4000 and 10,000 pula a month. Nurses, who start at 6000 pula in the past had their own associations, though they have recently formed their own union. Many work overtime to increase their pay. NGO workers, often women, earn relatively modest salaries, despite their middle-class status, about 120,000 to 150,000 pula per annum (about £11,000) or even less.
11. They are: employment injury benefit, sickness benefit, medical benefit, invalidity benefit, maternity benefit, unemployment benefit, old age benefit, survivors' benefit and family benefit. See Ntseane and Solo (2007: 24).
12. The code was formulated in 2005 but was still under review in 2007. The statement issued at the meeting in Zambia on 8/9 February 2007 reads: 'To address the issue of Social Security in the region, the Ministers and Social Partners approved the SADC Code on Social Security and recommended it to the ICM for adoption and urged

Member States to involve Social Partners in the domestication process of the Code'. The full text of the Code is unavailable, but see SADC (2007).

13. See Livingstone (2012: 12–18) on universal health care in Botswana. Minimal school fees were reintroduced in 2006, which are a heavy burden for low-income earners. Nevertheless, by contrast to neighbouring South Africa (see Barchiesi 2011), the non-commodified welfare state is undoubtedly a good deal more robust in Botswana.
14. See Republic of Botswana portal for Lobatse Town Hall (www.gov.bw/en/Ministries--Authorities/Ministries/Ministry-of-Local-Government-MLG1/Local-Authorities/Lobatse-Town-Council/Tools-and-Services/Services/DESTITUTION/, accessed 15 December 2011). I assume rates are comparable across the county.
15. I refer to the situation until August 2007. Since then, terms of employment have been renegotiated, with most industrial-class workers under the age of 50 moving on to a 'permanent and pensionable' scheme. Low-paid workers have been shifted to rolling, three-year contracts, not yet fully settled at the time of writing, meaning that gratuities are paid every three years and the contract renewed. I was told by unionist leaders that the terms are more favourable than before, with contract workers' gratuities calculated at 25 per cent of their annual salary multiplied by three. This means that a contract worker on 2000 pula a month would get 18,000 pula as a lump-sum gratuity payment after three years, an improvement on the above. The new contract also allows for six months sick leave with pay, as against one month previously. On the other hand, in calculating gratuities, pay rises are not reflected back over a working person's whole working career as before.
16. See also note 10 (above).
17. This means that each income earner has close to 24 dependants on average.
18. This was recently redefined to allow the scheme to employ only select skilled workers, excluding most rural women who relied on the relief works to subsidise their livelihoods from remittances. In 2010 the scheme was converted into the Ipelegeng Project, with workers earning 18 pula a day, or 360 pula a month, raised to 400 pula (less than £40) in March 2011.
19. On destitute allowances in 2011, see www.gov.bw/en/Ministries--Authorities/Ministries/Ministry-of-Local-Government-MLG1/Services/Destitude-allowance/ (accessed 5 October 2011).
20. For the implications of this, see van Driel (2003: 64), where she argues convincingly in the case of South Africa, as elsewhere, that privatisation has allowed for lucrative transfers from the state to a crony 'bourgeoisie' and financier class, often at less than actual value.
21. The women were among a cohort of union members interviewed in depth in 2007 and 2008, with repeat interviews in 2011, apart from MaJune, whom I visited in 2005 when she was living in the Old Naledi shanty town, but interviewed in 2011. I also attended their meetings and those of the union in which they participated. Some women I knew better than others, and I had many conversations with them over several years. One case study omitted here appears in P. Werbner (2010a).
22. All names used in the case studies are pseudonyms apart from the names of salaried union officials.
23. *Seriti* meaning 'dignity' in Setswana, as discussed in a later chapter.
24. Form 5 is the final year of senior high school which, in the state system, marks the achievement of a Cambridge Junior Certificate (the equivalent of GCSE), enough to be considered a candidate at the University of Botswana.
25. Interview with MaSeriti, 11 July 2005.

26. In Botswana, respect for elders is an important principle. The counterpart to it is that elders are expected to be wise and responsible.
27. Interview with Grace MaMolemo, 16 August 2005.
28. For MaSiame's case, see P. Werbner (2010a).
29. In other regions, such as Kanye and Gaborone, there have been female union chairpersons.
30. The eligibility of experienced storekeepers without academic qualifications to attend the course was successfully negotiated by the MWU (see Chapter 4). MaPelotona had been educated to Junior Certificate level but had failed the exams, and thus was originally barred from the course. Salaries presented here are all at the 2005 rates, and have been subject to revision since 2006. They are also raised annually in line with inflation.
31. Interview with MaPelotona, 17 August 2005.
32. The brigades are for pupils learning technical and trade subjects, including building and carpentry.
33. A diploma given after the first three years of Junior high school in Botswana.
34. On Mozambique, see Sender et al. (2006); on South Africa's 'peripheral' workforce, see Dibben (2007: 112–13).

Chapter 3

1. A version of this chapter was first published in *African Identities* (P. Werbner 2009b). It was presented as a keynote address at the conference on 'Self and Subject: African and Asian Perspectives', 20–23 September 2005, at the Ferguson Centre, Edinburgh, and to a workshop convened by the ESRC Programme on Non-Governmental Public Action (NGPA) on 14–16 March 2006. I am grateful to participants at both events for their comments and encouragement. The article also responded to comments from reviewers of the *Journal of Southern African Studies*, *Comparative Studies in Society and History* and *African Identities*.
2. It is beyond this chapter to discuss *seriti* here in all its complexity. It differs, however, from the Gikuyu *wiathi* described by Lonsdale, which refers to moral value attributed by Kikuyu to control over their labour in self-mastery, a precondition for gerontocratic rural sub-clan authority, and secondarily to freedom (Lonsdale 1992: 356), a notion which later, in the context of labour migration and the struggle for independence, was expanded to include strikers' 'struggle for self-mastery' (ibid.: 416), the Mau Mau fight for self-mastery and freedom (ibid.: 446) and even the *wiathi* right to vote (ibid.: 461). *Seriti*, by contrast, is, like charisma, an embodied notion of the self as inherited 'shade', protected by the ancestors, which stresses dialogical features of respect and self-respect, compassion and generosity, as well as vulnerability to attack by others (see R. Werbner 2007, 2011, n.d.).
3. McNay argues that Bourdieu's notion of embodied habitus allows for the capacity to change in the encounter with the 'field', a complex and changing social formation. She also appeals to Ricoeur's notion of narrativity and Castoriadis's notion of the radical social imaginary to spell out the possibility of agency outside discourse.
4. On the dialogical, see also Bakhtin (1984). Bakhtin means by 'dialogical' the fact that personal world-views always contain implicitly a consciousness of others' views in a never fully resolved argument, which arises in response to moral ordeals and crucibles (see Holquist & Clark 1984). Jeffery Nealton (1998: 31–52) compares this to Emmanuel Levinas's dialogics which – like the present chapter – posits the necessity of subjection to alterity along with responsibility for the other.

5. Lonsdale (2000) thus rejects the sceptical view of agency propounded by Fanon (1970), which is based on his belief that only violent revolution would free the self from mimetically reflecting the colonial master.
6. Anthropological examples include Shostak (1981).
7. Often interviews are combined thematically, as in Bozzoli (1991).
8. See Wells (1991) on early women's campaigns. For a recent review of feminist movements in post-independent Southern African countries, see Walsh et al. (2006).
9. See P. Werbner (2009b) for a portrayal of Joy Phumaphi, who rose from MP to Minister of Health and who instituted the free ARV treatment of HIV-positive patients; Phumaphi subsequently moved on to top positions at the World Health Organisation and the World Bank before returning to Botswana as the executive secretary of the African Leaders Malaria Alliance and co-chair of Aspen, the Global Leaders Council for Reproductive Health.
10. Perhaps not coincidentally, Unity Dow challenged the state on the new citizenship law in the High Court at about the same time, on 4 May 1990, in a landmark case for women's rights in Botswana (see Dow 1995).
11. Virtually all studies of trade unions mark the passage of time via a union's historically significant strikes. This seems unavoidable, if repetitive, since these remembered mobilisation events shape members' consciousnesses.
12. In November 2006, however, she was excluded from the executive committee, and, after she went to the press, from the union. Ultimately, she joined a third union.
13. The law was changed in the Public Service Act (2010).
14. On African intellectuals, nationalism and pan-Africanism, see Mkandawire (2005).
15. It later left the BFTU; see Chapter 7 and subsequent chapters on the creation of BOFEPUSU.
16. In Botswana, the women's movement is mainly concerned with rights issues (see Geisler 2004; Selolwane 1998, 2000). Legal rights do, of course, have economic implications. However, as most of the contributors to the *Journal of Southern African Studies* special issue on 'Women and the Politics of Gender in Southern Africa' (Walsh et al. 2006) argue, despite highly progressive constitutions and legal reform, implementation is still a challenge across the whole spectrum of family law reforms. Moreover, few of these movements outside trade unions significantly impact on the economic circumstances of poor women. In South Africa, for example, the demand for inclusion of domestic workers in the Law on Unemployment Insurance, likely to have huge benefits for women, was spearheaded by the South African Domestic Service and Allied Workers' Union, who joined a coalition organised by the Commission for Gender Equality, as Jennifer Fish (2006: 107–28) documents.
17. Some had lost faith in him, as Chapter 7 outlines.

Chapter 4

1. I speak of my own youthful experience as a member of the youth labour movement in Israel, where I witnessed the passion with which such ideologies were celebrated in the past. Many of the songs were written in Setswana by a former labour unionist and activist, Klass Motshidisi, later a government-appointed labour commissioner. I interviewed Motshidisi in his home in Palapye in 2005 and was struck by his idealism, despite being close to 70 years old. He is a prominent member of the Botswana National Front, an opposition party with, in the past, Marxist tendencies.

2. See also Chapter 8. Moodie reports of the South African miners' union that, 'Singing in union meetings, led by the comrades, was important for union solidarity' (Moodie 1994: 265).
3. More generally on cosmopolitanism, particularly beyond the West, see P. Werbner (2008).
4. Possibly included are also the treasurer, vice-chairperson and deputy secretary general.
5. Morning shifts were from 5 AM to 1 PM, afternoon shifts from 12 PM to 8 PM, and the twelve-hour night shift ran from 8 PM.
6. See the report, 'Tempers Flare as Workers Resist Transfers,' *Botswana Daily News*, 26 April 2005. Retrieved from: www.olddailynews.gov.bw/cgi-bin/news.cgi?d=20050426 (accessed 26 February 2014).
7. Ibid.
8. See also Chapter 3. The formula related to the fact that many industrial-class workers in hospitals worked twelve-hour shifts. For the night shift they were paid a third more; then, for 4 hours out of the 12, they got paid time and a half. In total, people are expected to work five night shifts a month.
9. Sally Engle Merry shows similar involvement in small claims courts by working-class Americans, although she appears to think this is a peculiarly American tendency: 'The consciousness of legal entitlement and the consequent turning to the law are profoundly democratic, radically egalitarian, and *fundamentally American*. This legal entitlement is an outgrowth of a faith in the law, a faith observed early by Tocqueville and other commentators on the American scene' (Merry 1990: 181, emphasis added). Botswana is another country where such faith in legal entitlement clearly prevails.
10. There is a vast literature on this topic, starting with Isaac Schapera's foundational oeuvre. References to this literature are made throughout the book.

Chapter 5

1. The present debate was initiated by Laidlaw (2002).
2. The 'post' refers to his additional stress on language, an issue taken up by later legal scholars.
3. For a review of the moral dimensions of legal realism, see Dagan (2005). See also the entry on 'Legal Realism' in *West's Encyclopedia of American Law* (see also http://legal-dictionary.thefreedictionary.com/legal+realism (accessed 6 April, 2014)). Tamanaha (2009: 734) considers the historical antecedents of the movement; for a critical historical review, see Horwitz (1992: 169–92).
4. Gluckman engages primarily with Cardozo (1921). Gluckman (1967) also argues against the realist sceptic Jerome Frank (1930). Later he engaged the realists as a movement more generally (Gluckman 1973).
5. Gluckman discusses the place of legal case studies versus rules in the legal realists' and his own work, in a masterly tribute to Hoebel in which he argues that a combination of both is essential in the 'triad of case–rule–praxis' (Gluckman 1973: 617). By 1973, it was clear that he was aware of Dworkin's work (ibid.: 616).
6. In trying to argue that Barotse legal concepts were imposed by the British who 'needed native courts', Conley and O'Barr (2004: 209–10) equate the very different mode of incorporation of state and stateless societies into the colonial state. They misrecognise the fact that indigenous, hierarchical Barotse courts (*kuta*), like Tswana

courts (*kgotla*), preceded colonial indirect rule, and thus differed radically from the stateless Tiv 'government' courts which were a British invention. Prins, for example, while mentioning debates in the Barotse *kuta* only in passing, tells us that 'white power never attained a high intensity in BuBarotse' (Prins 1980: 2). Schapera reports that 'apart from certain changes regarded as essential, there has been as little interference as possible with the traditional forms of government and jurisdiction' (Schapera 1956: 39–40).

7. This is evident, most recently, in an article by Maurer (2005), in which 'reasonable man' is opposed to 'economic man', a clear misunderstanding of the highly abstract notion of reasonableness as a yardstick embodied in particular situations, that informs judicial reasoning.
8. As Gluckman himself comments, 'I cannot help feeling that it is lamentable that so-called "legal anthropologists" should be so ignorant of those [American realist] jurisprudential controversies' (Gluckman 1973: 616).
9. On this feature in Botswana, see Mogalakwe (1997: 106).
10. In his masterly account of the development of early American labour law, Daniel Ernst (1995) shows that the move from common law-based universal individualism, with its anti-trust and closed-shop-floor ideology to political 'pluralism', which recognised organised labour and in which the rights of workers to unionise were increasingly hedged by legislation and regulation, began early in the twentieth century, and was subject to fierce disagreement and political contestation between progressive and conservative jurists. On the later history of labour relations in America, see also Tomlins (1985, 1993).
11. On the legal issues surrounding the 1991 strike, see also P. Werbner (2014).
12. Quoted from p.1 of the Conclusions in Molaudi (1992).
13. Last quote from p.1 of the Conclusions to Molaudi (1992). By 2011, the wage gap had increased to a ratio of 73:1.
14. Mogalakwe (1997: 12) claims 40,000. The names of all the places that went on strike are listed by Molaudi (1992: 12).
15. According to Molaudi, however, the DPSM telephoned the MWU chairman once, but did not call back until the strike was over (Molaudi 1992: 12). Molosiwa gets the date wrong. The meeting took place after the strike was over, on 11 November.

    In an interview with Ronald Baipidi, then head of the BFTU, at the time the procedure for calling a strike legally was 'too long. First you have to register a dispute with the commissioner of labour. Then you have to wait 21 days. Having attempted and failed to negotiate a settlement you would have to go to the industrial court'. There was, he said, 'a loophole in the law – after 21 days, in the short space of time before the commissioner of labour gave the certification to go to the Industrial Court, you could declare a strike, but once he issued the certificate you could no longer strike – you had to go to court and then the ruling made there was binding, whatever was awarded was binding. The strike, if declared in time, could thus be at most between the twenty-first day and the day for the hearing set by the court' (interview, 19 August 2005).
16. By 2011, the law had been amended considerably, but the indeterminacy regarding employers' legitimate responses to illegal strikes appears to have persisted, a matter pointed out by the presiding judge. The matter arose again in the court cases surrounding the 2011 strike, discussed in Chapter 12.

17. This is odd given that the chronology recorded above shows that the MWU repeatedly postponed a strike to allow more time for negotiations, without ever rejecting the action. Moreover, legal strikes were almost impossible.
18. For a full discussion of the legally plural aspects of this case, see P. Werbner (2014).
19. *National Amalgamated* versus *Attorney General* (1991). High Court Civil Case 1991, No. 1604, Lobatse. All references to this document in this section are given in the main text in parentheses.
20. See *National Amalgamated* versus *Attorney General* (1995), Court of Appeal Civil Appeal 1995, No. 26/93 of High Court Civil Case No. 1604/91, Lobatse. All subsequent references to this document in this section and the next are given in the main text in parentheses.
21. It should be noted that in 1997, two years after this court case, South Africa passed the Basic Conditions of Employment Act 75 (the BCEA), in recognition that 'lawfulness does not necessarily equal fairness' (Garbers 2004: 400). This followed the adoption of the Constitution of the Republic of South Africa and Bill of Rights in 1996, in which the requirement of fairness in employment became a 'constitutional imperative' (ibid.) in recognition of the fact that high unemployment leaves employees vulnerable to exploitation. Among the mechanisms imposed is 'legislation that promotes collective bargaining to ensure a greater measure of equality', protections against unfair dismissal, labour practices and discrimination, and the creation of specialist tribunals (ibid.: 400–1). The Court of Appeal verdict could thus be seen as reflecting an emerging regional trend in labour relations.
22. Notably the 1992 Unity Dow citizenship case and the San Central Kalahari Game Reserve cases in 2006 and 2011, both of which the government lost (on the 2006 case, see Saugestad 2011; Solway 2009).
23. Quoted from page 2 of the Conclusion to Molaudi (1992).
24. The Comaroffs do, however, admit that the law can be a 'weapon of the weak' (Comaroff & Comaroff (2006: 144–5).

Chapter 6

I would like to thank the editor of *Critical African Studies* for his useful comments on an earlier version of this chapter.

1. On the BNF, see Makgala (2006: 147–68); on the BDP, see Makgala (ibid.: 169–96). The autobiographies of former President Masire (2008) and David Magang (2008) both report on the 'malignant', 'unbridgeable' factional politics within the ruling BDP.
2. I base these figures on income from subscriptions divided by 60 pula, which was the annual subscription rate (5 pula per month). Obviously, this does not take account of numbers joining or retiring from the union, which in 2005, for example, claimed 40,000 members, a number that does not quite tally with income.
3. I have removed names for these politicians to preserve anonymity.
4. Ian Khama, the vice-president of the ruling BDP, succeeded Festus Mogae as president in 2008.
5. Nevertheless, they admitted on another occasion: 'Later we discovered that he [Ian Khama] had been telling the truth all along, when he said that he had no involvement in the union's disputes. Even if he had, back in the beginning, he wasn't [involved] at present'.

6. Details of the factional politics appear in Makgala et al. (2007), a book commissioned and paid for by the MWU, which contains very useful information; and in MWU (2007), also union-commissioned and written by John Makgala.
7. See MWU (2007) for an excellent detailed account.
8. Gratuity payments substitute for retirement pensions and are paid as lump sums every five years. This arrangement followed an agreement with the government.
9. A *sangoma* is a traditional healer or witchdoctor, claiming to communicate with the ancestors. In this instance, one is needed to interpret Motshwarakgole's dream.
10. The rebels had withdrawn 173,000 pula from the MWU's Barclays Bank account in four tranches. They also took 123,000 pula by intercepting registered mail cheques. Of this, only 20,000 pula had been left in the Standard Bank account. They then managed to extract another 10,000 pula after the accounts were frozen.
11. She was finally jailed for contempt of court in 2009.
12. See Makgala (2006: 173–4) on a similar north/south factional division within the ruling party, with some exceptions.
13. Even this was subject to government interference, as the case of BOPEU in 2011 showed, when the government threatened to withdraw its perks and secondment salaries.
14. The MWU had joined PSI, and the accounts officer had been elected the regional 'titular'.
15. Gratuities, normally paid every five years, are calculated by multiplying five weeks pay per annum for the full working career of a worker, and then subtracting the total of all earlier gratuities paid in the past. This means that a rise in pay of 2000 pula a month reflected over a 30-year career can amount to a substantial sum.
16. The committee of enquiry was chaired by Baatlhodi Molatlhegi, and the three other members were Nelson Mokgethi, Keitumele Gabonewe and Godiramang Makhaya. Their report was submitted on 23 October 2004.
17. *Monitor,* 20 November 2006, p.1.
18. By 2011 she had made friends with the national organising secretary and blamed her ex-comrade from the region for fomenting trouble between them. The latter, in turn, was keen to make friends with her.
19. I was never able to verify an actual kinship relationship, but both Minister Kwelagobe and Johnson came from Molepolole, and it was clear that Johnson was a family friend of the minister since I was told that he had attended the minister's son's wedding.
20. Lt. General Mompati Merafhe, later vice-president, was said to have 'burnt his fingers with clashes with the Government's and parastatal organisation industrial workers' when he first entered politics in 1991 (Makgala 2006: 176).
21. Alliances change, however. Years later, this same minister led the defence of the MWU and other public service unions in parliament, and was described by the national organising secretary as a 'great friend'!
22. On the history of these two factions of the BDP since 1991 and their ramifications in the youth and women's wings of the party, see Makgala (2006: 173 *et passim*).
23. See *Botswana Gazette*, 29 July 2005.
24. *Botswana Gazette*, 17–23 October 2007, p.3.

Chapter 8

1. For a detailed account of the miners' strike, if in places unclear with regard to internal union leadership battles, and exaggerated with regard to claims about management

bonuses, see Marobela (2011: 8–11), who details the ultimately failed negotiations to reach a compromise (ibid.: 9).

2. *Debswana* versus *BMWU* (2004), Industrial Court Case 2004 (2), BLR 129 (IC), Gaborone.
3. *Debswana* versus *BMWU* (2004), p.9.
4. Public Service Act (2008), A.207, §58.1.
5. Interview with Golekanye Mokeng, 4 September 2007. All other quotes in this paragraph come from this interview.
6. *BMWU* versus *Debswana* (2009), Court of Appeal 2009, 1 BLR 138 CA, Lobatse.
7. *National Amalgamated* versus *Attorney General* (1995), Court of Appeal Civil Appeal 1995, No. 26/93 of High Court Civil Case No. 1604/91, Lobatse, p.51.
8. *National Amalgamated* versus *Attorney General* (1995), p.48.
9. *National Amalgamated* versus *Attorney General* (1995), p.51.
10. Kenneth Good, lecturer in political science at the University of Botswana, was deported from Botswana unilaterally and at short notice on 'grounds of national security'. He had allegedly supported Survival International, which had taken the government of Botswana to court for expelling Basarwa from the Central Kalahari Game Reserve, allegedly in order to secure diamond mining there, a claim tantamount to accusing Botswana of trading in 'blood' diamonds. For more on this, see: www.interights.org/good/index.html (accessed December 2012).
11. See the report on the petition in Mooketsi (2005).
12. Interview with Pelotsweo Baeng, 30 August, 2007.
13. Interview with Golekanye Mokeng, 4 September 2007.
14. Interview with Gadzani Mhotsha, 30 August 2007. All other quotes in this paragraph come from this interview.
15. To the tune of 15 per cent, I was told, with a worker contributing 5 per cent.
16. Thus the Friedrich Ebert Stiftung country report on unions in Botswana in 2003, before the changes in the legislation in 2004, notes that 'the trade union movement does not have any significant negotiating power, especially since the extent of the trade unions' negotiating power is not prescribed by law. The law merely recognizes the right of trade unions to negotiate with employers on matters that have a bearing on the terms and conditions of employment of their members. As to what the exact extent of the negotiation process is, the law is silent. This has often resulted in confusion between employers and trade unions on the scope of negotiable (as opposed to consultative) matters. At the tripartite level, the Government, Employers and Employees, the machinery used is consultative, they are not bargaining. They recommend to a minister (FES 2004: 26).
17. Interview with Andrew Motsamai, 11 September 2007. All other quotes in this paragraph come from this interview.
18. I heard reports of the conference from various sources.
19. See Gabathuse (2008).
20. *Botswana Guardian*, 19 October 2007, p.5.

Chapter 9

1. Here Johnson is referring to Batswana who did labour studies in the eastern bloc. On the early role of the Comintern and the centrality of education for leadership in the ANC and trade unions in South Africa, see Suttner (2005: 126–7 *et passim*).
2. Motshidisi was for some time labour commissioner and is currently also chairman of the opposition party, the Botswana National Front and Chief of Palapye.

3. There are 100 thebe in the Botswana pula, usually valued slightly higher than the South African rand, which is divided into 100 cents. In 1970 the exchange rate was approximately 1.4 rands to one dollar, and $2.50 to £1 sterling.
4. Kenneth Kaunda was the first president of Zambia following independence in 1964.
5. The original biblical text is as follows: 'If it seem good unto thee to come with me into Babylon, come, and I will look well unto thee; but if it seem ill unto thee to come with me into Babylon, forbear: behold, all the land is before thee; whither it seemeth good and right unto thee to go, thither go' (Jer. 40: 3).
6. I am grateful to Neil Bernstein and Paul Losensky for this insight.
7. By 2012, one of their daughters had established herself as a successful actress in South Africa and was appearing on the popular soap-opera *Generations*, as well as acting in the theatre.
8. See 'Motshwarakgole and Others Walk Out of GCC Meeting', *Botswana Daily News*, 30 July 1999. The MWU wanted to resolve the dispute with the government rather than extend it.
9. The rally took place on Saturday, 14 May 2011 (see Keoreng 2011a).
10. Interview with Johnson Motshwarakgole, 14 June 2011.

Chapter 10

This chapter greatly benefited from participants' comments during a panel I co-convened at the ASA conference on 'Beyond the Arab Spring: The Aesthetics and Poetics of Popular Revolt and Protest', Delhi, 2012, and a Wenner-Gren conference at Aga Khan University in 2013 with a similar title. For further details of the strike see Makgala (2014).

1. On Africa more generally, see Cooper (1996) and Schler (2009); on South Africa see, Southall (1995).
2. On the process of 'citation', see Manoukian (2011).
3. On performative iteration in relation to Foucault's notion of 'discourse', see Butler (1993: 15); on the power of mimesis see Taussig (1993: 250); on hybridity as a displacement or the 'doubling up' of signs, see Bhabha (1994: 119) and also P. Werbner (2001: 136).
4. Thus, in a critique of social movement theory, Armstrong and Bernstein (2008) argue against the privileging in some social movement theory of the state, and argue that the state, like other institutions, is always culturally constituted. See also Sartwell (2010: 15–47) on the political aesthetics of dictatorial and authoritarian states.
5. These included the Ipelegeng Project, a welfare work scheme, a 'back garden' vegetable-growing scheme and a ploughing-subsidy scheme.
6. Support came from individuals as well: Sidney Pilane, a leading advocate, donated 5000 pula. In Kanye, councillors and MPs donated beasts to feed assembled strikers.
7. Teachers' union representative, 25 May 2011.
8. BOFEPUSU delegates conference, 28 May 2011.
9. Speech made at the GSS strike grounds, 28 April 2011.
10. Shade in Botswana has ritual meaning, linked to notions of dignity, and people avoid going bareheaded into the sun (R. Werbner n.d.).
11. For a fine discussion of the significance of occupying space in protests, see Butler (2011).
12. Juris (2008), among others, notes the capacity of popular culture to create 'affective solidarity'.
13. 'He/it' here refers to the government and/or Ian Khama.

14. *Makgolela* ('snatches') is the name for one of the divining throws. See R. Werbner (1989 and n.d.) on Tswana divination.
15. 'Ian' refers to President Ian Khama. At this point in the song, the singers raised their right arms and made a downward throwing gesture in unison.
16. 'Insult' is used here and throughout in the anthropological sense since 'there is no insult in a song' (see below, main text).
17. This was particularly offensive since Khama has been one of the few African leaders who has consistently refused to recognise Mugabe and who supported the Libyan uprising, unlike his counterpart in neighbouring South Africa.
18. The individuals named in the second verse were all in government at the time: Mokgweetsi Masisi, minister of presidential affairs, Kenneth Matambo, minister of finance, and Ian Khama, president.
19. The line 'When searching for the workers' presumably refers to efforts to call them back to work.
20. The explanation was suggested to me by my assistant, Queen Gasitsiwe.
21. In this line, the word *madi* means both 'blood' and 'money'.
22. Dungarees are usually worn casually by young people; to wear them 'with one arm missing' refers to a dress style.
23. Speech by Johnson Motshwarakgole at the GSS strike grounds, 3 May 2011.
24. See *Guardian* (London), 10 April 2011 (www.guardian.co.uk/world/2011/apr/10/hands-up-to-protest, accessed 28 February 2014). The gestures spread widely to the *indignados* demonstrations in Spain in May 2011, and later to the Israeli protests (see Werbner et al. 2014).
25. Lute (2011a) reports a total of 1951 dismissed workers including 65 medical and dental staff, 531 nursing personnel, and others, including allied health workers (211), health support staff (668), water services (55), fire, sewerage and electrical (252), workers from the Ministry of Information, Science and Technology (136) and Botswana Defence Force civilian personnel (33).
26. Indeed, there was some confusion, so even those who had gone back to work had their pay withdrawn, while others on strike were paid their usual salaries.
27. But see van Holdt (2002), who stresses that in the case of South Africa an emphasis in social movement theory on external alliances neglects internal divisions within unions based on ethnic divisions, with only some members of the unions joining forces with anti-apartheid activists in the community. Both Lambert and Webster (2001) and Waterman (2004) document the rise of international social movement unionism.
28. In the USA, powerful and effective social movement unionism has been documented, for example, in alliances among trade unions, churches and other religious groups in the Living Wage Movement (see Snarr 2011: esp. 66–101), and among trade unionists, civil rights activists and the women's movement in the Pay Equity Movement (McCann 1994).
29. To this list one might add human rights and indigenous peoples' movements.
30. The accusation was made during an address to the High Level Consultative Council, broadcast on BTV, 20 May 2011 (see also *Mmegi*, 20 May 2011, p.11). Kanani (2011a: 1) reports that in late June Khama claimed 93 per cent of Batswana were unemployed!
31. 'Parliament Seeks Way to End Strike', *Monitor*, 6 June 2011, p.2.
32. According to the press, the churches' document 'urged the government to re-consider its approach from the point of view of paying wider attention to social justice and narrowing the income disparities in Botswana' (Motseta & Makgapha 2011: 1).

The report also condemned the 'abuse of state media to mislead the nation', which undermined democracy (Moeng 2011b: 2).

33. The captions are taken from Kavahematui (2011b), Keoreng (2011b), Keoreng and Baputaki (2011) and Sereetsi (2011).
34. See Makghapa (2011a) and 'Parliament Seeks Way to End Strike', *Monitor*, 6 June 2011, p.2.
35. The word *mpimpi* ('traitors, stooges') is a Zulu/Xhosa word.

Chapter 11

1. Mogalakwe argues that, historically, the introduction of 'mediation-conciliation-compulsory arbitration procedures to break bargaining deadlocks, as well as the creation of the position of Permanent Arbitrator who was empowered to settle disputes and make awards that were binding' had the 'cumulative effect' of making 'strikes in Botswana unlawful even if the right to strike remained enshrined in the statute books' (Mogalakwe 2011a).
2. In the end, representation on the bargaining council, when it finally met in 2012, was based on numerical strength.
3. Public Service Act (2008), A.188, §5.5.
4. 'Govt Suspends BOFEPUSU Leader over "Umbrella Talks"', *Mmegi*, 23 November 2011.
5. Public Service Act (2008), A.200, §§ 36, 37e and 37f.
6. My printed copy of the Public Service Act (2008) omits §15.3. See Lute (2009) and Modise (2010) on the delays in implementing the act.
7. Public Service Act (2008), A.197, §28a.
8. The newly appointed chief justice appeared to be a conservative. His was the minority voice in the San case in 2006, finding for the government, overruled by the two other judges. The grounds for the judge's decision in the present case seem to have been that the dismissal was not based on the applicants' service record. It is worth noting, perhaps, that the Ministry of Works and Transport had a poor record of petty corruption in issuing driving licences and other permits: see the editorial in *Mmegi*, 24 September 2009 (http://mmegi.bw/index.php?sid=9&aid=35&dir=2009/September/Thursday24, accessed 28 February 2014), and the 2001 World Economic Forum corruption survey report on Botswana (www.fordham.edu/economics/vinod/cie/%5Cbotswana.htm, accessed 28 February 2014). On the bare facts of the San case, see Chapter 8, note 10. For detailed analysis, see Saugestad (2011) and Solway (2009).
9. Budget speech by O.K. Matambo, minister of finance and development planning, delivered to the National Assembly on 7 February 2011 (see paragraphs 67, 71 and 73, pp.15, 17). This was applied retrospectively from 1 May 2010, costing the treasury an additional 700 million pula. In order to finance the shortfall recruitment was temporarily frozen (ibid., p.17). It is conceivable that the implementation of the Public Service Act was delayed because of budget constraints.
10. PSOP (2011: p.11, paragraphs 46 and 49); see also MFDP (2000).
11. After the strike was suspended without a pay settlement, President Khama and his government were praised by the IMF, the Bank of Botswana and Moody's Investors Service, the credit-rating agency, who retained Botswana's A2 credit rating, See 'Botswana Refusal to Cave in to Striking Unions Supports Rating, Moody's Says', *Echo*, 16–22 June 2011, p.15; and 'Experts Applaud Botswana's Economic Management,' *Botswana Daily News*, 17 June 2011. See also : www.gov.bw/en/

Ministries--Authorities/Ministries/State-President/Office-of-the-President/Tools--Services/Inside-the-Presidency/Inside-the-Presidency-Issue-No-12-of-2011/ (accessed 28 February 2014).

12. 'Working poverty' is defined as full-time work that pays wages so low they cannot cover workers' basic living expenses (see Snarr 2011).
13. On the Millennium Development Goals, see: www.bw.one.un.org/index.php/millennium-development-goals/botswana-status (accessed 25 October 2013).
14. The Integrated Support Programme for Arable Agricultural Development (ISPAAD) was launched in 2008; it provided subsidised services and inputs to farmers, such as ploughing and planting services, seeds, fertiliser, seasonal loans and fencing. ISPAAD aimed, *inter alia*, to increase national grain production, commercialize agriculture through mechanization and promote food security.
15. But see Pheko (2011), who claims that with drip irrigation, the scheme would be sustainable and would target so-called destitutes. See also *Development News*, 29 April 2011, pp.9–10
16. Expenditure on the Ipelegeng Project was 330 million pula in 2011/12, targeting 50,000 workers a month (*Development News*, 29 April 2011, p.16). In Gaborone, the majority (19,500 of approximately 24,000) were reported to be women.
17. *Mmegi Monitor*, 5 December 2011.
18. Of the 730 million pula, 330 million were said by the president to be for Ipelegeng, 200 million for ISPAAD and 100 million for poverty eradication, which includes a range of social security and benefit schemes. I take backyard gardens to be an additional 100 million pula. No aggregate figures were available. See President Khama's address to the High Level Consultative Council (*Botswana Daily News*, 20 May 2011, p.3).
19. See 2011 budget speech, p.10.
20. See 'Consigning Botswana to Perpetual Poverty?' *Botswana Gazette*, 3 August 2011.
21. This first place was maintained in 2012. See the minister of finance's 2011 budget speech (www.gov.bw/en/Ministries--Authorities/Ministries/State-President/Office-of-the-President/Tools--Services/Speeches-/201112-Budget-Speech/, accessed 28 February 2014) and the president's 2011 state of the nation address (www.gov.bw/en/News/State-of-the-Nation-Address-to-the-3rd-Session-of-the-10th-Parliament/, accessed 28 February 2014) for details of many of these developmental programmes.
22. Botswana's first-past-the-post constituency system has meant that representation in parliament does not necessarily reflect the winning party's overall proportion of the popular vote. In 2009, the BDP won more than 75 per cent of parliamentary seats but only some 53 per cent of the vote.
23. The anonymous website www.iankhama.com, clearly hostile to the president, lists the network of relatives and close friends holding positions of power in 2009 in an article entitled 'Botswana: Of the Khamas, by the Khamas, for the Khamas' (www.iankhama.com – this website now his limited access). In 2012 he appointed his brother, Tshekedi Khama, as minister of wildlife and tourism.
24. Later, however, in June 2011, the Botswana Defence Force officers who had killed him were convicted and sentenced by the High Court to 11 years in jail, thus reasserting publicly the rule of law and judicial independence even in the case of the military. Five months into their sentence, however, they were pardoned by the president and released.
25. As will be seen in Chapter 12, not only the president but the Director of the DPSM made no attempt to meet unions during the first three weeks of the strike, while issuing a series of five ultimatums, breaking strike rules and taking BOFEPUSU

to court. A new book by the Speaker of the House, Margaret Nasha, condemns BDP politicians and MPs for being unwilling to stand up to Khama or criticise his decisions (Nasha 2014).

26. These can be found online. I have not tried to detail them specifically.
27. Amounts in Botswana pula are indicated in the quoted passages with a capital P.
28. In July 2011, for example, the permanent secretary in the Ministry of Infrastructure, Science and Technology was caught by 'secret agents' of the Directorate of Corruption and Economic Crime taking a substantial bribe from a Chinese civil engineering firm (Pitse 2011). Such rare instances confirmed workers' suspicions.
29. The article appeared on the same page as Otlogetswe's article (above).
30. Via Statutory Instrument No. 49 of 2011, an extraordinary gazette of the Trade Disputes Act, issued by the government of Botswana, Gaborone.
31. This expansion was rejected by the Botswana High Court in 2012, as detailed in Chapter 12.
32. See Chapter 10, note 39.
33. See Wilenius (2004) for a retrospective evaluation.
34. Notably, among others, Ditshwanelo, Botswana's human rights NGO.
35. The text of Bishop Mwamba's speech was conveyed to me in an e-mail by Jennifer Anderson, British high commissioner to Botswana.
36. 'Parliament Seeks Ways to End Strike', *Monitor*, 6 June 2011, p.2.
37. This was the figure I was given over the telephone in September 2011. In November, Motshwarakgole was reported in the press as saying that 700 workers had not been reinstated. Seventeen of the dismissed nurses had found work in Namibia. See *Botswana Daily News*, 24 November 2011 (www.olddailynews.gov.bw/cgi-bin/news.cgi?d=20111124 (accessed 28 February 2014).

Chapter 12

1. Sandy Smith-Nonini (2010) reports that protests against the Ministry of Health in 2000 and 2002 in San Salvador took the form of huge 'White Coat' marches. I'm not certain whether the Botswana unions were aware of this.
2. I was told that BOFEPUSU was relying on a case between the Botswana Power Corporation Union and the Botswana Power Corporation.
3. My husband knew Tubu well, and I had actually met him in 1968.
4. This in fact happened several months later, in November 2011.
5. A summary of these arguments can be found in Lobel (2007) and McCann (1994: 177, 288–303).
6. See Morewagae (2011b), as well as Toka (2008) on the start of the dispute.
7. On the court cases, see also Sapignoli (2012).
8. *Public Service Unions* versus *Attorney General* (2012), High Court Case 2012, No. MAHLB 000631–11, Lobatse. All references to this document in this section are given in the main text in parentheses.
9. One of the cases concerned the legality of essential workers striking is the Maruping case; and the other, their dismissal without a hearing, is the Dingake dismissal case.
10. Judge Amissah's comment occurs in *National Amalgamated* versus *Attorney General* (1995), Court of Appeal Civil Appeal 1995, No. 26/93, of High Court Civil Case No. 1604/91, Lobatse, p.51. It was cited in *BMWU* versus *Debswana* (2009), Court of Appeal 2009, 1 BLR 138 CA, Lobatse (see Chapter 8).
11. Details of the proceedings of the case are taken from my notes.

12. *Public Service Unions* versus *Minister of Labour and Home Affairs* (2012), High Court Case 2012, MAHLB-000674-li, Lobatse. All references to this document in this section are given in the main text in parentheses. It should be noted that Judge Dingake wrote his doctoral thesis and published a book on constitutional issues in Botswana (Dingake 1999).
13. Trade Disputes Act (2004), §49.
14. See www.elaws.gov.bw/wondersbtree.php?m=PRINCIPAL&v=I&t=STATUTORY INSTRUMENTS#1402 (accessed 1 March 2014).
15. The two cases were *Attorney General* versus *Public Service Unions* (2013), Court of Appeal Civil Appeal 2013, No. CACGB–053–12, Gaborone (reversing the Dingake case) and *Public Service Unions* versus *DPSM and Attorney General* (2013), Court of Appeal Civil Appeal 2013, No. CACLB–043–11, Gaborone (reversing the Maruping case); see above, note 9. Until further notice, all references in the main text are to *Attorney General* v. *Public Service Unions* (2013), with page numbers given in parentheses.
16. This was not entirely accurate as we saw in the previous chapter. A large proportion of civil servants had had a 10 per cent adjustment rise.
17. Quotation from the Public Service Act (2008), §27.2; the relevant part of the Trade Disputes Act (2004) is §45.1.
18. See *Public Service Unions* v. *DPSM and Attorney General* (2013). All references to this document are given in the main text in parentheses, and hereafter all such references are to this document.
19. See *Minister of Labour and Home Affairs and Attorney General* v. *Public Service Unions* (2014).
20. RIPCO was a public company in the process of being dissolved and fused with the Botswana Technology Centre (BOTEC), another public company. Some workers were being transferred to the new company, but they nevertheless required exit packages, as did those who would not be re-employed. The MWU had agreed a package and signed a deal that was later disputed.

Chapter 13

1. For a similar argument on Pakistanis in the diaspora, see P. Werbner (2002: 189, 267).

References

Adler, G., and E. Webster (1999) 'The Labour Movement, Radical Reform and the Transition to Democracy in South Africa', In R. Munch and P. Waterman (eds), *Labour Worldwide in the Era of Globalization: Alternative Union Models in the New World Order*. London: Macmillan, pp.133–57.

Alavi, H. (1987) 'Politics of Ethnicity in India and Pakistan', in F. Haliday and H. Alavi (eds), *State and Ideology in the Middle East and Pakistan*. London: Macmillan, pp.64–111.

Alexander, A. (2011) 'The Gravedigger of Dictatorship', *Socialist Review*, March 2011. Retrieved from: www.socialistreview.org.uk/article.php?articlenumber=11580 (accessed 20 July 2013).

Arigghi, G., and J.S. Saul (1963) *Essays on the Political Economy of Africa*. New York: Monthly Review Press.

Armstrong, E.A., and M. Bernstein (2008) 'Culture, Power, and Institutions: A Multi-institutional Politics Approach to Social Movements', *Sociological Theory* 26(1): 74–99.

Baaitse, F. (2011) 'Songs of a Revolution', *The Voice*, 27 May, p.12.

Bach, S., and D. Winchester (2003) 'Industrial Relations in the Public Sector', in P. Edwards (ed.), *Industrial Relations: Theory and Practice*. Oxford: Blackwell, pp.285–12.

Bakhtin, M. (1984) *Problems of Dostoevsky's Poetics*, ed. and trans. C. Emerson. Minneapolis: University of Minnesota Press.

Baputaki, C. (2010) 'Public Service Unions Decide to Merge', *Mmegi*, 18 March. Retrieved from: www.mmegi.bw/index.php?sid=1&aid=1019&dir=2010/march/thursday18 (accessed 19 April 2010).

Barchiesi, F. (2003) 'Social Citizenship, the Decline of Waged Labour and Changing Worker Strategies', in T. Bramble and F. Barchiesi (eds), *Rethinking the Labour Movement in the 'New South Africa'*. London: Ashgate, pp.113–31.

—— (2011) *Precarious Liberation: Workers, the State, and Contested Social Citizenship in Postapartheid South Africa*. Albany: State University of New York Press.

Basedau, M. (2005) 'Botswana', in A. Mehler, H. Melber and K. Van Walraven (eds), *Africa Yearbook*, Vol 2. Leiden: Brill, pp.409–16.

Basimanebotlhe, T. (2011a) 'Strike Costs BOFEPUSU over P200,000', *Echo*, 19–25 May, p.15.

—— (2011b) 'Khama, Merafhe Differ on Strike Resolution', *Echo*, 9–15 June, pp.1, 5.

Benjamin, W. (1968) *Illuminations: Essays and Reflections*, trans. H. Zohn. New York: Schocken Books.

Beresford, D. (2006) 'A Law unto Himself', *Guardian* (London), 23 November 2006. Retrieved from: www.guardian.co.uk/world/2006/nov/23/worlddispatch.southafrica (accessed 4 February 2013).

Berger, I. (1986) 'Sources of Class Consciousness: South African Women in Recent Labor Struggles', in C. Robertson and I. Berger (eds), *Women and Class in Africa*. London: Africana Publishing, pp.216–36.

—— (1992) *Threads of Solidarity: Women in South African Industry 1900–1980*. London: James Currey.

Beynon, H., and T. Austrin (1989) 'The Iconography of the Durham Miners' Gala', *Journal of Historical Sociology* 2(1): 66–81.

Bhabha, H.K. (1994) *The Location of Culture*. London: Routledge.

Bohannan, P. (1957) *Justice and Judgement among the Tiv*. London: Oxford University Press
—— (1969) 'Ethnography and Comparison in Legal Anthropology' in L. Nader (ed.), *Law in Culture and Society*. Berkeley: University of California Press, pp.401–18.
Bosaletswe, C. (2013) 'Botswana Climbs Down on Basarwa Issue', *Botswana Telegraph*, 30 January, p.1.
Botswana Government (1990) *The Revised National Policy on Income, Employment, Prices and Profits*. Gaborone: Government Printer.
Bozzoli, B. (1991) *Women of Phokeng: Consciousness, Life Strategy, and Migrancy in South Africa, 1900–1983*. London: James Currey.
Bourdieu, P. (1984) *Distinction: A Social Critique of the Judgement of Taste*, trans. R. Nice. London: Routledge and Kegan Paul.
Bratton, M. (1994) 'Civil Society and Political Transition in Africa', in J.W. Haberson, D. Rothchild and N. Chazan (eds), *Civil Society and the State in Africa*. Boulder, CO: Reinner, pp.51–82.
Brewster, C., and G. Wood (2007) 'Introduction: Comprehending Industrial Relations in Africa', in G. Wood and C. Brewster (eds), *Industrial Relations in Africa*. London: Palgrave Macmillan, pp.1–14.
Butler, J. (1993) *Bodies that Matter: On the Discursive Limits of 'Sex'*. London: Routledge.
—— (2011) 'Bodies in Alliance and the Politics of the Street', Institut Européen pour des Politiques Culturelles en Devenir, September. Retrieved from: www.eipcp.net/transversal/1011/butler/en (accessed 14 March 2014).
Cardozo, B.J. (1921) *The Nature of the Judicial Process*. New Haven: Yale University Press.
Carolan, E. (2009) *The New Separation of Powers: A Theory of the Modern State*. Oxford: Oxford University Press.
Carpenter, M. (2000) 'Between Elation and Despair: UNISON and the New Social Policy Agenda', in M. Terry (ed.), *Redefining Public Sector Unionism: UNISON and the Future of Trade Unions*. London: Routledge, pp.193–214.
Cheater, A.P. (1986) *The Politics of Factory Organisation*. Gweru: Mambo Press.
—— (1988) 'Contradictions in Modelling "Consciousness": Zimbabwean Proletarians in the Making', *Journal of Southern African Studies* (special issue) 14(2): 291–303.
Chwaane, T. (2005) 'Judge Leaves as Court of Appeal Session Ends', *Mmegi*, 1 February.
Cohen, J.L., and A. Arato (1992) *Civil Society and Political Theory*. Cambridge, MA: MIT Press.
Cohen, R. (1991) *Contested Domains: Debates in International Labour Studies*. London: Zed Books.
Cole, G.D.H. (1926) *A Short History of the British Working Class Movement 1789–1947*. London: Allen and Unwin.
Collins, J. (2012) 'Theorizing Wisconsin's 2011 Protests: Community-based Unionism Confronts Accumulation by Dispossession', *American Ethnologist* 39(1): 6–20.
Comaroff, J.L. (1978) 'Rules and Rulers: Political Processes in a Tswana Chiefdom', *Man* 13(1): 1–20.
Comaroff, J.L., and J. Comaroff (2006) 'Law and Disorder in the Postcolony', *Social Anthropology* 15(2): 133–52.
Comaroff, J.L., and S. Roberts (1981) *Rules and Processes: The Cultural Logic of Dispute in an African Context*. Chicago: University of Chicago Press.
Conley, J.M., and W.M. O'Barr (2004) 'A Classic in Spite of Itself: The Cheyenne Way and the Case Method in Legal Anthropology', *Law and Inquiry* 29(1): 179–217.
Constantin, C. (1979) 'The Puritan Ethic and the Dignity of Labor: Hierarchy vs. Equality', *Journal of the History of Ideas* 40(4): 543–61.

Cooper, D. (1978) 'The State, Mineworkers and Multi-nationals: The Selebi Pikwe Strike, Botswana, 1975', in P.C.W. Gutkind, R. Cohen and J. Copans (eds), *African Labour History*. London: Sage, pp.244–77.

Cooper, F. (1996) *Decolonization and African Society: The Labour Question in French and British Africa*. Cambridge: Cambridge University Press.

Cummings, S.L. (2007) 'Critical Legal Consciousness in Action', *Harvard Law Review* 120(4): 62–71.

Dagan, H. (2005) 'The Realist Conception of Law', *Tel Aviv University Law Faculty Papers*, No. 21.

Desai, A. (2002) *We Are the Poors: Community Struggles in Post-Apartheid South Africa*. New York: Monthly Review Press.

Dibben, P. (2007) 'Industrial Relations and Employment Insecurity in South Africa: The Possibilities of Social Justice Unionism', in G. Wood and C. Brewster (eds), *Industrial Relations in Africa*. London: Palgrave Macmillan, pp.111–24.

Dingake, O.K. (1999) *Key Aspects of the Constitutional Law of Botswana*. Gaborone: O.K. Dingake.

Dow, Unity (1995) *The Citizenship Case: The Attorney General of the Republic of Botswana V. Unity Dow*, ed. U. Dow. Gaborone: Lentswe La Lesedi.

Durham, D., and F. Klaits (2002) 'Funerals and the Public Space of Sentiment in Botswana', *Journal of Southern African Studies* 28(4): 755–76.

Durrenberger, E.P., and S. Erem (2005) *Class Acts: An Anthropology of Service Workers and their Union*. Boulder, CO: Paradigm Publishers.

Durrenberger, E.P., and K.S. Reichart, eds (2010) *The Anthropology of Labor Unions*. Boulder: University Press of Colorado.

Earthtrends (2003) *Country Profile: Botswana: Agricultural Production*. Retrieved from: http://earthtrends.wri.org/gsearch.php?kw=Botswana (accessed 11 May 2009).

Edelman, M. (2001) 'Social Movements: Changing Paradigms and Forms of Politics', *Annual Review of Anthropology* 30: 285–317.

Edmunds, J., and B. Turner (2002) *Generations, Culture and Society*. Milton Keynes: Open University Press.

Englund, H. (2006) *Prisoners of Freedom: Human Rights and the African Poor*. Berkeley: University of California Press.

Epstein, A.L. (1958) *Politics in an Urban African Community*. Manchester: Manchester University Press.

—— (1973) 'The Reasonable Man Revisited: Some Problems in the Anthropology of Law', *Law and Society Review* 7(4): 643–66.

Ernst, D.R. (1993) 'The Critical Tradition in the Writing of American Legal History', *Yale Law Journal* 102(4): 1019–76.

—— (1995) *Lawyers against Labor: From Individual Rights to Corporate Liberalism*. Champaign: University of Illinois Press.

Evens, T.M.S., and D. Handelman, eds (2006) *The Manchester School: Practice and Ethnographic Praxis in Anthropology*. Oxford: Berghahn Books.

Fanon, F. (1970) *Wretched of the Earth*. Harmondsworth: Penguin.

Ferguson, J. (1999) *Expectations of Modernity: Myths and Meanings of Modern Life on the Zambian Copperbelt*. Berkeley: University of California Press.

FES (2004) *Trade Unions in Botswana: Country Report 2003*. Gaborone: Friedrich Erbert Stiftung.

Fischman, G.E., and P. Mclaren (2005) 'Rethinking Critical Pedagogy and the Gramscian and Freirean Legacies: From Organic to Committed Intellectuals, or Critical Pedagogy, Commitment, and Praxis', *Cultural Studies/Critical Methodologies* 5(4): 425–47.

Fish, J.N. (2006) 'Engendering Democracy: Domestic Labour and Coalition-building in South Africa', *Journal of Southern African Studies* (special issue) 32(1): 107–28.

Fones-Wolf, K. (1989) *Trade Union Gospel: Christianity and Labor in Industrial Philadelphia 1865–1915*. Philadelphia: Temple University Press.

Foucault, M. (1972) *The Archaeology of Knowledge*. London: Routledge.

—— (1977 [1975]) *Discipline and Punish: The Birth of the Prison*, trans. A. Sheridan. London: Penguin.

—— (1980) *The History of Sexuality*, Vol. 1: *An Introduction*. New York: Vintage Books.

—— (1983) 'The Subject and Power', in H. Dreyfus and P. Rabinow (eds), *Beyond Structuralism and Hermeneutics*. Chicago: University of Chicago Press, pp.208–26.

—— (1987 [1984]) *The Uses of Pleasure: The History of Sexuality*, Vol. 2. London: Penguin.

—— (1990 [1984]) *The Care of the Self: The History of Sexuality*, Vol. 3. London: Penguin.

—— (1991 [1984]) *The Foucault Reader*, ed. P. Rabinow. London: Penguin.

—— (1997a [1994]) 'The Ethics of the Concern of the Self as the Practice of Freedom', in *Ethics: Subjectivity and Truth*, Vol. 1: *The Essential Works of Michel Foucault, 1954–1984*, ed. P. Rabinow. trans. R. Hurley et al. New York: New Press, pp.281–301.

—— (1997b [1994]) *Ethics: Subjectivity and Truth*, ed. P. Rabinow, trans. R. Hurley et al. New York: New Press.

Frank, J. (1930) *Law and the Modern Mind*. New York: Coward-McCann.

Fraser, N. (1992) 'The Uses and Abuses of French Discourse Theories for a Feminist Politics', in N. Fraser and S.L. Bartky (eds), *Revaluing French Feminism: Critical Essays on Difference, Agency, and Culture*. Bloomington: Indiana University Press, pp.177–94.

Fumanti, M. (2007) 'Burying E.S: Educated Elites, Subjectivity and Distinction in Rundu', *Journal of Southern African Studies* 33(3): 469–83.

—— (in press) *The Politics of Distinction: African Elites From Colonialism to Liberation in a Namibian Frontier Town*. Canon Pyon, UK: Sean Kingston Publishing.

Gabathuse, R. (2008) 'Public Sector Unions Clash at Congress', *Mmegi,* 1 April.

—— (2011) 'Charges against Baeng Dropped', *Monitor,* 5 December. Retrieved from: www.mmegi.bw/index.php?sid=1&aid=448&dir=2011/december/monday5 (accessed 20 December 2011).

Gaitskell, D. (2000a) 'Hot Meetings and Hard Kraals: African Biblewomen in Transvaal Methodism, 1924–60', *Journal of Religion in Africa* 30(3): 277–309.

—— (2000b) 'Female Faith and the Politics of the Personal: Five Mission Encounters in Twentieth-century South Africa', *Feminist Review* 65: 68–91.

Galanter, M. (1983) 'The Radiating Effects of Courts', in K.D. Boyum and L. Mather (eds), *Empirical Theories of Courts*. New York: Longman, pp.117–42.

Galeitse, T. (2011) 'Police Detain 25 "Strikers"', *Botswana Gazette*, 15–21 June, p.3.

Ganetsang, G. (2007a) 'Labour Movement Splinters as Unions Form Another Federation', *Sunday Standard*, 14 October. Retrieved from: www.sundaystandard.info/article.php?NewsID=2170&GroupID=1 (accessed 14 March 2014).

—— (2007b) 'Union War Intensifies', *Sunday Standard*, 17 December, p.1.

—— (2011) 'Tafa Offsets Molokomme Yet Again', *Sunday Standard*, 15 December. Retrieved from: www.sundaystandard.info/article.php?newsid=12765&groupid=1 (accessed 14 March 2014).

Gaotlhobogwe, M. (2011) 'More Than 50,000 Fall on Hard Times', *Monitor*, 23 May, p.9.

Garbers, C. (2004) 'Labor Law', in C.G. van der Merswe and J.E. du Plessis (eds), *Introduction to the Law of South Africa*. The Hague: Kluwer Law International, pp.399–429.

Garbett, K.G. (1970) 'The Analysis of Social Situations', *Man* 5(2): 214–27.

Geisler, G. (2004) *Women and the Remaking of Politics in Southern Africa: Negotiating Autonomy, Incorporation and Representation*. Uppsala: Nordic Africa Institute.

Gluckman, M. (1963a) 'The Reasonable Man in Barotse Law', in *Order and Rebellion in Tribal Africa*. London: Cohen and West, pp.178–206.

—— (1963b) *Order and Rebellion in Tribal Africa*. London: Cohen and West.

—— (1964) 'Natural Justice in Africa', *American Journal of Jurisprudence* 9(1): 25–44.

—— (1967 [1955]) *The Judicial Process among the Barotse of Northern Rhodesia (Zambia)*. Manchester: Manchester University Press.

—— (1973) 'Limitations of the Case-method in the Study of Tribal Law', *Law and Society Review* 7(4): 611–42.

Good, K. (2002) *The Liberal Model and Africa: Elites against Democracy*. London: Palgrave.

Graeber, D. (2009) *Direct Action: An Ethnography*. Edinburgh: AK Press.

Greener, R., K. Jeffries and H. Siphambe (2000) 'The Impact of HIV/AIDS on Poverty and Inequality in Botswana', *South African Journal of Economics* 68(5): 888–915.

Griffiths, A.M.O. (1998) *In the Shadow of Marriage: Gender and Justice in an African Community*. Chicago, IL: University of Chicago Press.

—— (2006) 'A Second Liberation: Lobbying for Women's Political Representation in Zambia, Botswana and Namibia', *Journal of Southern African Studies* (special issue), 32(1): 69–84.

Grillo, R. (1973) *African Railwaymen: Solidarity and Opposition in An East African Labour Force*. Cambridge: Cambridge University Press.

—— (1974) *Race, Class and Militancy: An African Trade Union, 1939–1965*. London: Chandler.

Gulbrandsen, O. (1995) 'The King Is King by the Grace of the People: The Exercise and Control of Power in Subject–Ruler Relations', *Comparative Studies in Society and History* 37(3): 415–44.

—— (1996) 'Living Their Lives in Courts: The Counter-hegemonic Force of the Tswana Kgotla in a Colonial Context', in O. Harris (ed.), *Inside and Outside the Law: Anthropological Studies of Authority and Ambiguity*. London: Routledge, pp.125–56.

—— (2012) *The State and the Social: State Formation in Botswana and Its Precolonial and Colonial Genealogies*. Oxford: Berghahn.

Gutman, H.G. (1966) 'Protestantism and the American Labor Movement: the Christian Spirit in the Gilded Age', *American Historical Review* 72(1): 74–101.

Handelman, D. (2006) 'The Extended Case: Interactional Foundations and Prospective Dimensions', in T.M.S. Evens and D. Handelman (eds), *The Manchester School: Practice and Ethnographic Praxis in Anthropology*. Oxford: Berghahn, pp.94–117.

Hansen, S. (2008) 'Botswana: An African Success Story Shows Strains', *Council On Foreign Relations*, 10 January 2008. Retrieved from: www.cfr.org/publication/15108/ (accessed 11 May 2009).

Harries, P. (1994) *Work, Culture, and Identity: Migrant Laborers in Mozambique and South Africa, c. 1860–1910*. London: James Currey.

Hays, M.J. (1988) 'Queens, Prostitutes and Peasants: Historical Perspectives on African Women, 1971–1986', *Canadian Journal of African Studies* 22(3): 431–47.

Hirschsohn, P. (1998) 'From Grassroots Democracy to National Mobilization: COSATU as a Model of Social Movement Unionism', *Economic and Industrial Democracy* 19(4): 663–66.

—— (2007) 'Union Democracy and Shopfloor Mobilization: Social Movement Unionism in South African Auto and Clothing Plants', *Economic and Industrial Democracy* 28(1): 6–48.

Hitchcock, R.K., M. Sapignol and W.A. Babchuk (2011) 'What About Our Rights? Settlements, Subsistence and Livelihood Security among Central Kalahari San and Bakgalagadi', *International Journal of Human Rights* 15(1): 72–88.

Hobsbawm, E.J. (1959) *Primitive Rebels: Studies in Archaic Forms of Social Movement in the Nineteenth and Twentieth Centuries*. Manchester: Manchester University Press.

Hodgson, D. (2008) 'Cosmopolitics, Neoliberalism and the State: The Indigenous Rights Movement in Africa', in P. Werbner (ed.), *Anthropology and the New Cosmopolitanism*. Oxford: Berg, pp.215–30.

Holquist, M., and K. Clark (1984) *Mikhail Bakhtin*. Cambridge, MA: Harvard University Press.

Horwitz, M.J. (1992) *The Transformation of American Law 1870–1960: The Crisis of Legal Orthodoxy*. Oxford: Oxford University Press.

Hunyepa, J.C. (2009) 'State of Botswana Trade Unions: Trials and Tribulations: A Background', *Mmegi*, 25 September 2009. Retrieved from: www.mmegi.bw/index.php?sid=6aid=308dir=2011/september/wednesday14&aid=84&dir=2009/september/friday25 (accessed 17 December 2011).

Iliffe, J. (1975) 'The Creation of Group Consciousness among the Dockworkers of Dar Es Salaam 1929–1950', in R. Sandbrook and R. Cohen (eds), *The Development of an African Working Class*. Toronto: University of Toronto Press, pp.21–48.

—— (2005) *Honour in African History*. Cambridge: Cambridge University Press.

ILO (2007) Case No. 2500, Governing Body, International Labour Organisation GB.299/4/1, 299th Session. Geneva: International Labour Organisation.

Jeffries, K. (2011) 'Road Ahead Not Rosy, Part I', *Economic Express*, 14–20 May, p.6.

Jeffries, R. (1978) *Class, Power and Ideology in Ghana: The Railwaymen of Sekondi*. Cambridge: Cambridge University Press.

Jones, M. (2000) 'Working with Labour: The Impact of UNISON's Political Settlement', in M. Terry (ed.), *Redefining Public Sector Unionism: UNISON and the Future of Trade Unions*. London: Routledge, pp.119–27.

Jordan, J., C. Mills, T. Moy, C. Keshav, and J. Ndoziya (1992) 'Classification of Jobs into Levels of Work: Four Reliability Studies', *Zambezia* 29(2): 139–44.

Juris, J.S. (2008) 'Performing Politics: Image, Embodiment, and Affective Solidarity During Anti-Corporate Globalization Protests', *Ethnography* 9: 61–97.

Kanani, K. (2011a) 'Let's Meet in 2014!' *Echo*, 23–29 June, pp.1, 3.

—— (2011b) 'Nasha in Trouble for Convening MP Meeting?' *Echo*, 9–15 June, p.4.

Kapferer, B. (1972) *Strategy and Transaction in an African Factory*. Manchester: Manchester University Press.

—— (2006) 'Situations, Crisis, and the Anthropology of the Concrete: The Contribution of Max Gluckman', in T.M.S. Evens and D. Handelman (eds), *The Manchester School: Practice and Ethnographic Praxis in Anthropology*. Oxford: Berghahn, pp.94–117.

Kaplow, L. (1992) 'Rules versus Standards: An Economic Analysis', *Duke Law Journal* 42(3): 557–629.

Kasmir, S. (2005) 'Activism and Class Identity: The Saturn Auto Factory Case', in J. Nash (ed.), *Social Movements: An Anthropological Reader*. Oxford: Blackwell, pp.78–95.

Kavahematui, J. (2011a) '35,000 Govt Jobs on the Line', *Botswana Guardian*, 18 February. Retrieved from: www.botswanaguardian.co.bw/newsdetails.php?nid=1375&cat=bg news (accessed 17 December, 2011).

—— (2011b) 'Ministers Run For Cover', *Botswana Guardian*, 3 June, pp.1, 7.

—— (2011c) '17 Axed Directors Lose Case', *Botswana Guardian*, 24 June, p.3.

Kelebonye, G. (2011) 'Public Service Strike a Major Turning Point', *Mmegi*, 13 May, p.22.

Keoreng, E. (2011a) 'Unionists Pour Scorn on Khama's Leadership Credentials', *Monitor*, 16 May. Retrieved from: www.mmegi.bw/index.php?sid=1&aid=864&dir=2011/may/monday16 (accessed 27 April 2011).

—— (2011b) 'Ministers Flee from Audience', *Mmegi*, 3 June, pp.2, 6.

Keoreng, E., and C. Baputaki (2011) 'Masisi Runs for Dear Life as Talks Collapse', *Mmegi*, 1 June, pp.1–2.

Khabo, F.M. (2008) 'Collective Bargaining and Labour Disputes Resolution: Is SADC Meeting the Challenge?' Harare: ILO Sub-Regional Office For Southern Africa.

Khunwane, T. (2011) 'Govt Cannot Afford Salary Increase', *Botswana Daily News*, 20 May, pp.1–2.

Kiragu, K., R. Mukandala, and D. Morin (2004) 'Reforming Pay Policy: Techniques, Sequencing, and Politics', World Bank report. Retrieved from: www1.worldbank.org/publicsector/civilservice/.../bsc_ch04.pdf (accessed 15 April 2011).

Klaits, F. (2010) *Death in a Church of Life: Moral Passion During Botswana's Time of AIDS*. Berkeley: University of California Press.

Klare, K.E. (1982) 'Critical Theory and Labour Relations Law', in D. Kairys (ed.), *The Politics of Law: A Progressive Critique*. New York: Basic Books, pp.539–68.

Kologwe, O. (2011) 'BOFEPUSU F'town Members Reject Move to Suspend the Strike', *Sunday Standard*, 12–18 June, p.2.

Kompe, L. (1985) 'Union Women', in J. Barrett et al. (eds), *South African Women on the Move*. London: Zed Books, pp.97–118.

Konopo, J. (2011) 'IMF Advises Govt Not to Increase Salaries', *Weekend Post*, 11–17 June, p.21.

Korobkin, R.B. (2000) 'Behavioral Analysis versus Legal Form: Rules versus Standards Revisited', *Oregon Law Review* 79: 23–60.

Kuper, A. (1970a) 'The Kgalagari and the Jural Consequences of Marriage', *Man* 5(3): 466–82.

—— (1970b) *Kalahari Village Politics: An African Democracy*. Cambridge: Cambridge University Press.

Laclau, E. (1990) *New Reflections on the Revolution of Our Time*. London: Verso.

Laidlaw, J. (2002) 'For an Anthropology of Ethics and Freedom', *Journal of the Royal Anthropological Insttute* 8: 311–32.

Lambert, R., and E. Webster (2001) 'Southern Unionism and the New Labour Internationalism', *Antipode* 33(3): 337–62.

Larmer, M. (2006) '"The Hour Has Come to the Pit": The Mineworkers' Union of Zambia and the Movement For Multi-party Democracy, 1982–1991', *Journal of Southern African Studies* 32(2): 293–312.

—— (2007) *Mineworkers in Zambia: Labour and Political Change in Post-colonial Africa*. London: Taurus Academic.

Lentz, C. (1994) 'Home, Death and Leadership: Discourses of an Educated Elite from North-western Ghana', *Social Anthropology* 2(2): 49–69.

Livingstone, J. (2005) *Debility and Moral Imagination in Botswana: Disability, Chronic Illness and Aging*. Bloomington, IN: Indiana University Press.

—— (2012) *Improvising Medicine: An African Oncology Ward in An Emerging Cancer Epidemic*. Durham, NC: Duke University Press.

Lobel, O. (2007) 'The Paradox of Extralegal Activism: Critical Legal Consciousness and Transformative Politics', *Harvard Law Review* 120(4): 937–88.

Lodge, T. (1983) *Black Politics in South Africa since 1945*. Harlow: Longman.

Lonsdale, J. (1992) 'The Moral Economy of Mau Mau: Wealth, Poverty and Civic Virtue in Kikuyu Political Thought', in B. Berman and J. Lonsdale (eds), *Unhappy Valley*, Vol.2: *Violence and Ethnicity*. Oxford: James Currey, pp.315–467.

—— (2000) 'Agency in Tight Corners: Narrative and Initiative in African History'. *Journal of African Cultural Studies* (special issue) 13(1): 5–16.

LRC (2008) 'Alec Freund Interview', Document ID AG3298-1-047, Legal Resources Centre, South Africa. Johannesburg: Historical Papers, William Cullen Library, University of the Witwatersrand.

Lute, A. (2009) 'Elusive Public Service Act: Unions to Meet Minister, PSP', *Botswana Gazette*, 26 May. Retrieved from: www.gazettebw.com/index.php?option=com_content&view=article&id=3261:elusive-public-service-act-unions-to-meet-minister-psp&catid=18:headlines&itemid=2 (accessed 17 December 2011).

—— (2011a) 'Government Takes War to Unions', *Weekend Post* 28 May–3 June, p.2.

—— (2011b) 'Top Civil Servants to Gain More From 16 Percent', *Weeknend Post* 7–13 May, p.3.

McCann, M.W. (1994) *Rights At Work: Pay Equity Reform and the Politics of Legal Mobilization*. Chicago, IL: University of Chicago Press.

McCaskie, T.C. (2000) 'The Consuming Passions of Kwame Boakye: An Essay on Agency and Identity in Asante History', *Journal of African Cultural Studies* (special issue) 13(1): 43–62.

McCracken, J. (1988) 'Labour in Nyasaland: An Assessment of the 1960 Railway Workers' Strike', *Journal of Southern African Studies* (special issue) 14(2): 257–78.

McIntyre, J. (2010) 'Christianity and the Labour Leadership', *New Statesman* (London), 7 July. Retrieved from: www.newstatesman.com/blogs/public-accounts/2010/07/labour-shall-faith-values (accessed 29 February 2012).

McNay, L. (2000) *Gender and Agency: Reconfiguring the Subject in Feminist and Social Theory*. Cambridge: Polity Press.

Magang, D. (2008) *The Magic of Perseverance*. Cape Town: Centre for Advanced Studies of African Society.

Mahmood, S. (2001) 'Feminist Theory, Embodiment, and the Docile Agent: Some Reflections on the Egyptian Islamic Revival', *Cultural Anthropology* 16(2): 202–36.

—— (2005) *Politics of Piety: The Islamic Revival and the Feminist Subject*. Princeton: Princeton University Press.

Majube, B. (2011) 'More Doctors Join the Strike', *Echo*, 12–18 May, p.5.

Makgala, C.J. (2006) *Elite Conflict in Botswana: A History*. Pretoria: African Institute of South Africa.

Makgala, C.J., and I.S. Malila (2014) *The 2011 BOFEPUSU Strike: A story of the Fight for the Restoration of Workers Purchasing Power*. Capetown: the Centre for Advanced Studies of African Society (CASAS).

Makgala, C.J., Z. Maundeni and P.P. Molosiwa (2007) *History of the Botswana Manual Workers' Union: A Story of Courageous Struggle for Democratic and Economic Advancement in Southern Africa*. Gaborone: NALCPGPMU/Bay Publishing.

Makgapha, S. (2011a) 'Luxury Cars Parked Where Strikers Meet – Merafhe', *Botswana Gazette*, 25–31 May, p.3.

—— (2011b) 'I Did Not Walk Out – Seretse', *Botswana Gazette*, 8 June.

—— (2011c) 'Political Statements Out for Civil Servants – Molale', *Botswana Gazette*, 31 August.

—— (2011d) 'Why We Are Suing', *Botswana Gazette*, 12 October. Retrieved from: www.gazettebw.com/index.php?option=com_content&view=article

&id=11542:why-we-are-suing&catid=18:headlines&itemid=2 (accessed 21 December 2011).
—— (2012) 'BOFEPUSU Turns Its Back On Party Politics', *Botswana Gazette*, 22 February. Retrieved from: www.gazettebw.com/index.php?option=com_content &view=article&id=12501:bofepusu-turns-its-back-on-party-politics&catid=18:headl ines&itemid=2 (accessed 27 April 2012).

Mannheim, K. (1997 [1952]) 'The Problem of Generation', in *Collected Works of Karl Mannheim*, Vol. 5. London: Routledge, pp.276–320.

Manoukian, S. (2010) 'Where Is This Place? Crowds, Audiovision and Poetry in Postelection Iran', *Public Culture* 22(2): 237–63.

—— (2011) 'Two Forms of Temporality in Contemporary Iran', *Sociologica* 3: 1–17.

Marks, S. (1988) *Not Either an Experimental Doll: The Separate Worlds of Three South African Women*. Bloomington, IN: Indiana University Press.

—— (1994) *Divided Sisterhood: Race, Class and Gender in the South African Nursing Profession*. London: St Martin's Press.

—— (2000) 'Changing History, Changing Histories: Separations and Connections in the Lives of South African Women', *Journal of African Cultural Studies* 13(1): 94–106.

Marks, S., and R. Rathbone (1982) 'Introduction', in S. Marks and R. Rathbone (eds), *Industrialisation and Social Change in South Africa*. New York: Longman, pp.1–44.

Marobela, M.N. (2011) 'Industrial Relations in Botswana – Workplace Conflict: Behind the Diamond Sparkle', *Emerald Emerging Markets Case Studies* 1(3): 1–16.

Mashinini, E. (1989) *Strikes Have Followed Me All My Life: A South African Biography*. London: Women's Press.

Masire, Q.K. (2008) *Masire: Memoirs of an African Democrat: Very Brave or Very Foolish?* ed. S.R. Lewis. Gaborone: Palgrave Macmillan.

Matumo, V., and T. Pheage (2013) 'How Accessible Is President Khama?' *Weekend Post*, 2–8 February, pp.A1, A4.

Maundeni, Z. (2004) *Civil Society, Politics and the State in Botswana*. Gaborone: Medi Publishers.

—— (2011) 'New Botswana Politics (III)', The *Telegraph*, June 22, p.9.

Maurer, B. (2005) 'Due Diligence and "Reasonable Man," Offshore', *Cultural Anthropology* 20(4): 474–505.

Mazonde, I.N. (1994) *Ranching and Enterprise in Eastern Botswana: A Case Study of Black and White Farmers*. Edinburgh: Edinburgh University Press.

——ed, (2003) *Minorities in the Millennium: Perspectives From Botswana*. African Books Collective, Botswana: Lightbooks.

Melucci, A. (1989) *Nomads of the Present: Social Movements and Individual Needs in Contemporary Society*. Philadelphia, PA: Temple University Press.

—— (1996) *Challenging Codes: Collective Action in the Information Age*. Cambridge: Cambridge University Press.

Merry, S.E. (1990) *Getting Justice and Getting Even: Legal Consciousness among Working-class Americans*. Chicago, IL: University of Chicago Press.

—— (2006) *Human Rights and Gender Violence: Translating International Law into Local Justice*. Chicago, IL: University of Chicago Press.

Mhotsha, G. (2008) 'Towards an Honest and Accountable Union', *Mmegi*, 15 August. Retrieved from: www.mmegi.bw/index.php?sid=1&aid=20&dir=2008/august/ friday15 (accessed 14 February 2010).

Ministry of Finance and Development Planning (2000) 'Privatisation Policy for Botswana', Government Paper No. 1, 2000. Gaborone: Government Printer.

Mitchell, J.C. (1966) 'Theoretical Orientations in African Urban Studies', in M. Banton (ed.), *The Social Anthropology of Complex Societies*. London: Tavistock, pp.37–68.
Mkandawire, T. (2005) *African Intellectuals*. Dakar/London: CODESRIA/Zed Books.
Modikwa, O. (2008) 'Trade Unions Demand Meeting with Minister', *Mmegi*, 7 April.
—— (2011a) 'BOFEPUSU Challenges Appointment of Industrial Court Judges', *Mmegi*, 22 November. Retrieved from: http://new.mmegi.bw/index.php?sid=1&aid=117&dir=2011/november/tuesday22 (accessed 21 December 2011).
—— (2011b) 'BOFEPUSU Defies Govt On Opposition Meeting', *Mmegi*, 23 November. Retrieved from: http://www.mmegi.bw/index.php?sid=1&aid=118&dir=2011/november/tuesday22 (accessed 27 April 2012).
Modise, O. (2010) 'Fired Directors Take Government to Court', *Sunday Standard*, 1 October. Retrieved from: www.sundaystandard.info/print_article.php?newsid=6662 (accessed 17 December 2011).
Moeng, G. (2011a) 'A Song to Spice the Struggle', *Mmegi*, 13 May, p.12.
—— (2011b) 'UCCSA Enters the Fray', *Mmegi*, 25 May, pp.1–2.
Mogalakwe, M. (1997) *The State and Organised Labour in Botswana: Liberal Democracy and Emergent Capitalism*. Aldershot: Ashgate.
—— (2011a) 'Lessons from the Public Sector Strike, Part 1', *Botswana Guardian*, 6 May 2011, p.7.
—— (2011b) 'Lessons from the Public Sector Strike, Part 2', *Botswana Guardian*, 13 May 2011, pp.9–10.
—— (2011c) 'The Awakening of the People, Part 3,' *Botswana Guardian*, 17 June 2011, pp.9–10.
Mokotedi, A. (2006) 'Labour Leaders Criticise Mogae', *Botswana Daily News*, 16 November , p.2.
Molaudi, S.K. (1992) *Chronological Events of 154% Wage Increase Demand*. Gaborone: National Amalgamated Local and Central Government and Parastatals Manual Workers' Union.
Molokomme, A. (1989) 'Political Rights in Botswana: Regression or Development?' in J. Holm and P. Molutsi (eds), *Democracy in Botswana*. Athens, OH: Ohio University Press, pp.163–73.
Molosiwa, P.P. (2007) 'Re Neeland Ditsa Rona! The Great 1991 Manual Workers Union Strike', in C.J. Makgala (ed.), *History of the Botswana Manual Workers' Union: A Story of Courageous Struggle for Democratic and Economic Advancement in Southern Africa*. Gaborone: National Amalgamated Local and Central Government and Parastatals Manual Workers' Union, pp.72–98.
Moodie, D.T., with V. Ndatshe (1994) *Going for Gold: Man, Mines and Migration*. Berkeley: University of California Press.
Mooketsi, L. (2005) 'BFTU Leads March to OP Over Sacked Workers', *Mmegi*, 9 June. Retrieved from: www.mmegi.bw/2005/june/thursday9/468490281337.html (accessed 27 February 2012).
—— (2011) 'OP Sets Record on Re-employment Straight', *Mmegi*, 19 December. Retrieved from: www.mmegi.bw/index.php?sid=1&aid=779&dir=2011/december/monday19 (accessed 27 April 2011).
Moore, S.F. (1978) *Law As Process: An Anthropological Approach*. London: Routledge and Kegan Paul.
—— (2001) 'Certainties Undone: Fifty Turbulent Years of Legal Anthropology, 1949–1999', *Journal of the Royal Anthropological Institute* 7(1): 95–116.
Moorsom, R. (1977) 'Underdevelopment, Contract Labour and Worker Consciousness in Namibia, 1915–1972' *Journal of Southern African Studies* 4(1): 52–87.

Morewagae, I. (2011a) 'Arrested Unionist Marvels at His Security Escort', *Monitor*, 30 May. Retrieved from: www.mmegi.bw/index.php?sid=1&aid=1255&dir=2011/may/monday30 (accessed 29 January 2013).

—— (2011b) 'NALCGPWU Wins Battle of the Unions', *Mmegi*, 9 August. Retrieved from: www.mmegi.bw/index.php?sid=1&aid=852&dir=2011/august/tuesday9 (accessed 28 January 2013).

Morula, M. (2005) 'Govt. Rebuffs Unions', *Botswana Guardian*, 26 August, p.4.

Mosikare, L. (2011a) 'BOFEPUSU Attacks Khama in His Stronghold', *Midweek Sun*, 25 May, p.1.

—— (2011b) 'BOFEPUSU Claims Diarrhoea Killed 120', *Botswana Gazette*, 28 September. Retrieved from: www.gazettebw.com/index.php?option=com_content&view=article&id=11405%3abofepusu-claims-diarrhoea-killed-120&catid=19%3anorthcast&itemid=2 (accessed 27 April 2011).

Mosikare, O. (2013) 'Essential Service Judgement in the Spotlight', *Mmegi*, 4 April. Retrieved from: www.mmegi.bw/index.php?sid=1&aid=275&dir=2013/april/thursday4 (accessed 11 October 2013).

Motlhabane, D., and N. Ntibinyane (2011) 'Strike Divides BDP', *Botswana Guardian*, 27 May, pp.1, 8.

Motlogelwa, T. (2010) 'Kirby's Dilemma: The Khama Association', *Mmegi*, 4 August. Retrieved from: www.mmegi.bw/index.php?sid=1&aid=3936&dir=2010/august/wednesday4 (accessed 29 January 2013).

—— (2011) 'Can BOFEPUSU Really Hurt BDP?' *Weekend Post*, 14–20 May, p.6.

Motzafi-Haller, P. (2002) *Fragmented Worlds, Coherent Lives: The Politics of Difference in Botswana*. London: Bergin and Garvey.

Motseta, S., and S. Makgapha (2011) 'Strike: Now Divine Intervention', *Botswana Gazette*, 1–7 June, pp.1–2.

Mpolokwa, E. (2012) 'Unionists Disappointed by Collapse of Umbrella Talks', *Monitor*, 9 January. Retrieved from: http://www.mmegi.bw/index.php?sid=1&aid=943&dir=2012/january/monday9 (accessed 27 April 2012).

MWU (2007) *Leadership Challenges at the Botswana Manual Workers' Union 2002–2007*. Gaborone: NALCPGPMU/Bay Publishing.

—— (2012) 'The Winning Month', *Lentswe La Baberke*, Vol. 1 No. 4 front page, 4 June 2012, Gaborone: National Amalgamated.

Nasha, M.N. (2014) *Madam Speaker, SIR! Breaking the Glass Ceiling: One Woman's Struggles*. Gaborone: Diamond Educational Publishers.

Nealton, J.F. (1998) *Alterity Politics: Ethics and Performative Subjectivity*. Durham, NC: Duke University Press.

Ngakane, G. (2011) 'The Day Striking Workers Invaded Tonota', *Mmegi*, 13 May, pp.21, 36.

Nugent, D. (2012) 'Commentary: Democracy, Temporalities of Capitalism, and Dilemmas of Inclusion in Occupy Movements', *American Ethnologist* 39(2): 280–83.

Ntseane, D., and K. Solo (2007) *Social Security and Social Protection in Botswana*. Gaborone: Bay Publishing.

Ontobetse, K. (2011) 'Union Leader Facing Assault Charges', *Weekend Post*, 28 May, p.2.

—— (2013) 'Unions to Mobilise Against Ministers, MPs', *Botswana Telegraph*, 30 January, p.1.

Otlogetswe, T. (2011) 'The BDP Does Not Need Ian Khama', *Botswana Telegraph*, June 15, p.9.

Parry, J. (1999) 'Lords of Labour: Working and Shirking in Bhilai', in J. Parry, J. Breman and K. Kapadia (eds), *The Worlds of Indian Industrial Labour*. Delhi: Sage.

—— (2008) 'Cosmopolitan Values in a Central Indian Steel Town', in P. Werbner (ed.), *Anthropology and the New Cosmopolitanism: Rooted, Feminist and Vernacular Perspectives*. Oxford: Berg, pp.325–44.

—— (2010) '"Sociological Marxism" in Central India: Polanyi, Gramsci, and the Case of the Unions', in C. Hann and K. Hart (eds), *Market and Society: The Great Transformation Today*. Cambridge: Cambridge University Press, pp.175–202.

Parsons, N., W. Henderson and T. Tlou (1995) *Seretse Khama 1921–1980*. Braemfontein: Macmillan.

Peace, A.J. (1975) 'The Lagos Proletariat: Labour Aristocrats or Populist Militants', in R. Sandbrook and R. Cohen (eds), *The Development of an African Working Class: Studies in Class Formation and Action*. Toronto: University of Toronto Press, pp.281–302.

—— (1979) *Choice, Class and Conflict: A Study of Southern Nigerian Factory Workers*. London: Harvester Press.

Pheko, I. (2011) 'Rich Pickings for Backyard Gardening', *Botswana Guardian*, 11 March. Retrieved from: www.botswanaguardian.co.bw/newsdetails.php?nid=1521&cat=bg%20news (accessed 12 December 2011).

Piet, B. (2007) 'Mogae Angers Trade Unions', *Mmegi*, 7 November, p.4.

—— (2008) 'Tough Laws For Motorists', *Mmegi*, 12 November. Retrieved from: http://mmegi.bw/index.php?sid=1&aid=1&dir=2008/november/wednesday12 (accessed 14 March 2014).

Pitse, Reuben (2011) 'DCEC Foils Attempted Bribery by China Civil Engineering', *Sunday Standard*, 3 July. Retrieved from: http://www.sundaystandard.info/article.php?NewsID=11209&GroupID=1 (accessed 1 March 2014).

Prins, G. (1980) *The Hidden Hippopotamus: Reappraisal in African History, the Early Colonial Experience*. Cambridge: Cambridge University Press.

PSOP (2011) 'Public Service Outsourcing Programme', policy document. Gaborone.

Raftopoulos, B., and I. Phimister (1997) *Keep On Knocking: A History of the Labour Movement in Zimbabwe, 1900–1997*. Harare: Baobab Books.

Rantsimako, S. (2011) 'BDP MPs "Against" Pyramid Salary Increases', *Botswana Gazette*, 8–14 June. Retrieved from: http://www.gazettebw.com/index.php?option=com_content&view=article&id=9982:bdp-mps-against-pyramid-salary-increases&catid=18:headlines (accessed 19 December 2012).

Richards, A., and A. Kuper (1971) *Councils in Action*. Cambridge: Cambridge University Press.

Riggs, R.E. (1988) 'Legitimate Expectation and Procedural Fairness in English Law', *American Journal of Comparative Law* 36(3): 395–436.

Rosenberg, G.K. (1991) *The Hollow Hope: Can Courts Bring About Social Change?* Chicago, IL: University of Chicago Press.

Rosenfeld, H., and S. Carmi (1990) 'The Privatization of Public Means: The State-made Middle Class, and the Realization of Family Value in Israel', *International Journal of Politics, Culture, and Society* 3(1): 139–51.

SADC (2007) 'Communique of the Meeting of SADC Ministers of Employment and Labour and Social Partners Held in Lusaka, Zambia On 8–9 February 2007'. Retrieved from: www.sadc.int/archives/read/news/940 (accessed 11 May 2009).

Saidy Khan, A. (n.d.) 'Hallowed Institutions: Reframing African Industrial Relations', *Critical African Studies* (forthcoming).

Sandbrook, R., and R. Cohen, eds (1975) *The Development of an African Working Class: Studies in Class Formation and Action*. London: Longman.

Sapignoli, M. (2012) 'The San, the State, and the International Community: Asserting Local Power through Globalised Indigenous Identities', PhD thesis. Colchester: University of Essex.

Sartwell, C. (2010) *Political Aesthetics*. Ithaca, NY: Cornell University Press.

Saugestad, S. (2011) 'Impact of International Mechanisms on Indigenous Rights in Botswana', *Intenational Journal of Human Rights* 15(1): 37–61.

Saul, J.S. (1975) '"The Labour Aristocray" Thesis Reconsidered', in R. Sandbrook and R. Cohen (eds), *The Development of an African Working Class*. London: Longman, pp.303–10.

Sawyer, T. (2000) 'UNISON and New Labour: Searching For New Relationships', in M. Terry (ed.), *Redefining Public Sector Unionism: UNISON and the Future of Trade Unions*. London: Routledge, pp.128–34.

Schapera, I. (1938) *A Handbook of Tswana Law and Custom*. London: Oxford University Press.

—— (1956) *Government and Politics in Tribal Society*. London: Watts and Co.

—— (1970) *Tribal Innovators: Tswana Chiefs and Social Change 1795–1940*. London: Athlone Press.

Schirmer, J. (1989) 'Those Who Die for Life Cannot Be Called Dead: Women and Human Rights Protest in Latin America', *Feminist Review* 32: 3–29.

—— (1993) 'The Seeking of Truth and the Gendering of Consciousness: The Comadres of El Salvador and the Conavigua Widows of Guatemala', in S.A. Radcliffe and S. Westwood (eds), *Viva: Women and Popular Protest in Latin America*. London: Routledge, pp.30–64.

Schler, L. (2009) 'Transnationalism and Nationalism in the Nigerian Seamen's Union', *African Identities* (special issue) 7(3): 387–98.

Schler, L., L. Bethlehem and G. Sabar (2009) 'Editorial: Rethinking Labour in Africa, Past and Present', *African Identities* (special issue) 7(3): 299–325.

Scipes, K. (1992) 'Understanding the New Labor Movements in the "Third World": The Emergence of Social Movement Unionism, a New Type of Trade Unionism', *Critical Sociology* 19(2): 81–101.

Scott, J.W. (1988) *Gender and the Politics of History*. New York: Columbia University Press.

—— (1991) 'The Evidence of Experience', *Critical Inquiry* 17(4): 773–97.

Selolwane, O.D. (1998) 'Equality of Citizenship and the Gendering of Democracy in Botswana', in W.A. Edge and M.H. Lekorwe (eds), *Botswana: Politics and Society*. Pretoria: Van Schaik, pp.397–411.

—— (2000) 'Civil Society, Citizenship and Civil Rights in Botswana', in S.M. Rai, (ed.), *International Perspectives on Gender and Democratisation*. London: Macmillan, pp.89–99.

Sender, J., C. Oya and C. Cramer (2006) 'Women Working for Wages: Putting Flesh on the Bones of a Rural Labour Market Survey in Mozambique', *Journal of Southern African Studies* 32(2): 313–33.

Sereetsi, T. (2011) 'Masisi, Rakhudu Booed Out of "Secret Meeting"', *Echo*, 2–8 June, p.3.

Shostak, M. (1981) *Nisa: The Life and Words of a !Kung Woman*. Cambridge, MA: Harvard University Press.

Simmonds, N.E. (2007) *Law as a Moral Idea*. Oxford: Oxford University Press.

Simons, J., and R. Simons (1969) *Class and Colour in South Africa 1850–1950*. Harmondsworth: Penguin.

Smith-Nonini, S. (2010) *Healing the Body Politic: El Salvador's Popular Struggle for Health Rights from Civil War to Neoliberal Peace*. New Brunswick, NJ: Rutgers University Press.

Snarr, C.M. (2011) *All You That Labor: Religion and Ethics in the Living Wage Movement*. New York, NY: New York University Press.

Solway, J.S. (2002) 'Navigating the "Neutral" State: "Minority" Rights in Botswana', *Journal of Southern Africa Studies* 28(4): 711–30.

—— (2009) 'Human Rights and NGO "Wrongs": Conflict Diamonds, Culture Wars and the "Bushman" Question', *Africa* 79(3): 321–46.

Southall, R. (1995) *Imperialism or Solidarity? International Labour and South African Trade Unions*. Cape Town: University of Cape Town Press.

Subramanian, A. (2009) *Shorelines: Space and Rights in South India*. Stanford, CA: Stanford University Press.

Suttner, R. (2005) 'The Character and Formation of Intellectuals within the ANC-led South African Liberation Movement', in T. Mkandawire (ed.), *African Intellectuals: Rethinking Politics, Langauge, Gender and Development*. London: Zed Books, pp.117–54.

Talib, M. (2010) *Writing Labour: Stone Quarry Workers in Delhi*. Delhi: Oxford University Press.

Tamanaha, B.Z. (2009) *Beyond the Formalist–Realist Divide: The Role of Politics in Judging*. Princeton, NJ: Princeton University Press.

Tate, W. (2007) *Counting the Dead*. Berkeley, CA: University of California Press.

Taussig, M.T. (1993) *Mimesis and Alterity: A Particular History of the Senses*. London: Routledge.

Taylor, A.J. (1989) *Trade Unions and Politics: A Comparative Introduction*. London: Macmillan.

Taylor, C. (1994) 'The Politics of Recognition', in A. Gutmann (ed.), *Multiculturalism*. Princeton, NJ: Princeton University Press, pp.25–74.

Terry, M., ed. (2000) *Redefining Public Sector Unionism: UNISON and the Future of Trade Unions*. London: Routledge.

Thompson, E.P. (1963) *The Making of the English Working Class*. Harmondsworth: Penguin.

Toka, G. (2008) 'Manual Workers' Union Takes Government to Court Over Recognition of BOGOWU', *Sunday Standard*, 12 October.

Tomlins, C.L. (1985) *The State and the Unions: Labour Relations, Law, and the Organized Labour Movement in America, 1880–1960*. Cambridge: Cambridge University Press.

—— (1993) *Law, Labour and Ideology in the Early American Republic*. Cambridge: Cambridge University Press.

—— (2007) 'How Autonomous Is Law?' *Annual Review of Law, Society and Science* 3: 45–68.

Tshukudu, I. (2011) '3 Days to Disaster', *The Voice*, 15 April.

Tsimane, E. (2011) 'Alleged P3.5 Million Govt. Legal Bill From Collins Newman Surfaces', *Sunday Standard*, 26 June–2 July. Retrieved from: www.sundaystandard.info/print_article.php?newsid=11138 (accessed 19 December 2012).

Turner, V.W. (1957) *Schism and Continuity in An African Society*. Manchester: Manchester University Press.

Van Driel, M. (2003) 'Unions and Privatisation in South Africa, 1990–2001', in T. Bramble and F. Barchiesi (eds), *Rethinking the Labour Movement in the 'New South Africa'*. London: Ashgate, pp.62–80.

Van Holdt, K. (2002) 'Social Movement Unionism: The Case of South Africa', *Work, Employment and Society* 16(2): 283–304.

Van Onselen, C. (1976) *Chibaro: African Mine Labour in Colonial Zimbabwe, 1900–1933.* London: Pluto Press.

Van Velsen, J. (1979) 'The Extended-case Method and Situational Analysis', in A.L. Epstein (ed.), *The Craft of Anthropology*. Oxford: Pergammon, pp.129–49.

Vaughan, O. (2003) *Chiefs, Power, and Social Change: Chiefship and Modern Politics in Botswana, 1880s–1990s.* Trenton, NJ: African World Press.

Waddington, J. (2003) 'Trade Union Organization', in P. Edwards (ed.), *Industrial Relations: Theory and Practice*, 2nd edn. Oxford: Blackwell, pp.214–56.

Walsh, D., P. Scully and D. Gaitskell, eds (2006) 'Women and the Politics of Gender in Southern Africa', *Journal of Southern African Studies* (special issue) 32(1).

Waterman, P. (1976) 'Third World Strikes: An Invitation to a Discussion', *Development and Change* 7(3): 331–44.

—— (1993) 'Social-movement Unionism: A New Union Model for a New World Order?' *Review* 16 (Summer), pp.245–78.

—— (1999) 'The New Social Unionism: A New Union Model For A New World Order', in R. Munch and P. Waterman (eds), *Labour Worldwide in the Era of Globalization: Alternative Union Models in the New World Order.* London: Macmillan, pp.247–64.

—— (2004) 'Adventures of Emancipatory Labour Strategy as the New Global Movement Challenges International Unionism'. *Journal of World System Research* 10(1): 217–53.

Wells, J. (1991) *We Have Done with Pleading: The Women's 1913 Anti-Pass Campaign.* Johannesburg: Ravan Press.

Werbner, P. (1998) 'Exoticising Citizenship: Anthropology and the New Citizenship Debate', *Canberra Anthropology* 21(2): 1–27.

—— (1999a) 'Political Motherhood and the Feminisation of Citizenship: Women's Activism and the Transformation of the Public Sphere', in N. Yuval-Davis and P. Werbner (eds), *Women, Citizenship and Difference*. London: Zed Books, pp.221–45.

—— (1999b) 'Global Pathways: Working Class Cosmopolitans and the Creation of Transnational Ethnic Worlds', *Social Anthropology* 7(1): 17–37.

—— (2001) 'The Limits of Cultural Hybridity: On Ritual Monsters, Poetic Licence, and Contested Postcolonial Purifications', *Journal of the Royal Anthropological Institute* 7(1): 133–52.

—— (2002) *Imagined Diasporas among Manchester Muslims*. Oxford: James Currey.

—— (2008) 'Introduction', in P. Werbner (ed.), *Anthropology and the New Cosmopolitanism: Rooted, Feminist and Vernacular Perspectives*. Oxford: Berg, pp.1–29.

—— (2009a) 'The Hidden Lion: Tswapong Girls' Puberty Rituals and the Problem of History', *American Ethnologist* 36(3): 441–58.

—— (2009b) 'Dialogical Subjectivities for Hard Times: Expanding Political and Ethical Imaginaries of Elite and Subaltern Southern African Women', *African Identities* 7(3): 299–325.

—— (2010a) 'Appropriating Social Citizenship: Women's Labour, Poverty, and Entrepreneurship in the Manual Workers' Union of Botswana', *Journal of Southern African Studies* 36(3): 693–710.

—— (2010b) 'Many Gateways to the Gateway City: Elites, Class, and Policy Networking in the London African Diaspora', *African Diaspora* (special issue) 3(1/2): 132–59.

—— (2014a) '"The Mother of all Strikes": Popular Protest Culture and Vernacular Cosmopolitanism in the Botswana Public Service Unions' Strike, 2011', in P. Werbner, M. Webb and K. Spellman-Poots (eds), *The Political Aesthetics of Global Protest: The Arab Spring and Beyond*. Edinburgh: Edinburgh University Press.

—— (2014b) '"The Duty to Act Fairly": Ethics, Legal Anthropology, and Labor Justice in the Manual Workers' Union of Botswana'. *Comparative Studies in Society and History* 56(2): 1–29.

Werbner, P., and N. Yuval-Davis (1999) 'Introduction: Women and the New Discourse of Citizenship', in N. Yuval-Davis and P. Werbner (eds), *Women, Citizenship and Difference*. London: Zed Books, pp.1–38.

Werbner, P., M. Webb and K. Spellman, eds (2014) *The Political Aesthetics of Global Protest: The Arab Spring and Beyond*. Edinburgh: Edinburgh University Press.

Werbner, R. (1977) 'Small Man Politics and the Rule of Law: Centre–Periphery Relations in East Central Botswana', *Journal of African Law* 21(2): 24–39.

—— (1980) 'The Quasi-judicial and the Experience of the Absurd: Remaking Land Law in North-eastern Botswana', *Journal of African Law* 24(1): 131–50.

—— (1984) 'The Manchester School in South Central Africa', *Annual Review of Anthropology* 13: 157–85.

—— (1988) 'Epilogue: Knowing the Power of Agency', *Journal of Southern African Studies* (special issue) 14(2): 323–29.

—— (1989) *Ritual Passage, Sacred Journey: The Process and Organization of Religious Movement*. Washington, DC: Smithsonian Institution Press.

—— (1991) *Tears of the Dead: The Social Biography of an African Family*. Washington, DC: Smithsonian Institution Press.

—— (2002a) 'Introduction: Postcolonial Subjectivities', in R. Werbner (ed.), *Postcolonial Subjectivities in Africa*. London: Zed Books, pp.1–21.

—— (2002b) 'Cosmopolitan Ethnicity, Entrepreneurship and the Nation: Minority Elites in Botswana', *Journal of Southern African Studies* 28(4): 731–54.

—— (2002c) 'Introduction', *Journal of Southern African Studies* (special issue) 28(4): 671–84.

—— (2004) *Reasonable Radicals and Citizenship in Botswana*. Bloomington, IN: Indiana University Press.

—— dir. (2007) *Shade Seekers and the Mixer*, film, 56 mins. Manchester: International Centre for Contemporary Cultural Research, University of Manchester.

—— (2008) 'Responding to Cosmopolitanism: Patriots, Ethnics and the Public Good in Botswana', in P. Werbner (ed.), *Anthropology and the New Cosmopolitanism: Rooted, Feminist and Vernacular Perspectives*. Oxford: Berg, pp.173–96.

—— (2011) *Holy Hustlers, Schism, and Prophecy: Apostolic Reformation in Botswana*. Berkeley, CA: University of California Press.

—— (n.d.) *Divination's Grasp: African Encounters with the Almost Said*. Bloomington, IN: Indiana University Press.

Wilenius, P. (2004) 'Enemies Within: Thatcher and the Unions', *BBC News*, 5 March. Retrieved from: http://news.bbc.co.uk/2/hi/uk_news/politics/3067563.stm (accessed 14 March 2014).

Wilson, R.A. (2001) *The Politics of Truth and Reconciliation in South Africa: Legitimizing the Post-Apartheid State*. Cambridge: Cambridge University Press.

Wright Mills, C. (1959) *The Sociological Imagination*. Oxford: Oxford University Press.

WTO (2007) *The WTO Building: The Symbolic Artwork of the Centre William Rappard Headquarters of the World Trade Organization*. Geneva: World Trade Organisation.

Yarrow, T. (2008) 'Life/History: Personal Narratives of Development amongst NGO Workers and Activists in Ghana', *Africa* 78(3): 334–58.

—— (2011) *Development Beyond Politics: Aid, Activism and Ngos in Ghana*. London: Palgrave Macmillan.

Newspapers

Botswana Daily News
Botswana Gazette
Botswana Guardian
Development News
Echo
Economic Express
Lentswe La Baberke
Midweek Sun
Mmegi
Monitor
Sunday Standard
The Telegraph
Voice
Weekend Post

Legal Cases

Attorney General versus *Public Service Unions [Botswana Landboards and Local Authorities Workers' Union, Botswana Public Employees' Union, National Amalgamated Workers' Union and Kefileng Toteng]* (2013). Court of Appeal Civil Appeal 2013, No. CACGB 053–12, Gaborone.

BMWU versus *Debswana* (2009). Court of Appeal 2009, 1 BLR 138 CA, Lobatse.

Debswana versus *BMWU* (2004). Industrial Court Case 2004 (2), BLR 129 (IC), Gaborone.

Minister of Labour and Home Affairs and Attorney General versus *Public Service Unions [BOPEU, NTU, BOSETU and National Amalgamated]* (2014). Court of Appeal Civil Appeal 2014, No. CACGB-083-12, Lobatse.

Mosetlanyane et al. versus *Attorney General* (2011). Court of Appeal Civil Appeal 2011, No. CACLB 074–10, MAHLB 000393–09, Lobatse.

National Amalgamated versus *Attorney General* (1991). High Court Civil Case 1991, No. 1604, Lobatse.

National Amalgamated versus *Attorney General* (1995), Court of Appeal Civil Appeal 1995, No. 26/93 of High Court Civil Case No. 1604/91, Lobatse.

Public Service Unions [Botswana Landboards and Local Authorities Workers' Union, Botswana Public Employees' Union, National Amalgamated Union and Kefilwe Toteng] versus *Attorney General* (2012). High Court Case 2012, No. MAHLB 000631–11, Lobatse.

Public Service Unions versus *Minister of Labour and Home Affairs* (2012). High Court Case 2012, MAHLB 000674–li, Lobatse.

Public Service Unions [Botswana Landboards and Local Authorities Workers' Union, Botswana Public Employees' Union, and the National Amalgamated Workers' Union] versus *DPSM and Attorney General* (2013). Court of Appeal Civil Appeal 2013, No. CACLB 043–11, Gaborone.

Index

Printed and bound by CPI Group (UK) Ltd, Croydon, CR0 4YY

16/04/2025

14658482-0005